Angel Diary

vol. 6

Kara · Lee YunHee

Yen Press

A WORD FROM THE CREATORS

IT SEEMS LIKE THERE'S ONLY BEEN A HANDFUL OF DEADLINES SINCE
WE BEGAN *ANGEL DIARY*, AND YET WE SOMEHOW MADE IT TO VOLUME
6. IF YOU LOOK AT OUR CALENDAR, THIS COMIC IS THE ONLY THING
ON IT. WE FORGOT ALL ABOUT PLANNING FOR A PERSONAL LIFE. IT'S
A TRAGIC STORY...

THIS YEAR IS ALREADY MAPPED OUT. (YES, WE'RE SCHEDULE FREAKS!
-_-;;;) IT LOOKS TO LIKE THIS YEAR IS GOING TO BE NOTHING BUT
DEADLINES, DEADLINES, DEADLINES.

BY KARA

WE'RE ALREADY ON VOLUME 6. EVERY TIME A NEW PAPERBACK COMES
OUT, I THINK, "HUH, ALREADY?!" IT'S TRUE, TIME REALLY DOES FLY. I
FEEL BAD FOR ALL THE DAYS I WASTED. (AND YET, I'M STILL LAZY AND
DON'T WANT TO DO ANYTHING. -_-;;)

BY YUNHEE LEE

C O N T E N T S

VI THE PRINCESS IS KIDNAPPED!

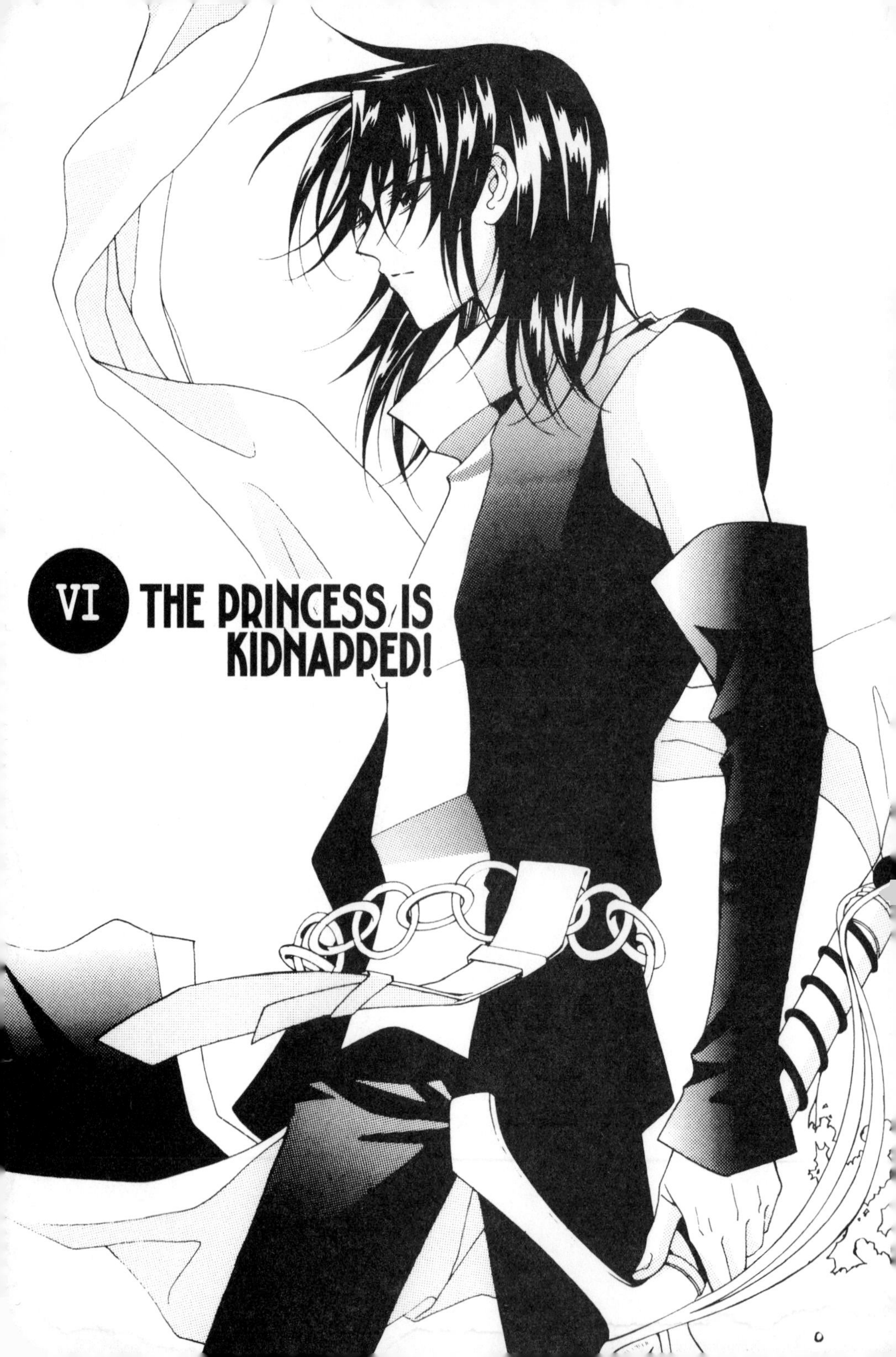

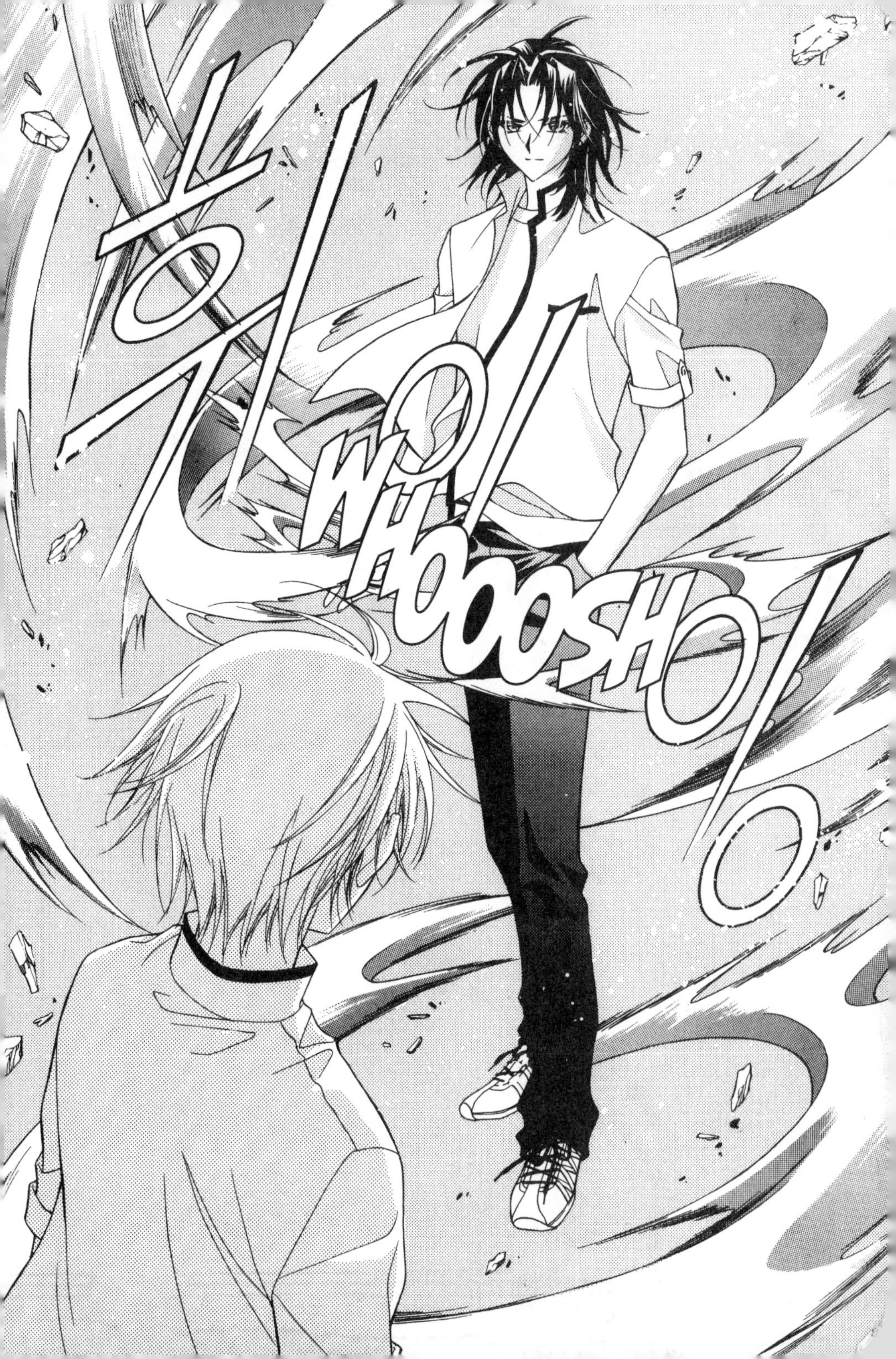
WHOOOSH

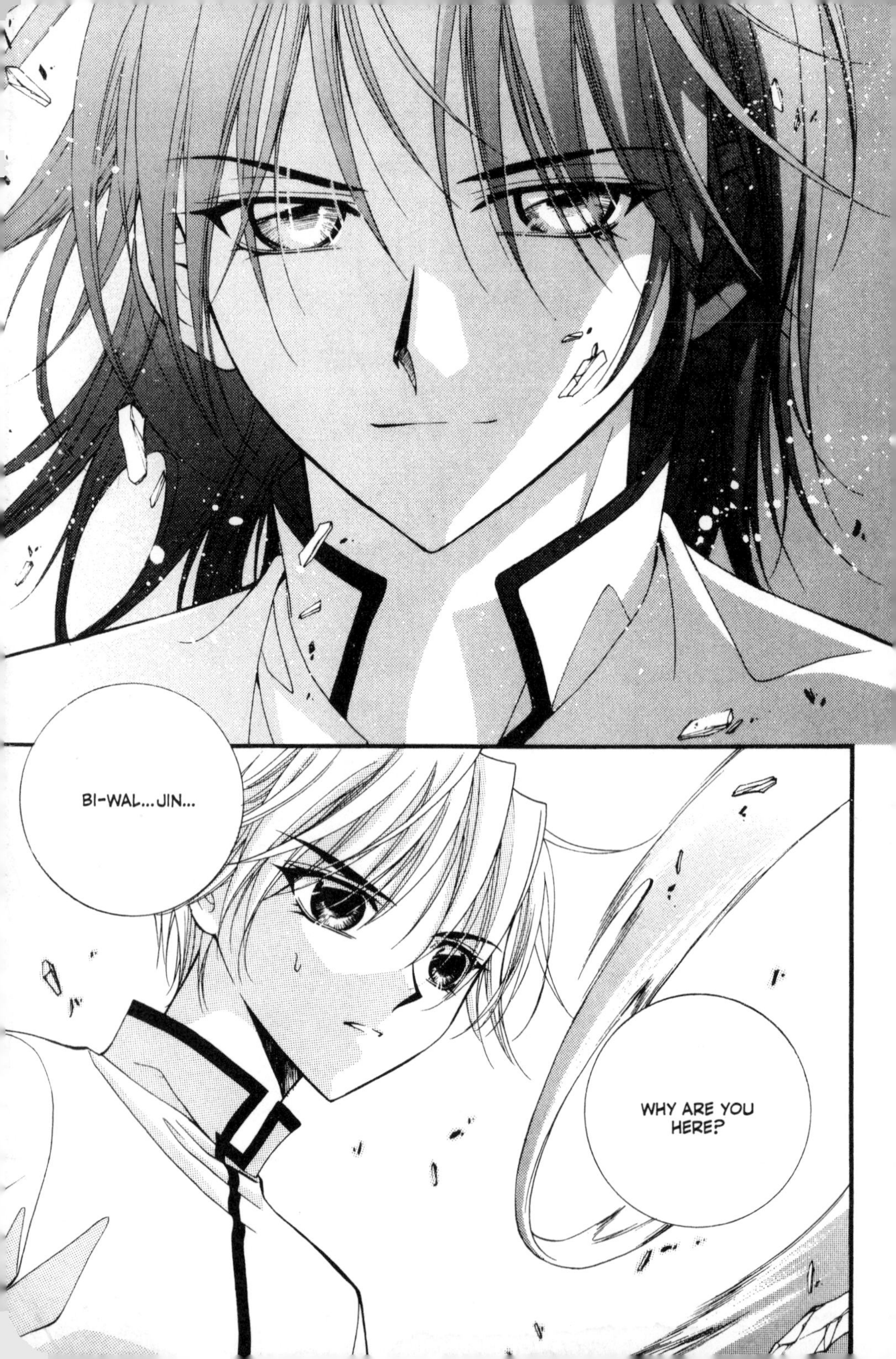
BI-WAL...JIN...
WHY ARE YOU HERE?

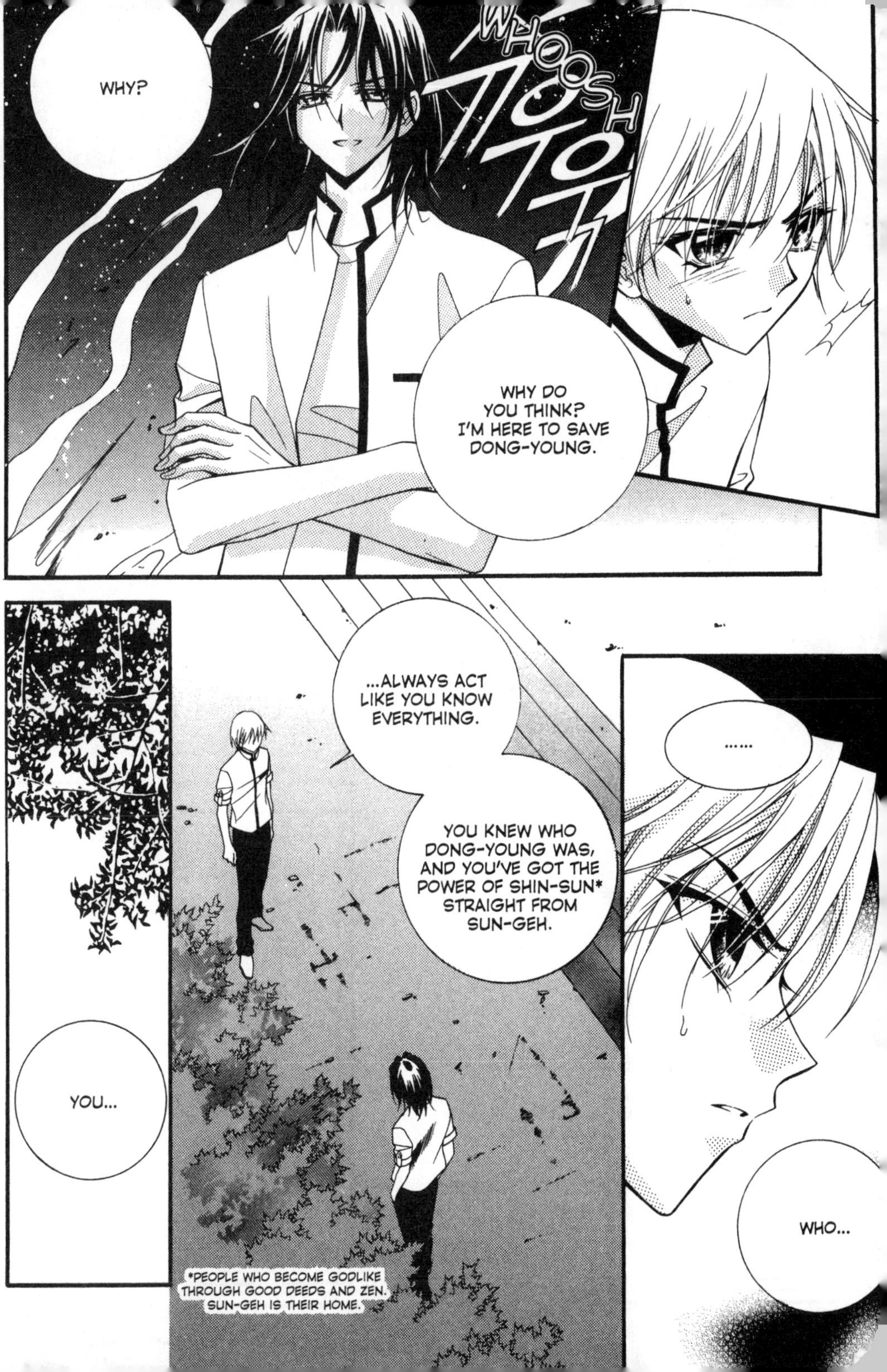
WHY?
WHOOSH
WHY DO YOU THINK? I'M HERE TO SAVE DONG-YOUNG.
YOU...
...ALWAYS ACT LIKE YOU KNOW EVERYTHING.
YOU KNEW WHO DONG-YOUNG WAS, AND YOU'VE GOT THE POWER OF SHIN-SUN* STRAIGHT FROM SUN-GEH.
......
WHO...
*PEOPLE WHO BECOME GODLIKE THROUGH GOOD DEEDS AND ZEN. SUN-GEH IS THEIR HOME.

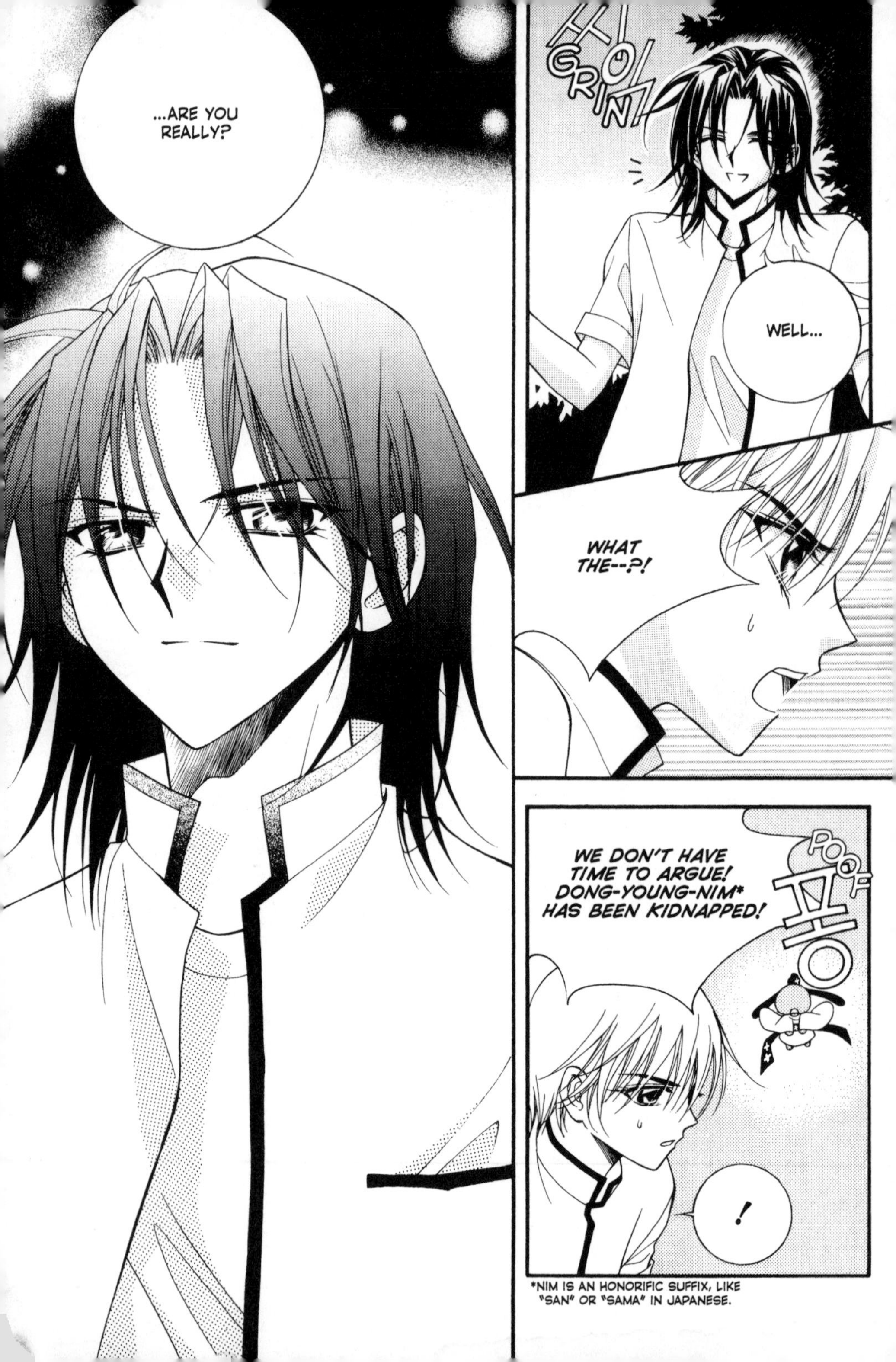
...ARE YOU REALLY?
GRIN
WELL...
WHAT THE--?!
WE DON'T HAVE TIME TO ARGUE! DONG-YOUNG-NIM* HAS BEEN KIDNAPPED!
POOF
!

*NIM IS AN HONORIFIC SUFFIX, LIKE "SAN" OR "SAMA" IN JAPANESE.

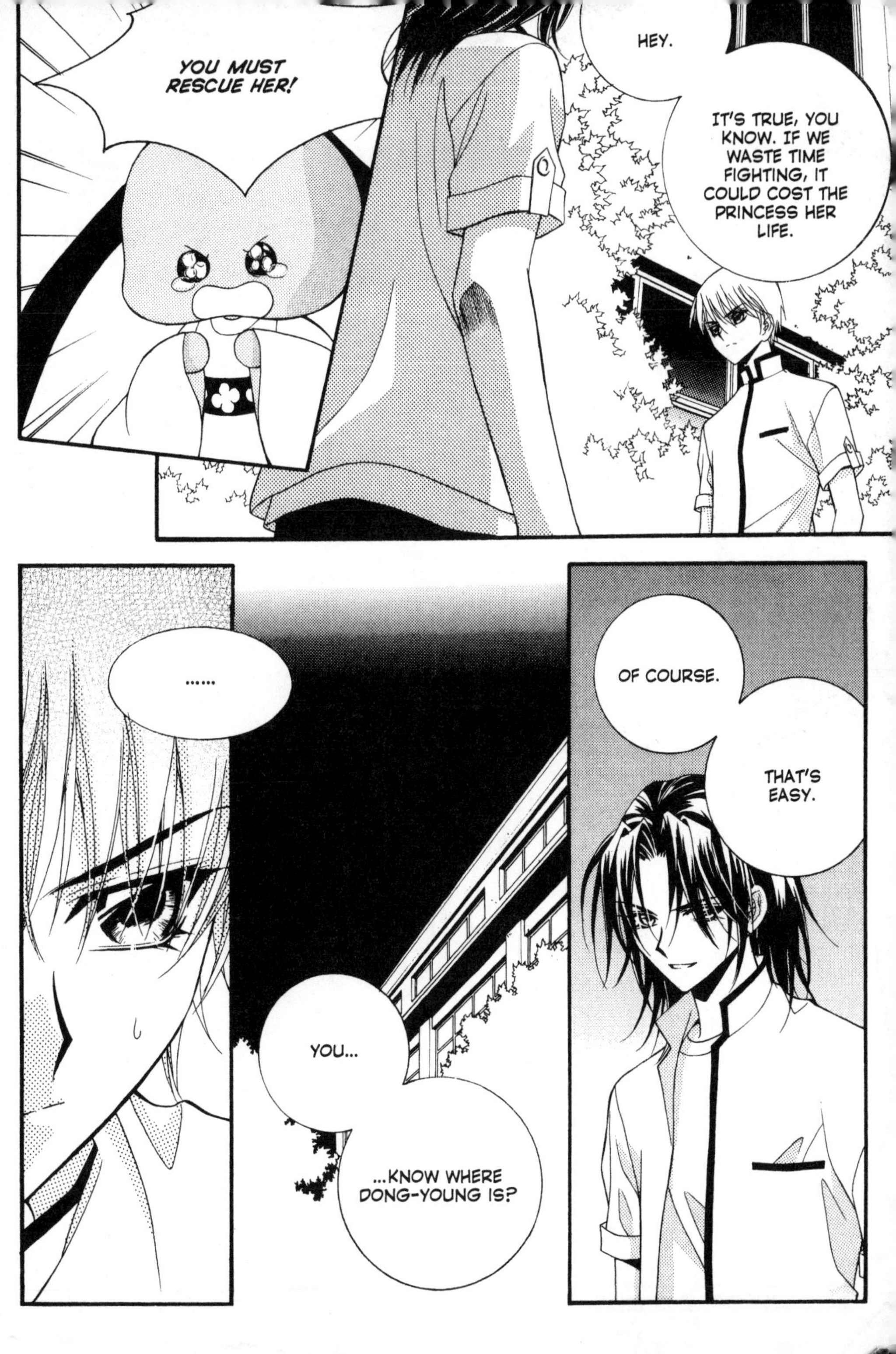
YOU MUST RESCUE HER!
HEY.
IT'S TRUE, YOU KNOW. IF WE WASTE TIME FIGHTING, IT COULD COST THE PRINCESS HER LIFE.
......
YOU...
...KNOW WHERE DONG-YOUNG IS?
OF COURSE.
THAT'S EASY.

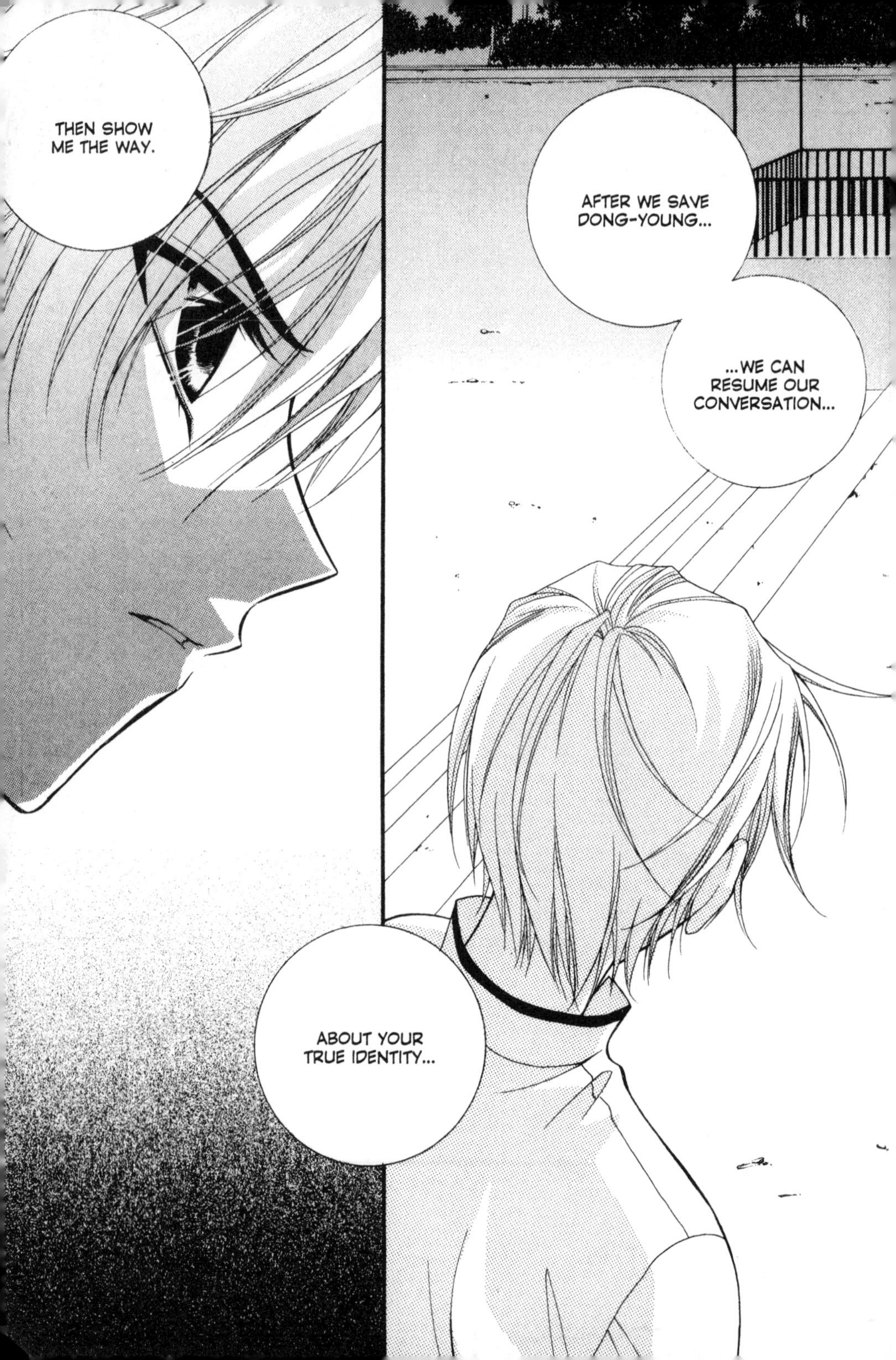
AFTER WE SAVE DONG-YOUNG...
...WE CAN RESUME OUR CONVERSATION...
THEN SHOW ME THE WAY.
ABOUT YOUR TRUE IDENTITY...

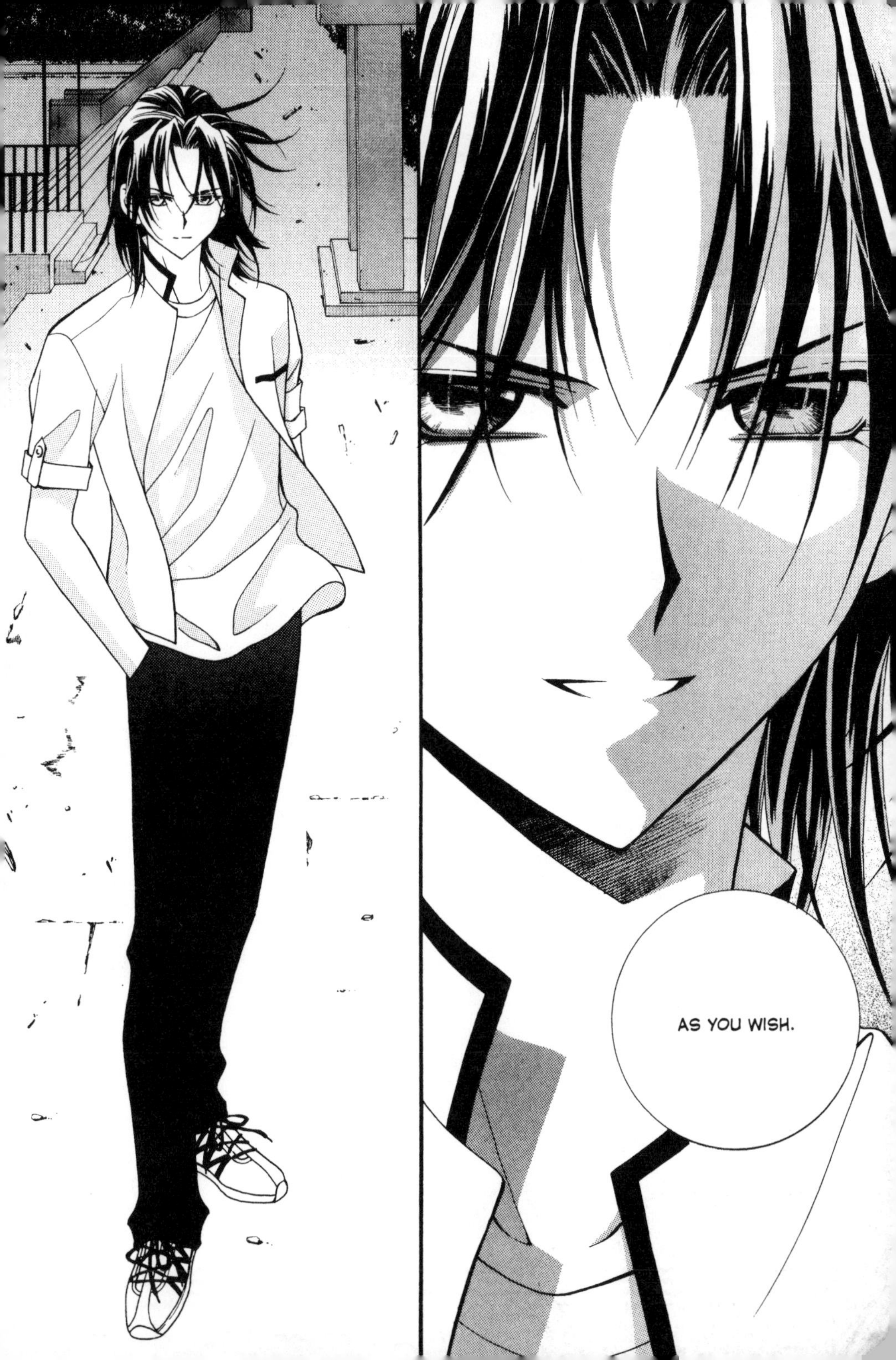
AS YOU WISH.

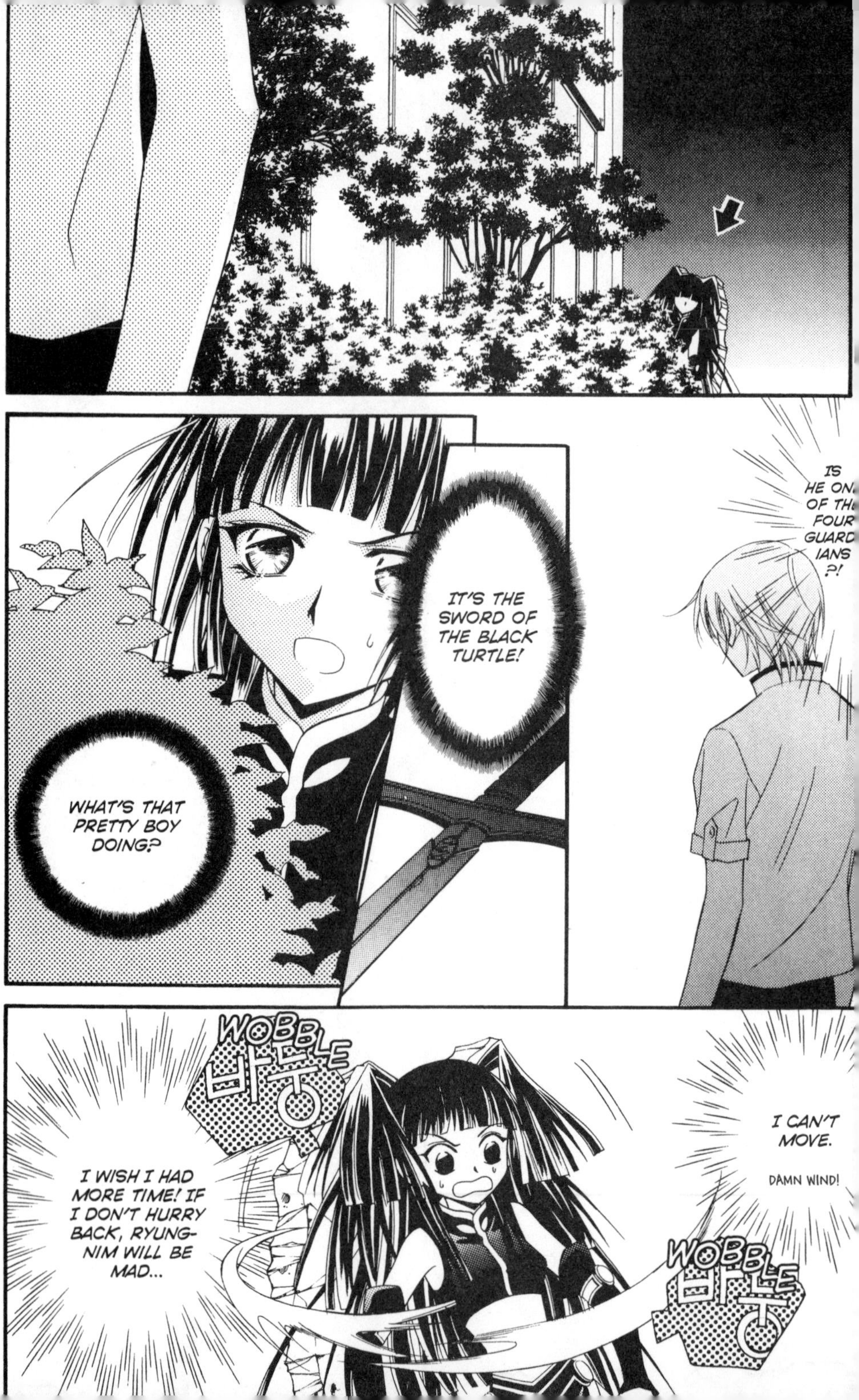
IS HE ON OF TH FOUR GUARD IANS ?!
IT'S THE SWORD OF THE BLACK TURTLE!
WHAT'S THAT PRETTY BOY DOING?
WOBBLE 바둥
I CAN'T MOVE.
DAMN WIND!
WOBBLE 바둥
I WISH I HAD MORE TIME! IF I DON'T HURRY BACK, RYUNG-NIM WILL BE MAD...

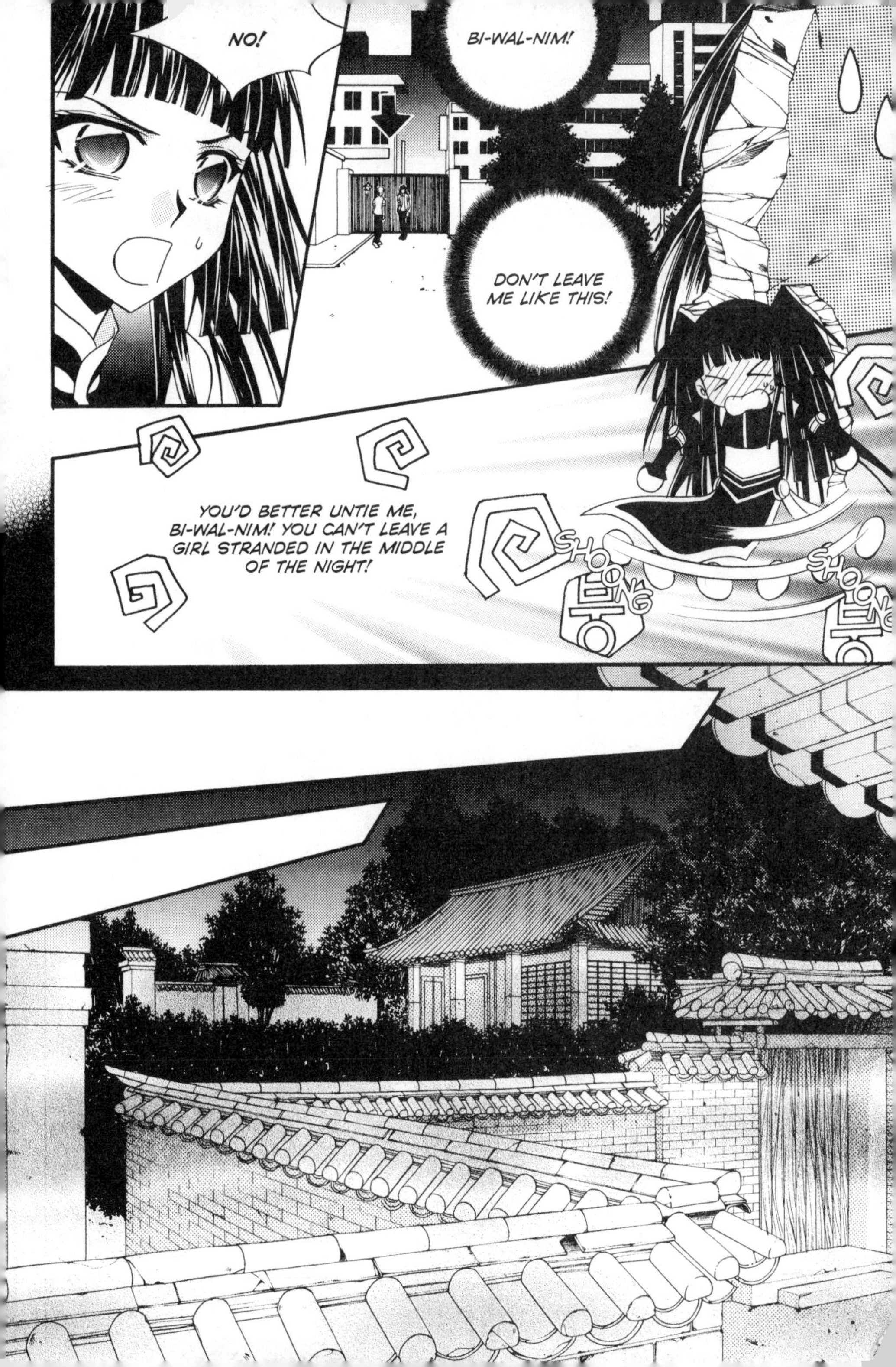
NO!
BI-WAL-NIM!
DON'T LEAVE ME LIKE THIS!
YOU'D BETTER UNTIE ME, BI-WAL-NIM! YOU CAN'T LEAVE A GIRL STRANDED IN THE MIDDLE OF THE NIGHT!
SHOOONG
SHOOONG

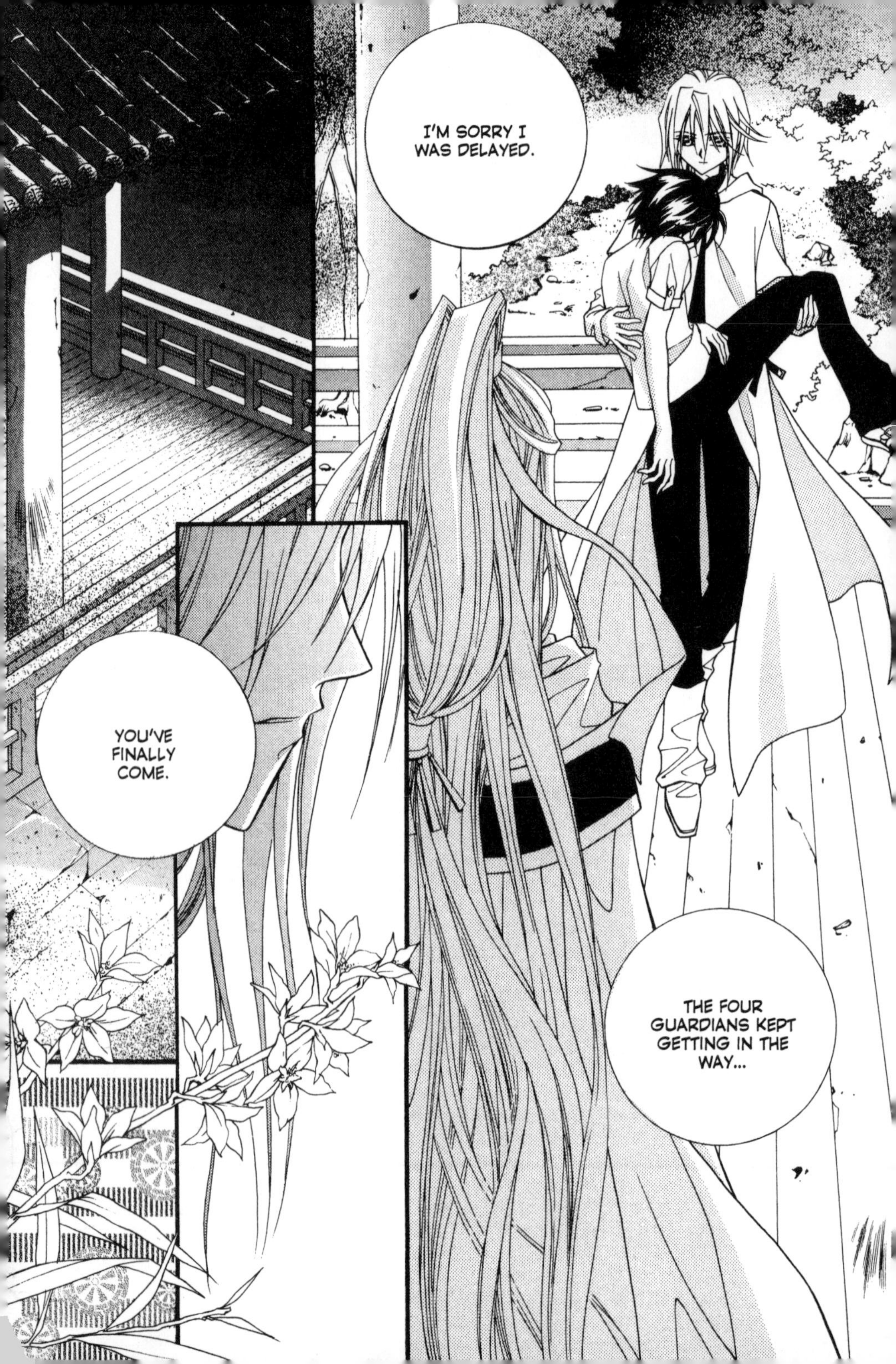
I'M SORRY I WAS DELAYED.
THE FOUR GUARDIANS KEPT GETTING IN THE WAY...
YOU'VE FINALLY COME.

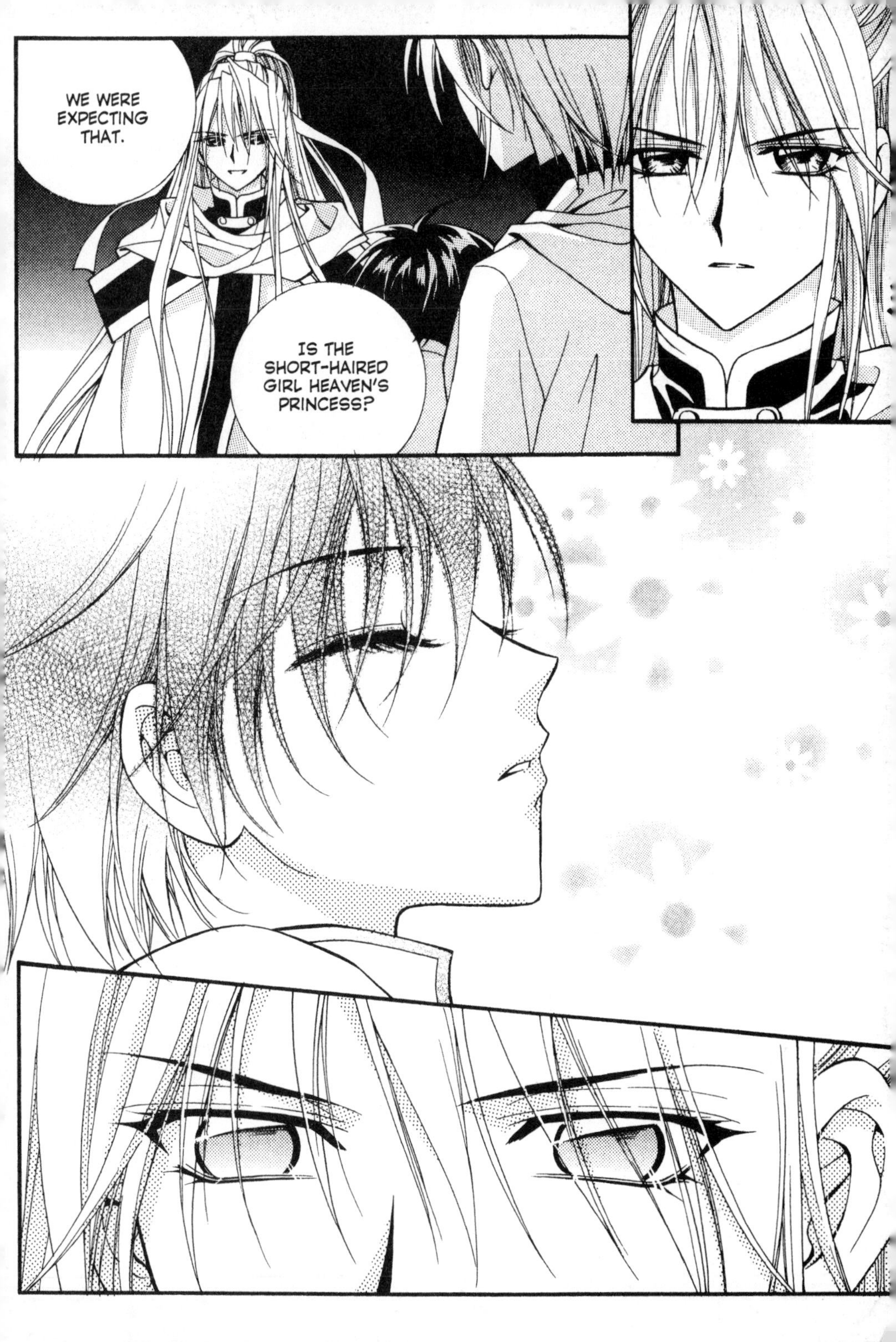
WE WERE EXPECTING THAT.
IS THE SHORT-HAIRED GIRL HEAVEN'S PRINCESS?

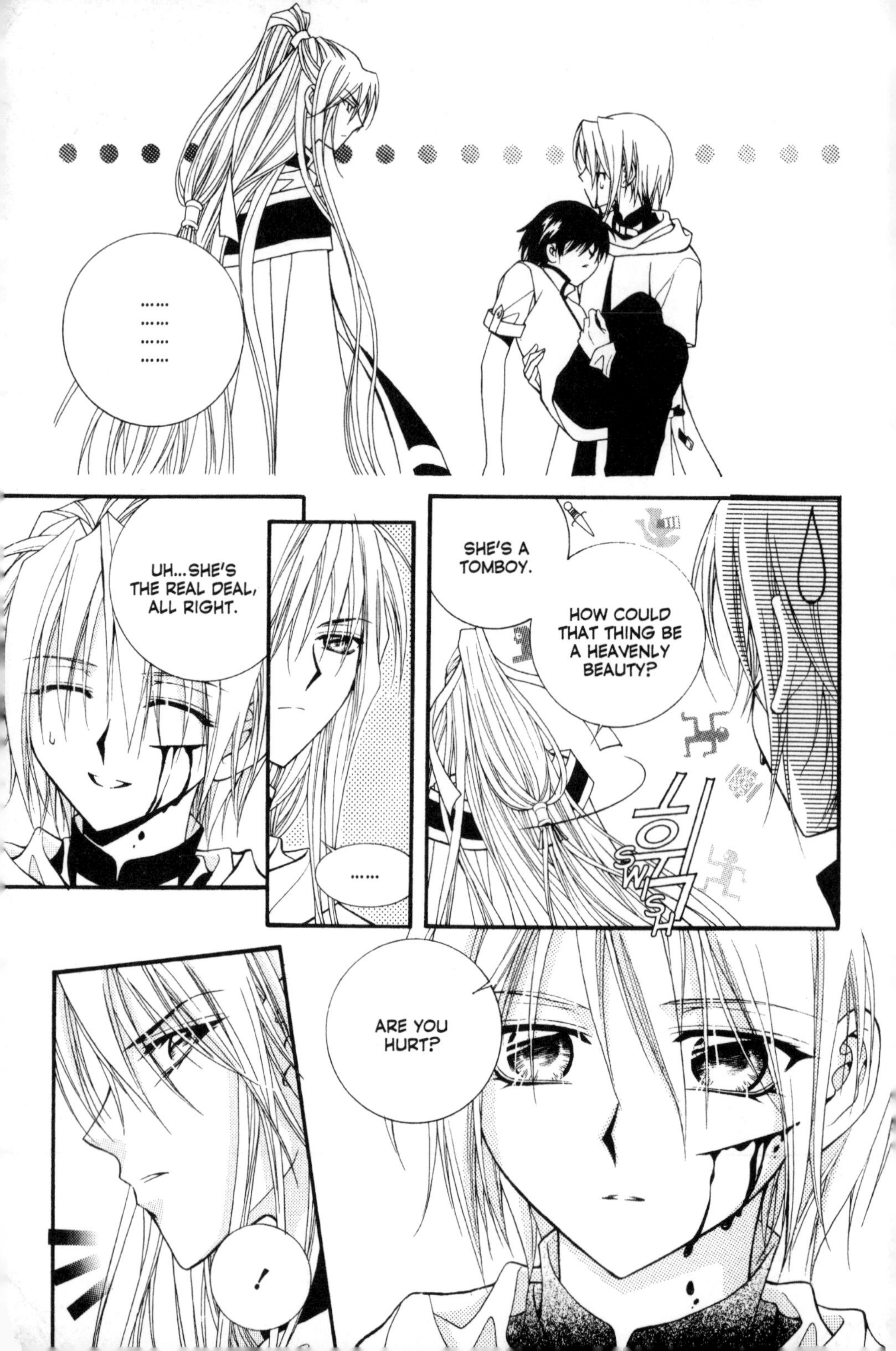

……
……
……
……
SHE'S A TOMBOY.
HOW COULD THAT THING BE A HEAVENLY BEAUTY?
SWISH
……
UH...SHE'S THE REAL DEAL, ALL RIGHT.
ARE YOU HURT?
!

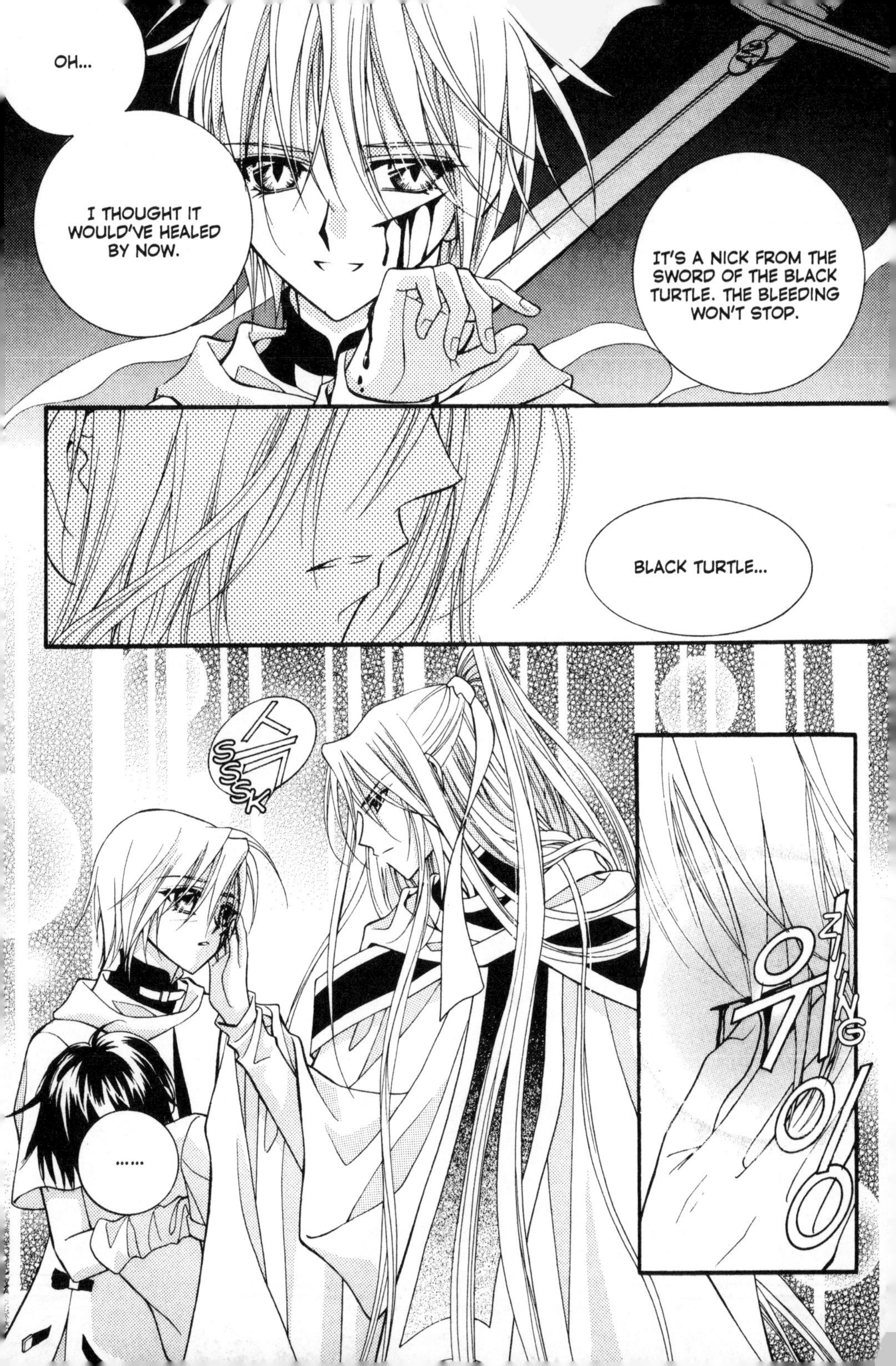
OH...
I THOUGHT IT WOULD'VE HEALED BY NOW.
IT'S A NICK FROM THE SWORD OF THE BLACK TURTLE. THE BLEEDING WON'T STOP.
BLACK TURTLE...
SSSK
ZING
......

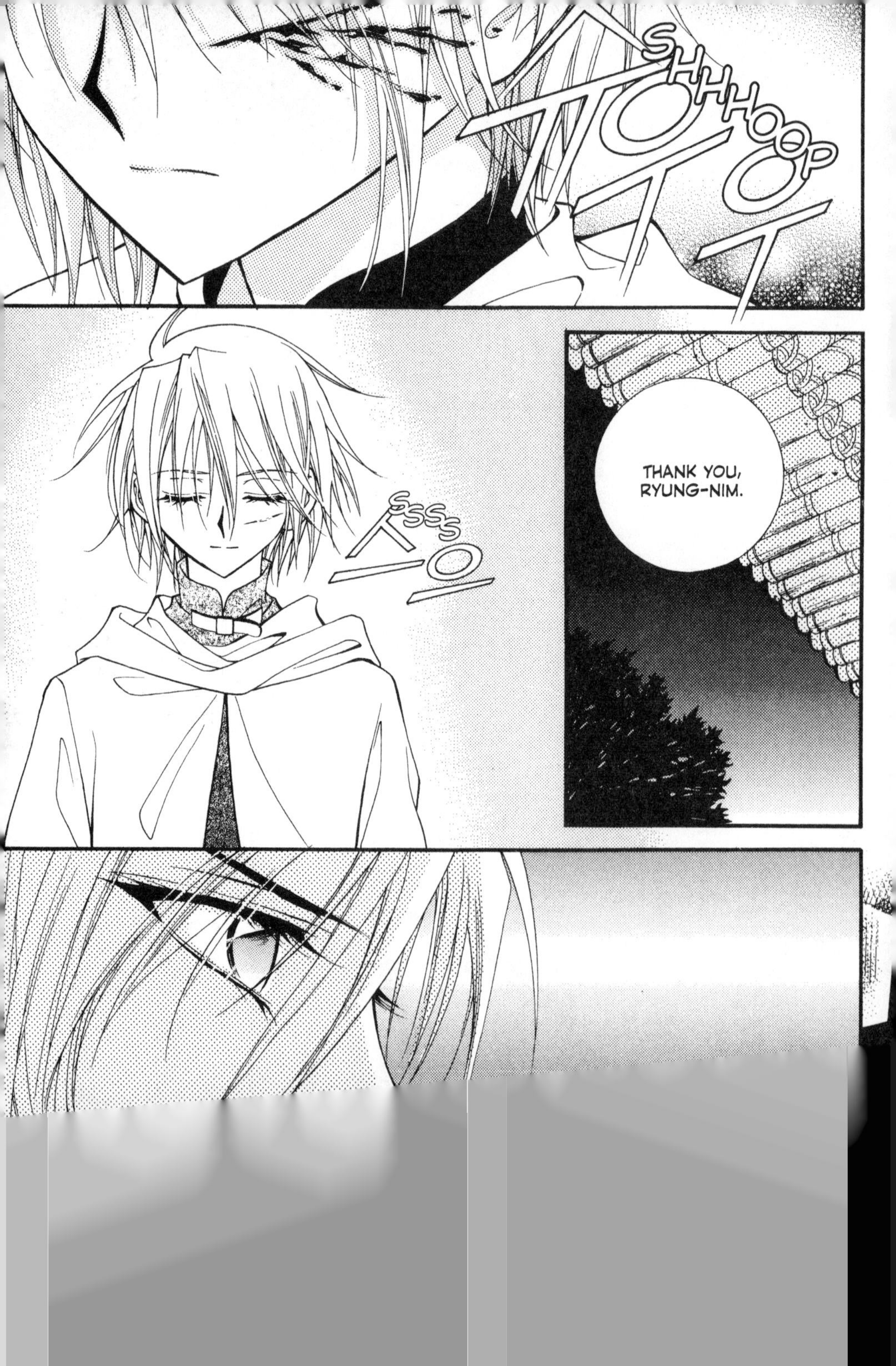
SHHHOOP
THANK YOU, RYUNG-NIM.
SSSS

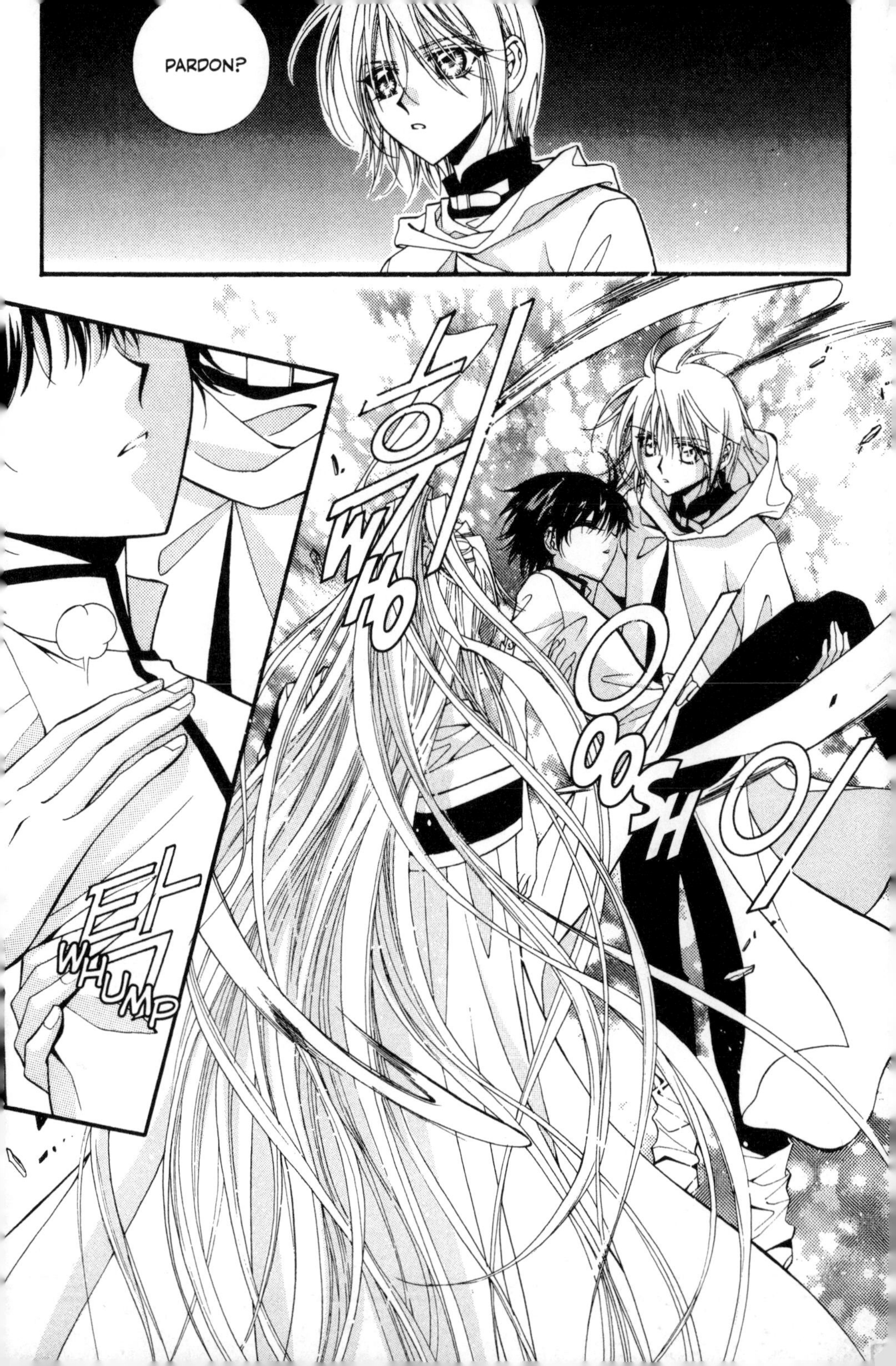
PARDON?
휘
WHOO
오오
OOSH
턱
WHUMP

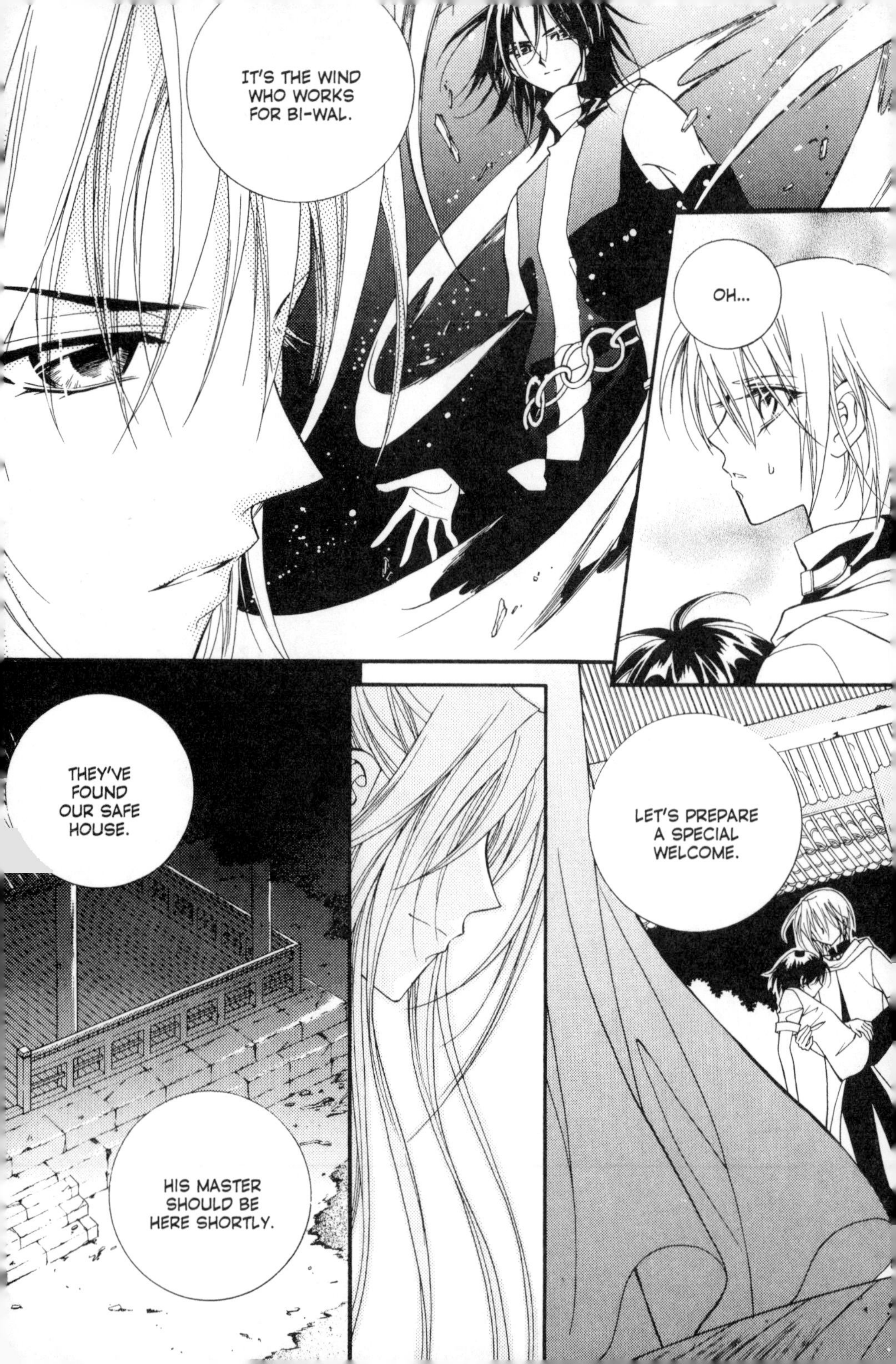
IT'S THE WIND WHO WORKS FOR BI-WAL.
OH...
LET'S PREPARE A SPECIAL WELCOME.
THEY'VE FOUND OUR SAFE HOUSE.
HIS MASTER SHOULD BE HERE SHORTLY.

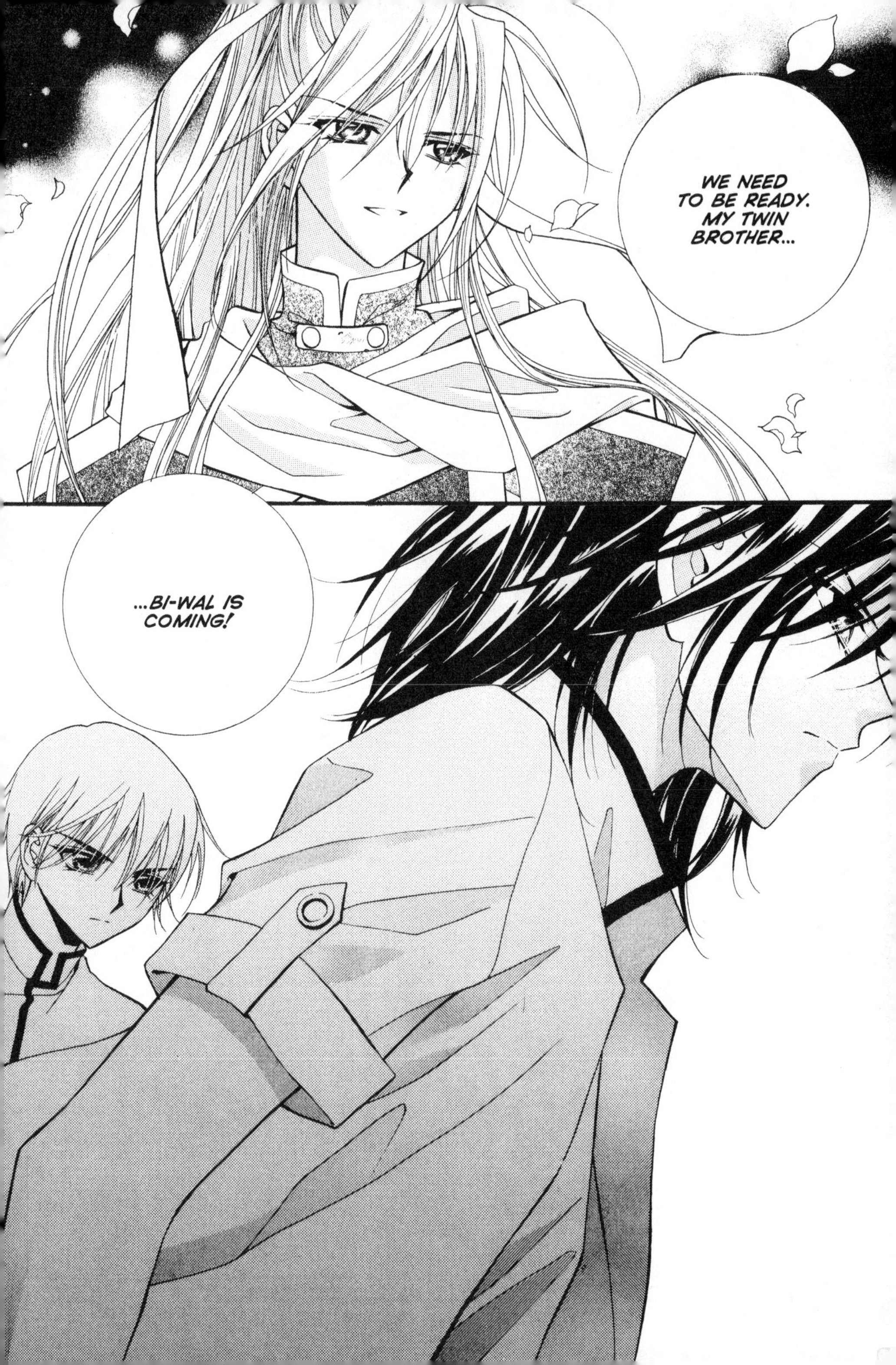
WE NEED TO BE READY. MY TWIN BROTHER...
...BI-WAL IS COMING!

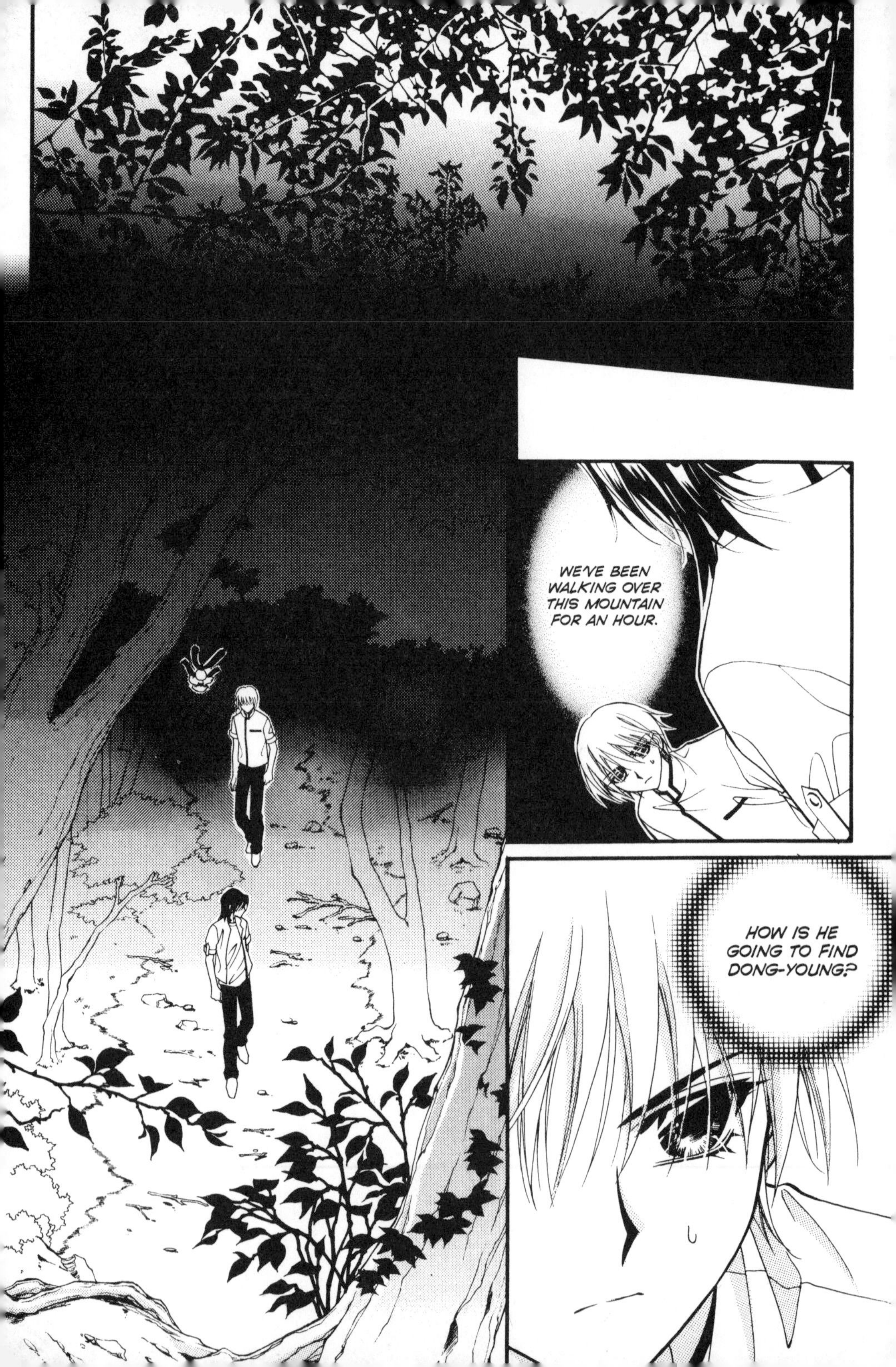
WE'VE BEEN WALKING OVER THIS MOUNTAIN FOR AN HOUR.
HOW IS HE GOING TO FIND DONG-YOUNG?

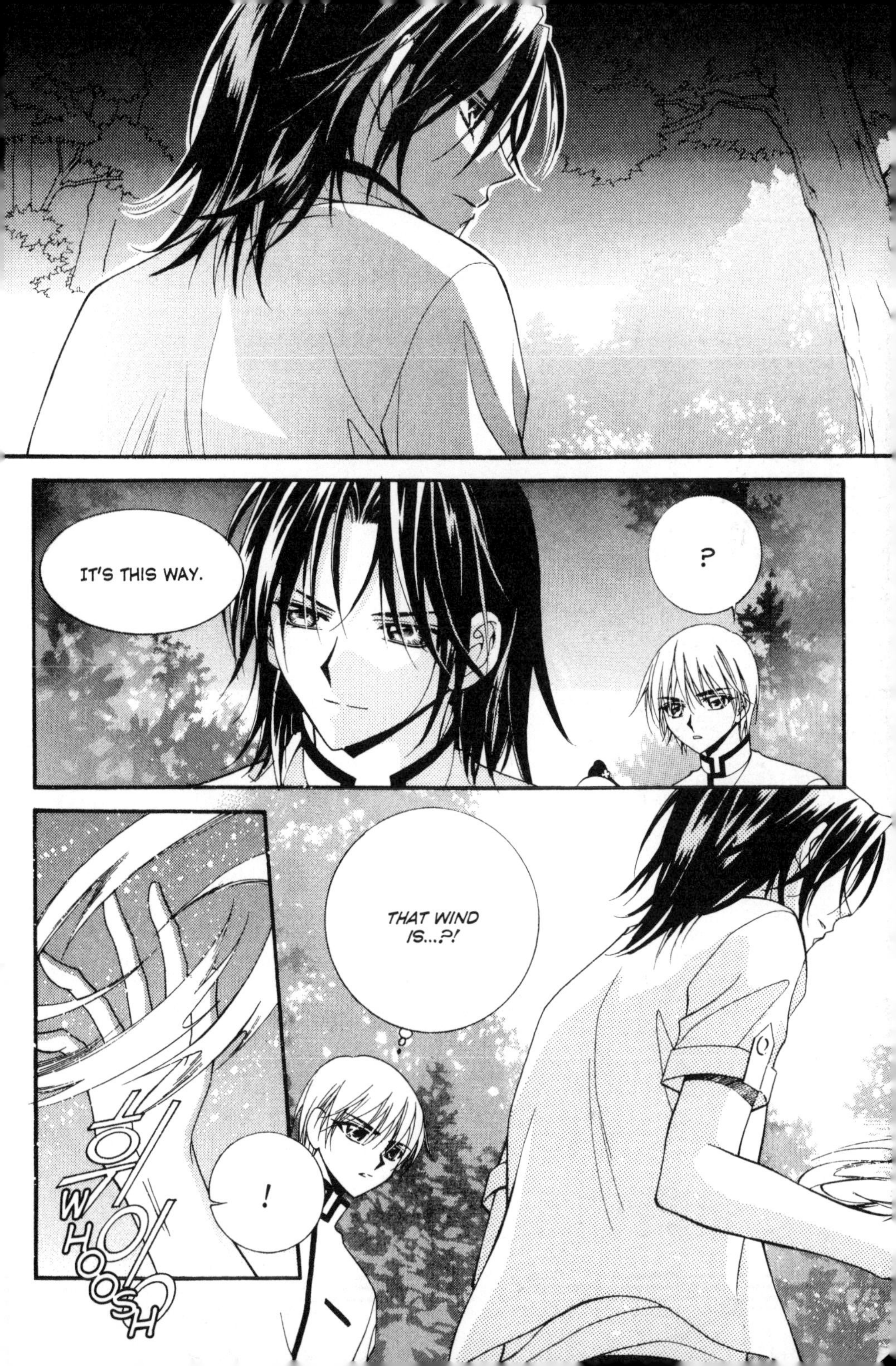
IT'S THIS WAY.
?
THAT WIND IS...?!
!
WHOOSH

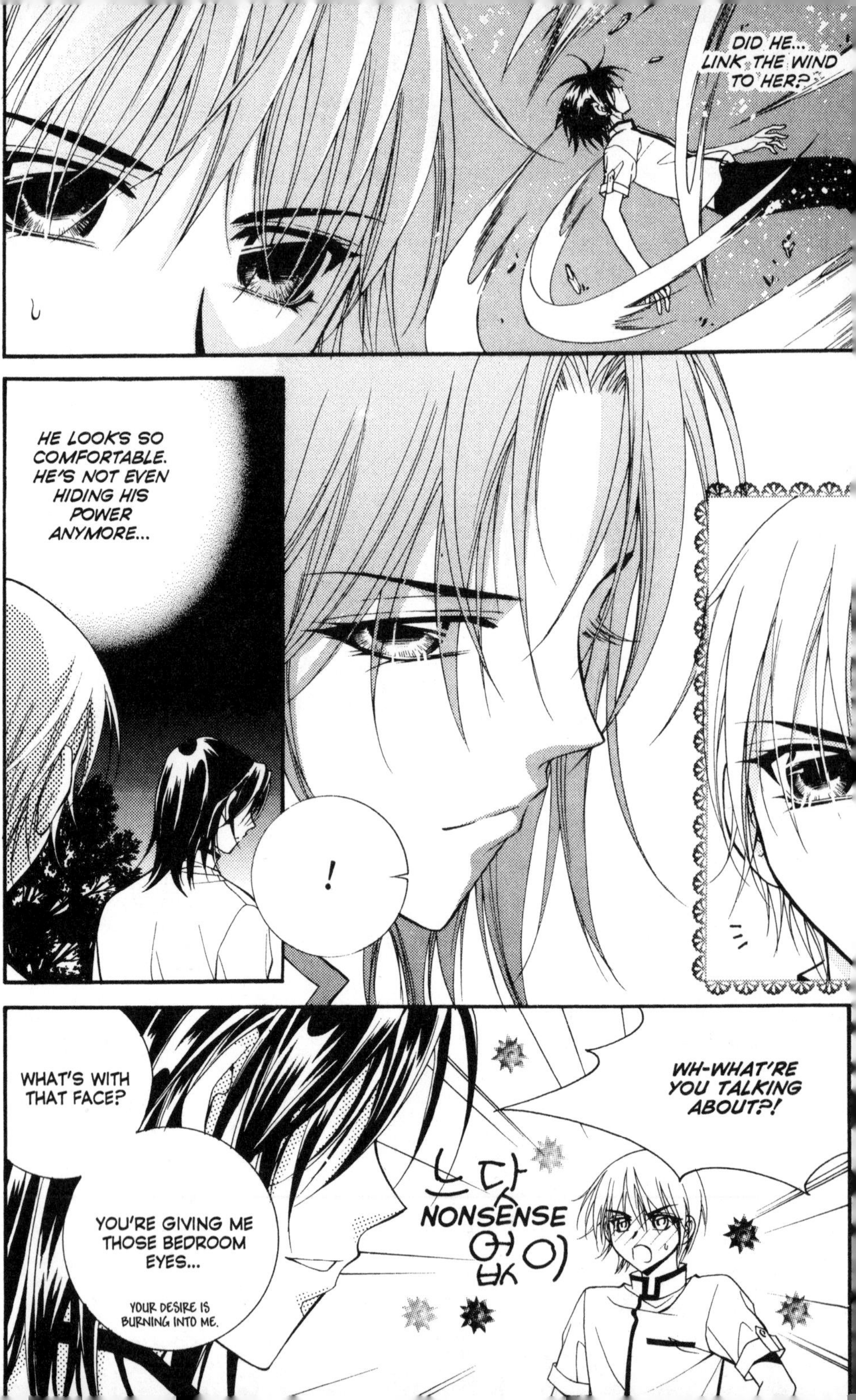
DID HE... LINK THE WIND TO HER?
HE LOOKS SO COMFORTABLE. HE'S NOT EVEN HIDING HIS POWER ANYMORE...
!
WHAT'S WITH THAT FACE?
YOU'RE GIVING ME THOSE BEDROOM EYES...
YOUR DESIRE IS BURNING INTO ME.
느닷없이
NONSENSE
WH-WHAT'RE YOU TALKING ABOUT?!

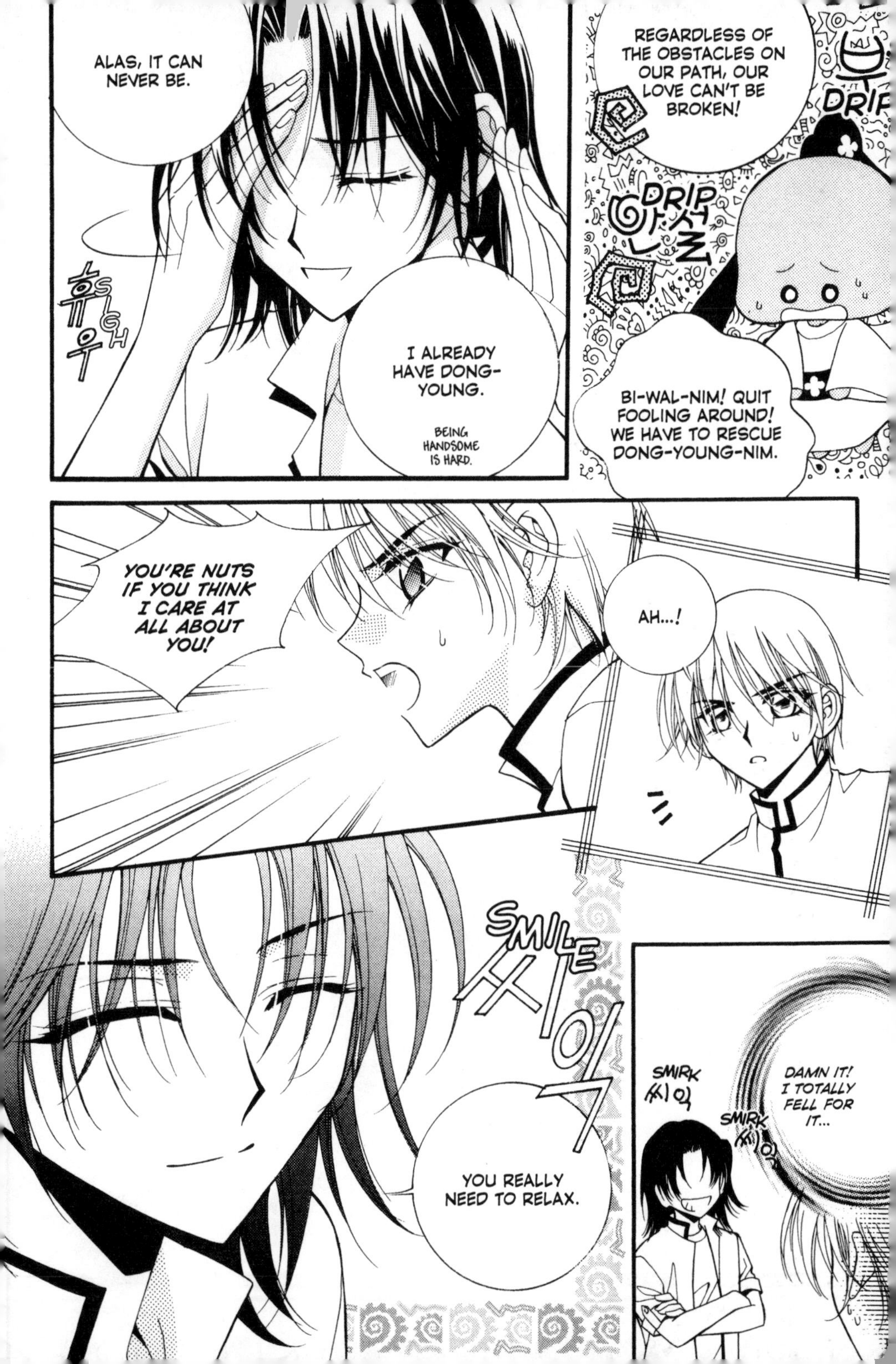
ALAS, IT CAN NEVER BE.
SIGH
I ALREADY HAVE DONG-YOUNG.
BEING HANDSOME IS HARD.
REGARDLESS OF THE OBSTACLES ON OUR PATH, OUR LOVE CAN'T BE BROKEN!
DRIP
DRIP
BI-WAL-NIM! QUIT FOOLING AROUND! WE HAVE TO RESCUE DONG-YOUNG-NIM.
YOU'RE NUTS IF YOU THINK I CARE AT ALL ABOUT YOU!
AH...!
SMILE
씨익
YOU REALLY NEED TO RELAX.
SMIRK
씨익
SMIRK
씨익
DAMN IT! I TOTALLY FELL FOR IT...

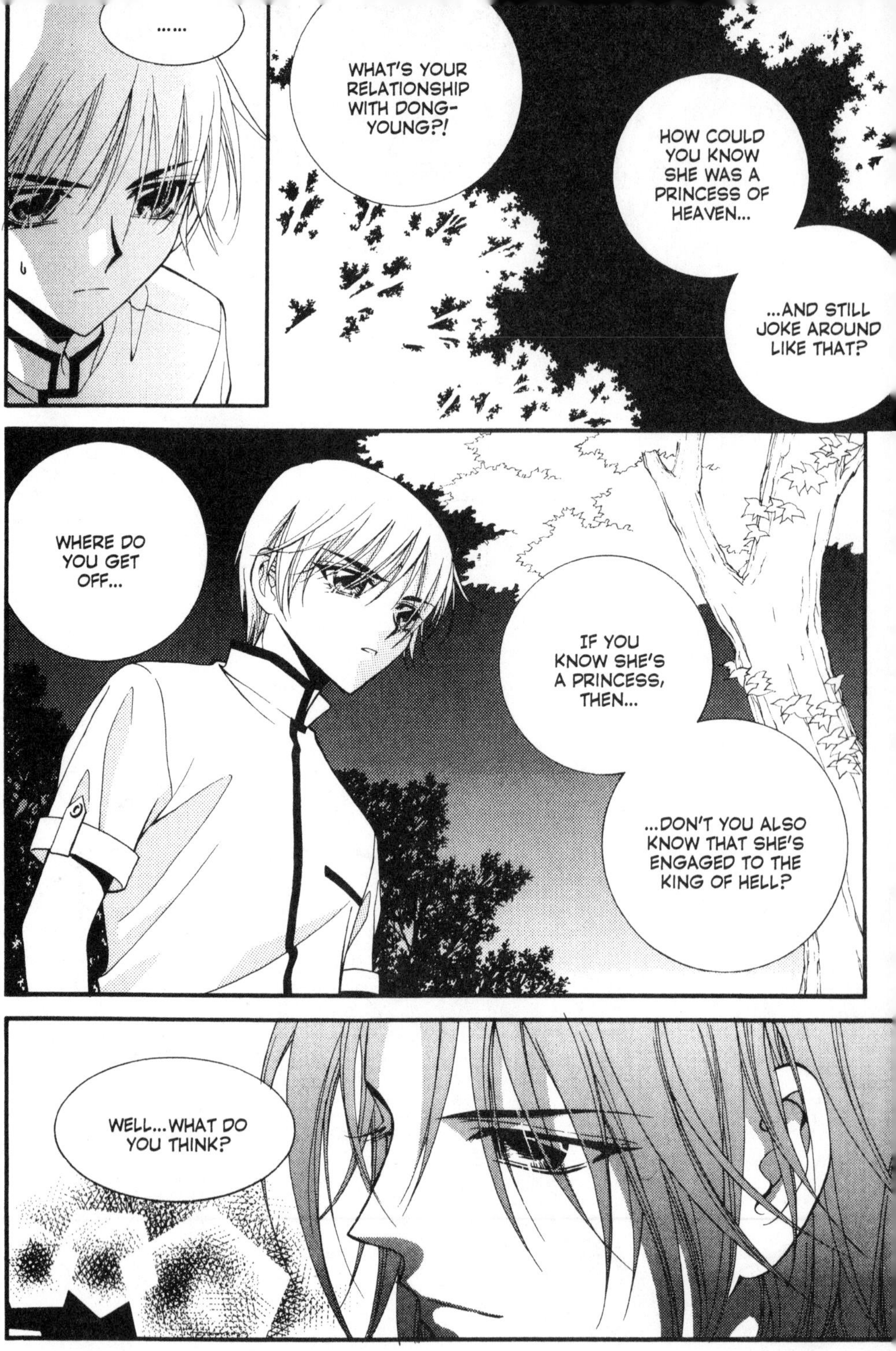
......
WHAT'S YOUR RELATIONSHIP WITH DONG-YOUNG?!
HOW COULD YOU KNOW SHE WAS A PRINCESS OF HEAVEN...
...AND STILL JOKE AROUND LIKE THAT?
WHERE DO YOU GET OFF...
IF YOU KNOW SHE'S A PRINCESS, THEN...
...DON'T YOU ALSO KNOW THAT SHE'S ENGAGED TO THE KING OF HELL?
WELL...WHAT DO YOU THINK?

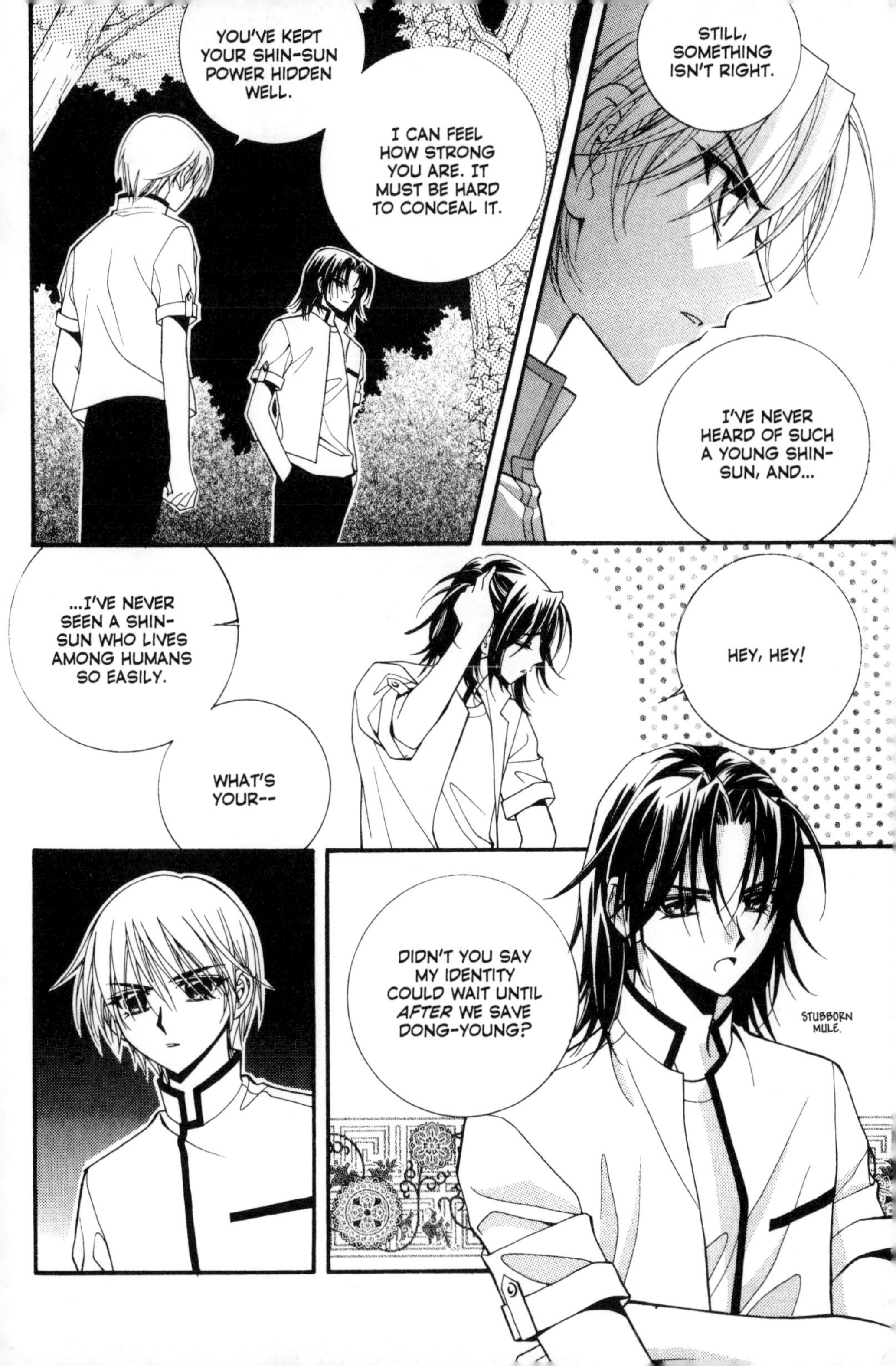

YOU'VE KEPT YOUR SHIN-SUN POWER HIDDEN WELL.
I CAN FEEL HOW STRONG YOU ARE. IT MUST BE HARD TO CONCEAL IT.
STILL, SOMETHING ISN'T RIGHT.
I'VE NEVER HEARD OF SUCH A YOUNG SHIN-SUN, AND...
...I'VE NEVER SEEN A SHIN-SUN WHO LIVES AMONG HUMANS SO EASILY.
WHAT'S YOUR--
HEY, HEY!
DIDN'T YOU SAY MY IDENTITY COULD WAIT UNTIL *AFTER* WE SAVE DONG-YOUNG?
STUBBORN MULE.

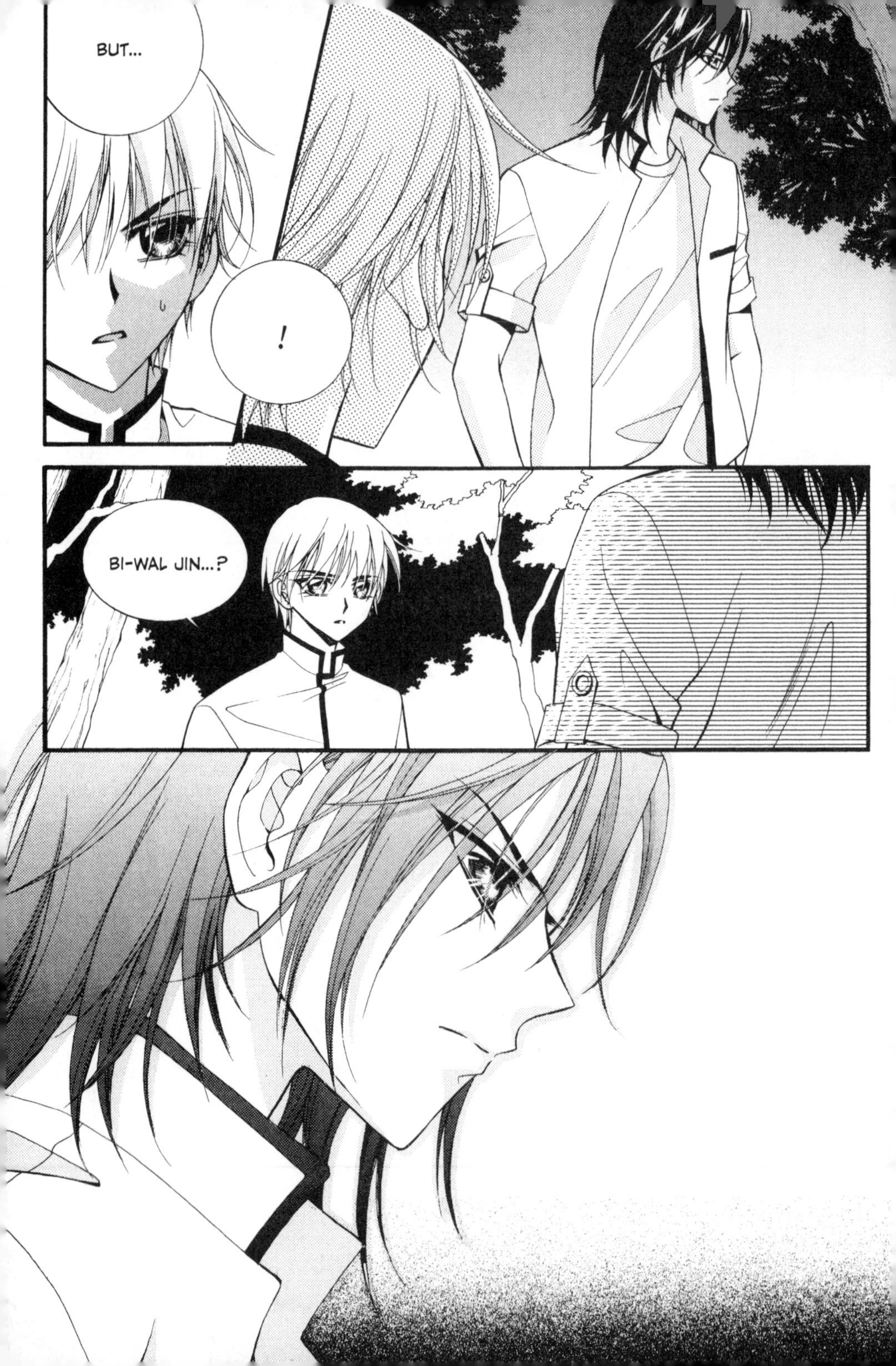
BUT...
!
BI-WAL JIN...?

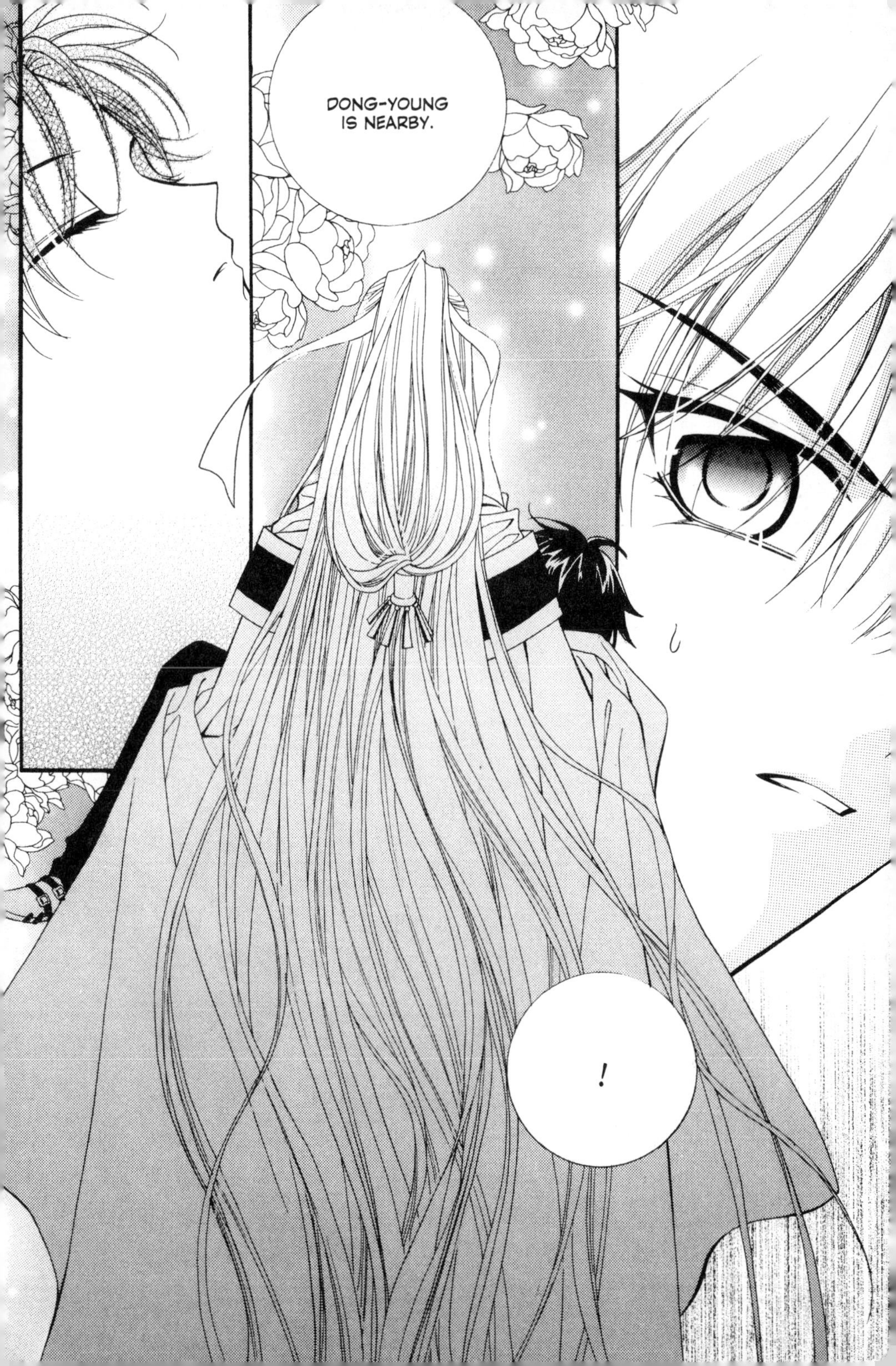
DONG-YOUNG IS NEARBY.
!

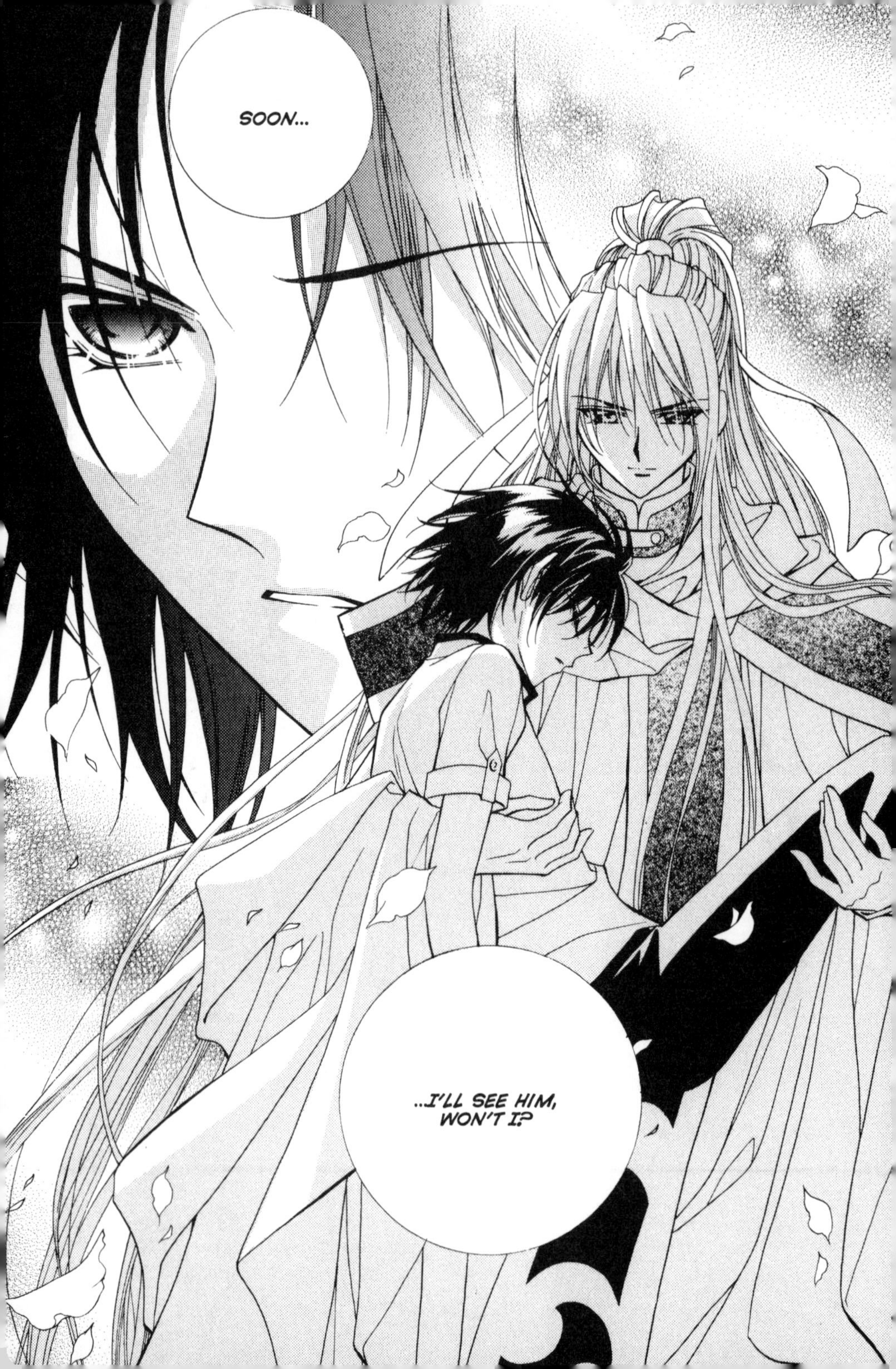
SOON...
...I'LL SEE HIM, WON'T I?

VII CHOOSING AND BEING CHOSEN

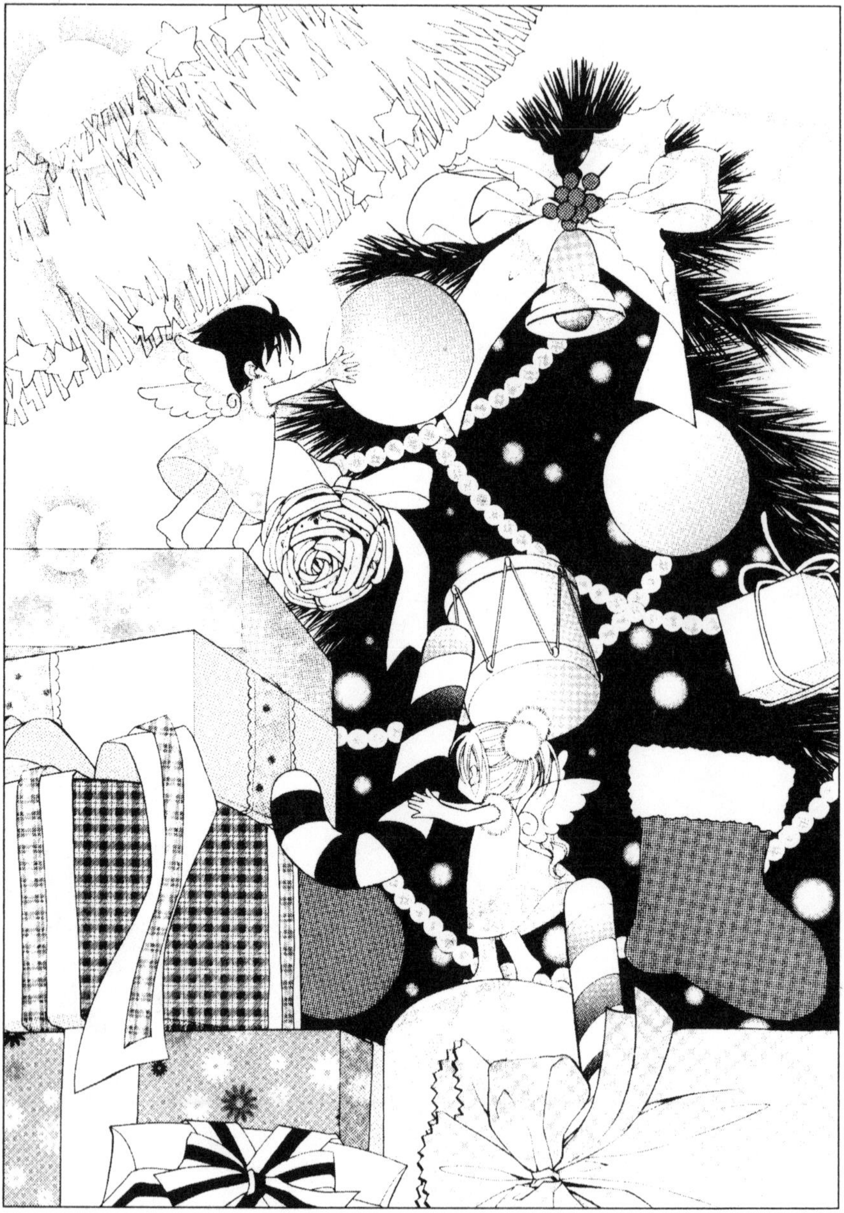

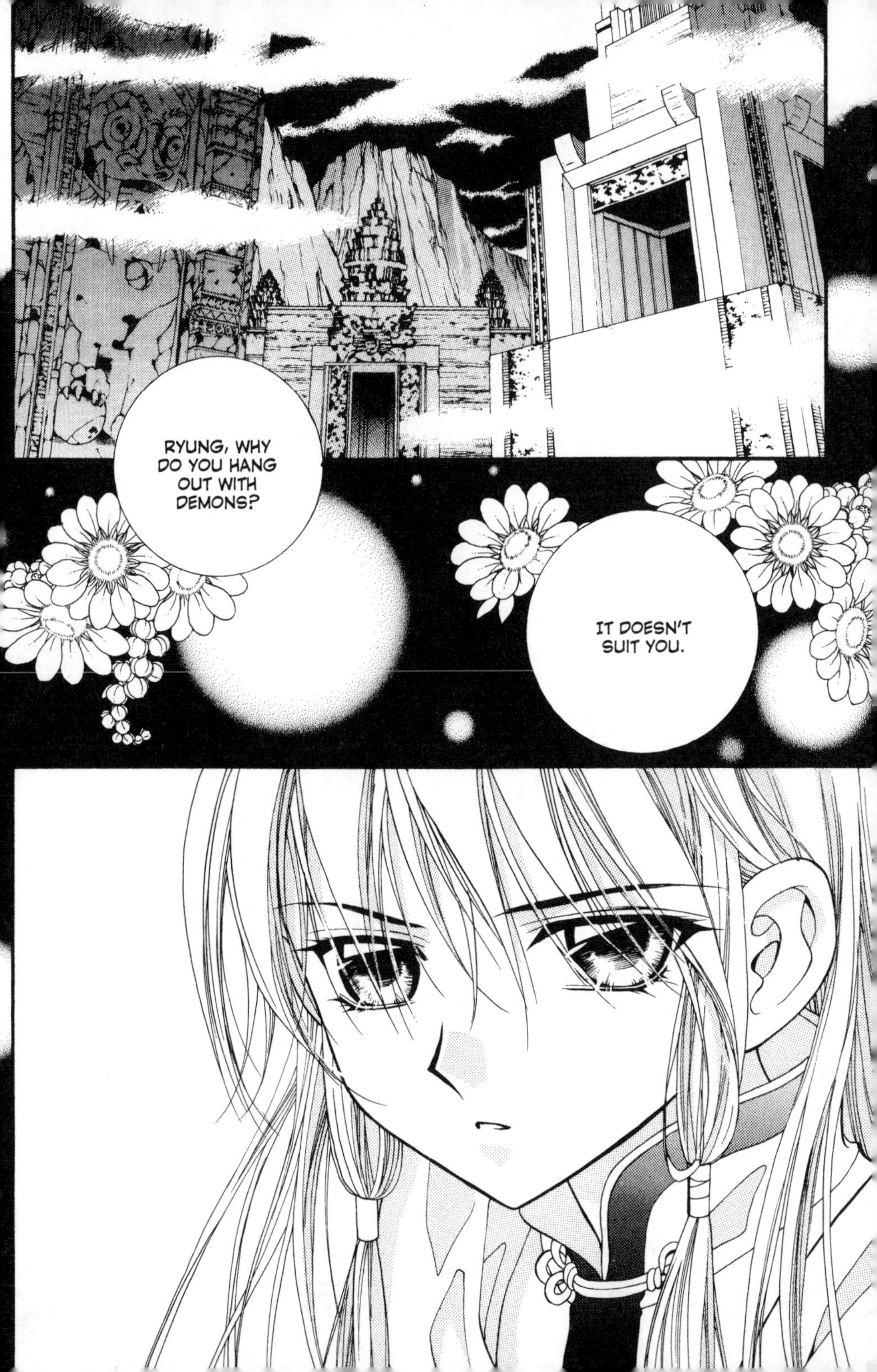
RYUNG, WHY DO YOU HANG OUT WITH DEMONS?
IT DOESN'T SUIT YOU.

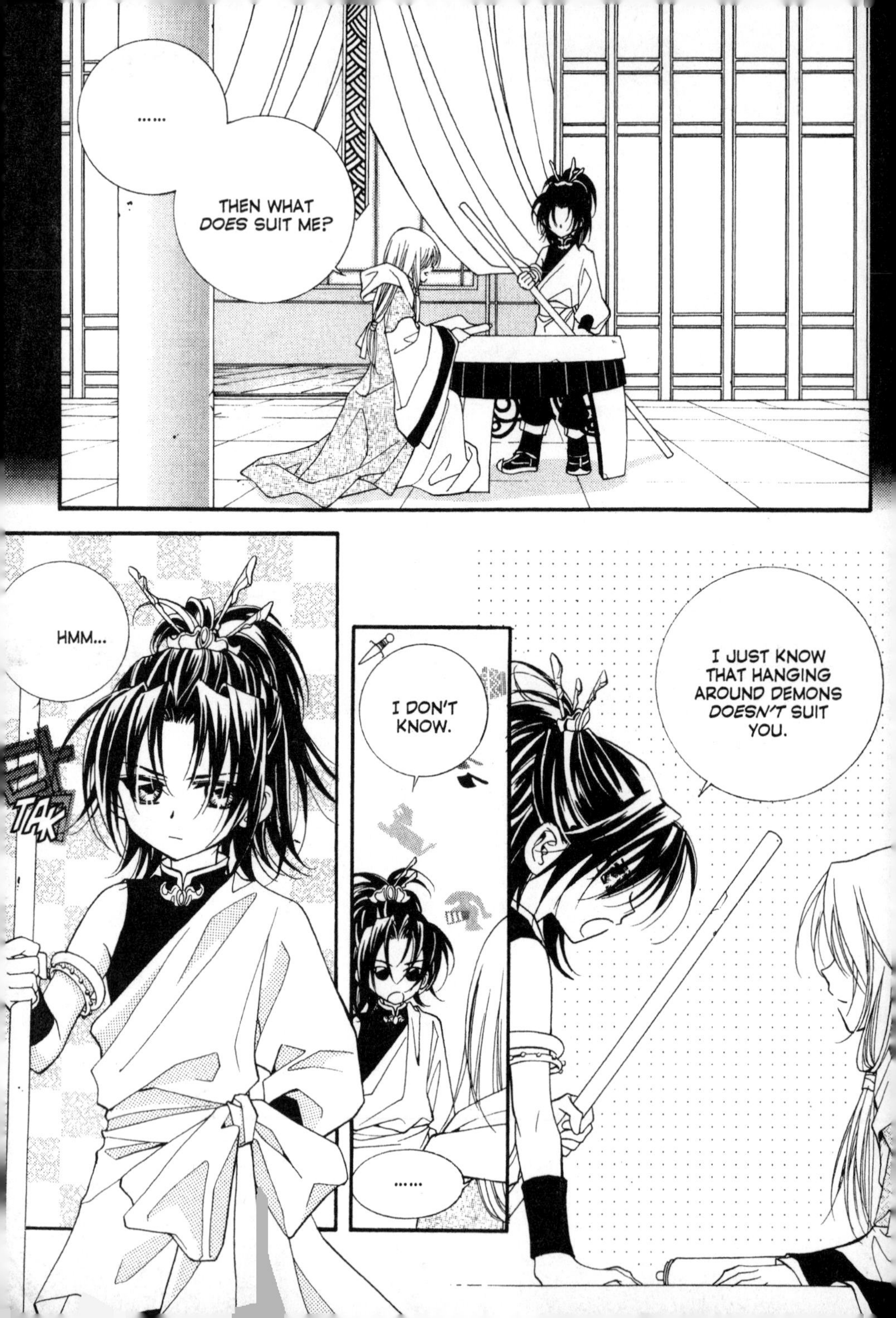
......
THEN WHAT DOES SUIT ME?
I JUST KNOW THAT HANGING AROUND DEMONS DOESN'T SUIT YOU.
I DON'T KNOW.
......
HMM...
TAK

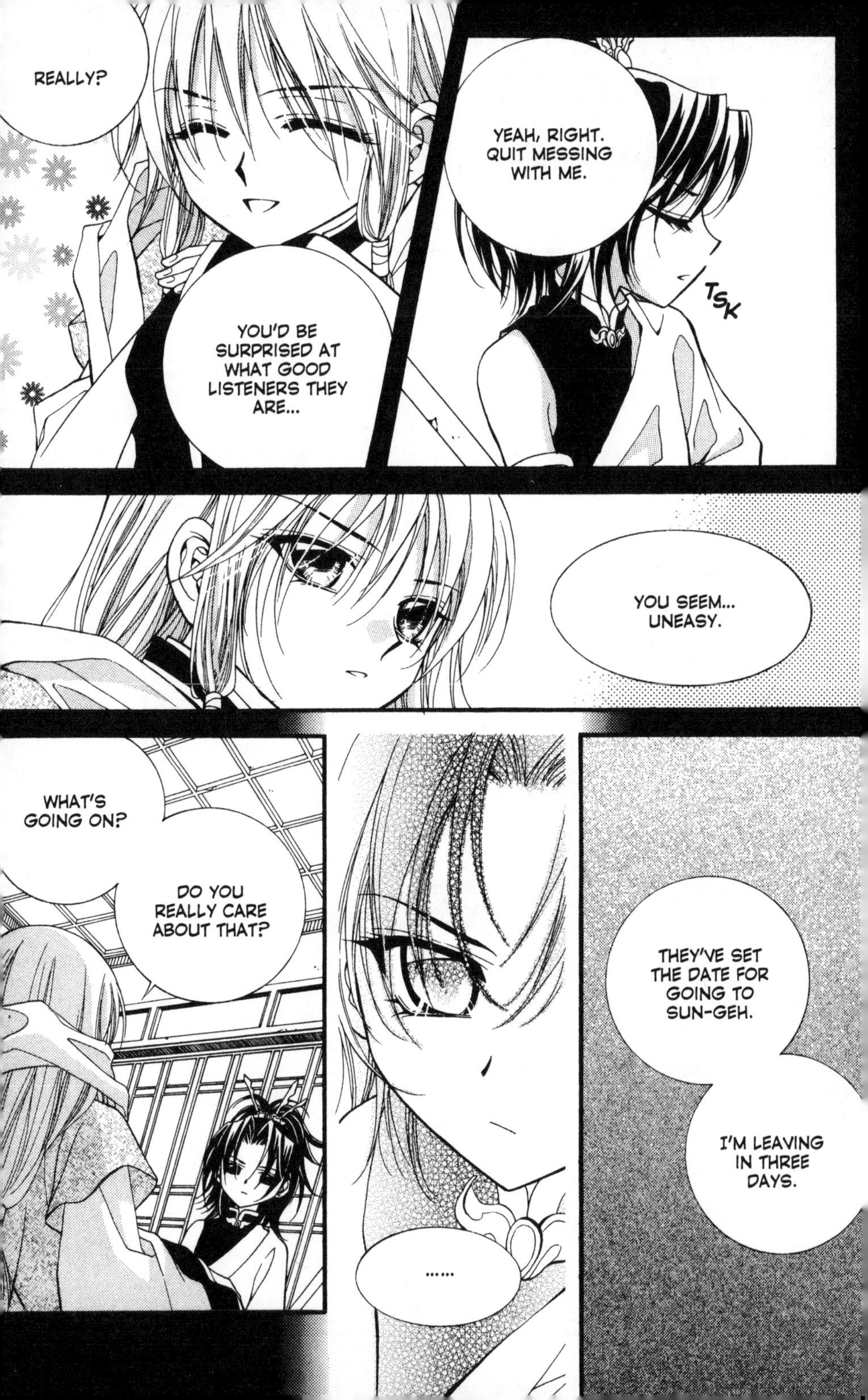
REALLY?
YOU'D BE SURPRISED AT WHAT GOOD LISTENERS THEY ARE...
YEAH, RIGHT. QUIT MESSING WITH ME.
TSK
YOU SEEM... UNEASY.
WHAT'S GOING ON?
DO YOU REALLY CARE ABOUT THAT?
......
THEY'VE SET THE DATE FOR GOING TO SUN-GEH.
I'M LEAVING IN THREE DAYS.

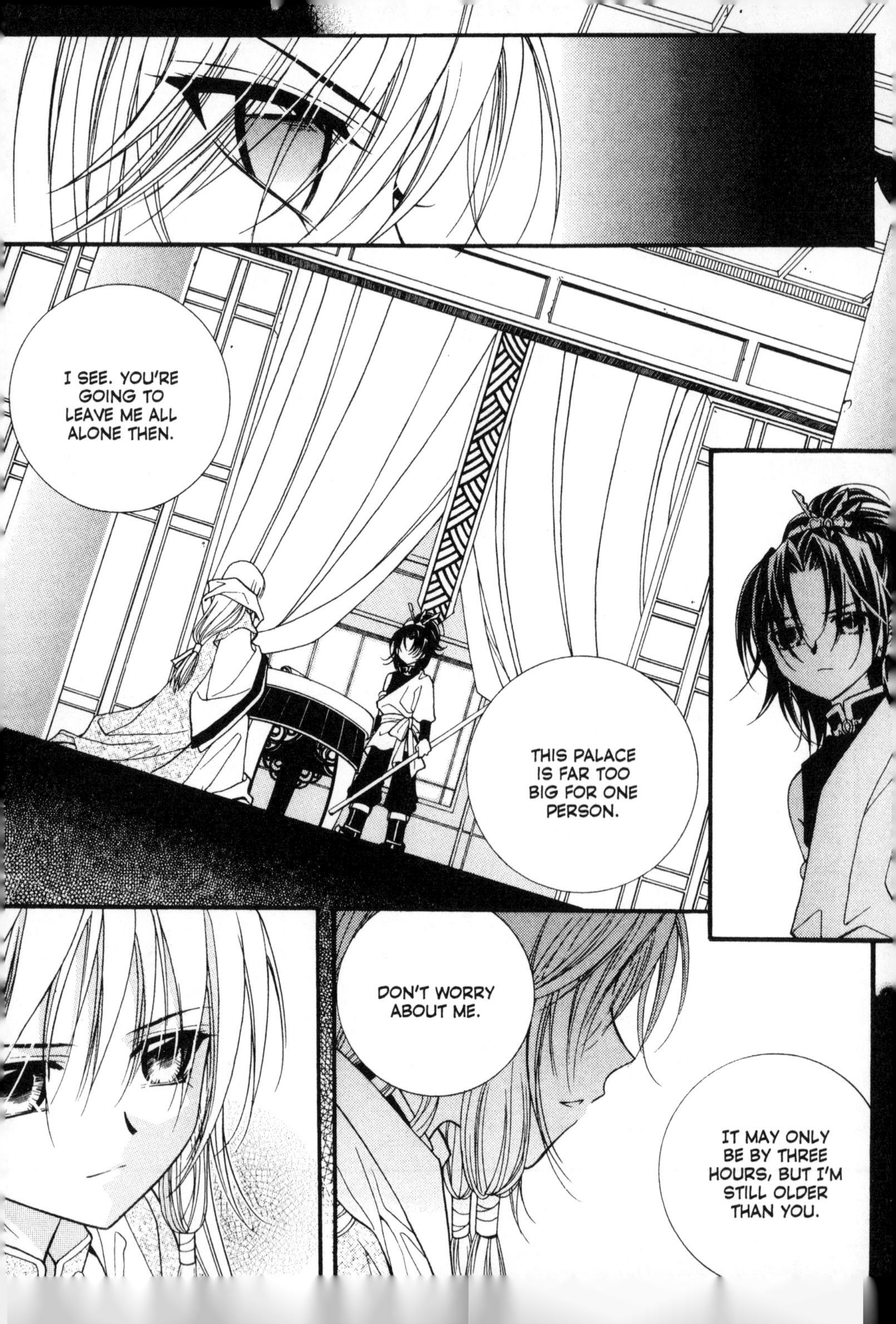

I SEE. YOU'RE GOING TO LEAVE ME ALL ALONE THEN.
THIS PALACE IS FAR TOO BIG FOR ONE PERSON.
IT MAY ONLY BE BY THREE HOURS, BUT I'M STILL OLDER THAN YOU.
DON'T WORRY ABOUT ME.

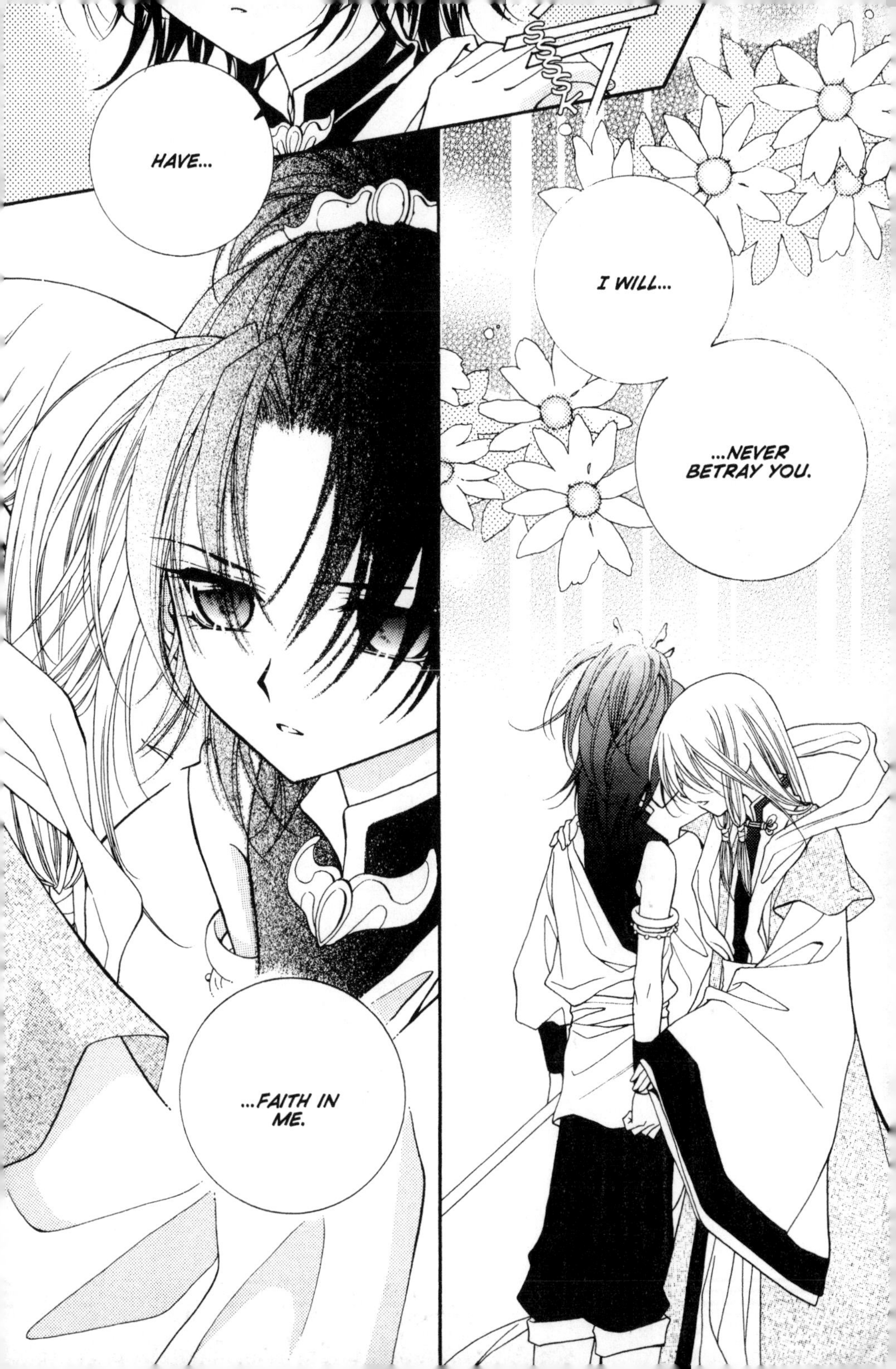
SSSSK
I WILL...
...NEVER BETRAY YOU.
HAVE...
...FAITH IN ME.

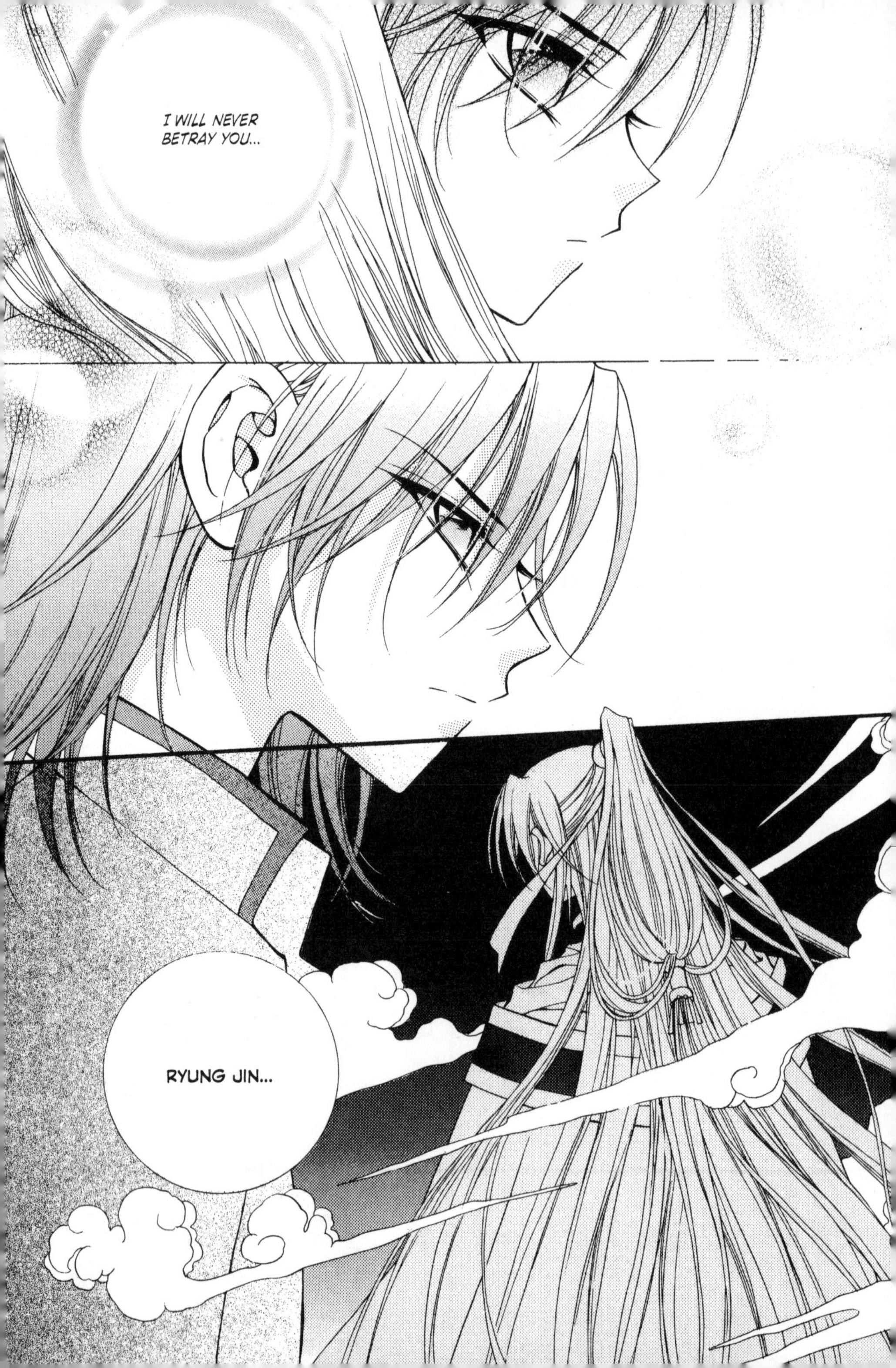
I WILL NEVER BETRAY YOU...
RYUNG JIN...

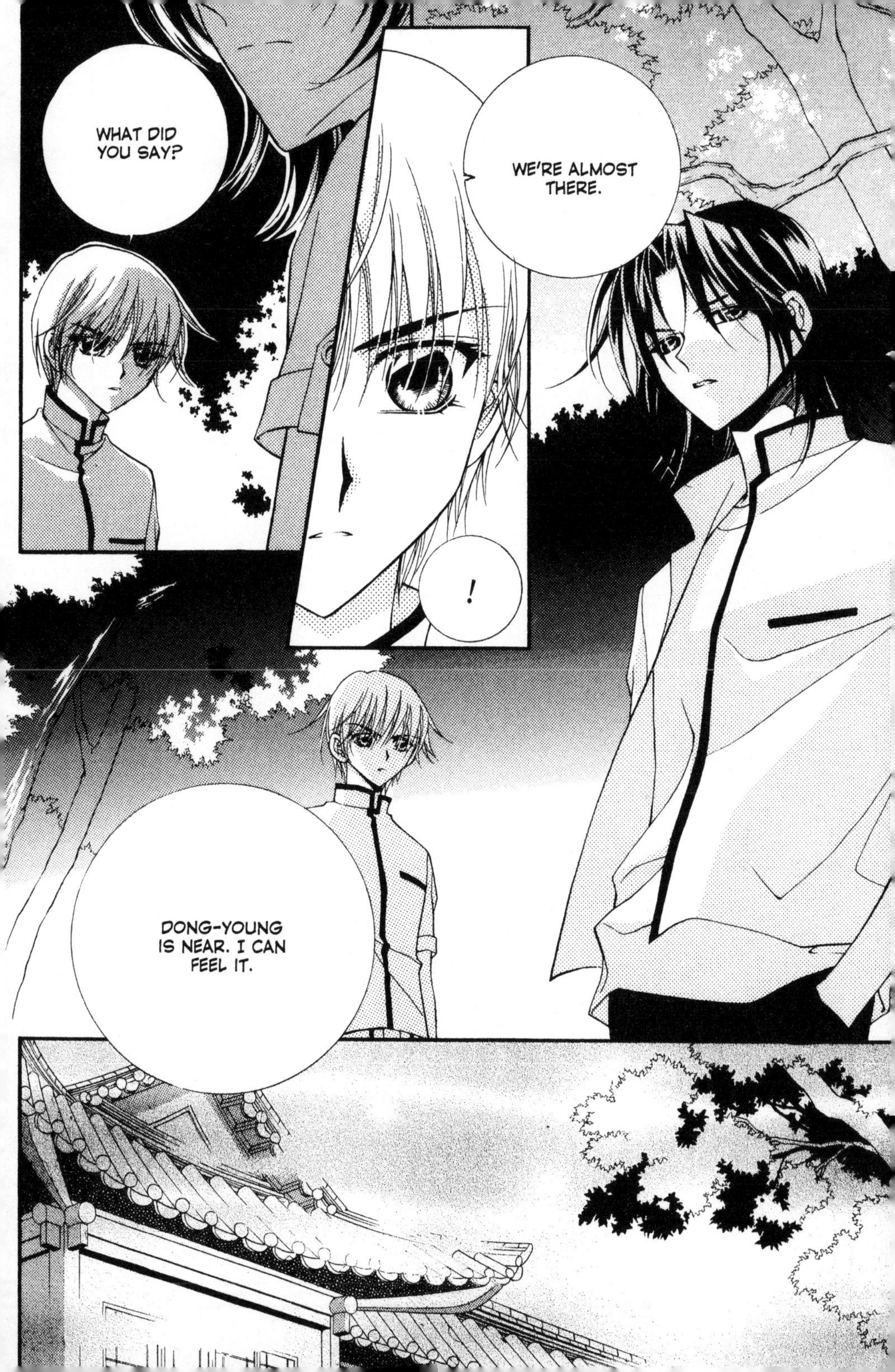
WHAT DID YOU SAY?
WE'RE ALMOST THERE.
!
DONG-YOUNG IS NEAR. I CAN FEEL IT.

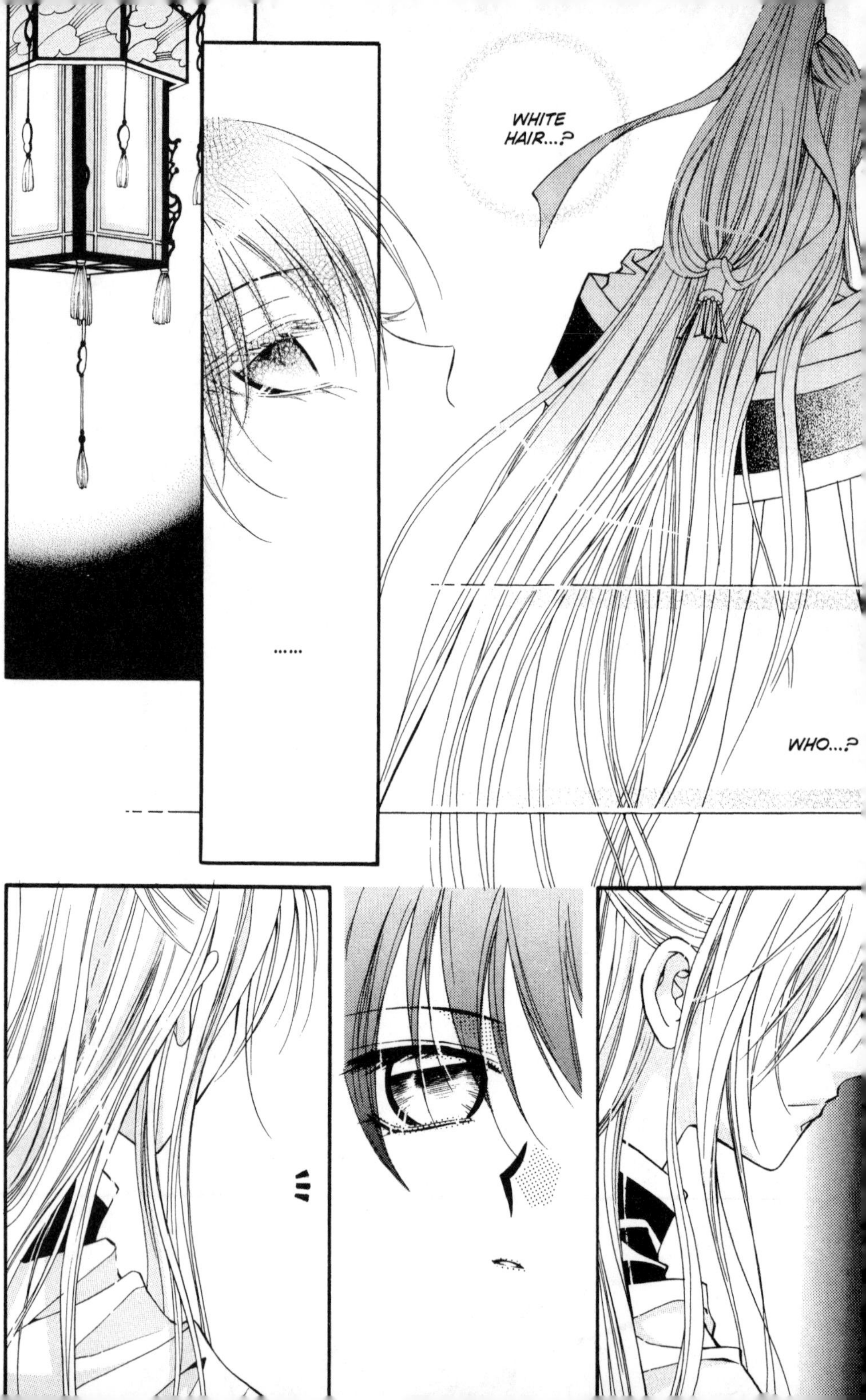
WHITE HAIR...?
......
WHO...?

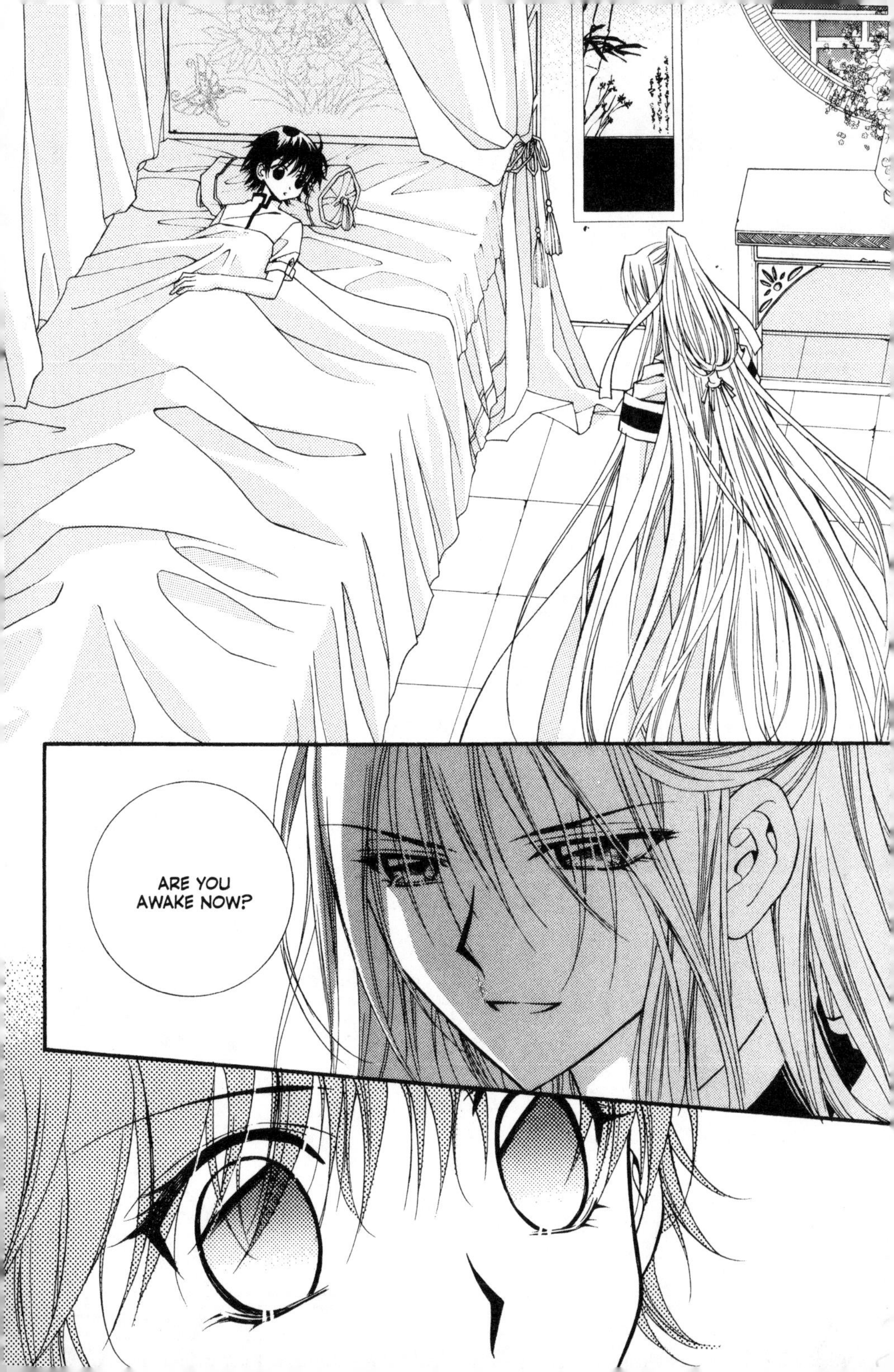
ARE YOU
AWAKE NOW?

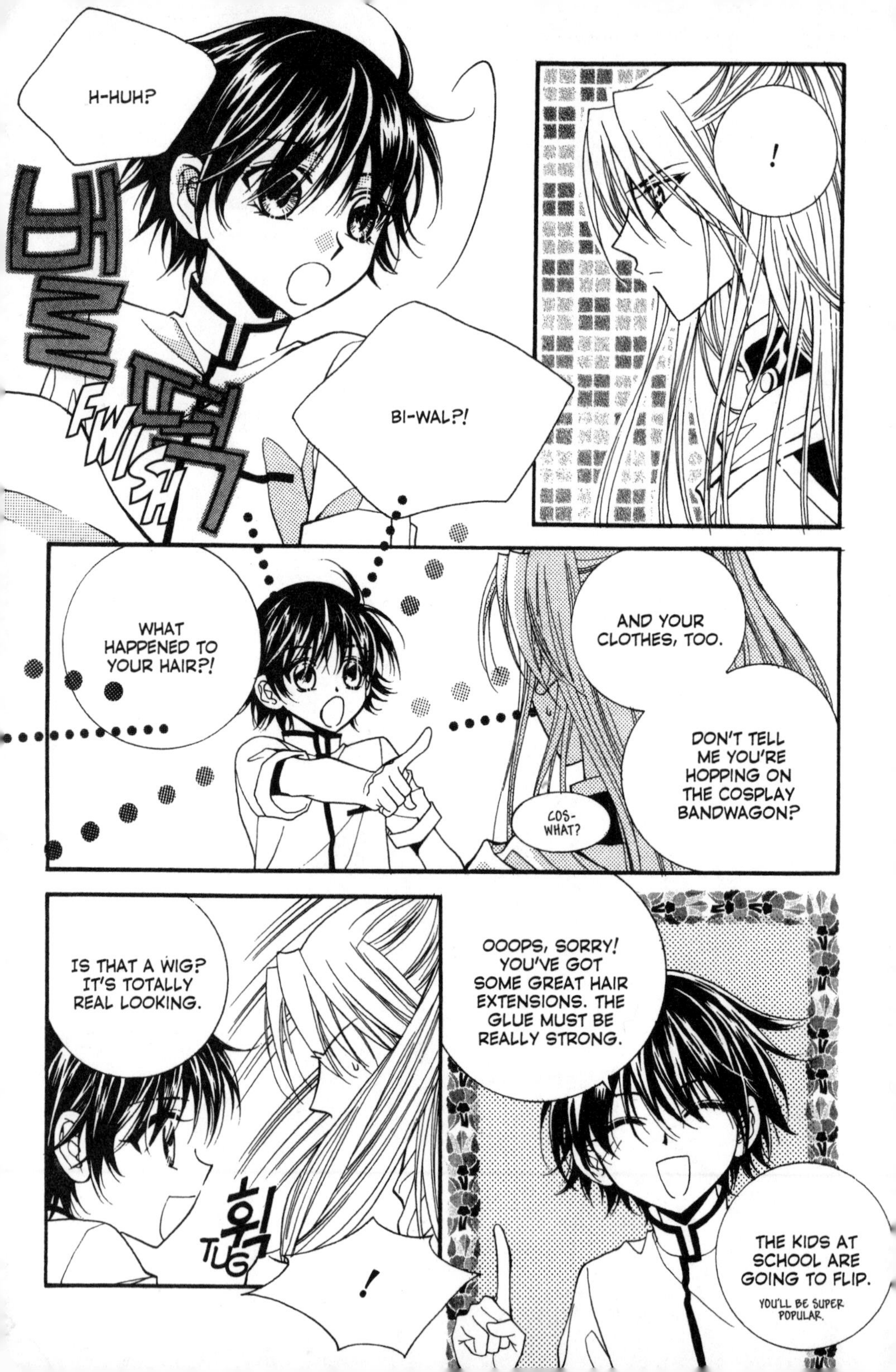
H-HUH?
FWISH
BI-WAL?!
!
WHAT HAPPENED TO YOUR HAIR?!
AND YOUR CLOTHES, TOO.
DON'T TELL ME YOU'RE HOPPING ON THE COSPLAY BANDWAGON?
COS-WHAT?
IS THAT A WIG? IT'S TOTALLY REAL LOOKING.
TUG
!
OOOPS, SORRY! YOU'VE GOT SOME GREAT HAIR EXTENSIONS. THE GLUE MUST BE REALLY STRONG.
THE KIDS AT SCHOOL ARE GOING TO FLIP.
YOU'LL BE SUPER POPULAR.

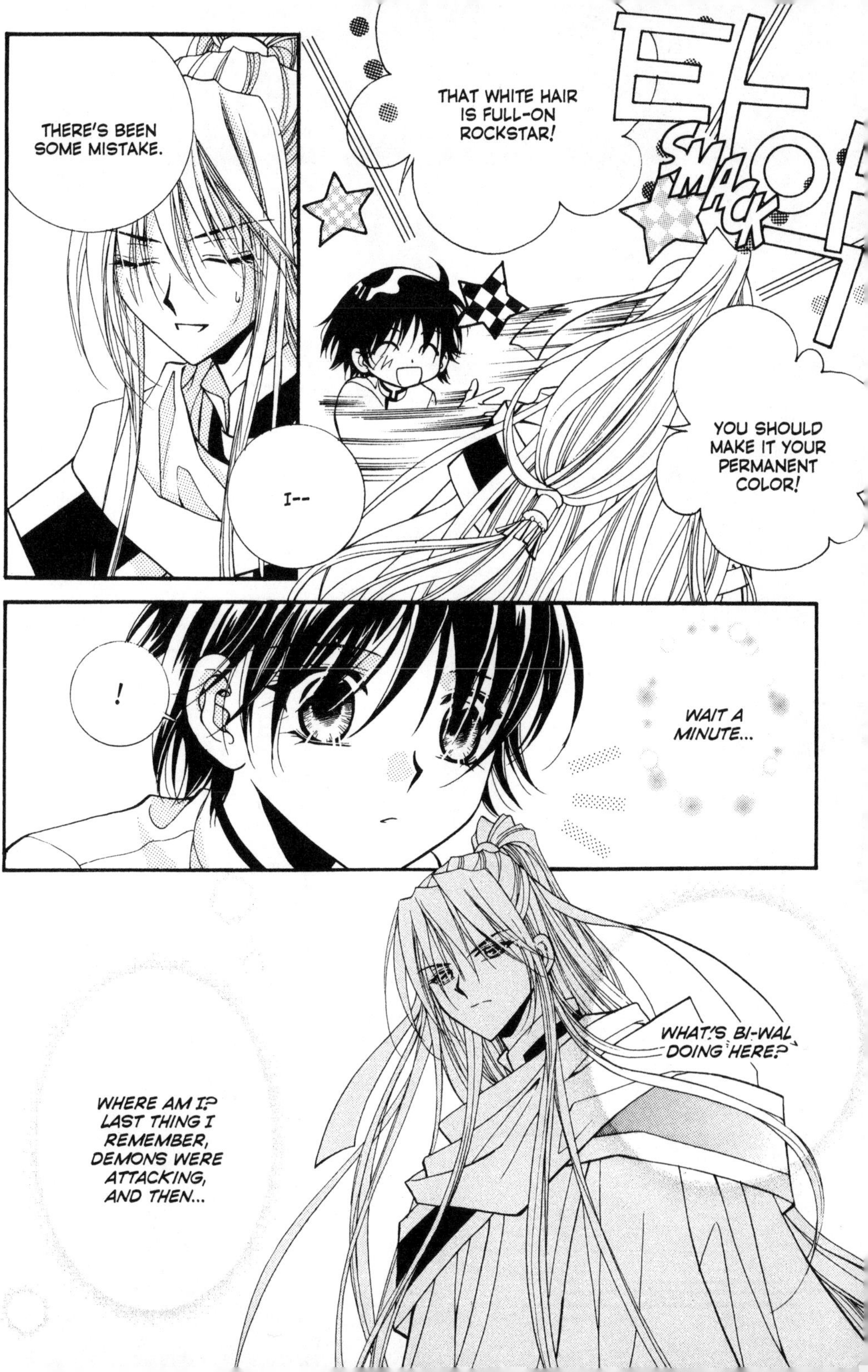
SMACK
THAT WHITE HAIR IS FULL-ON ROCKSTAR!
YOU SHOULD MAKE IT YOUR PERMANENT COLOR!
I--
THERE'S BEEN SOME MISTAKE.
!
WAIT A MINUTE...
WHAT'S BI-WAL DOING HERE?
WHERE AM I? LAST THING I REMEMBER, DEMONS WERE ATTACKING, AND THEN...

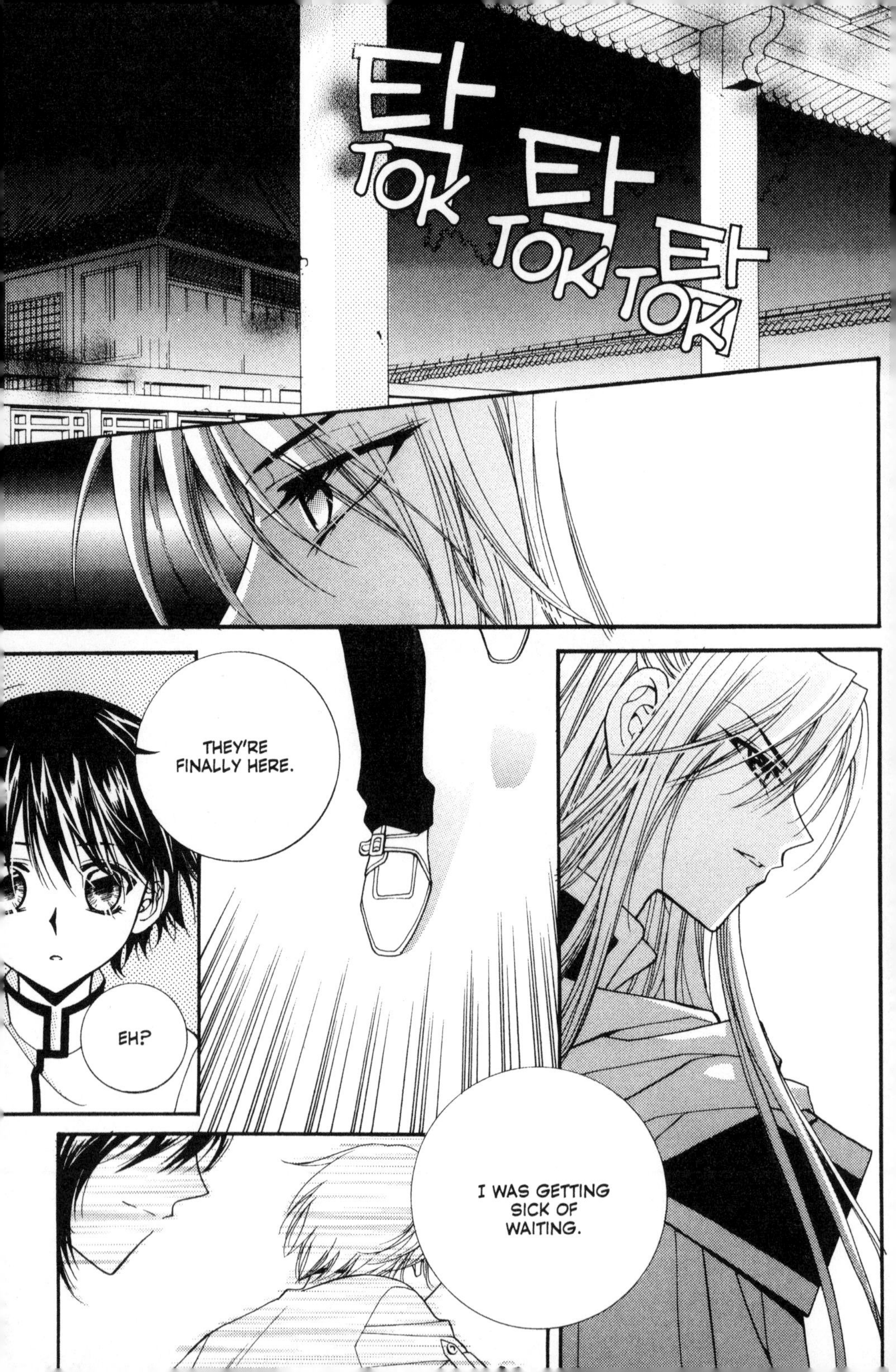

타 TOK
탁 TOK
타 TOK
탁 TOK
THEY'RE FINALLY HERE.
EH?
I WAS GETTING SICK OF WAITING.

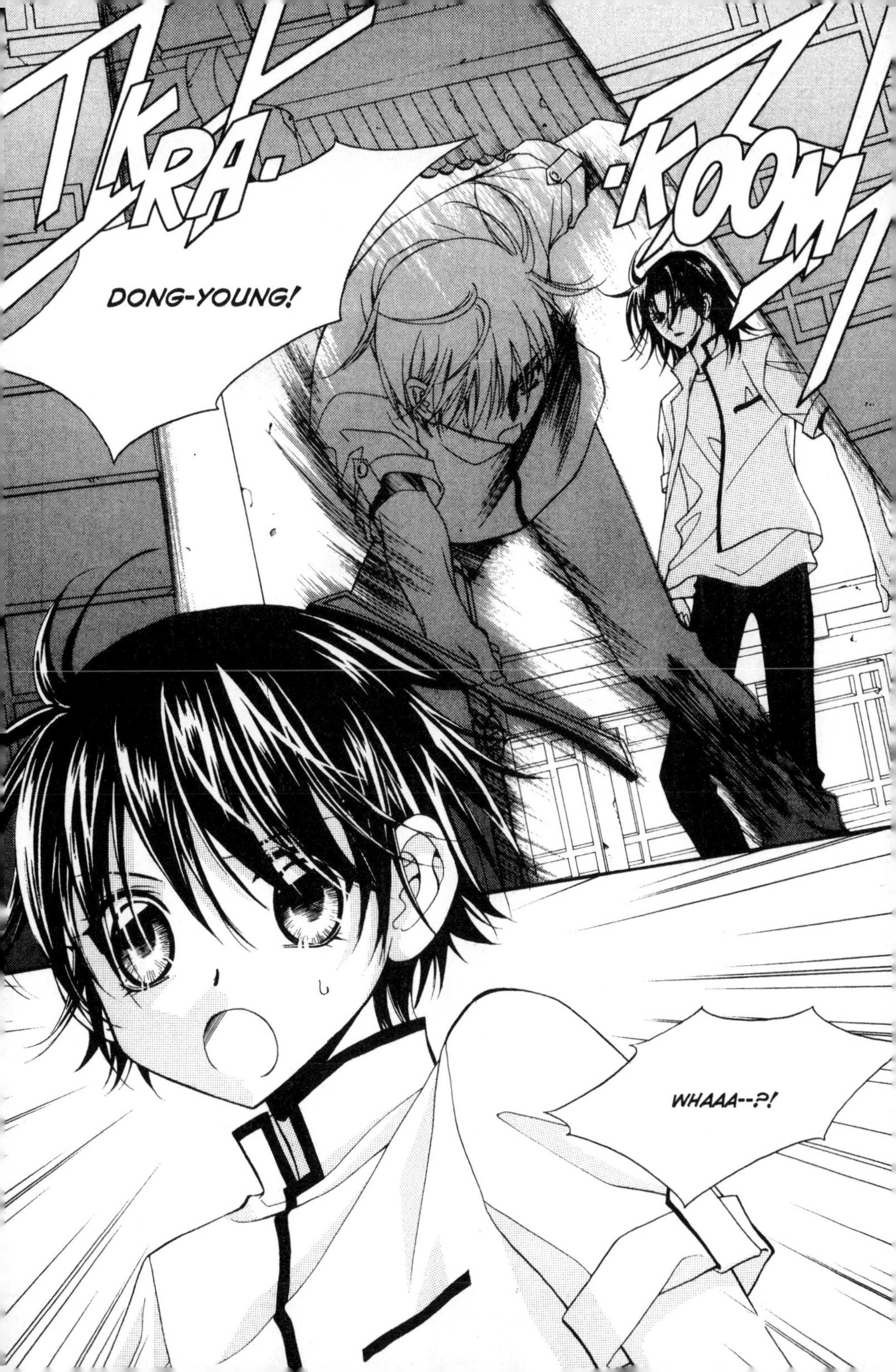
KRA-
-KOOM
DONG-YOUNG!
WHAAA--?!

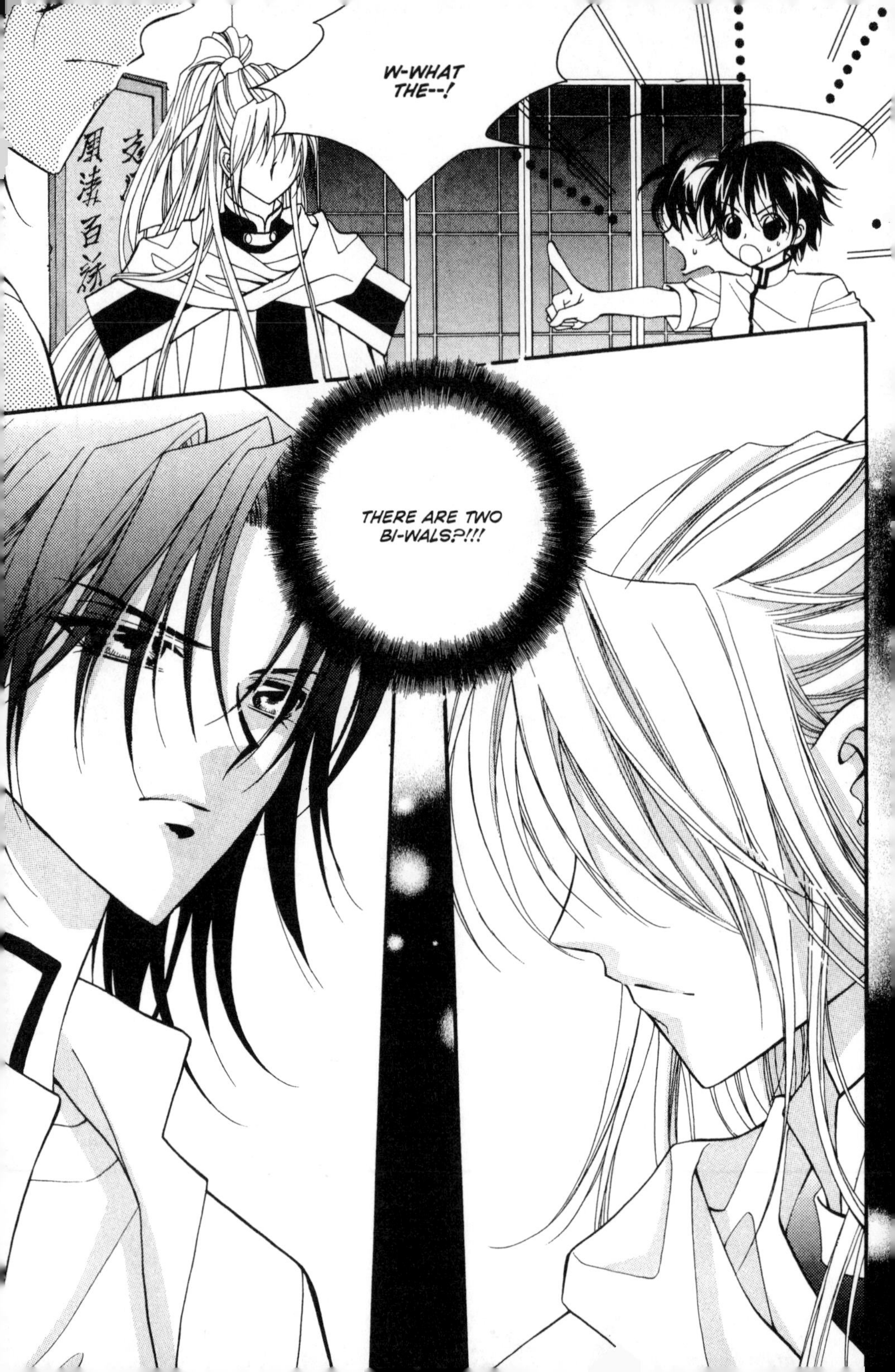
W-WHAT THE--!
THERE ARE TWO BI-WALS?!!!

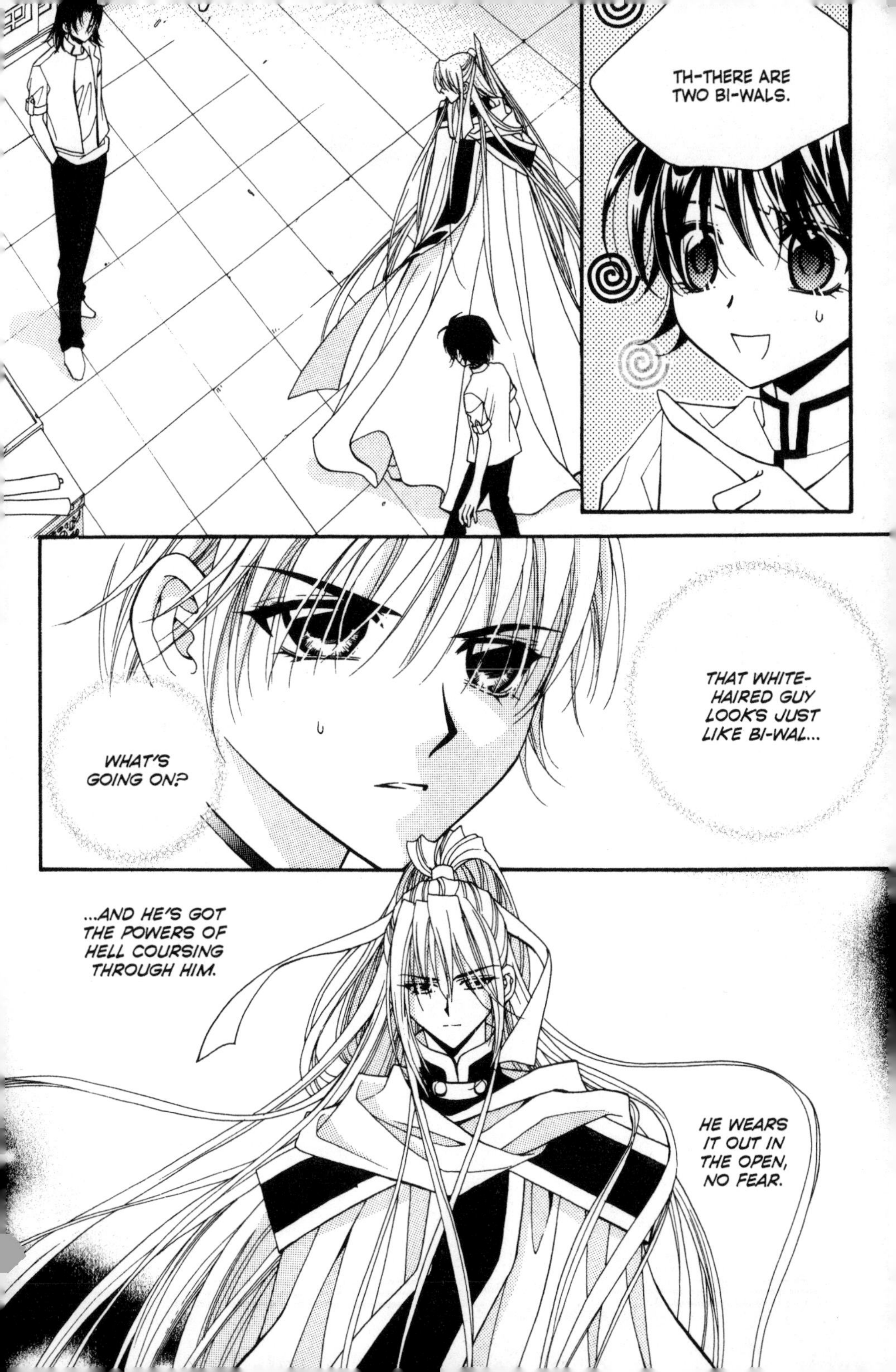
TH-THERE ARE TWO BI-WALS.
THAT WHITE-HAIRED GUY LOOKS JUST LIKE BI-WAL...
WHAT'S GOING ON?
...AND HE'S GOT THE POWERS OF HELL COURSING THROUGH HIM.
HE WEARS IT OUT IN THE OPEN, NO FEAR.

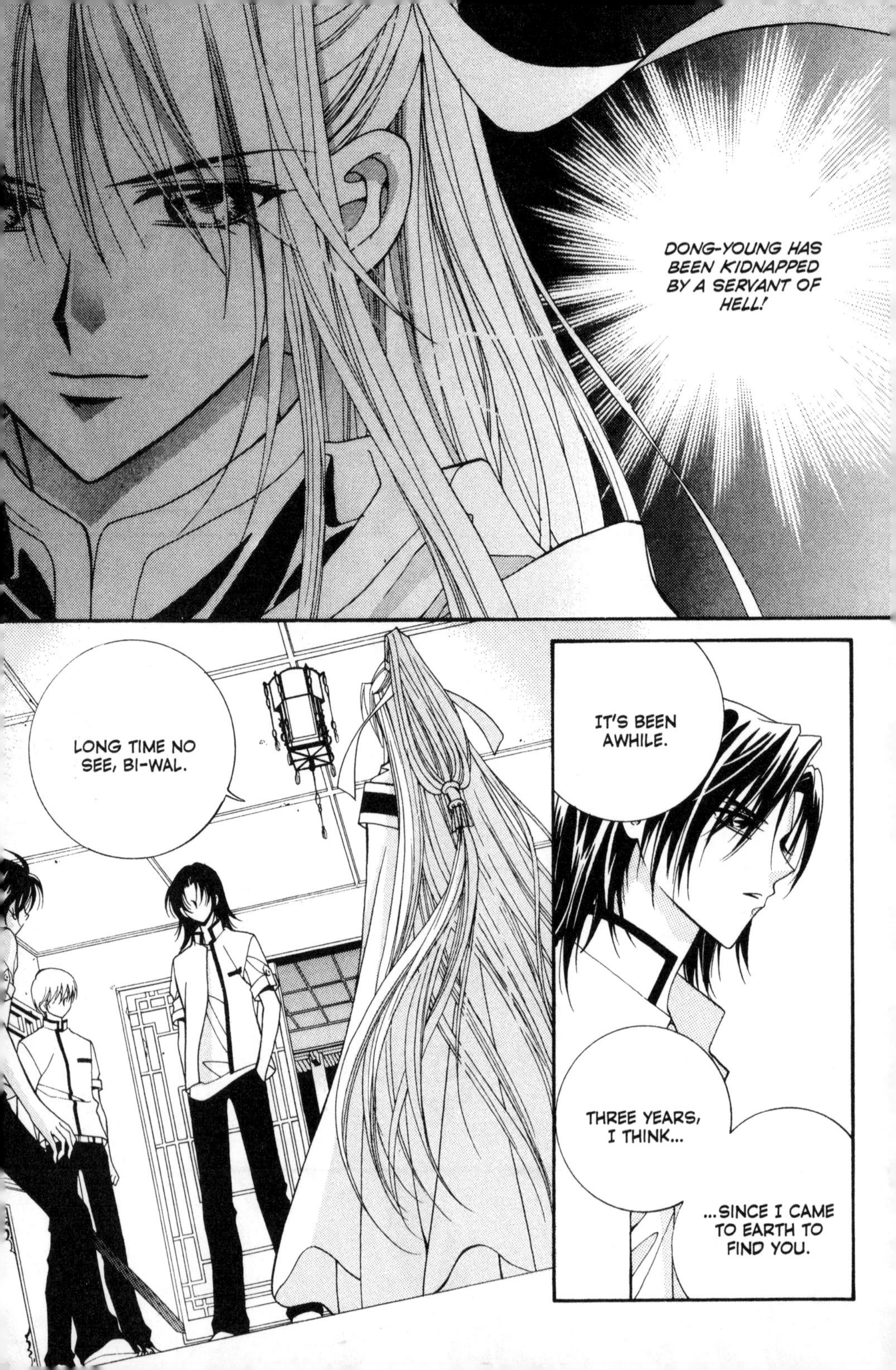
DONG-YOUNG HAS BEEN KIDNAPPED BY A SERVANT OF HELL!
IT'S BEEN AWHILE.
THREE YEARS, I THINK...
...SINCE I CAME TO EARTH TO FIND YOU.
LONG TIME NO SEE, BI-WAL.

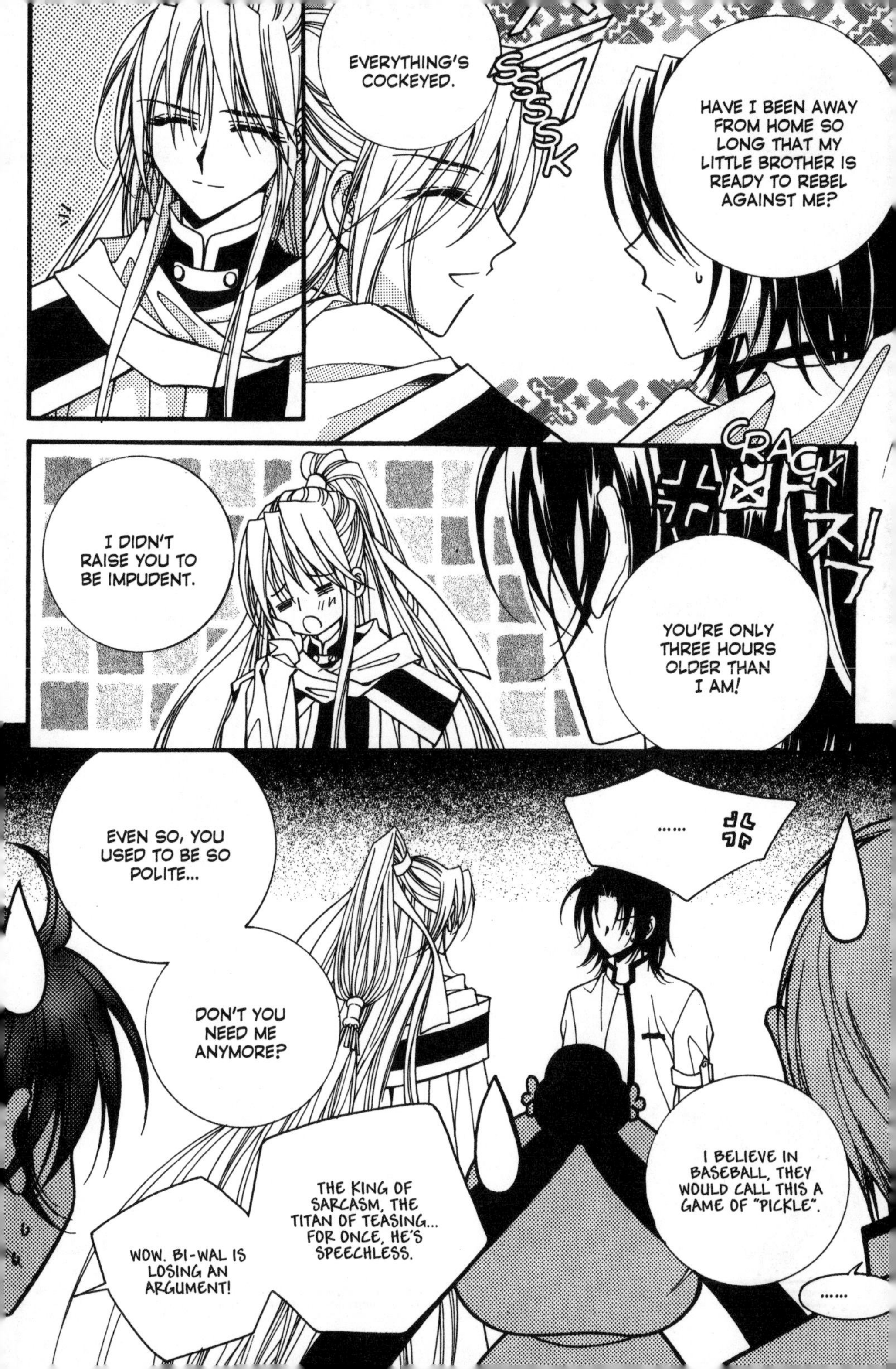
HAVE I BEEN AWAY FROM HOME SO LONG THAT MY LITTLE BROTHER IS READY TO REBEL AGAINST ME?
SSSSK
EVERYTHING'S COCKEYED.
CRACK
YOU'RE ONLY THREE HOURS OLDER THAN I AM!
I DIDN'T RAISE YOU TO BE IMPUDENT.
......
EVEN SO, YOU USED TO BE SO POLITE...
DON'T YOU NEED ME ANYMORE?
I BELIEVE IN BASEBALL, THEY WOULD CALL THIS A GAME OF "PICKLE".
THE KING OF SARCASM, THE TITAN OF TEASING... FOR ONCE, HE'S SPEECHLESS.
WOW. BI-WAL IS LOSING AN ARGUMENT!
......

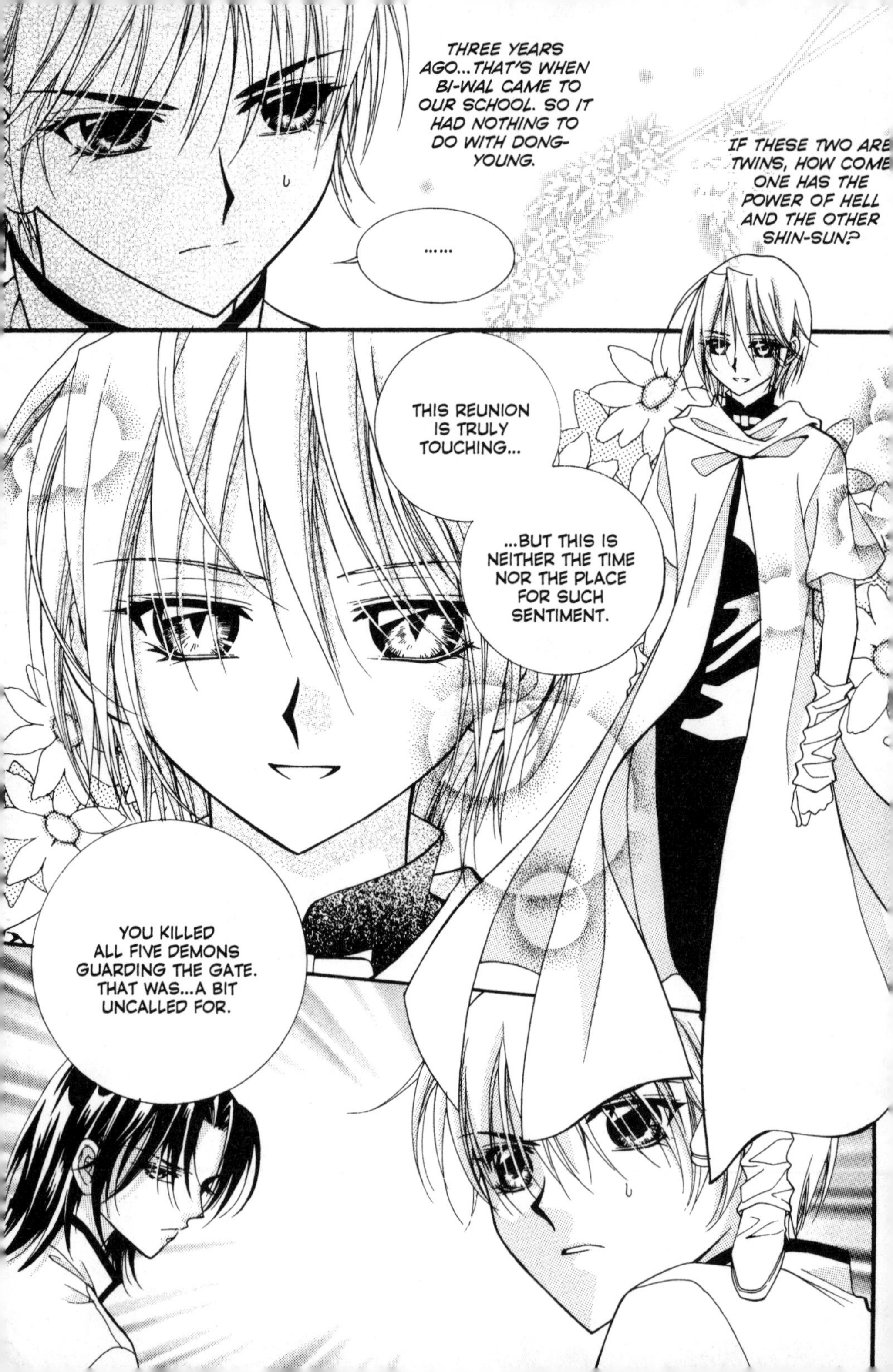
THREE YEARS AGO...THAT'S WHEN BI-WAL CAME TO OUR SCHOOL. SO IT HAD NOTHING TO DO WITH DONG-YOUNG.
IF THESE TWO ARE TWINS, HOW COME ONE HAS THE POWER OF HELL AND THE OTHER SHIN-SUN?
......
THIS REUNION IS TRULY TOUCHING...
...BUT THIS IS NEITHER THE TIME NOR THE PLACE FOR SUCH SENTIMENT.
YOU KILLED ALL FIVE DEMONS GUARDING THE GATE. THAT WAS...A BIT UNCALLED FOR.

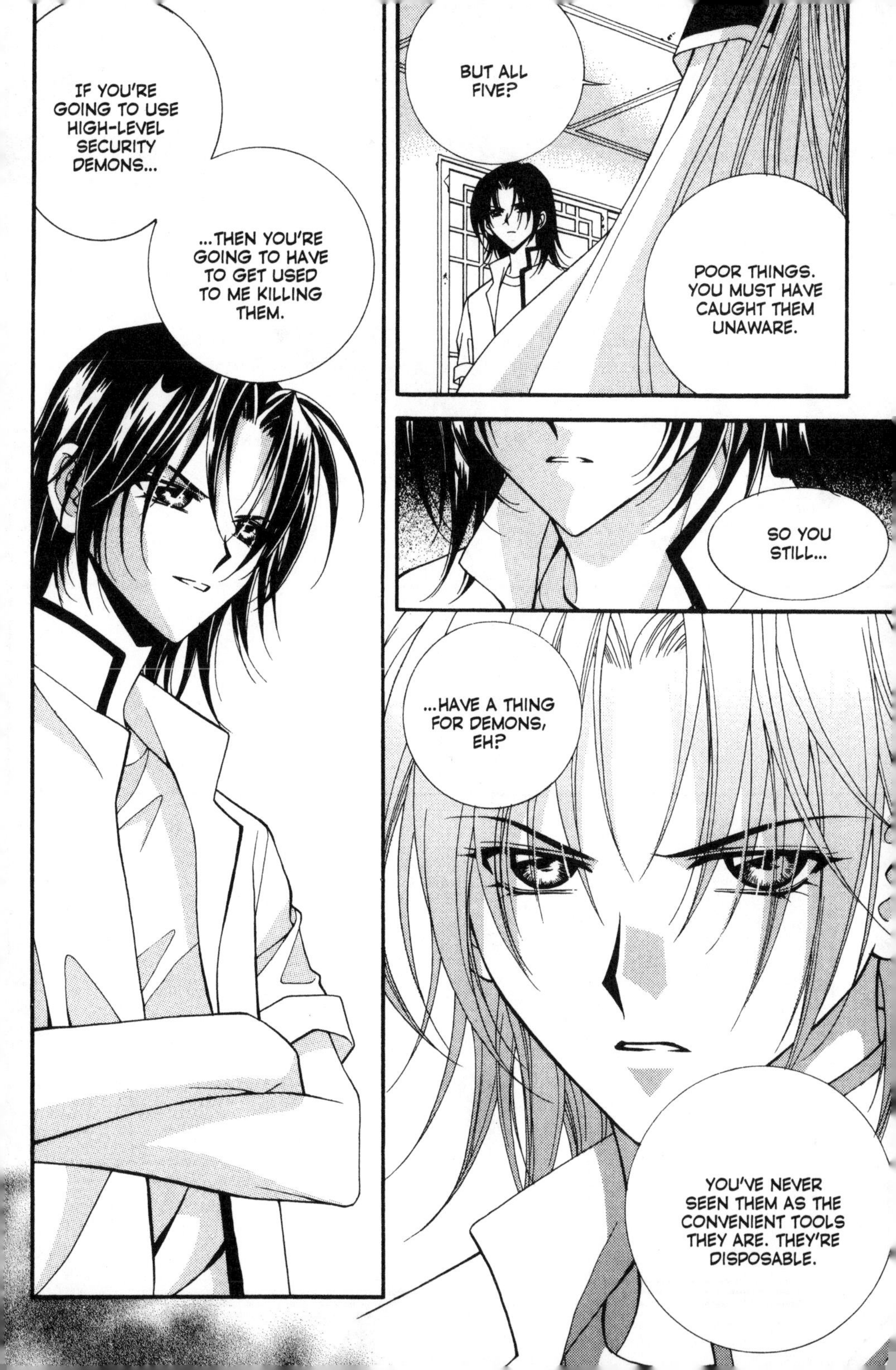

BUT ALL FIVE?
POOR THINGS. YOU MUST HAVE CAUGHT THEM UNAWARE.
IF YOU'RE GOING TO USE HIGH-LEVEL SECURITY DEMONS...
...THEN YOU'RE GOING TO HAVE TO GET USED TO ME KILLING THEM.
SO YOU STILL...
...HAVE A THING FOR DEMONS, EH?
YOU'VE NEVER SEEN THEM AS THE CONVENIENT TOOLS THEY ARE. THEY'RE DISPOSABLE.

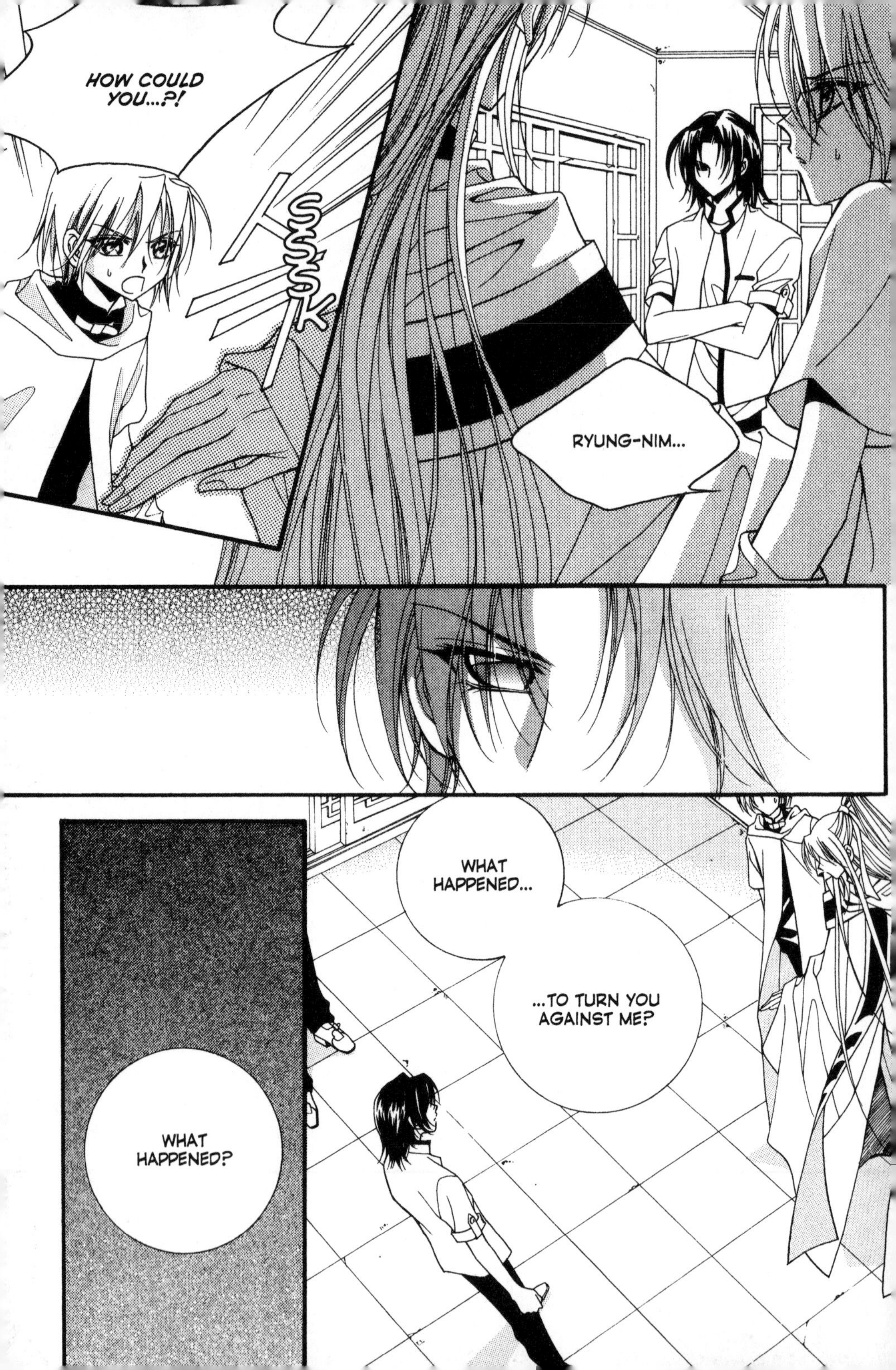
HOW COULD YOU...?!
SSSK
RYUNG-NIM...
WHAT HAPPENED...
...TO TURN YOU AGAINST ME?
WHAT HAPPENED?

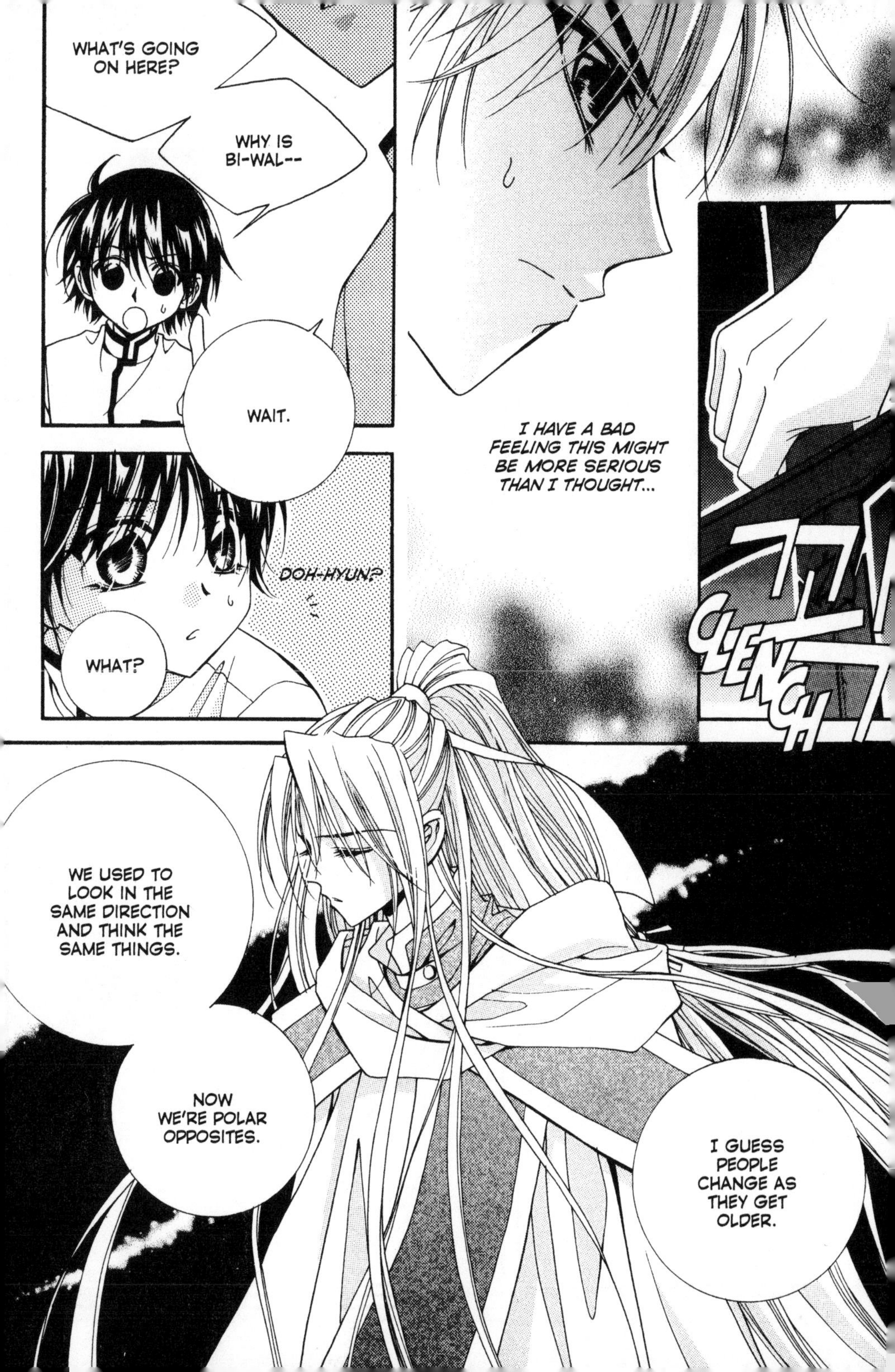
WHAT'S GOING ON HERE?
WHY IS BI-WAL--
WAIT.
DOH-HYUN?
WHAT?
I HAVE A BAD FEELING THIS MIGHT BE MORE SERIOUS THAN I THOUGHT...
CLENCH
WE USED TO LOOK IN THE SAME DIRECTION AND THINK THE SAME THINGS.
NOW WE'RE POLAR OPPOSITES.
I GUESS PEOPLE CHANGE AS THEY GET OLDER.

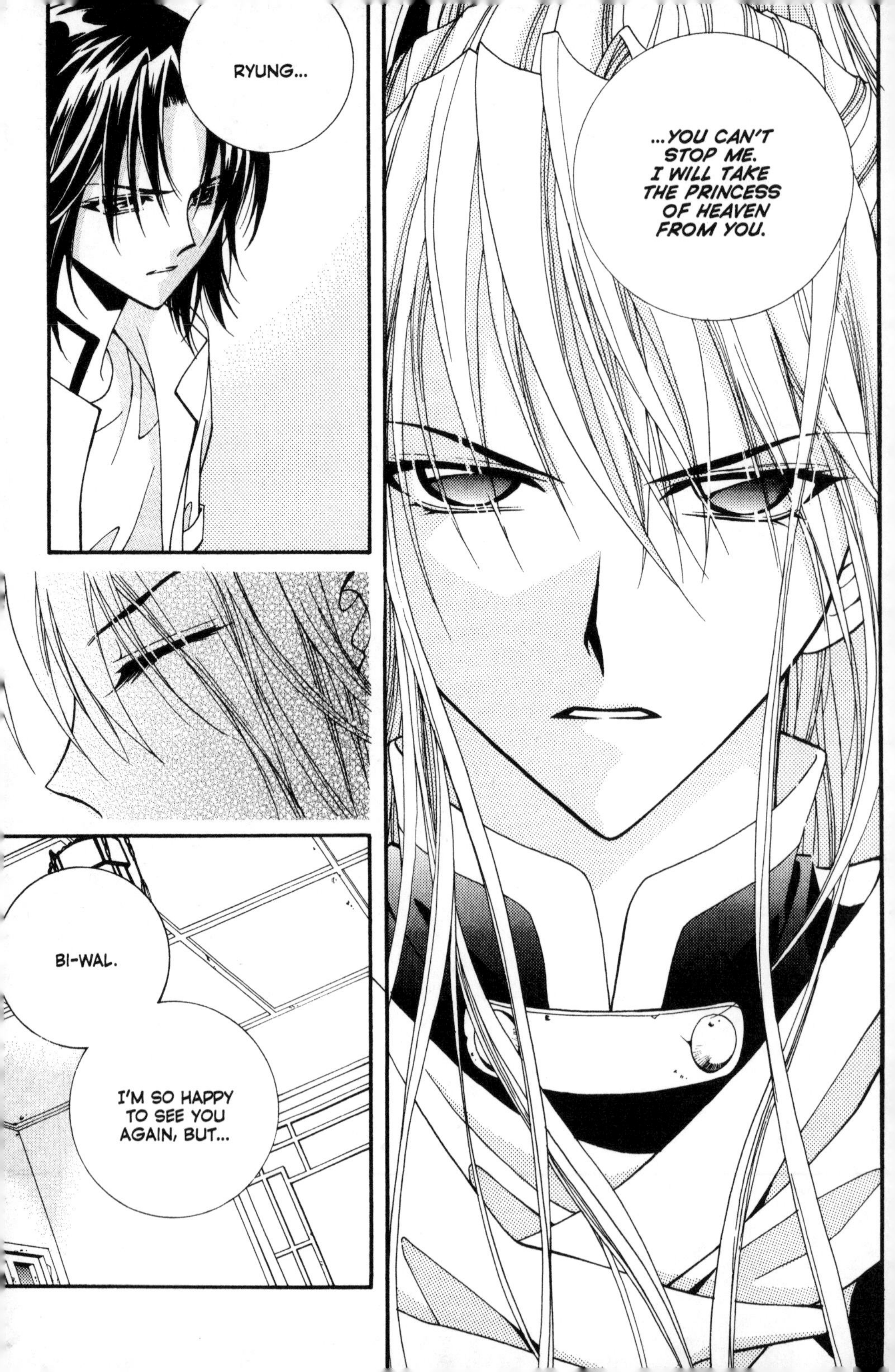
RYUNG...
BI-WAL.
I'M SO HAPPY TO SEE YOU AGAIN, BUT...
...YOU CAN'T STOP ME. I WILL TAKE THE PRINCESS OF HEAVEN FROM YOU.

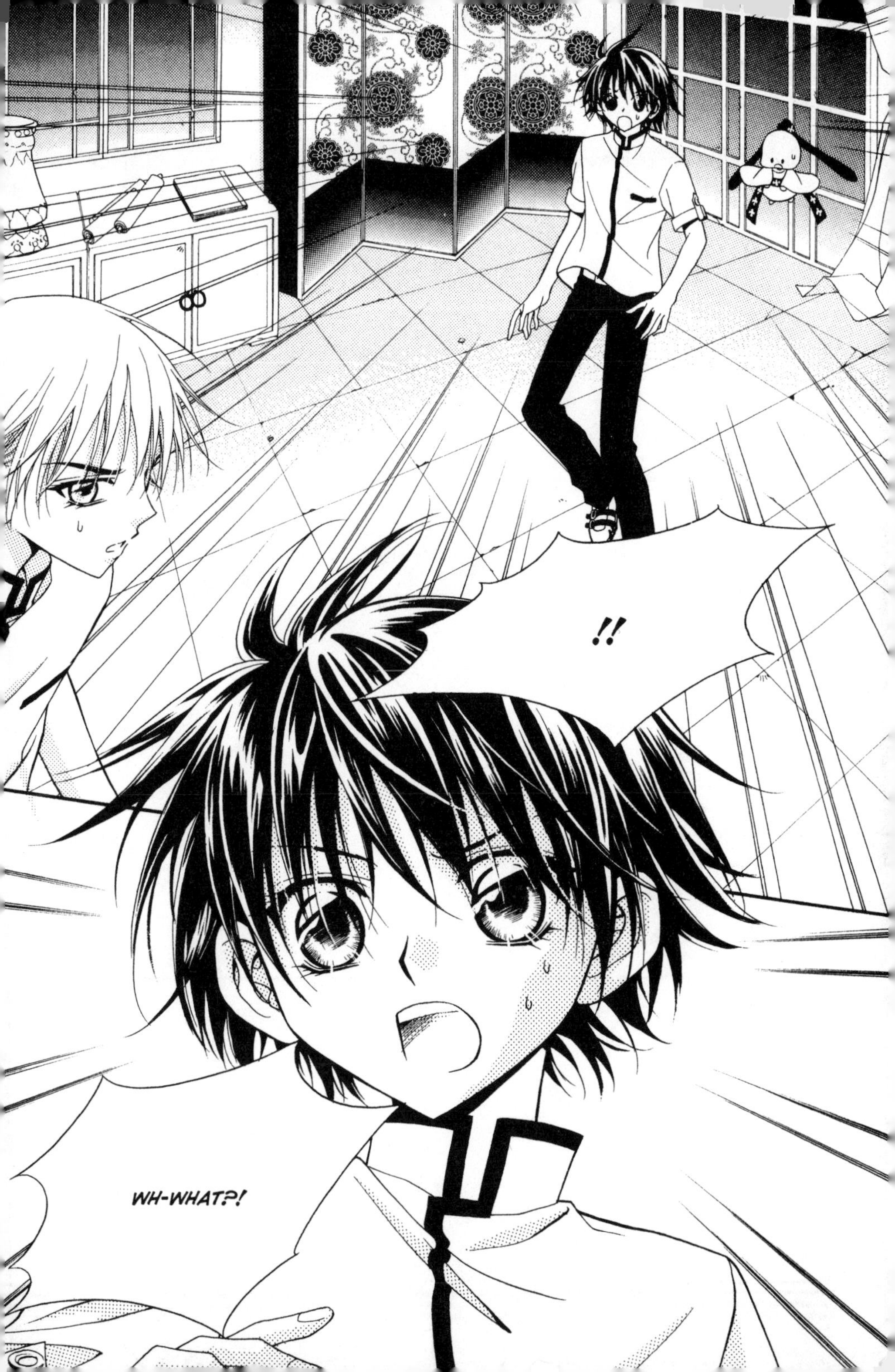
!!
WH-WHAT?!

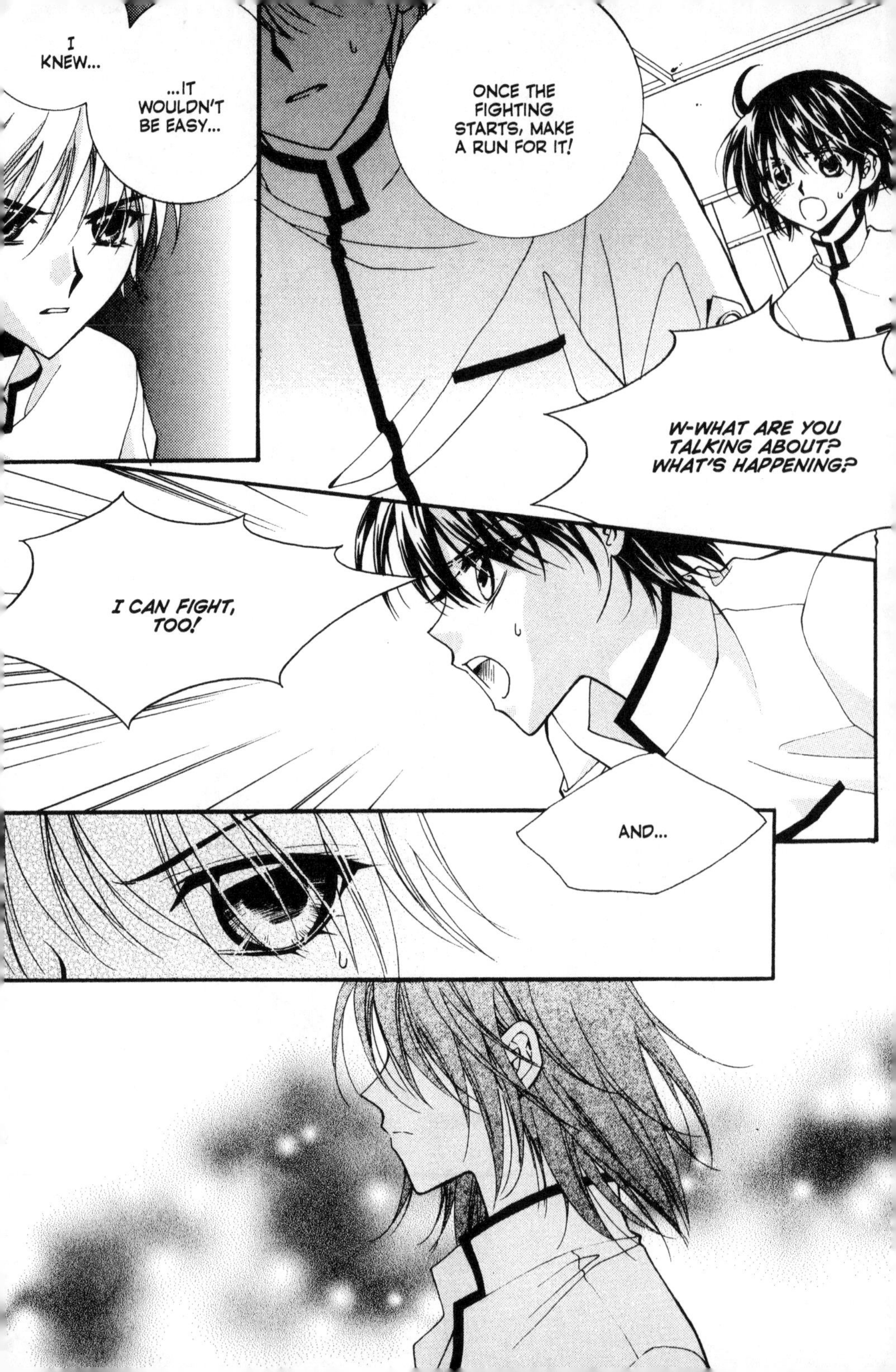
ONCE THE FIGHTING STARTS, MAKE A RUN FOR IT!
I KNEW...
...IT WOULDN'T BE EASY...
W-WHAT ARE YOU TALKING ABOUT? WHAT'S HAPPENING?
I CAN FIGHT, TOO!
AND...

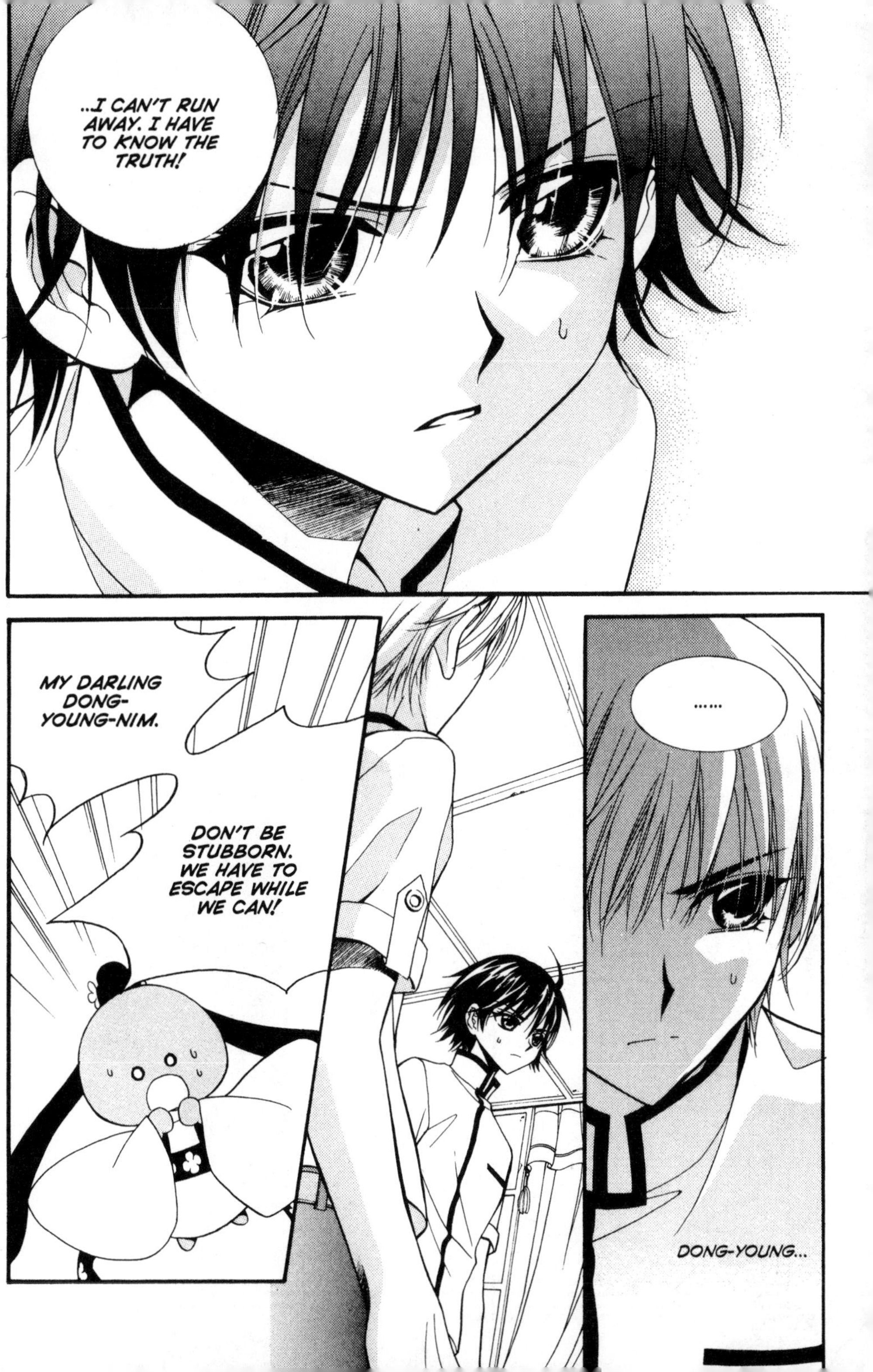

..I CAN'T RUN AWAY. I HAVE TO KNOW THE TRUTH!
......
MY DARLING DONG-YOUNG-NIM.
DON'T BE STUBBORN. WE HAVE TO ESCAPE WHILE WE CAN!
DONG-YOUNG...

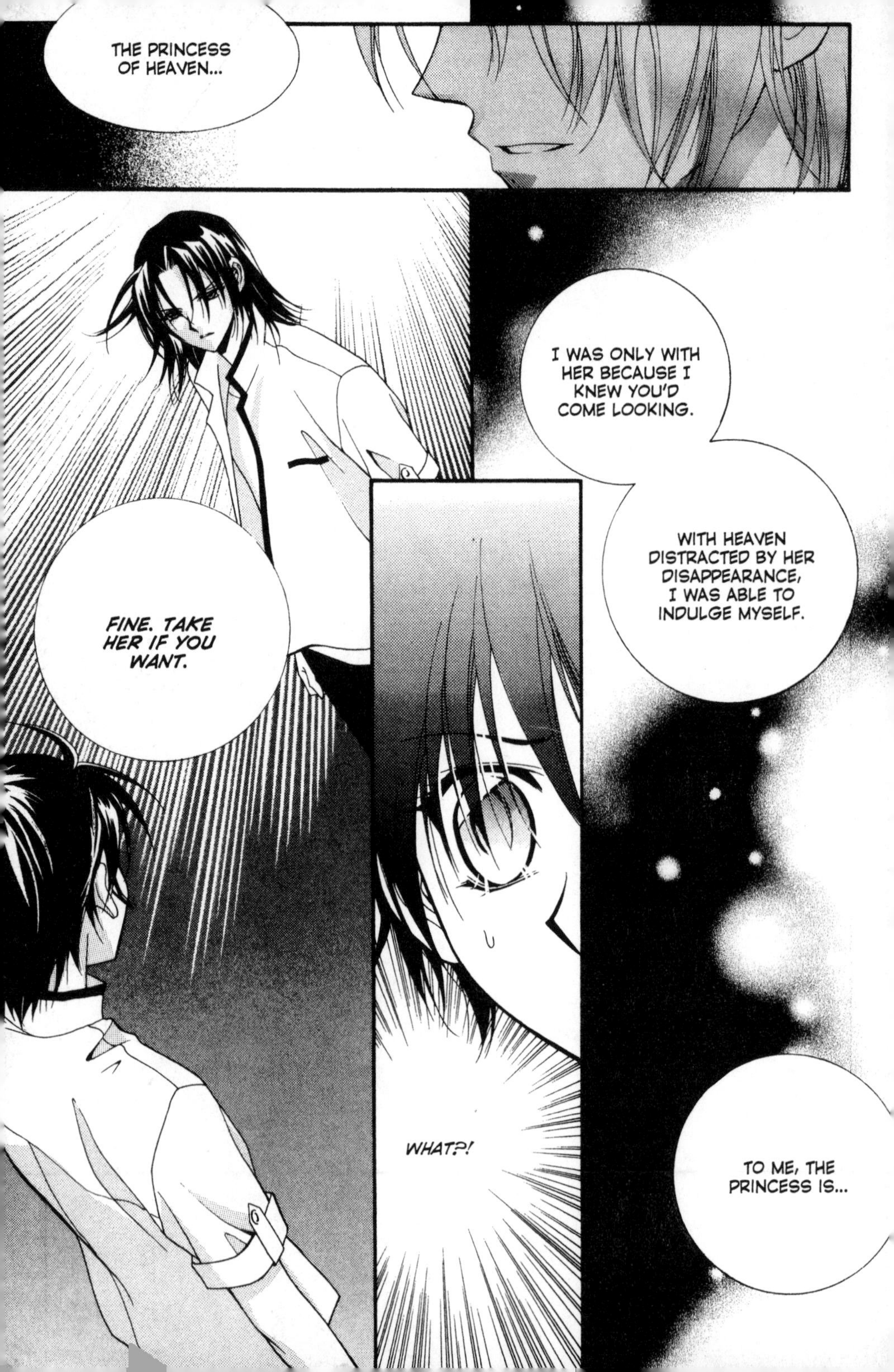
THE PRINCESS OF HEAVEN...
I WAS ONLY WITH HER BECAUSE I KNEW YOU'D COME LOOKING.
WITH HEAVEN DISTRACTED BY HER DISAPPEARANCE, I WAS ABLE TO INDULGE MYSELF.
TO ME, THE PRINCESS IS...
FINE. TAKE HER IF YOU WANT.
WHAT?!

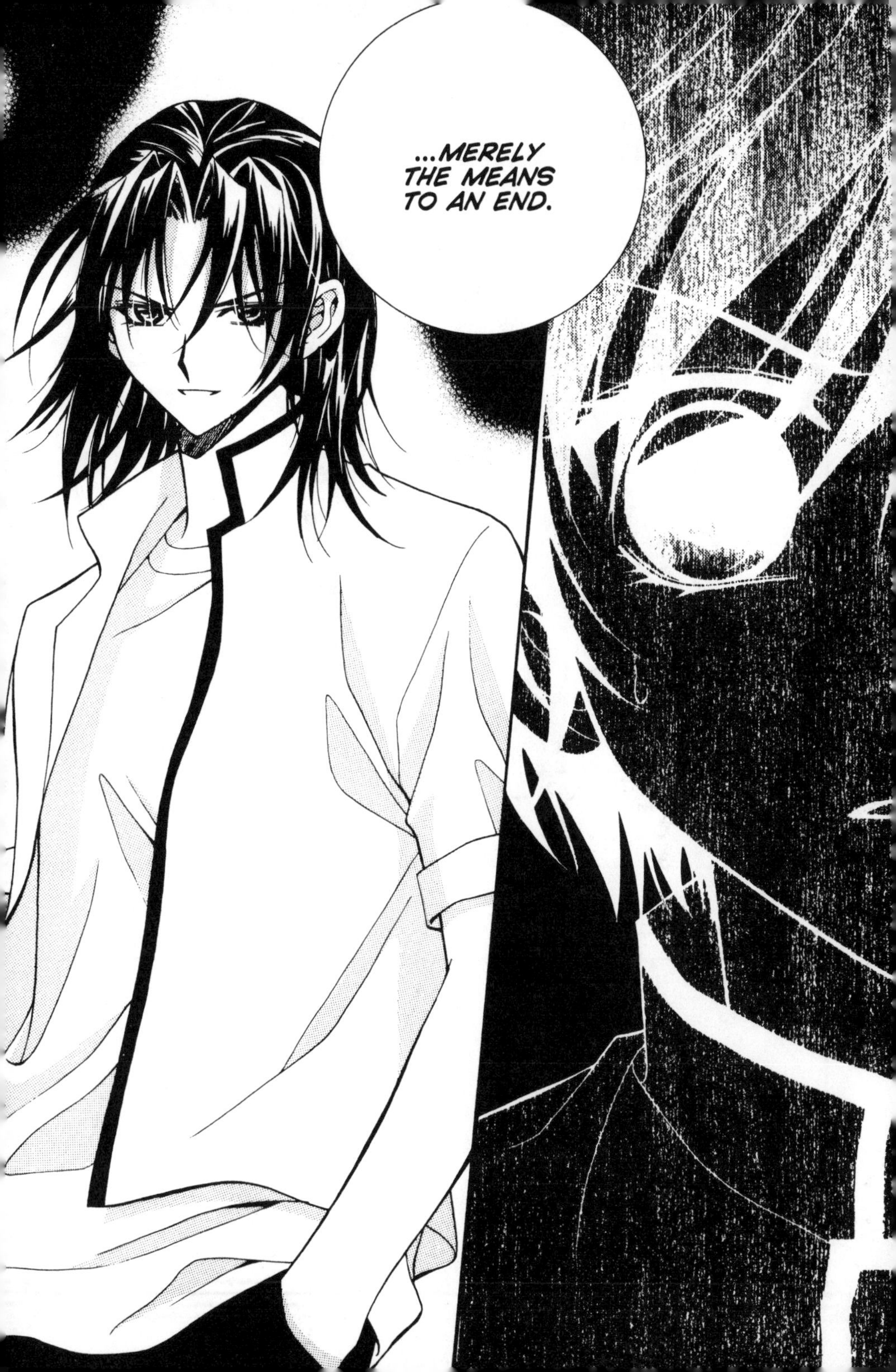
...MERELY THE MEANS TO AN END.

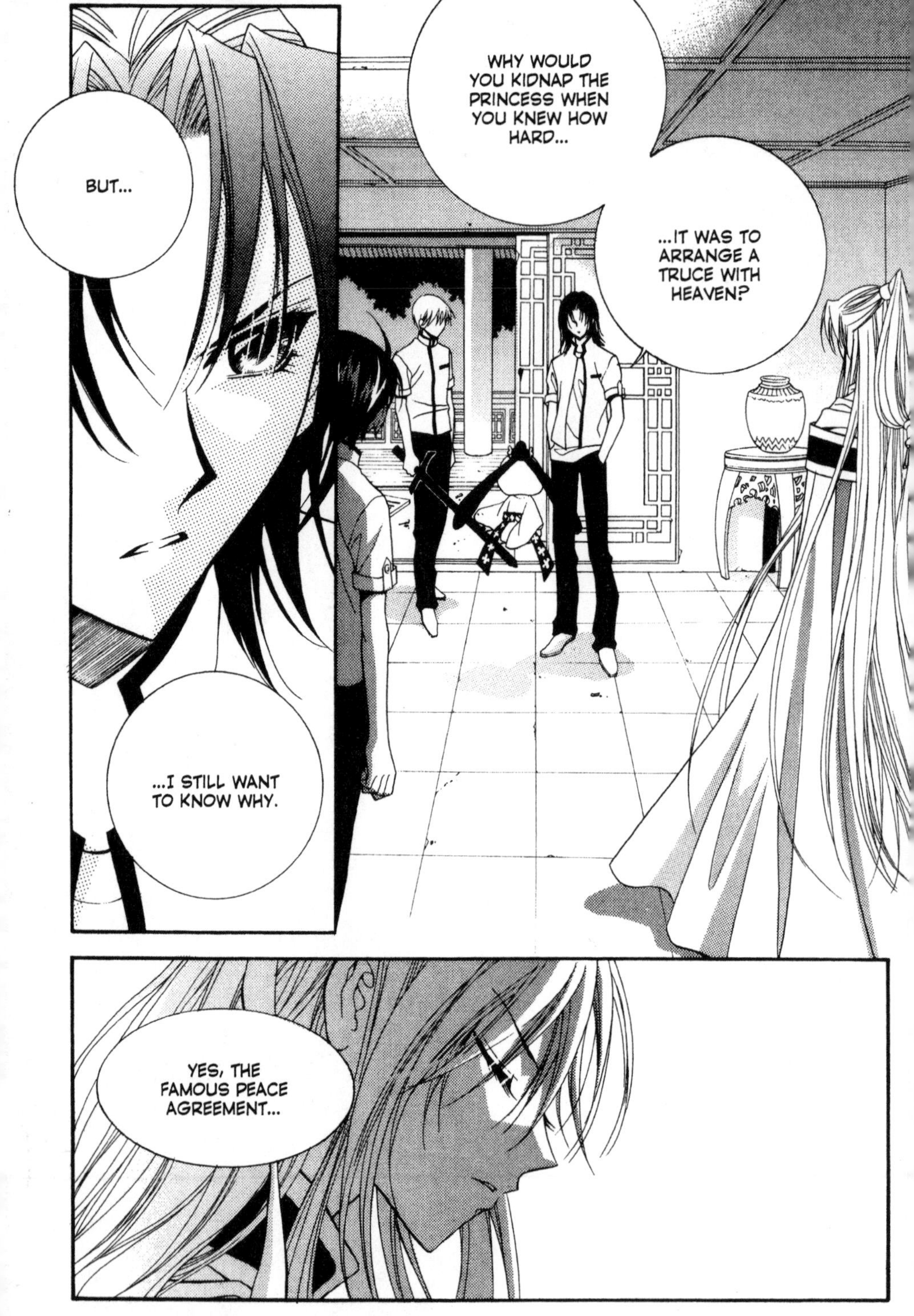
BUT...
WHY WOULD YOU KIDNAP THE PRINCESS WHEN YOU KNEW HOW HARD...
...IT WAS TO ARRANGE A TRUCE WITH HEAVEN?
...I STILL WANT TO KNOW WHY.
YES, THE FAMOUS PEACE AGREEMENT...

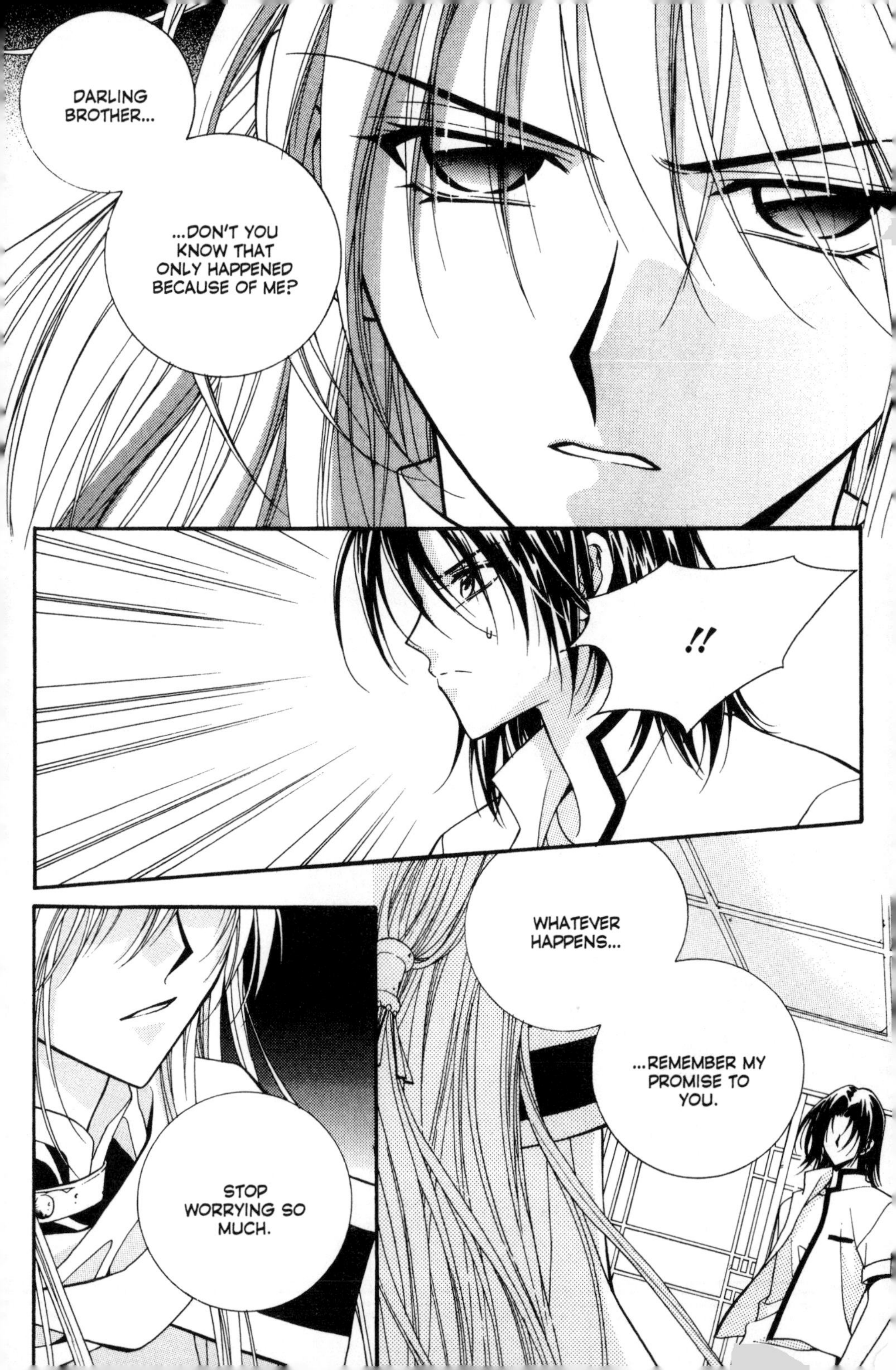
DARLING BROTHER...
...DON'T YOU KNOW THAT ONLY HAPPENED BECAUSE OF ME?
!!
WHATEVER HAPPENS...
...REMEMBER MY PROMISE TO YOU.
STOP WORRYING SO MUCH.

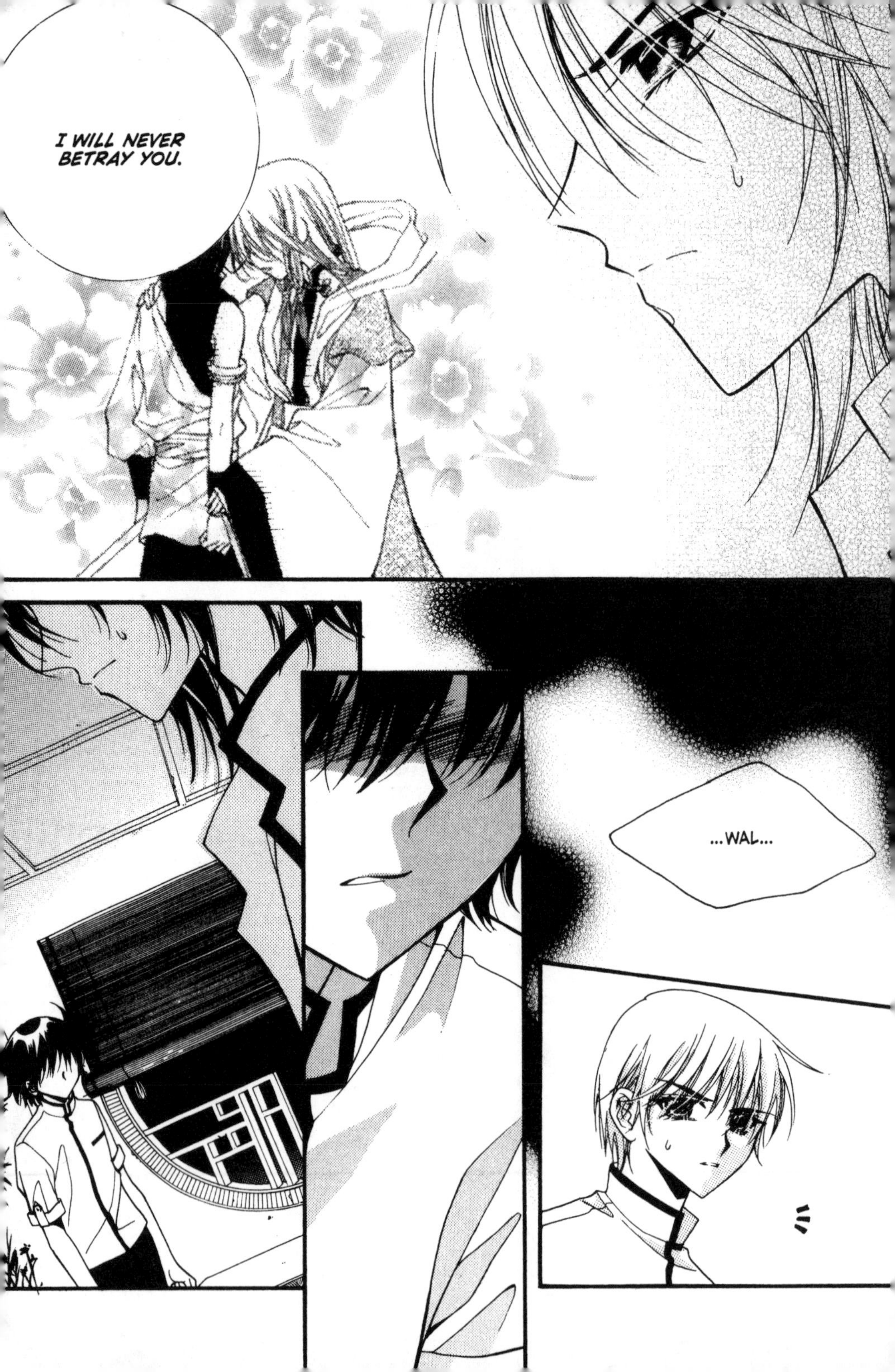
I WILL NEVER BETRAY YOU.
...WAL...

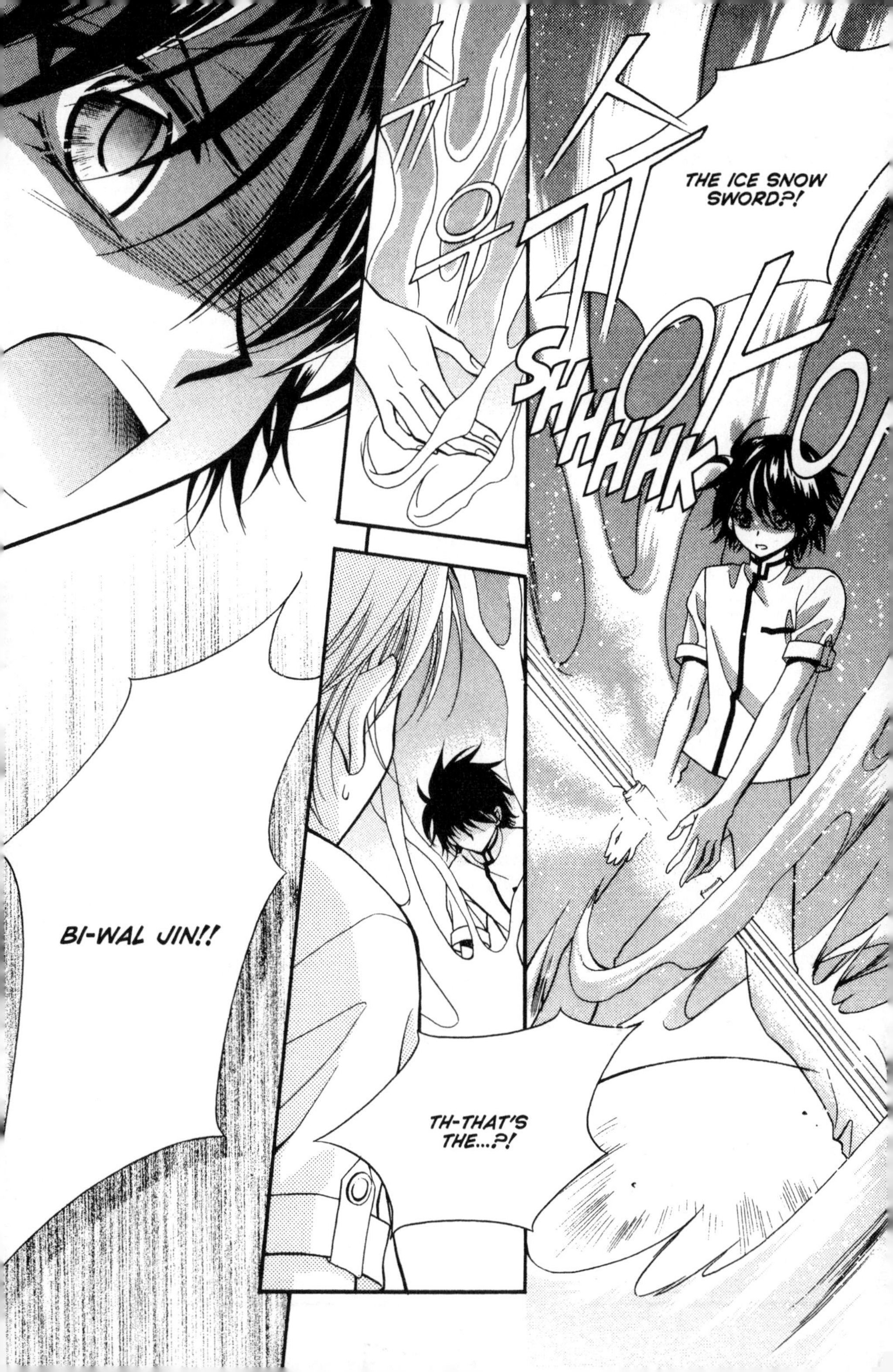
THE ICE SNOW SWORD?!
SHHHHHK
TH-THAT'S THE...?!
BI-WAL JIN!!

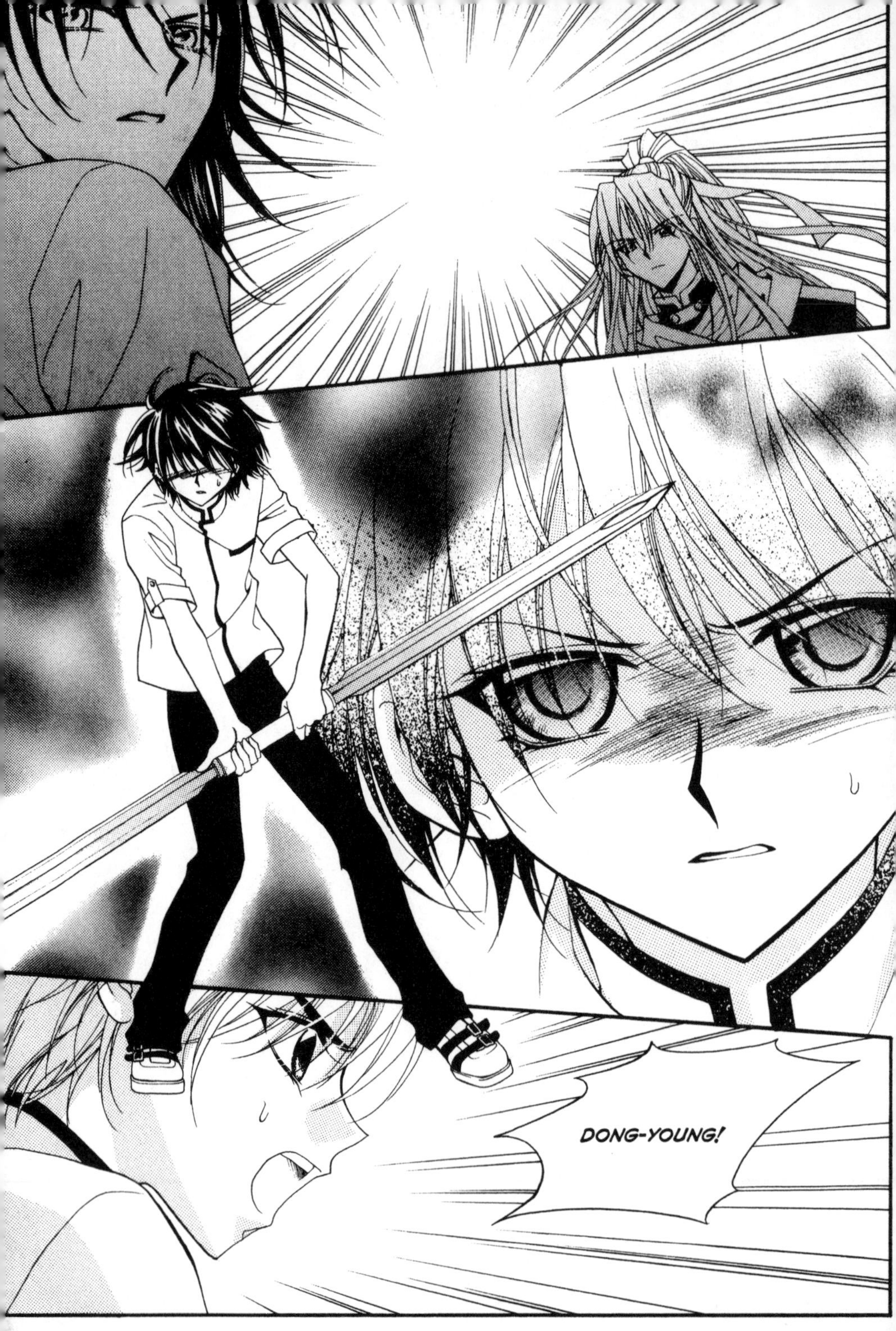
DONG-YOUNG!

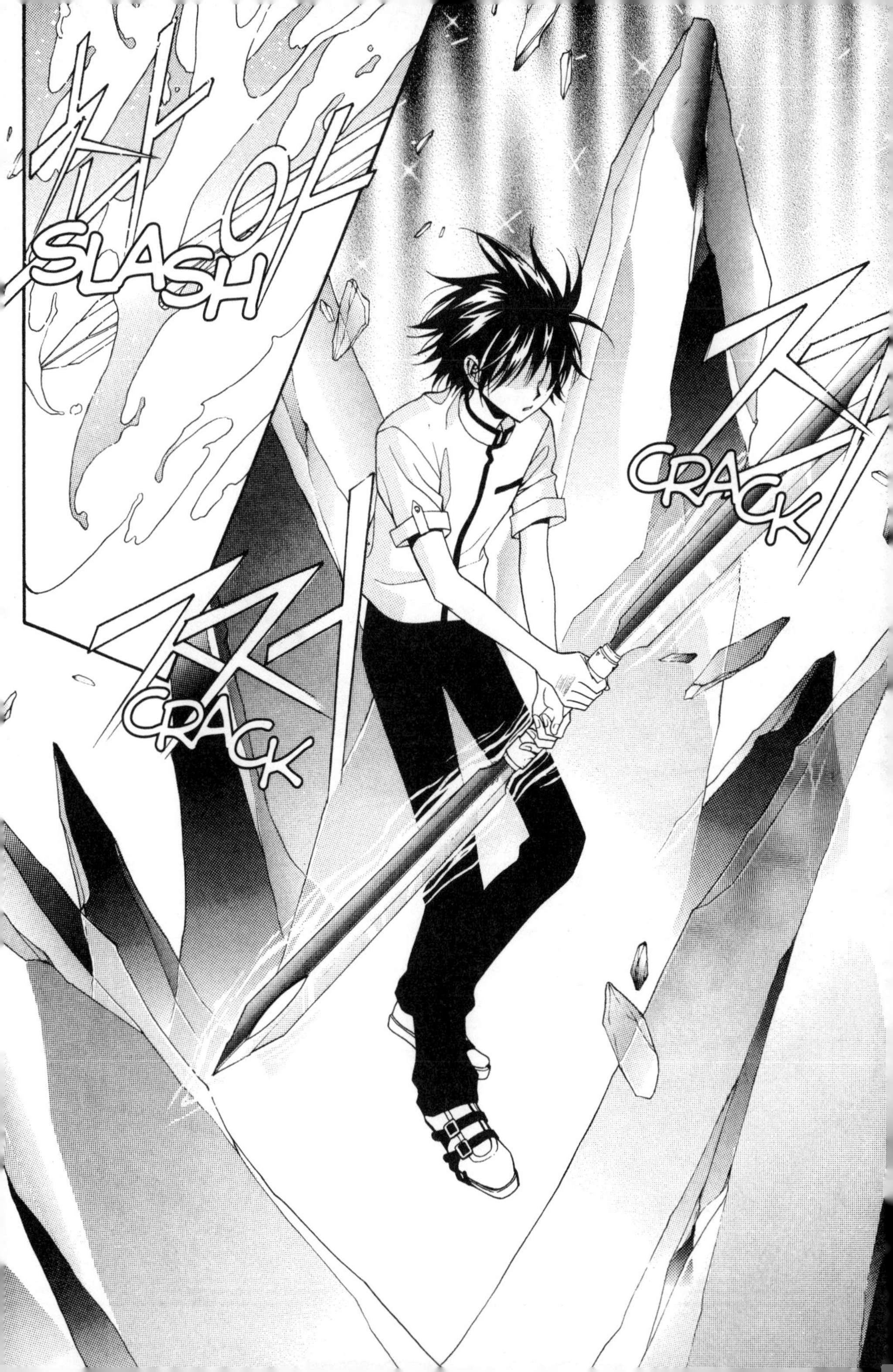
SLASH
CRACK
CRACK

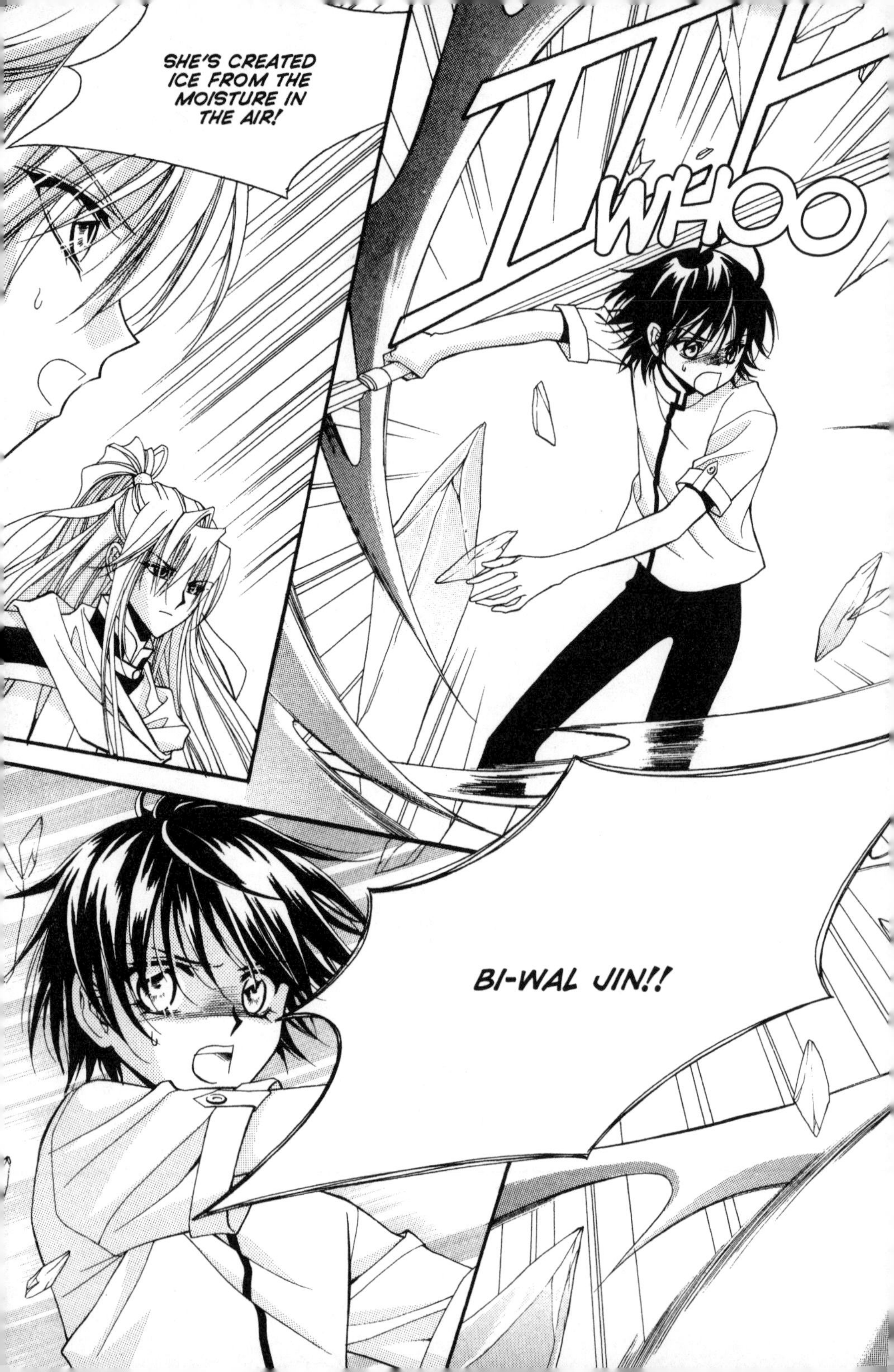
WHOO
SHE'S CREATED ICE FROM THE MOISTURE IN THE AIR!
BI-WAL JIN!!

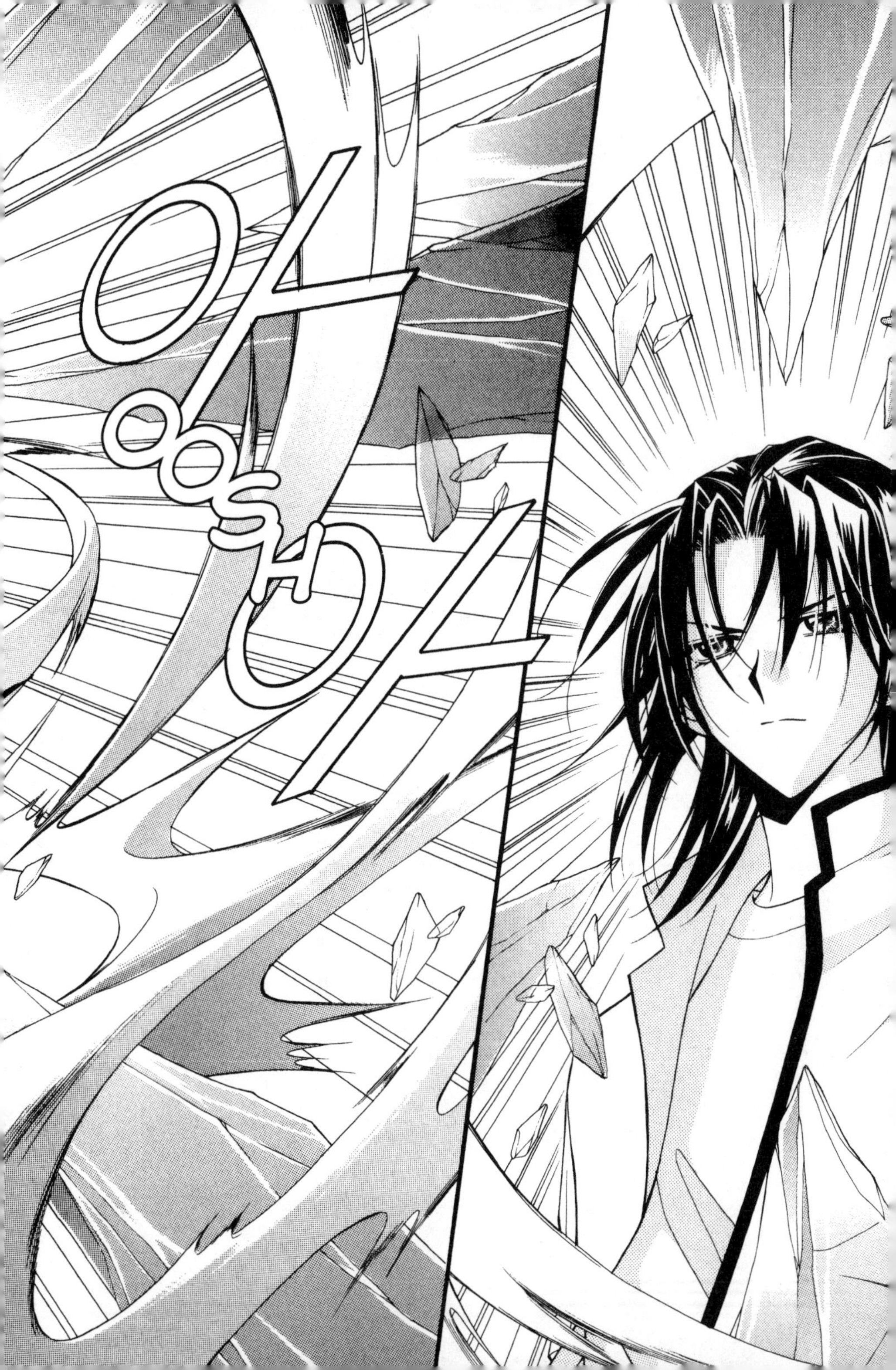
WHOOSH

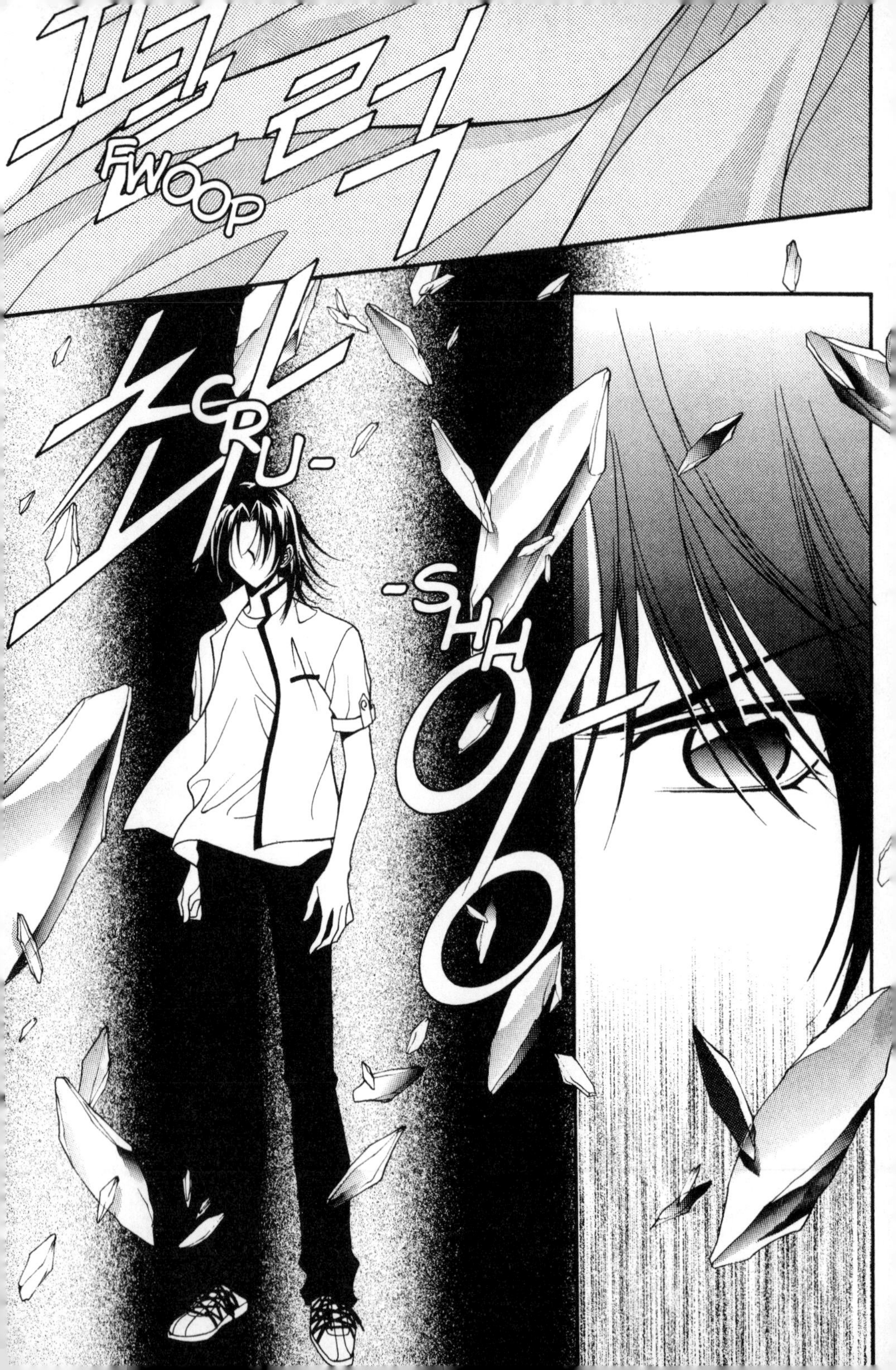

펄럭
FWOOP
CRU-
-SHH

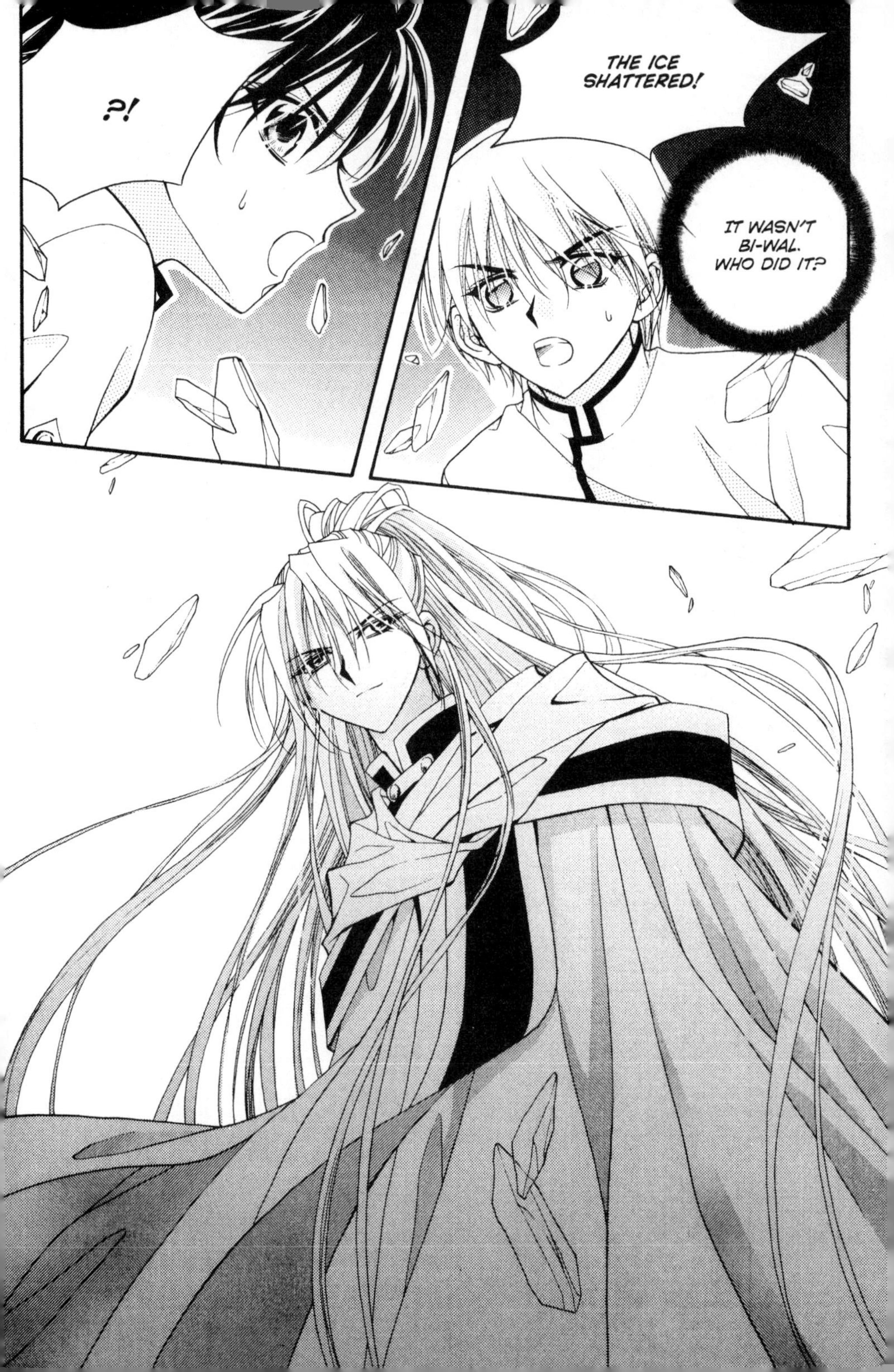
THE ICE SHATTERED!
IT WASN'T BI-WAL. WHO DID IT?
?!

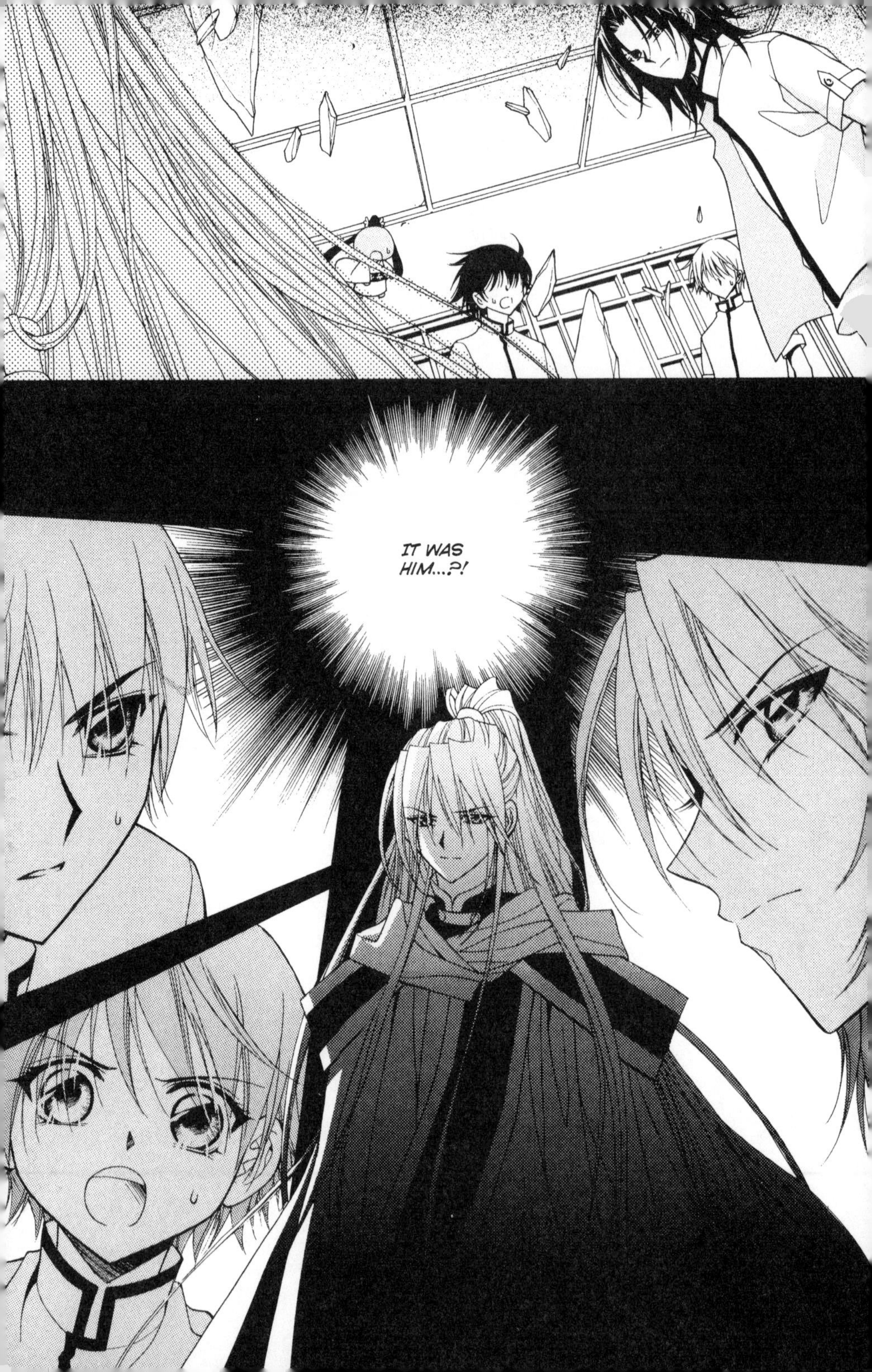
IT WAS HIM...?!

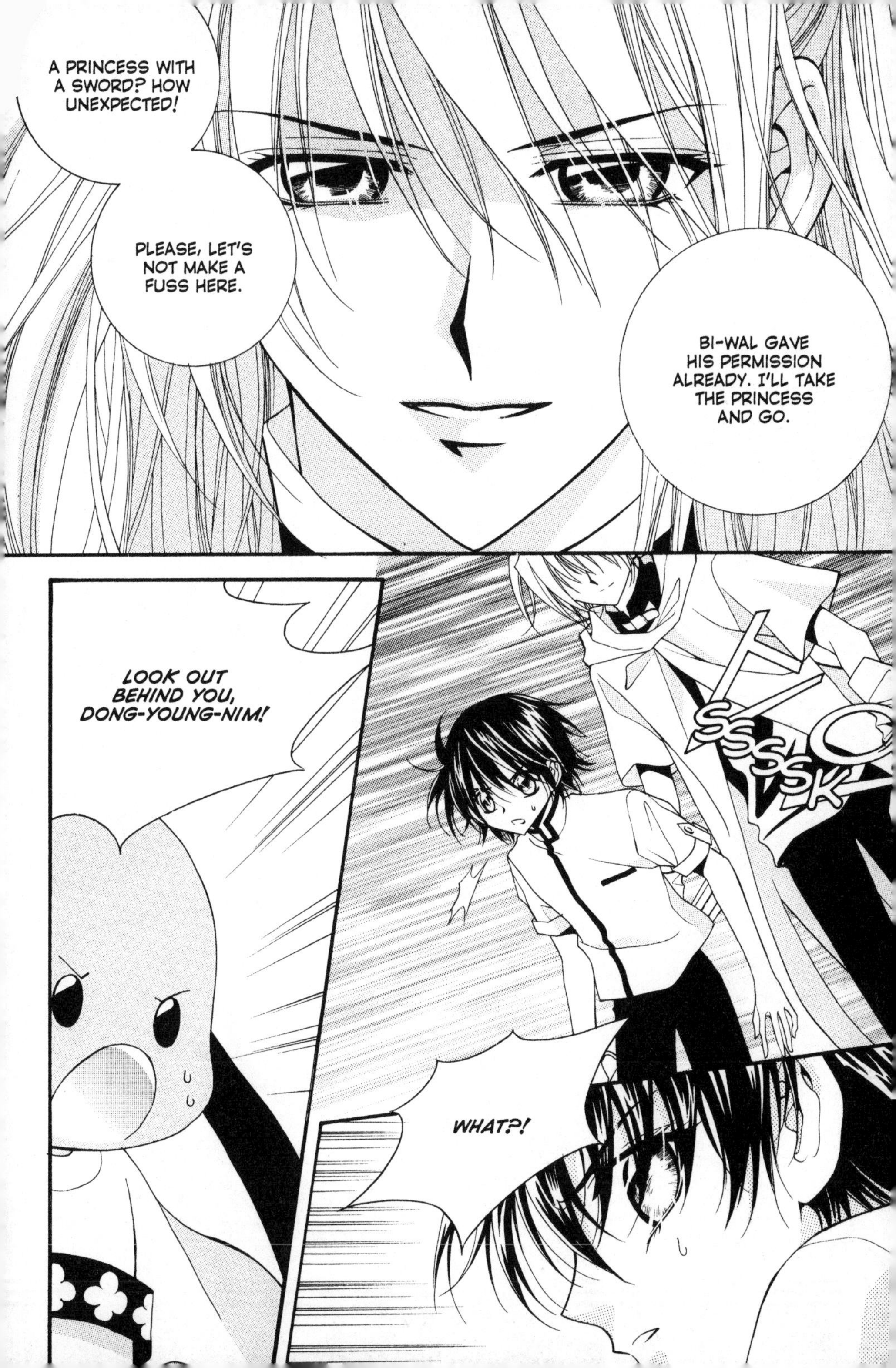
A PRINCESS WITH A SWORD? HOW UNEXPECTED!
PLEASE, LET'S NOT MAKE A FUSS HERE.
BI-WAL GAVE HIS PERMISSION ALREADY. I'LL TAKE THE PRINCESS AND GO.
SSSSK
LOOK OUT BEHIND YOU, DONG-YOUNG-NIM!
WHAT?!

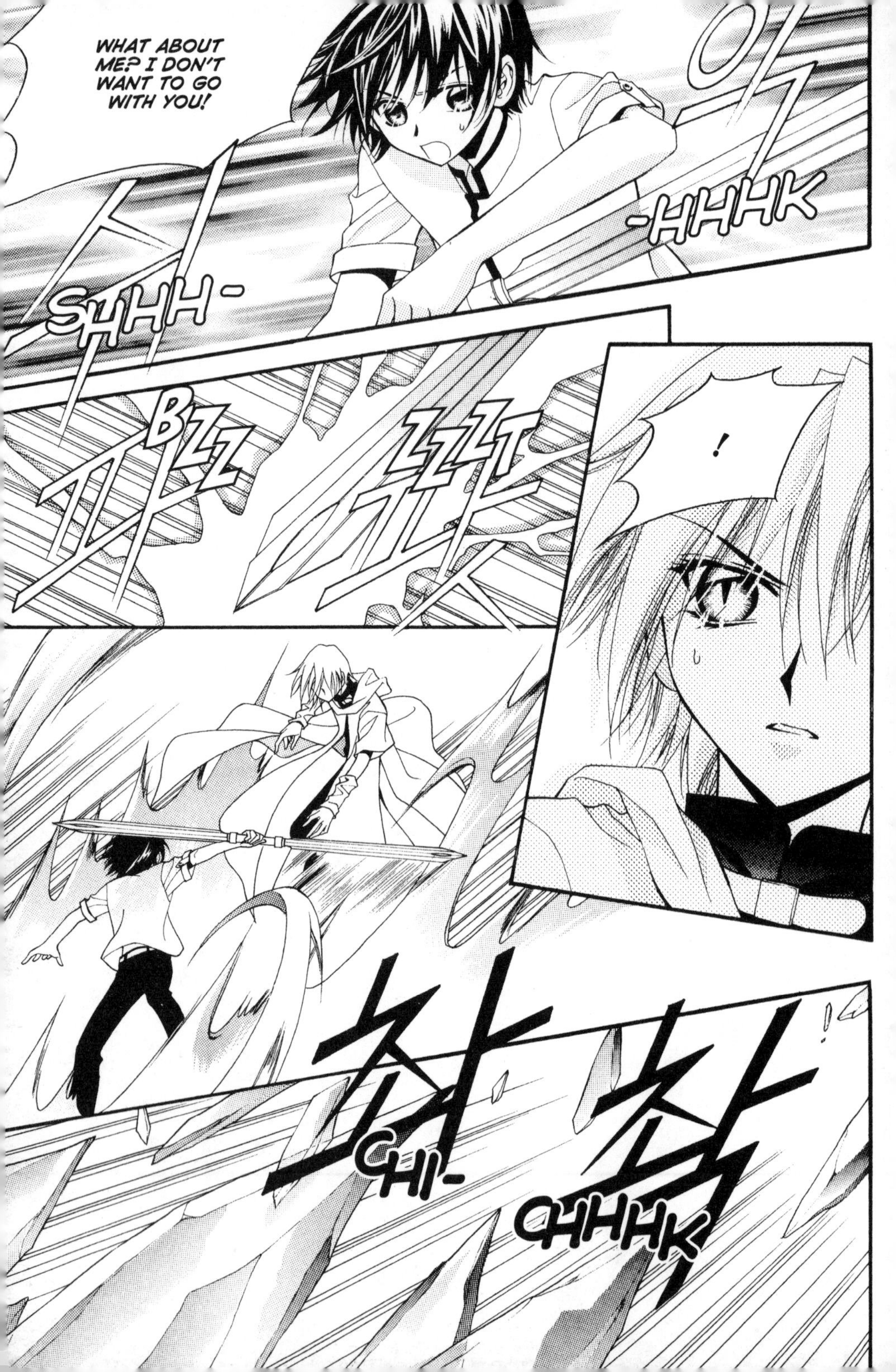
WHAT ABOUT ME? I DON'T WANT TO GO WITH YOU!
-HHHK
SHHH-
BZZZ
ZZZT
!
!
CHI-
CHHHK

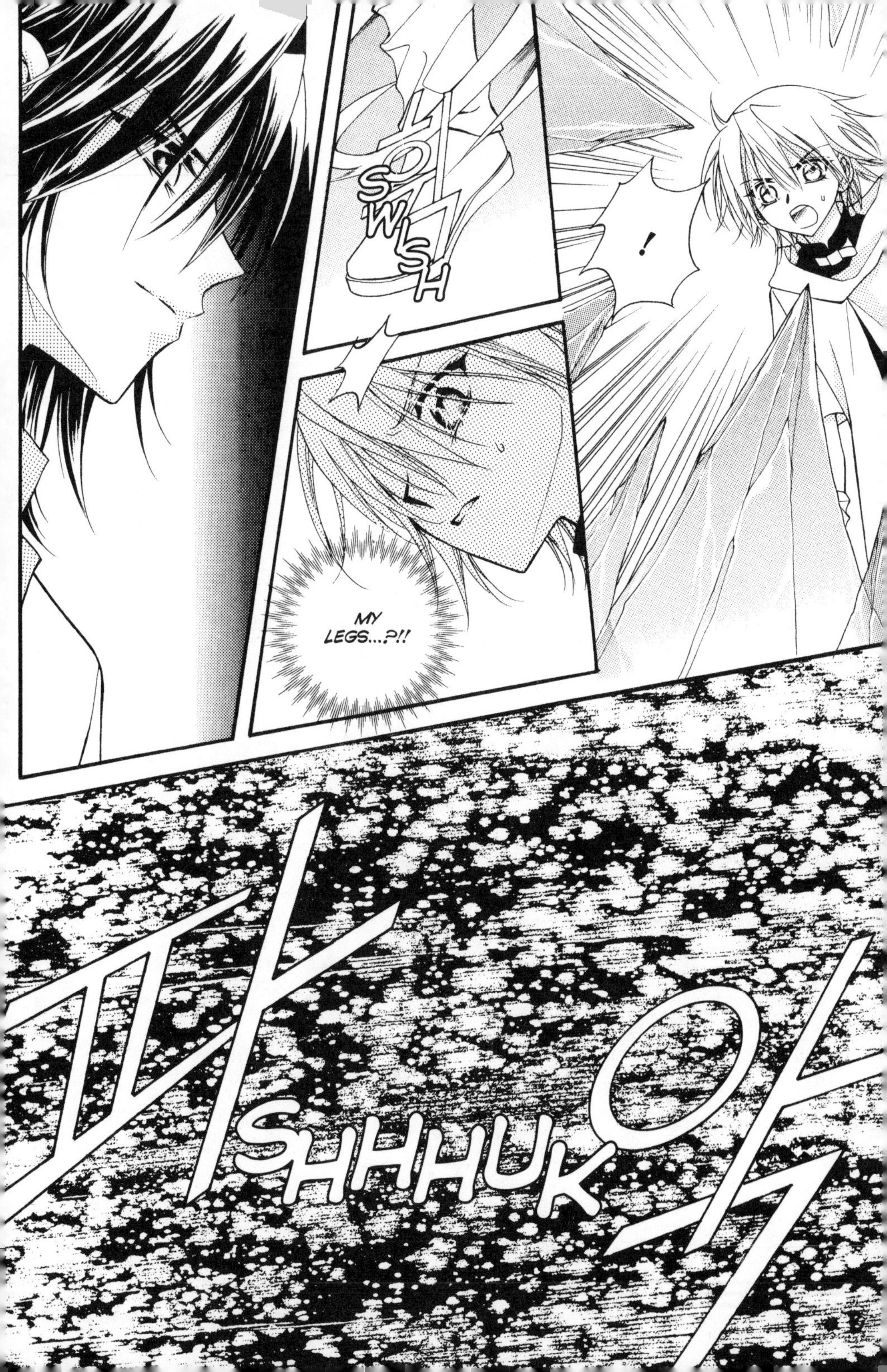
!
SWISH
MY LEGS...?!!
SHHHUK

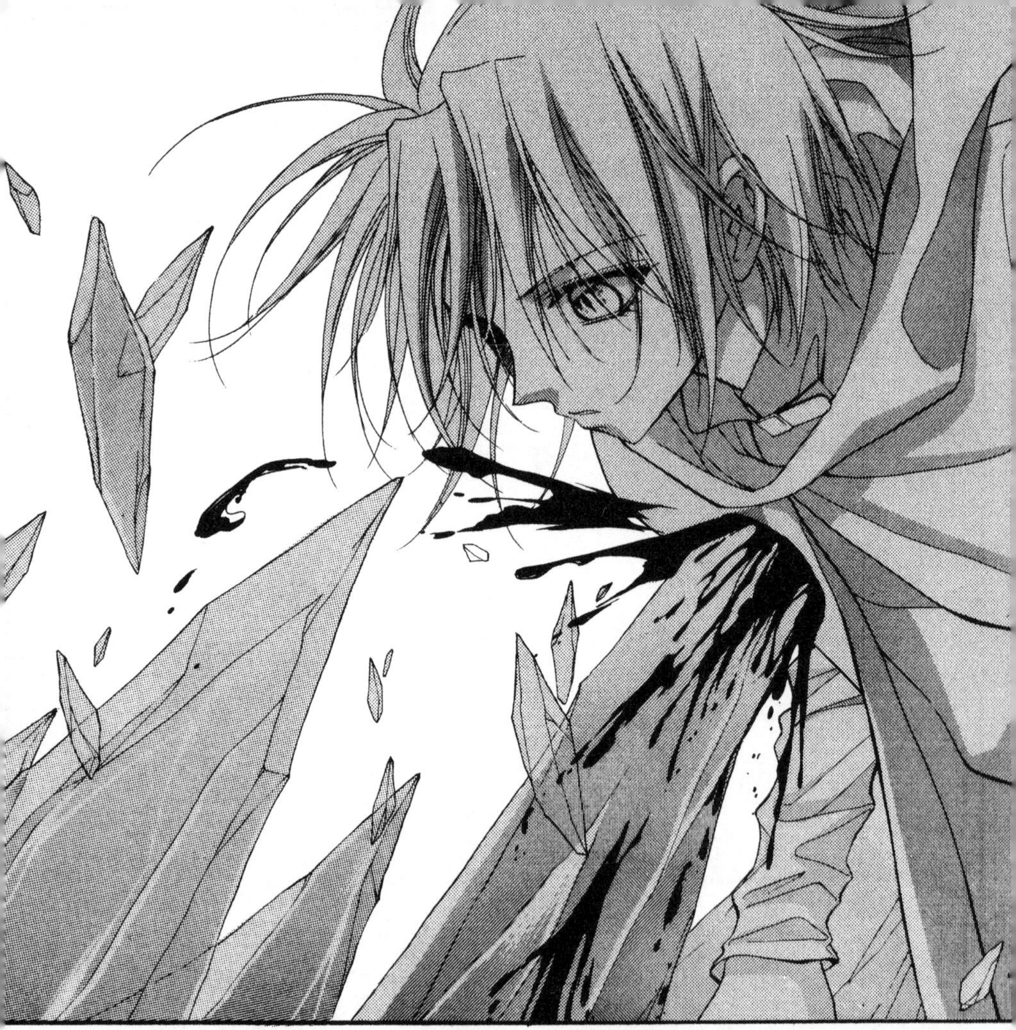
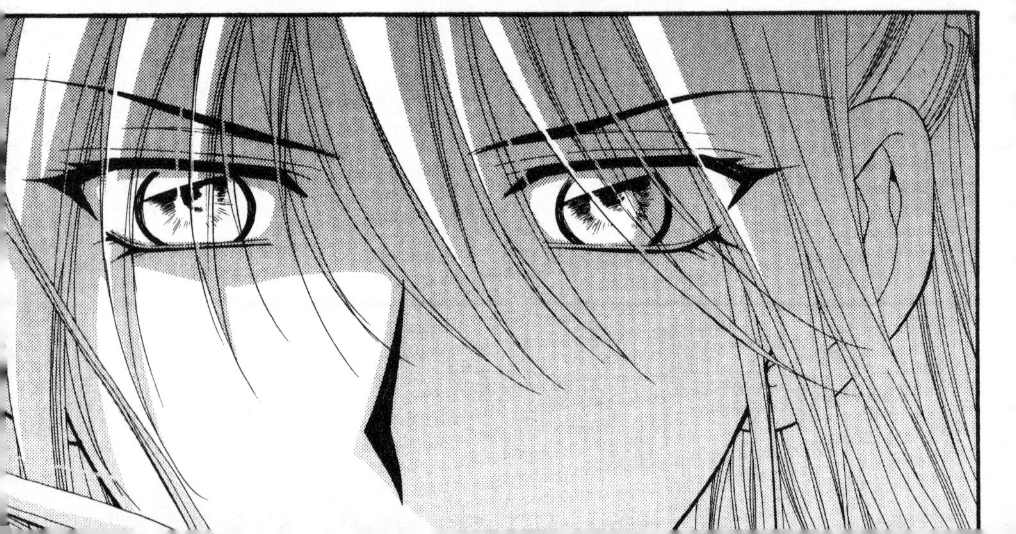

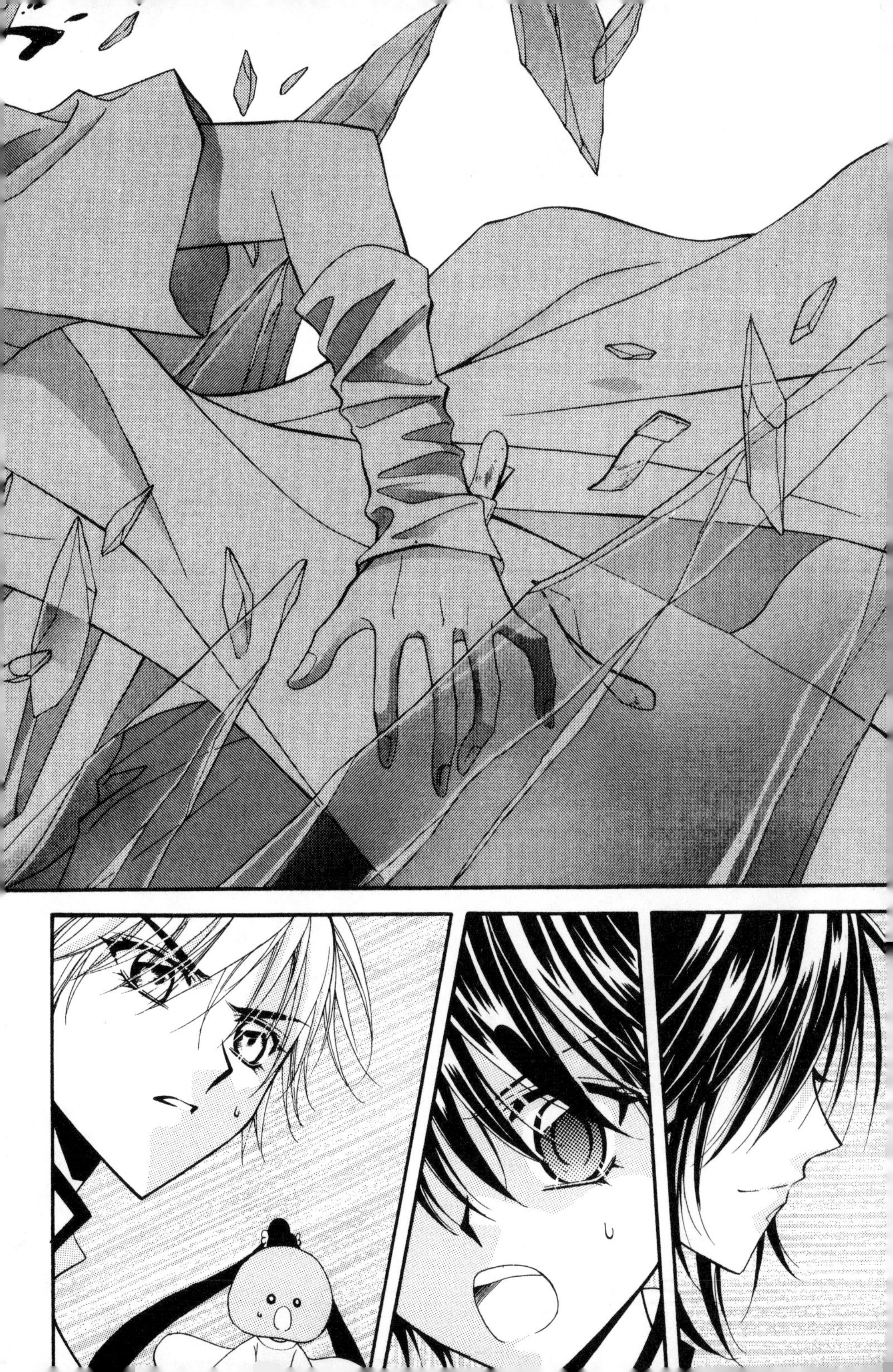

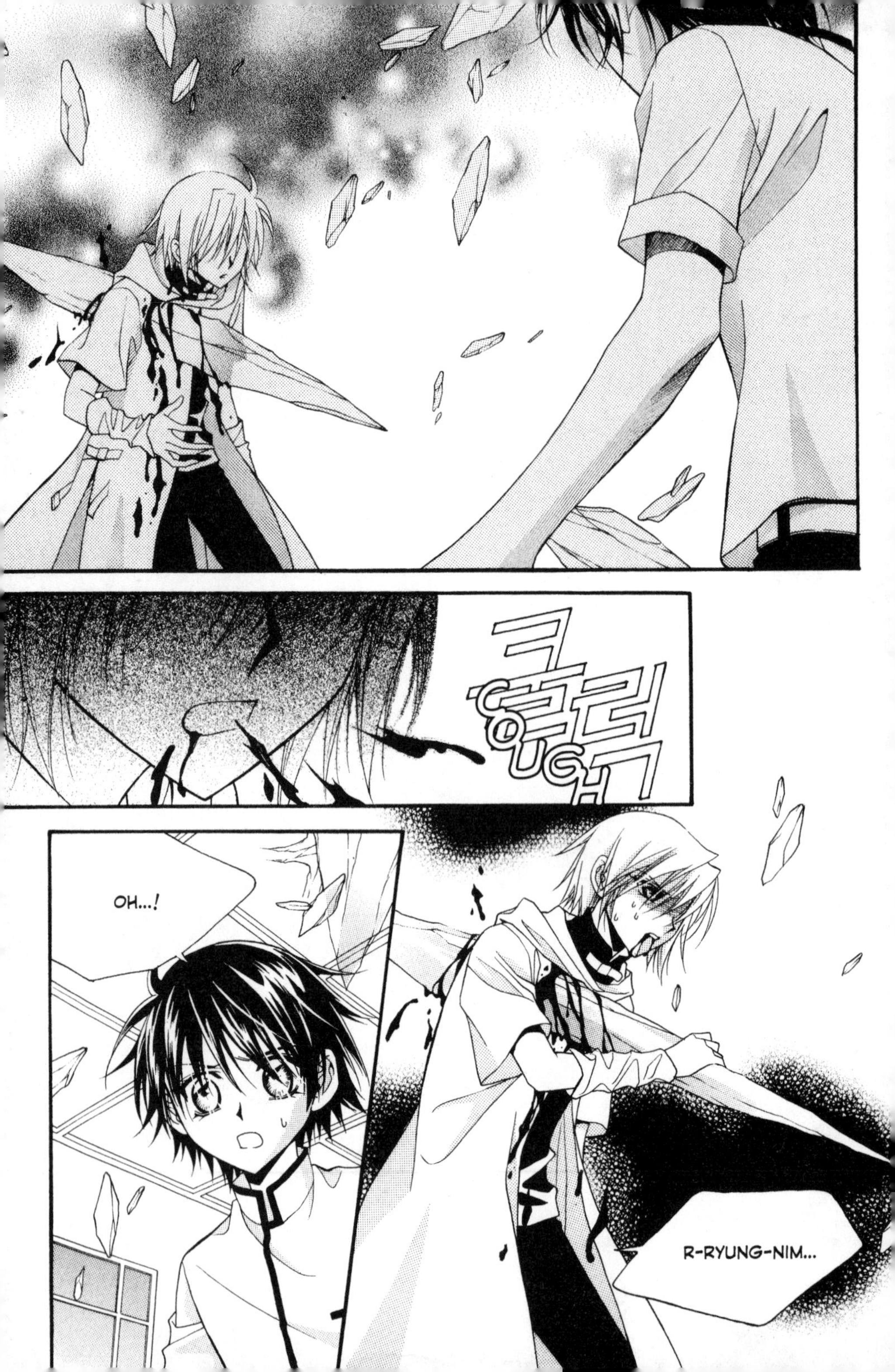

크헉
COUGH
R-RYUNG-NIM...
OH...!

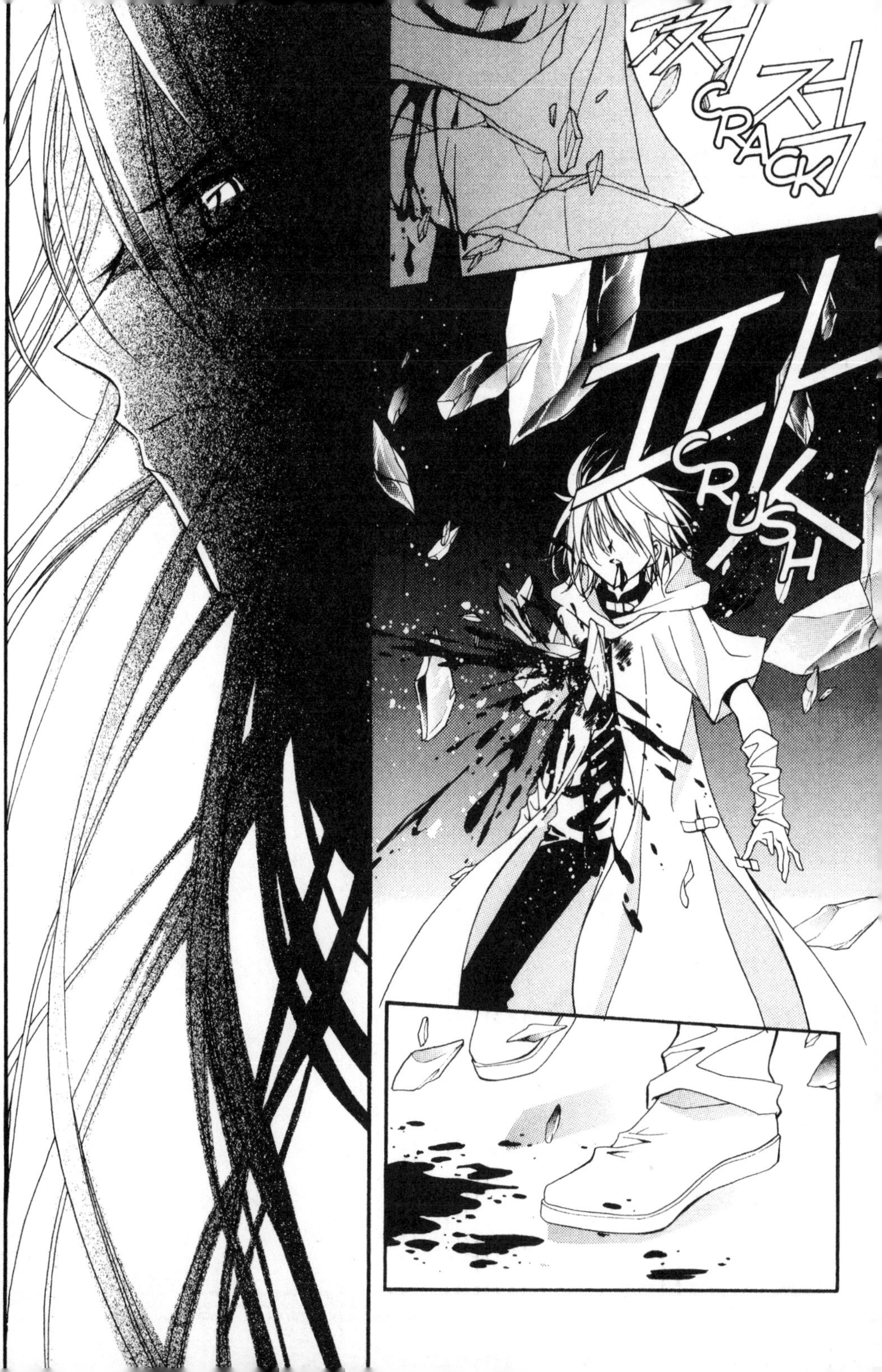
CRACK!
CRUSH

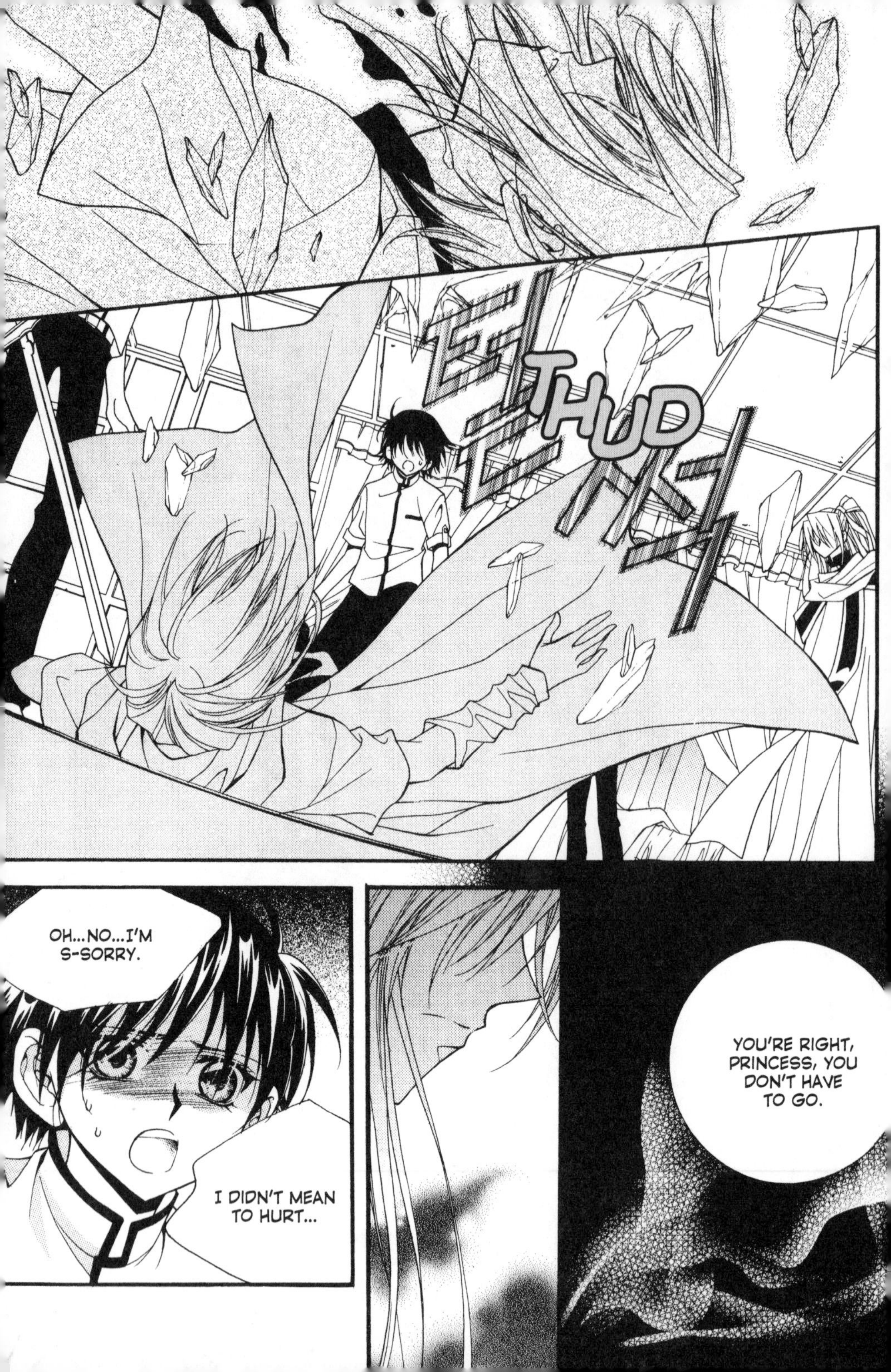
THUD
YOU'RE RIGHT, PRINCESS, YOU DON'T HAVE TO GO.
OH...NO...I'M S-SORRY.
I DIDN'T MEAN TO HURT...

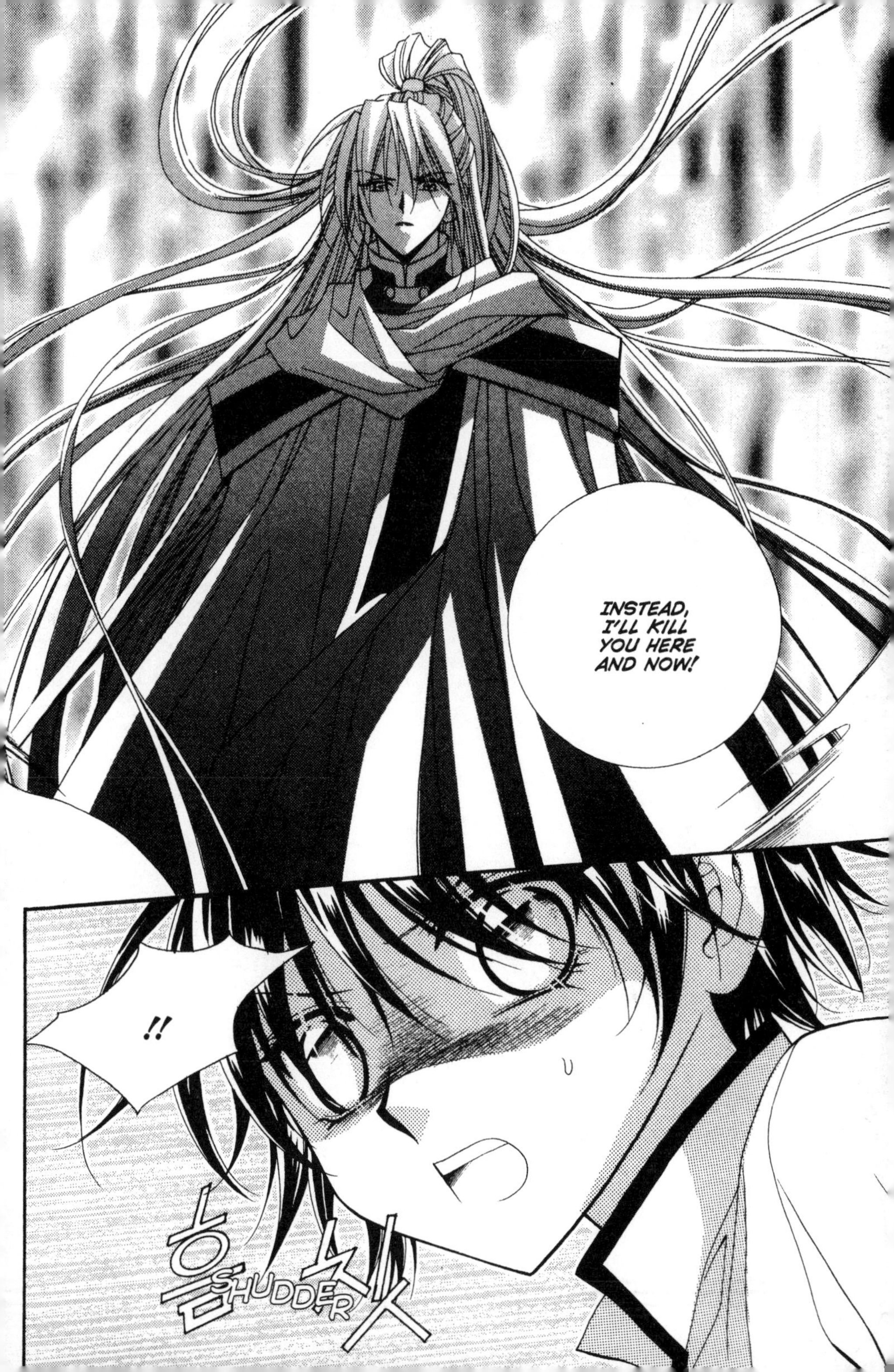
INSTEAD, I'LL KILL YOU HERE AND NOW!
!!
SHUDDER

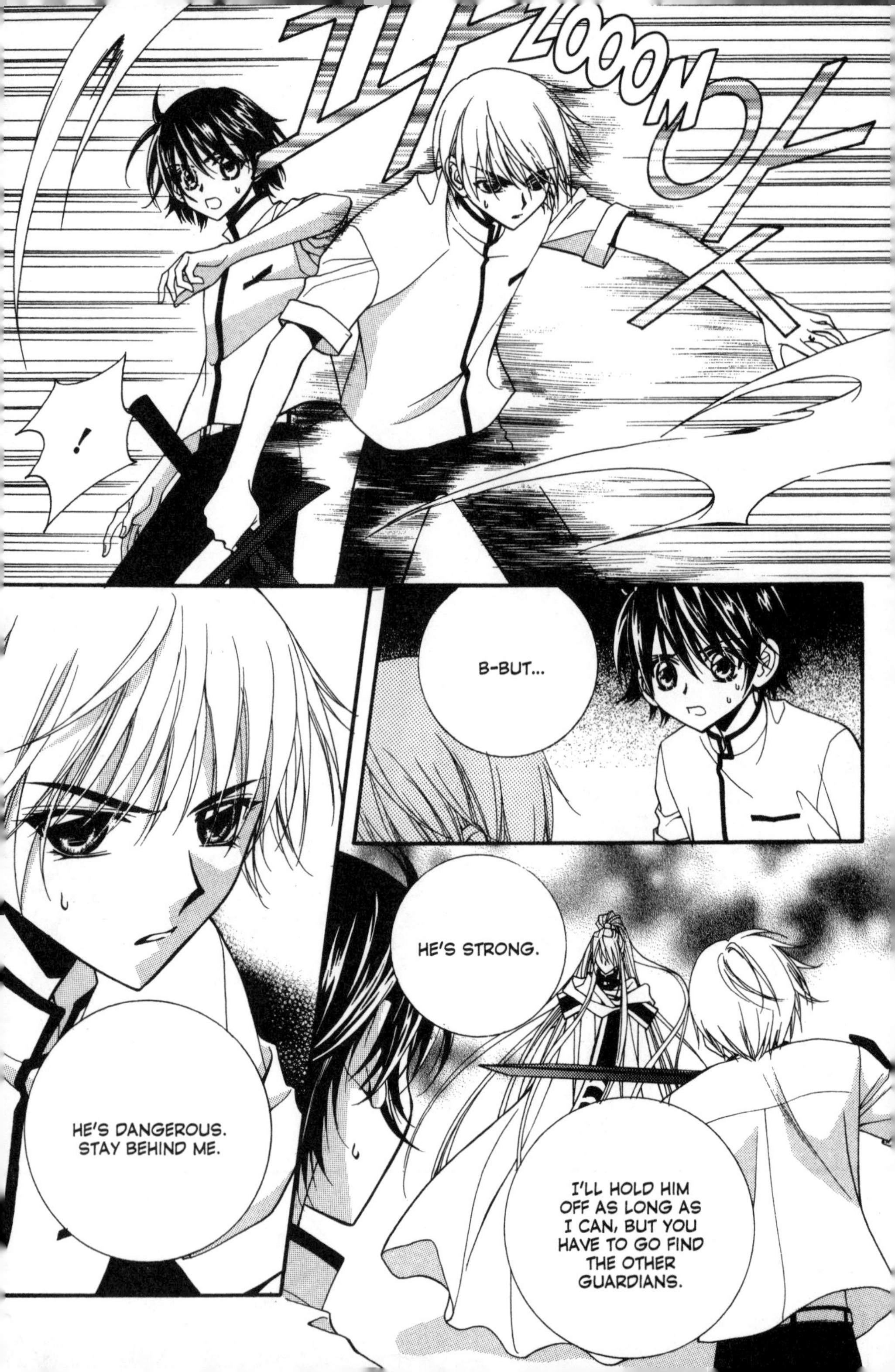
ZOOOM
!
B-BUT...
HE'S DANGEROUS. STAY BEHIND ME.
HE'S STRONG.
I'LL HOLD HIM OFF AS LONG AS I CAN, BUT YOU HAVE TO GO FIND THE OTHER GUARDIANS.

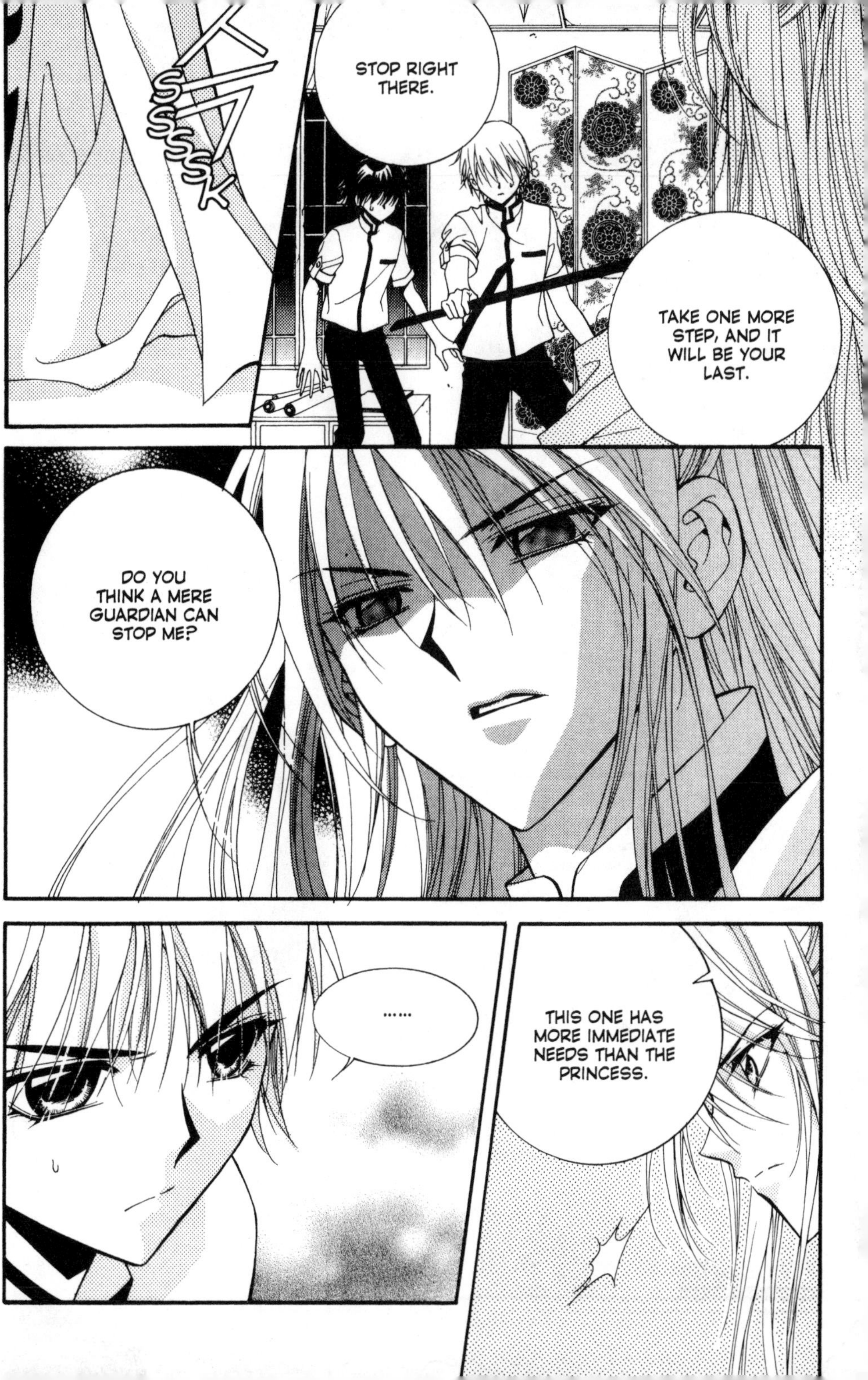
STOP RIGHT THERE.
SSSSSK
TAKE ONE MORE STEP, AND IT WILL BE YOUR LAST.
DO YOU THINK A MERE GUARDIAN CAN STOP ME?
THIS ONE HAS MORE IMMEDIATE NEEDS THAN THE PRINCESS.
......

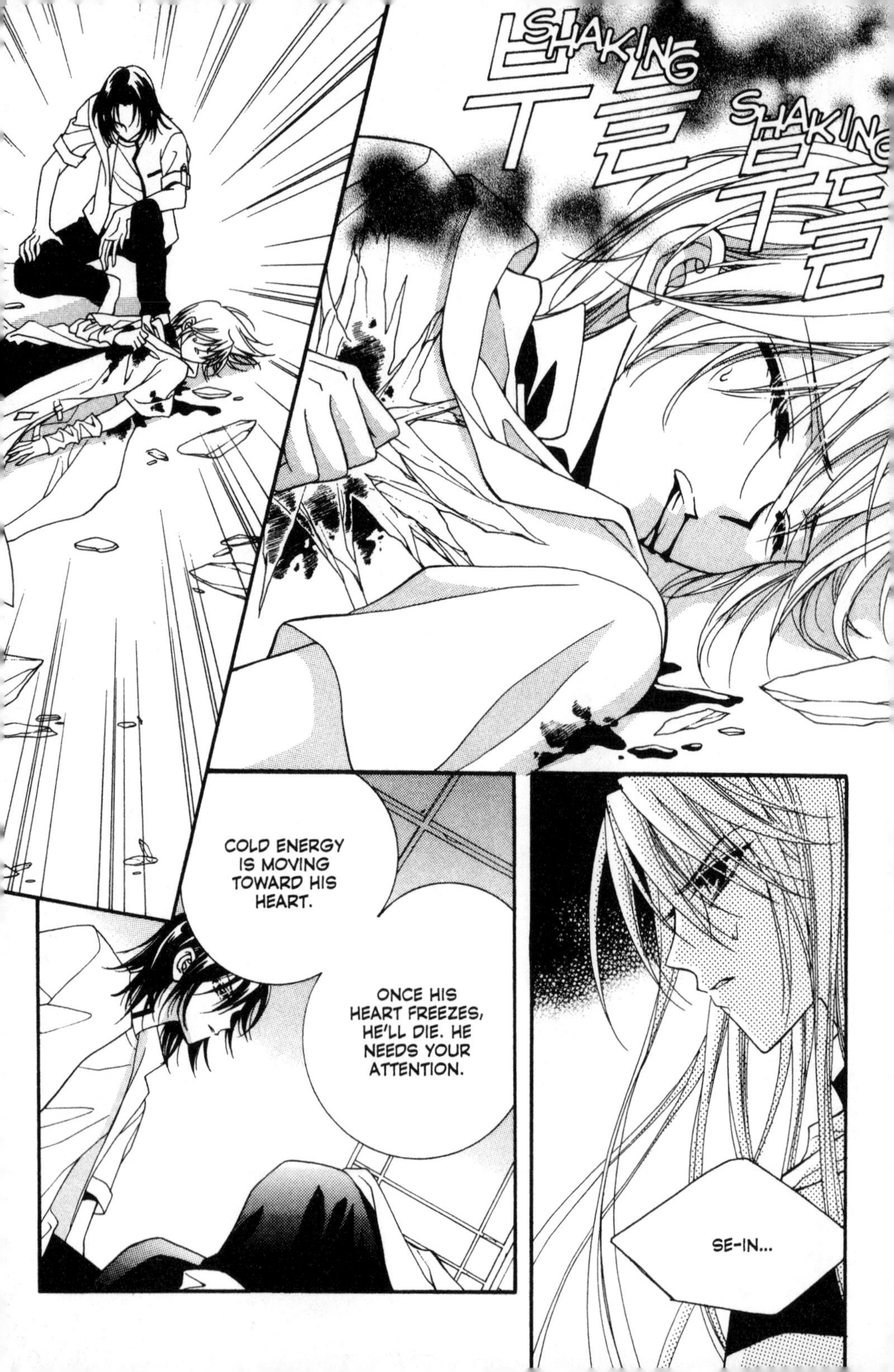
SHAKING
SHAKING
COLD ENERGY IS MOVING TOWARD HIS HEART.
ONCE HIS HEART FREEZES, HE'LL DIE. HE NEEDS YOUR ATTENTION.
SE-IN...

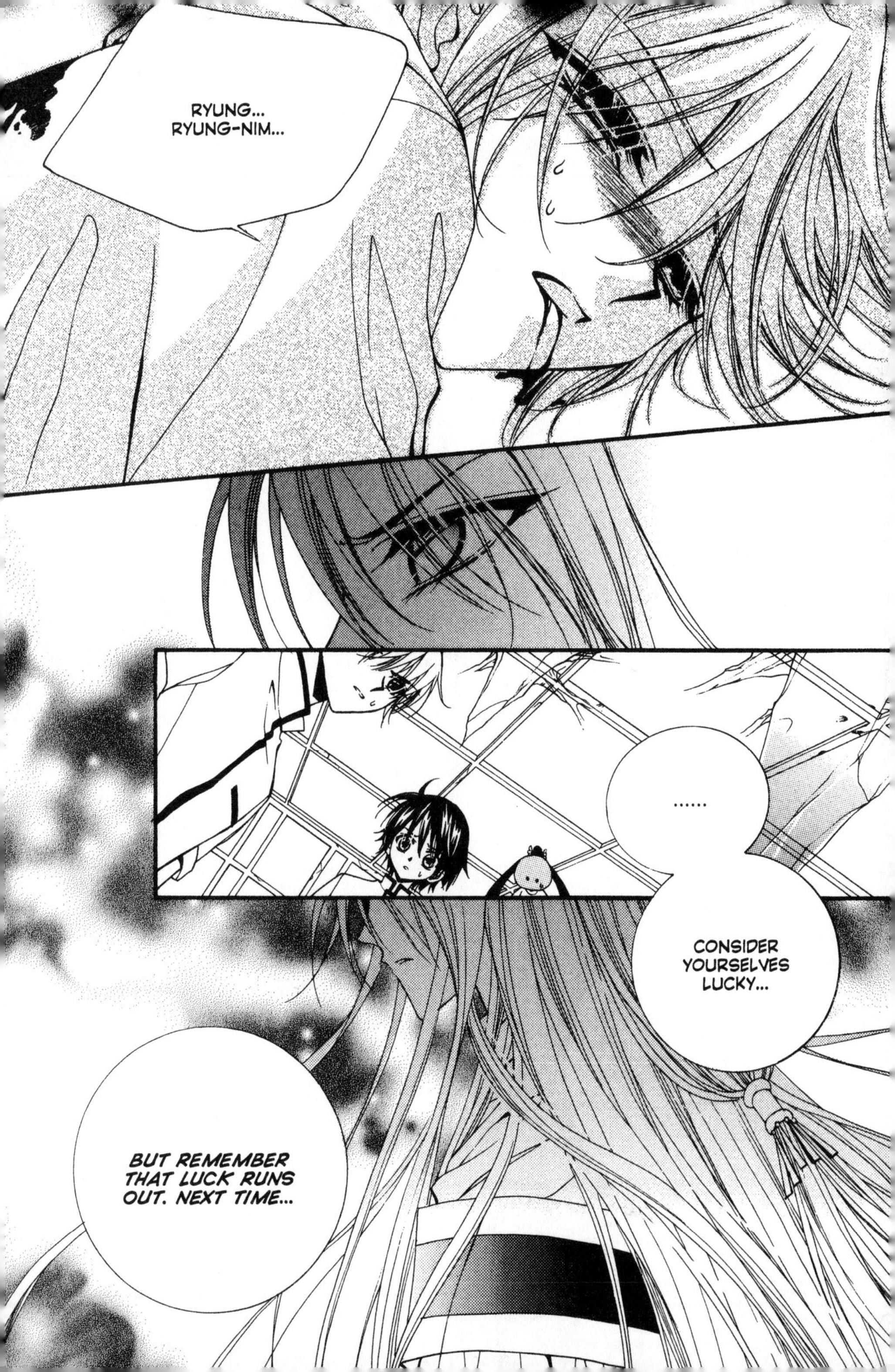

RYUNG... RYUNG-NIM...
......
CONSIDER YOURSELVES LUCKY...
BUT REMEMBER THAT LUCK RUNS OUT. NEXT TIME...

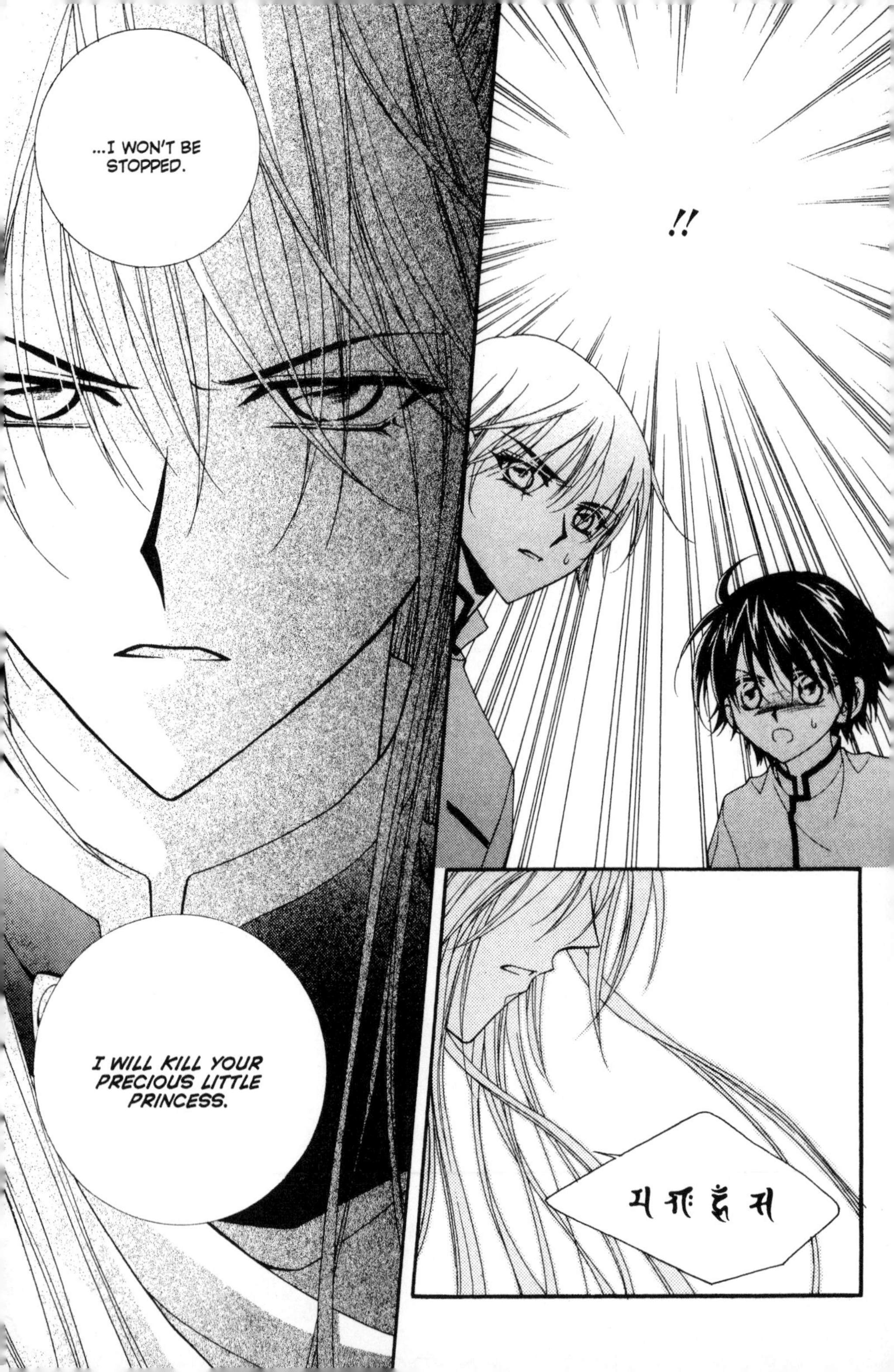

...I WON'T BE STOPPED.
!!
I WILL KILL YOUR PRECIOUS LITTLE PRINCESS.

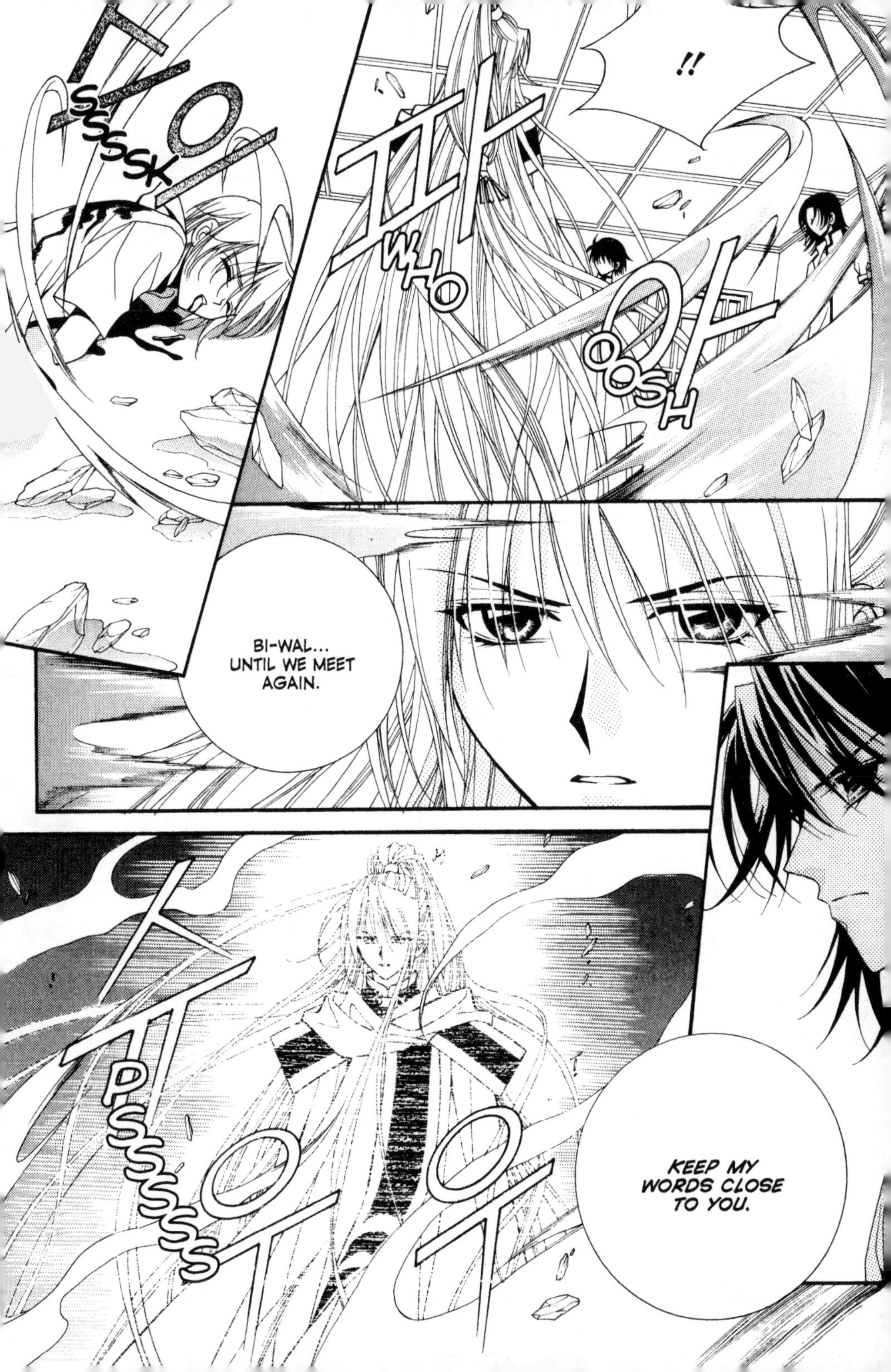

!!
WHO
OOSH
SSSSSK
BI-WAL... UNTIL WE MEET AGAIN.
KEEP MY WORDS CLOSE TO YOU.
PSSSSSS

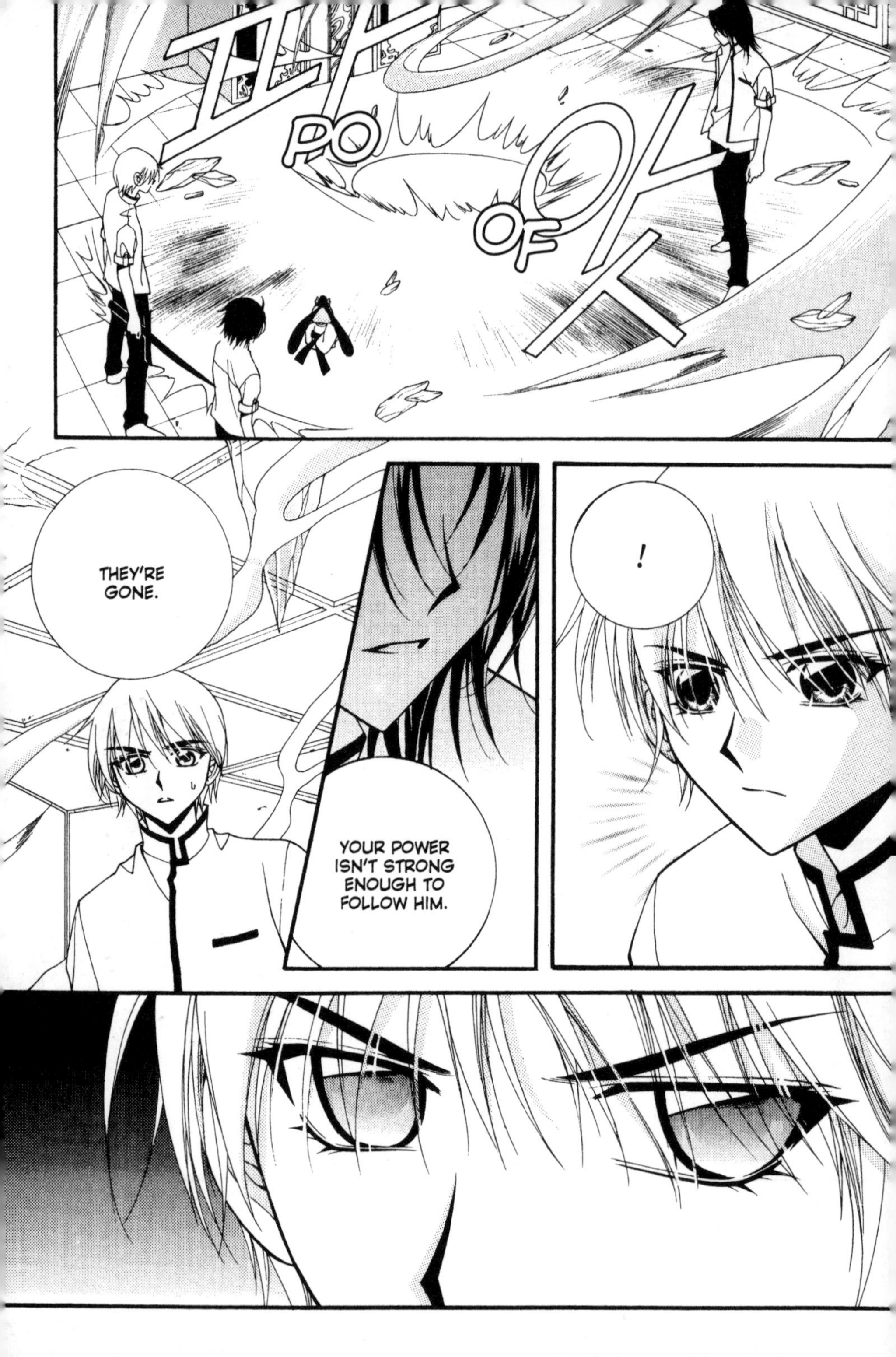
POOF
!
YOUR POWER ISN'T STRONG ENOUGH TO FOLLOW HIM.
THEY'RE GONE.

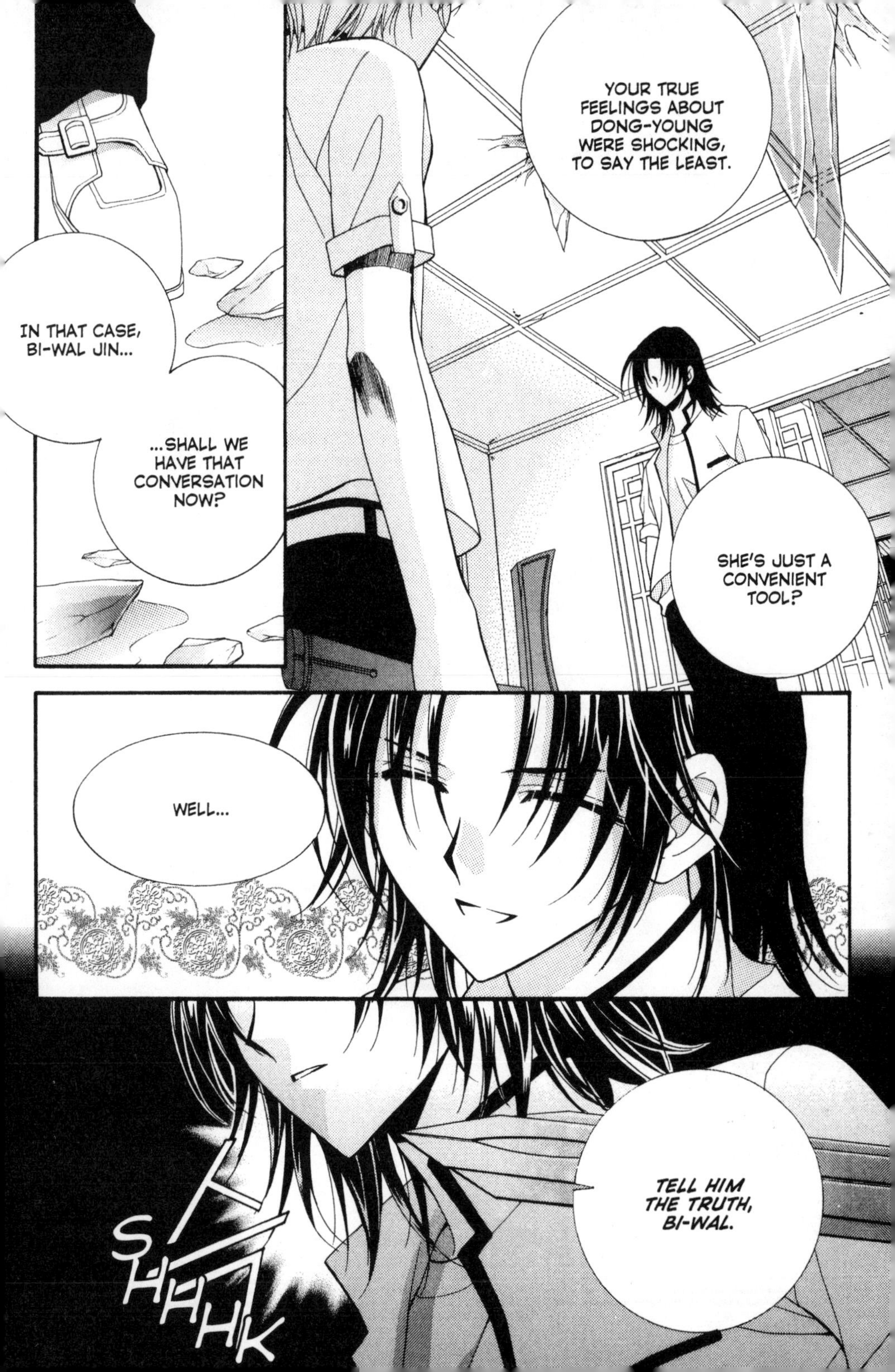

IN THAT CASE, BI-WAL JIN...
...SHALL WE HAVE THAT CONVERSATION NOW?
YOUR TRUE FEELINGS ABOUT DONG-YOUNG WERE SHOCKING, TO SAY THE LEAST.
SHE'S JUST A CONVENIENT TOOL?
WELL...
TELL HIM THE TRUTH, BI-WAL.
SHHHHK

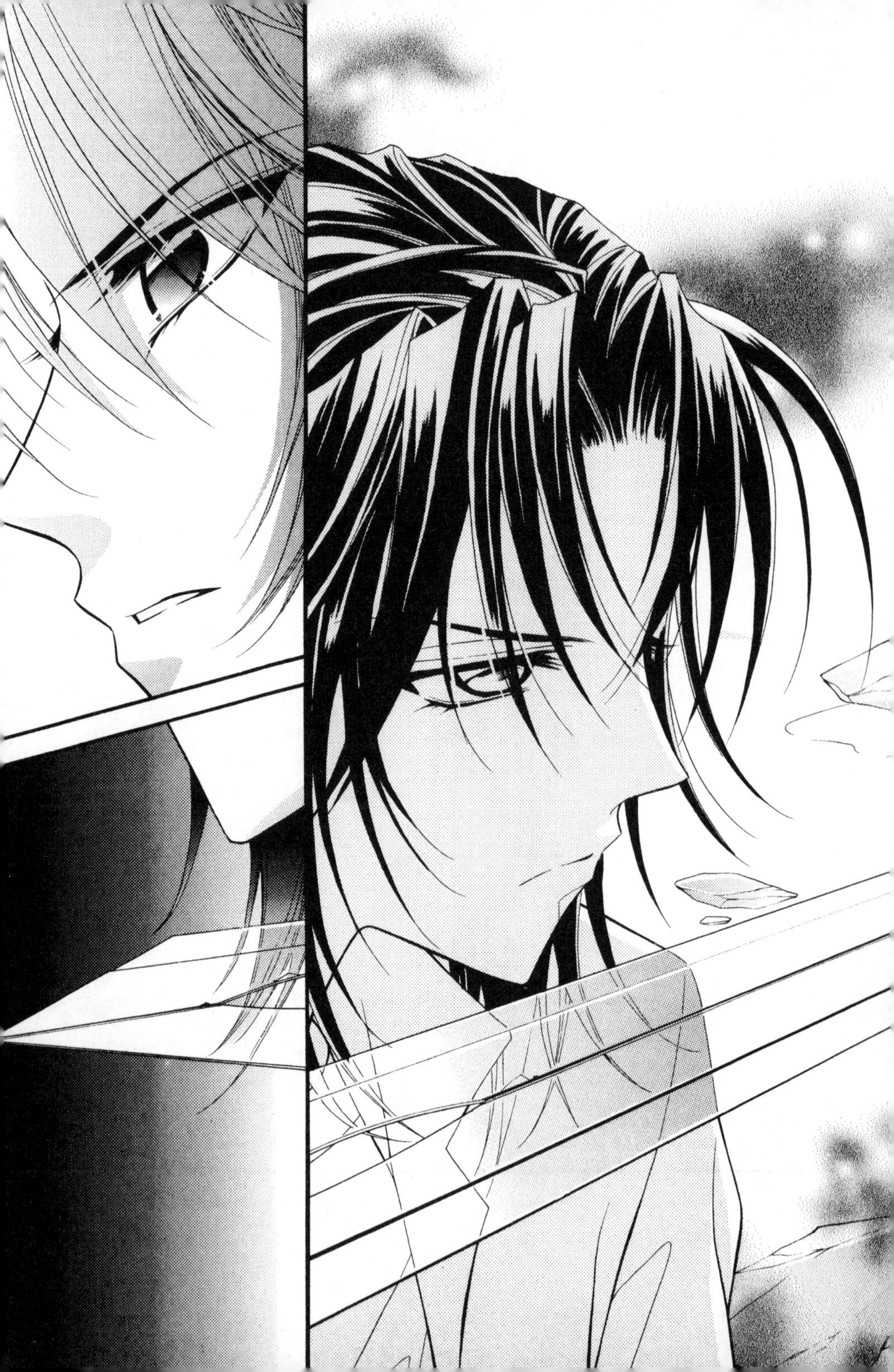

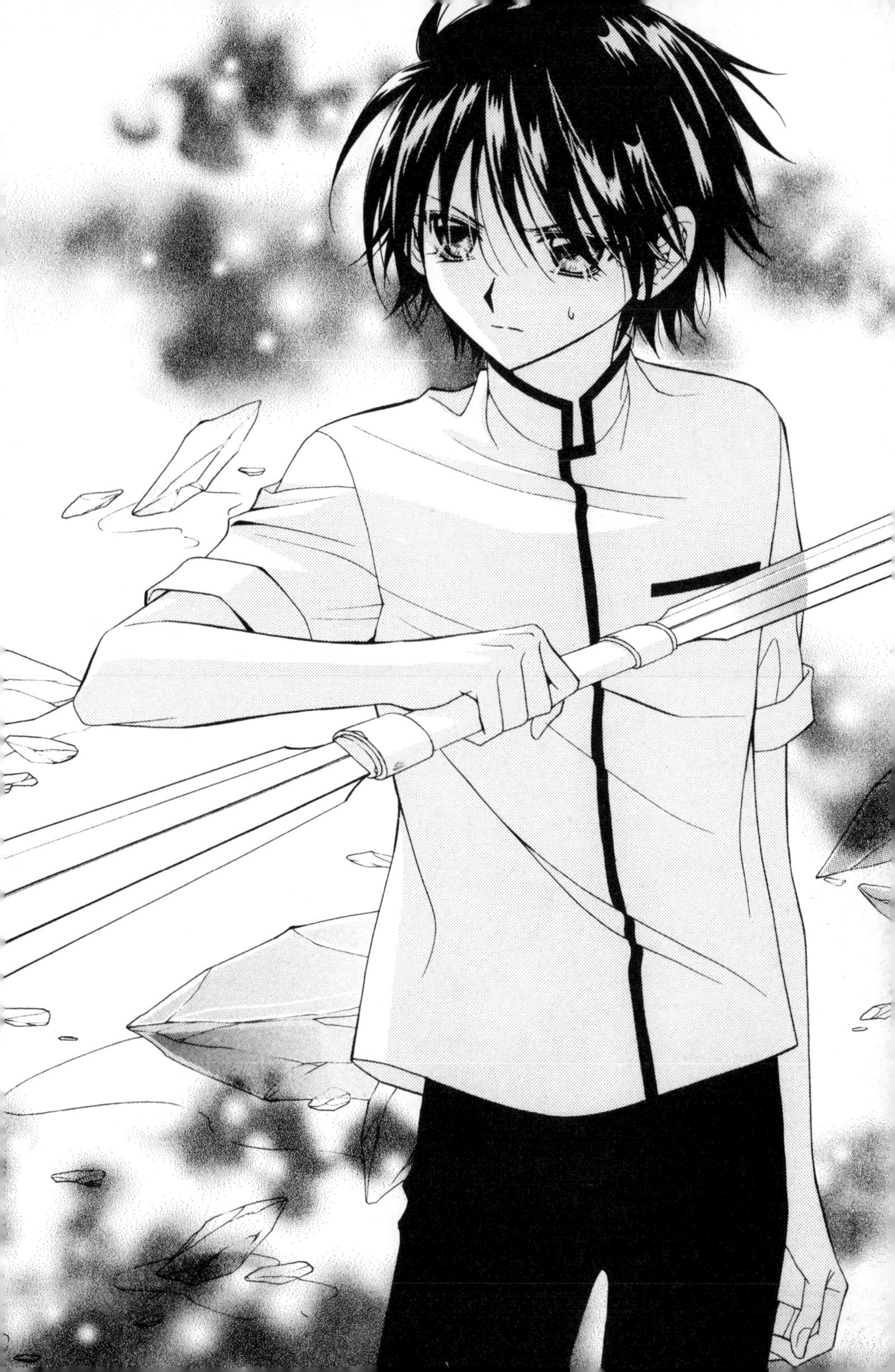

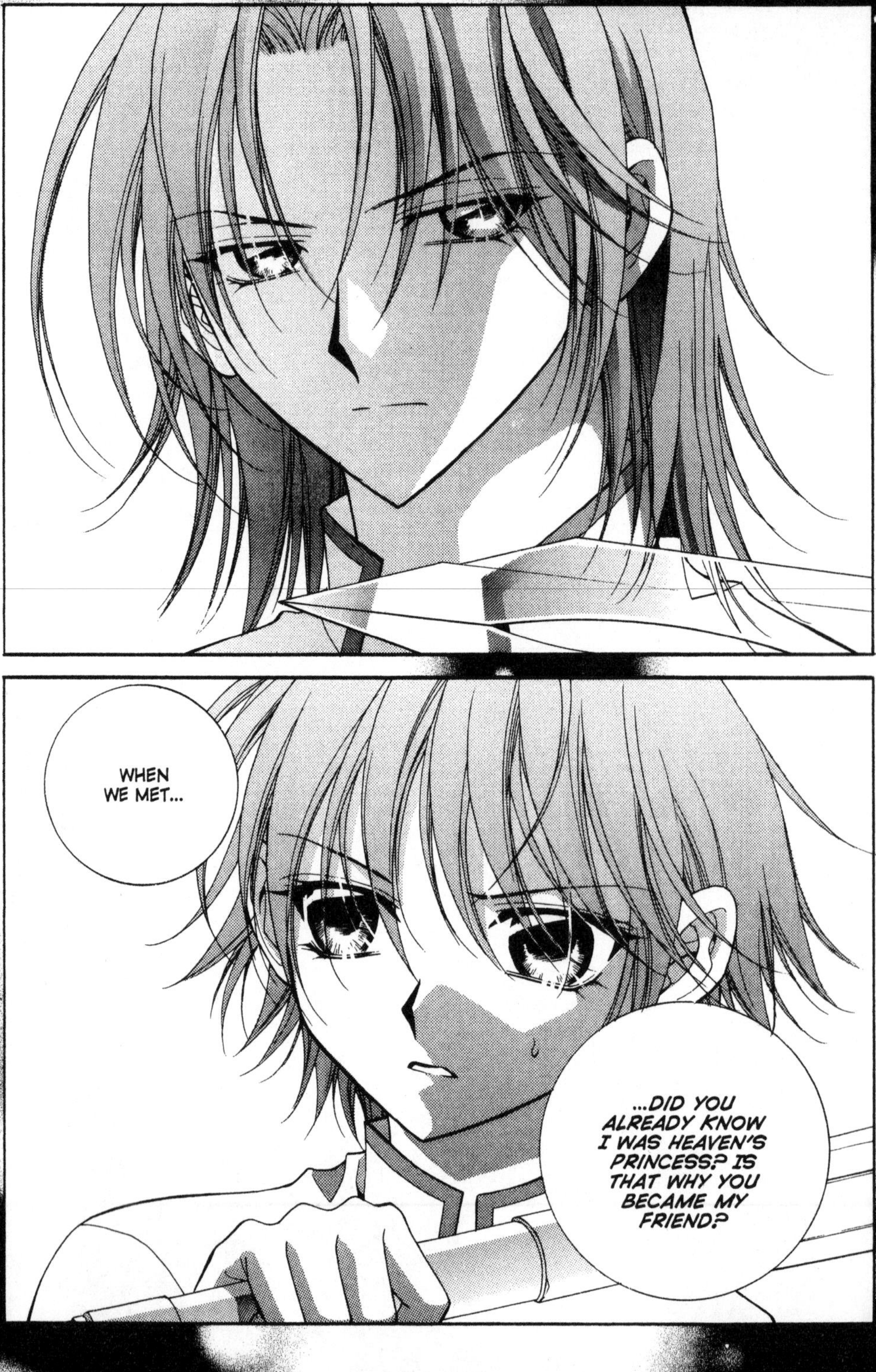
WHEN WE MET...
...DID YOU ALREADY KNOW I WAS HEAVEN'S PRINCESS? IS THAT WHY YOU BECAME MY FRIEND?

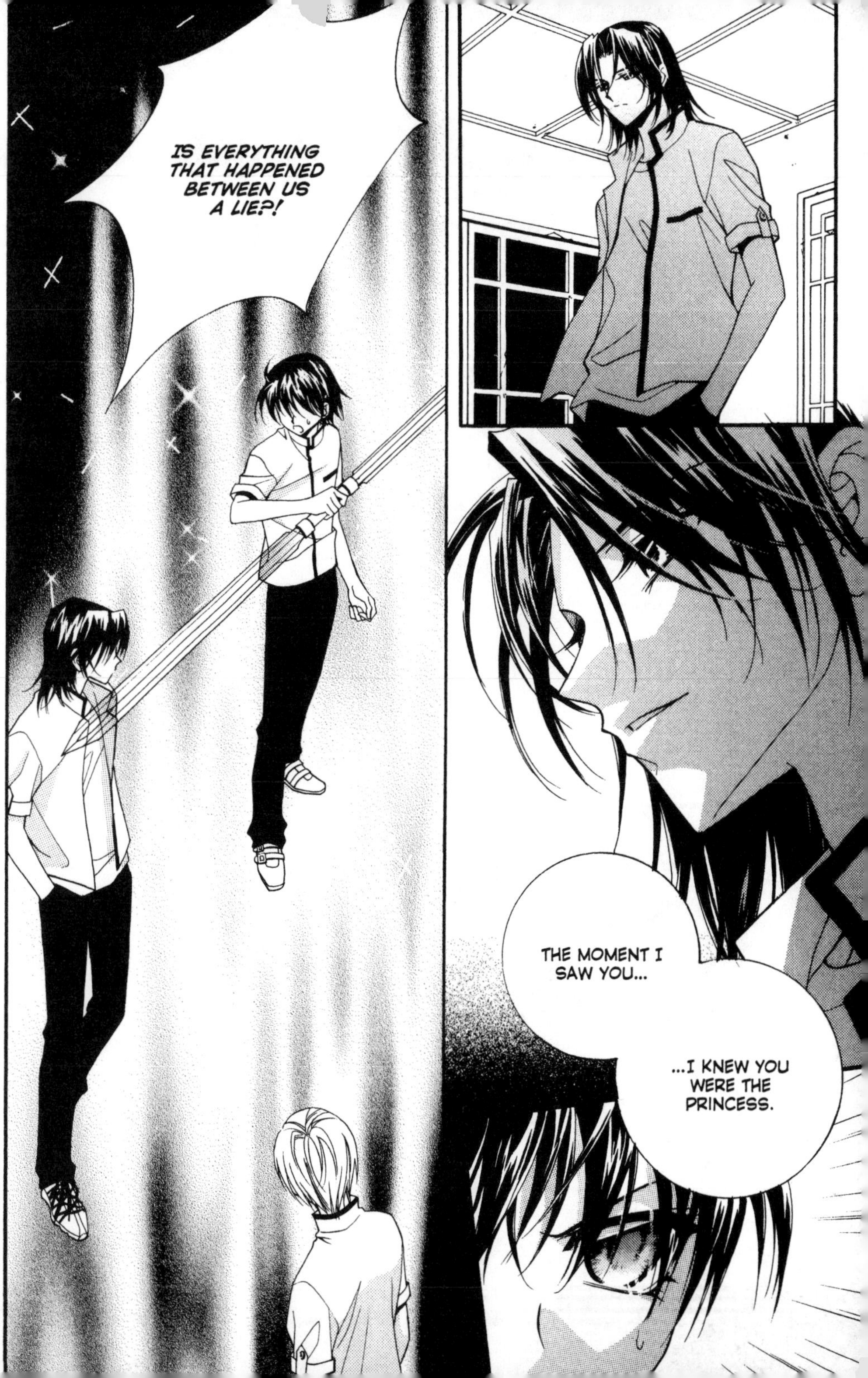
THE MOMENT I SAW YOU...
...I KNEW YOU WERE THE PRINCESS.
IS EVERYTHING THAT HAPPENED BETWEEN US A LIE?!

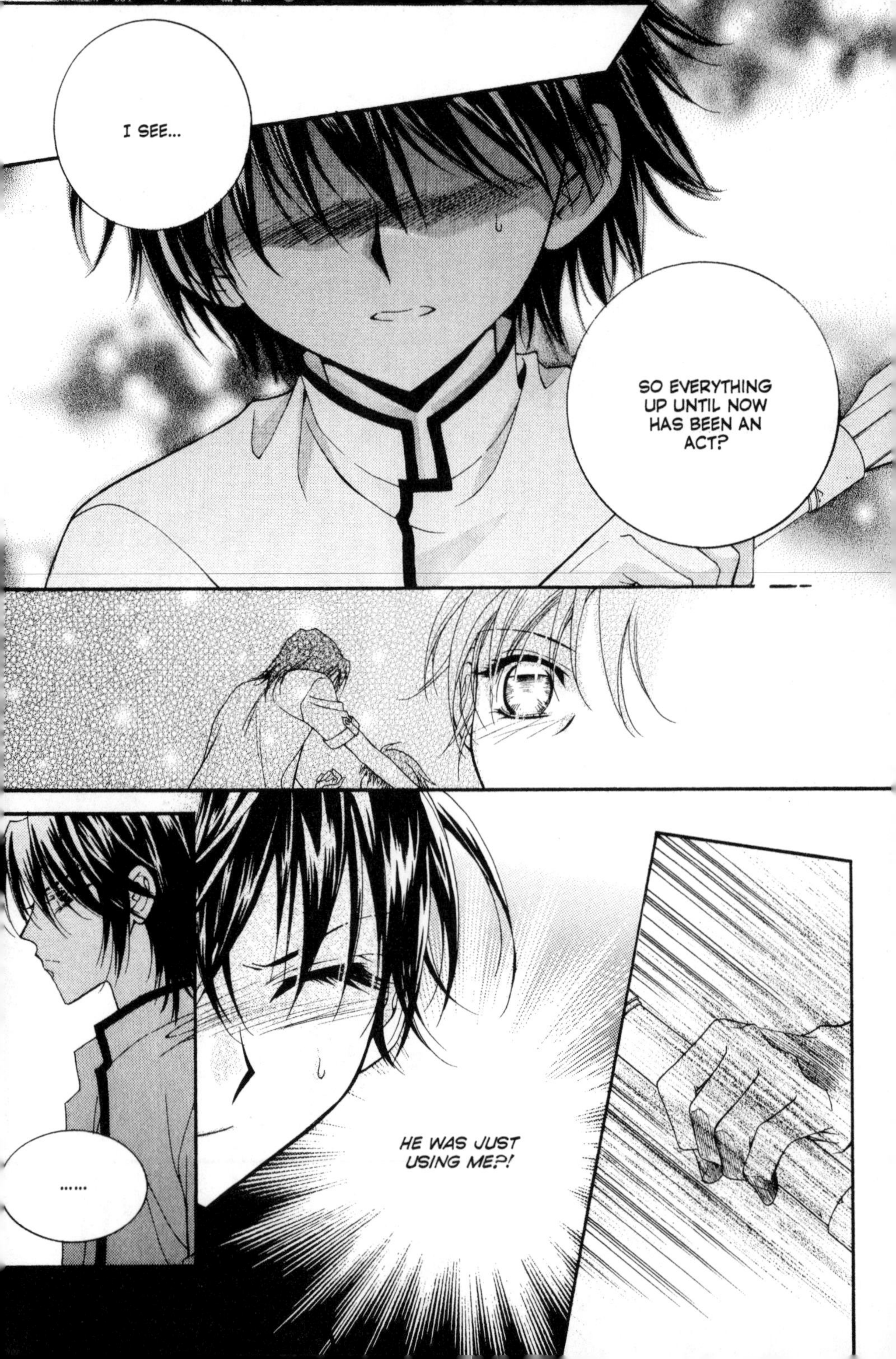

I SEE...
SO EVERYTHING UP UNTIL NOW HAS BEEN AN ACT?
HE WAS JUST USING ME?!
......

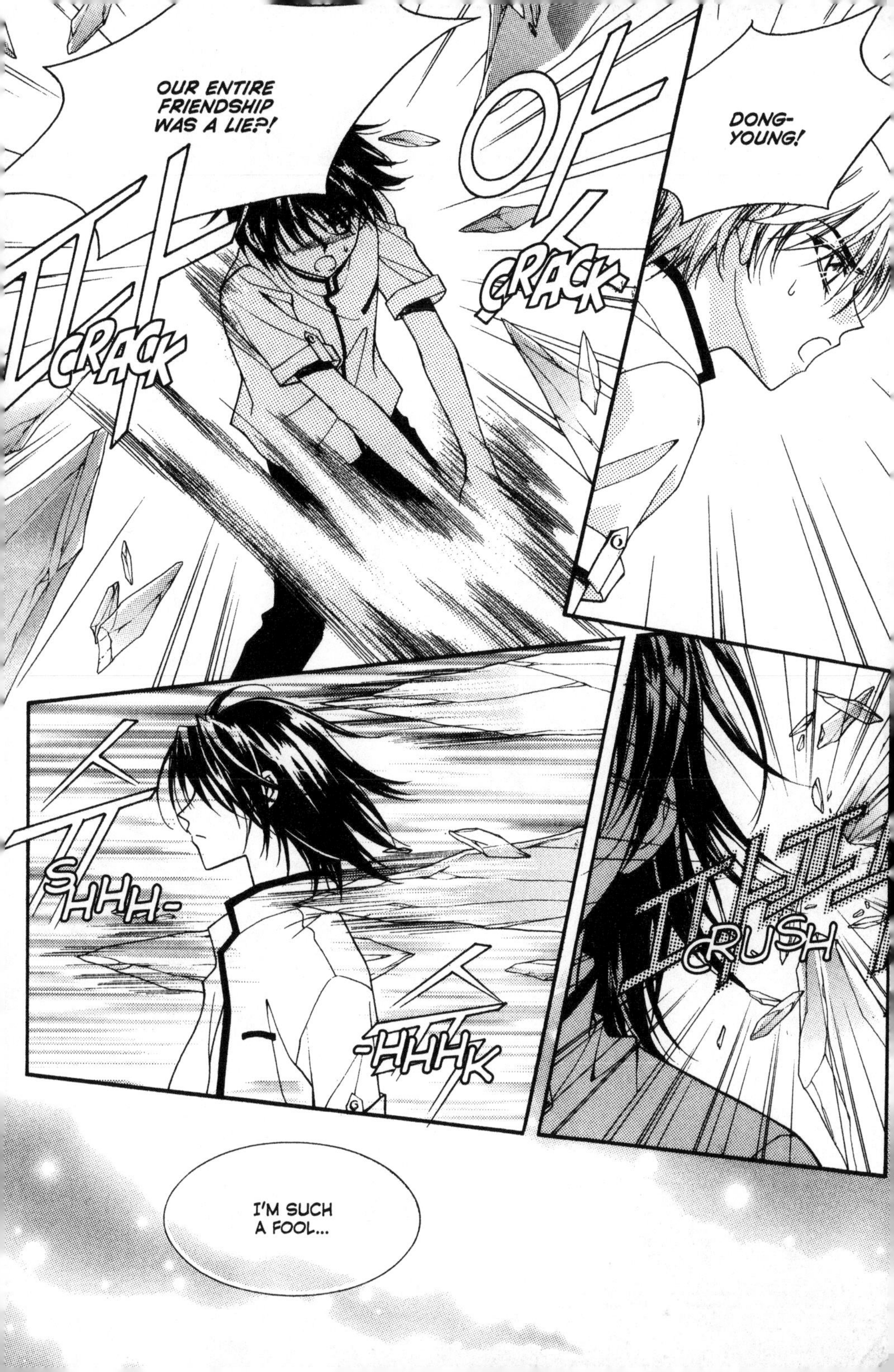

OUR ENTIRE FRIENDSHIP WAS A LIE?!
CRACK
CRACK
DONG-YOUNG!
SHHH-
-HHHK
CRUSH
I'M SUCH A FOOL...

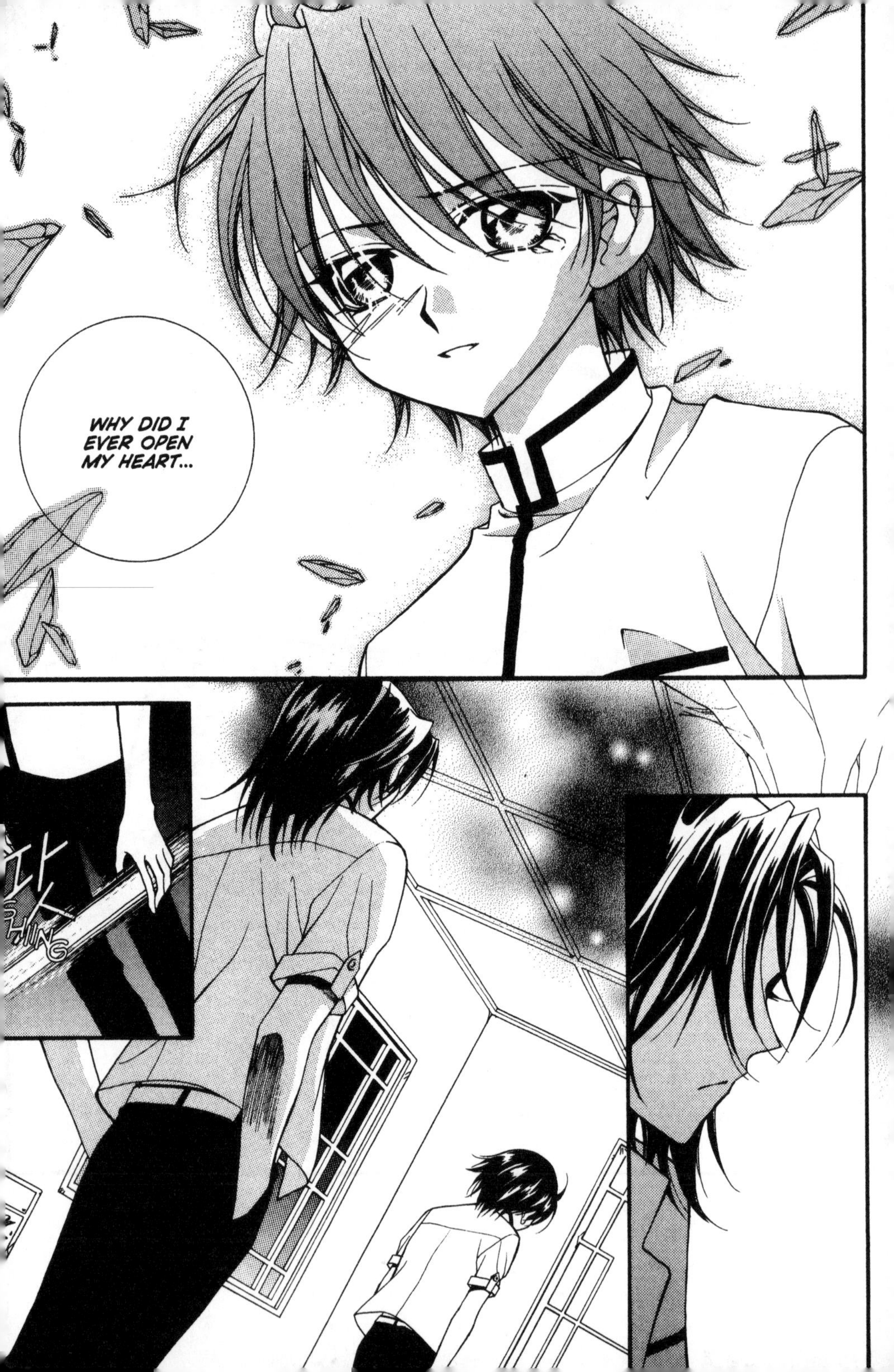
WHY DID I EVER OPEN MY HEART...

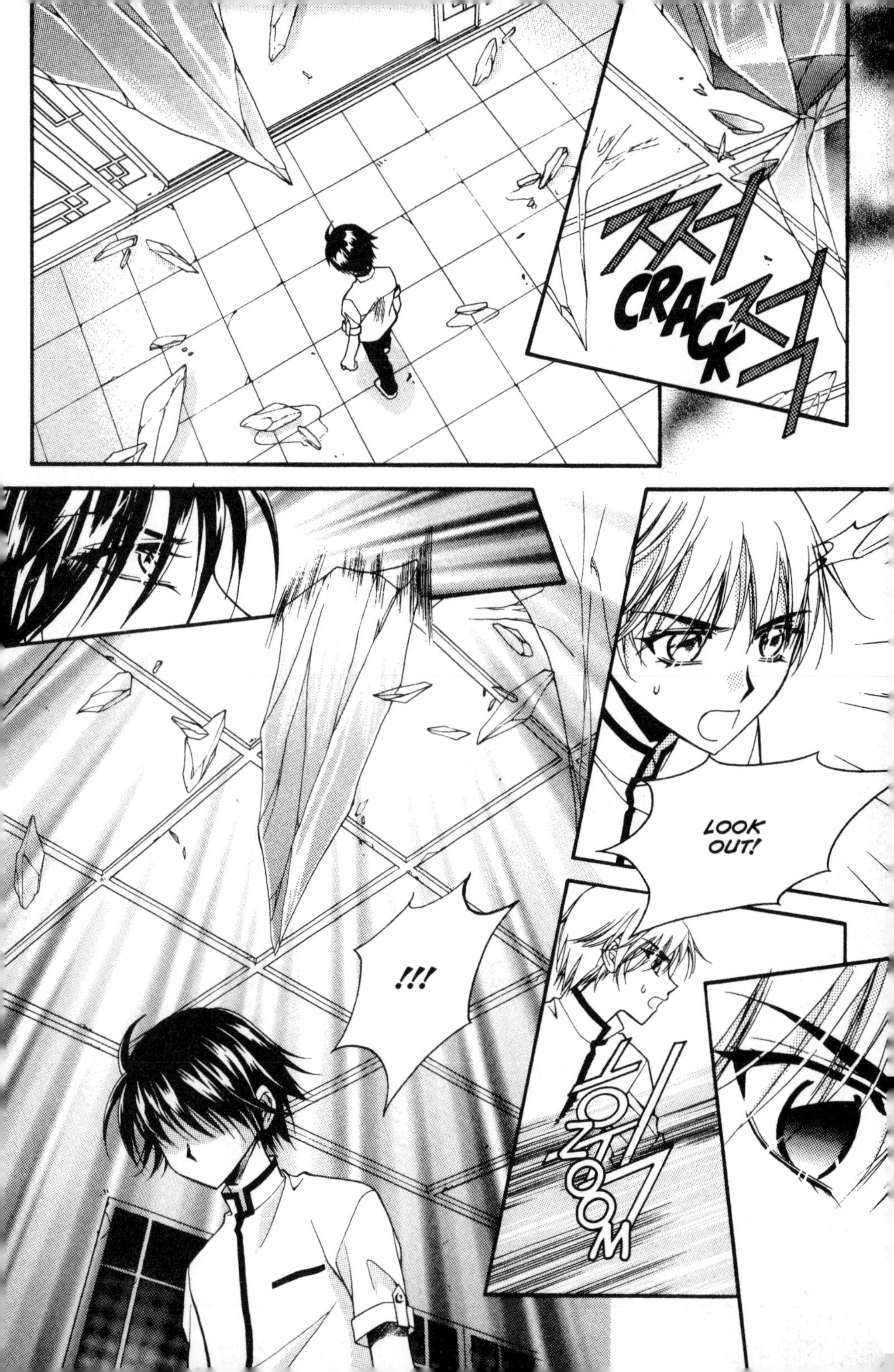
CRACK
LOOK OUT!
ZOOM
!!!

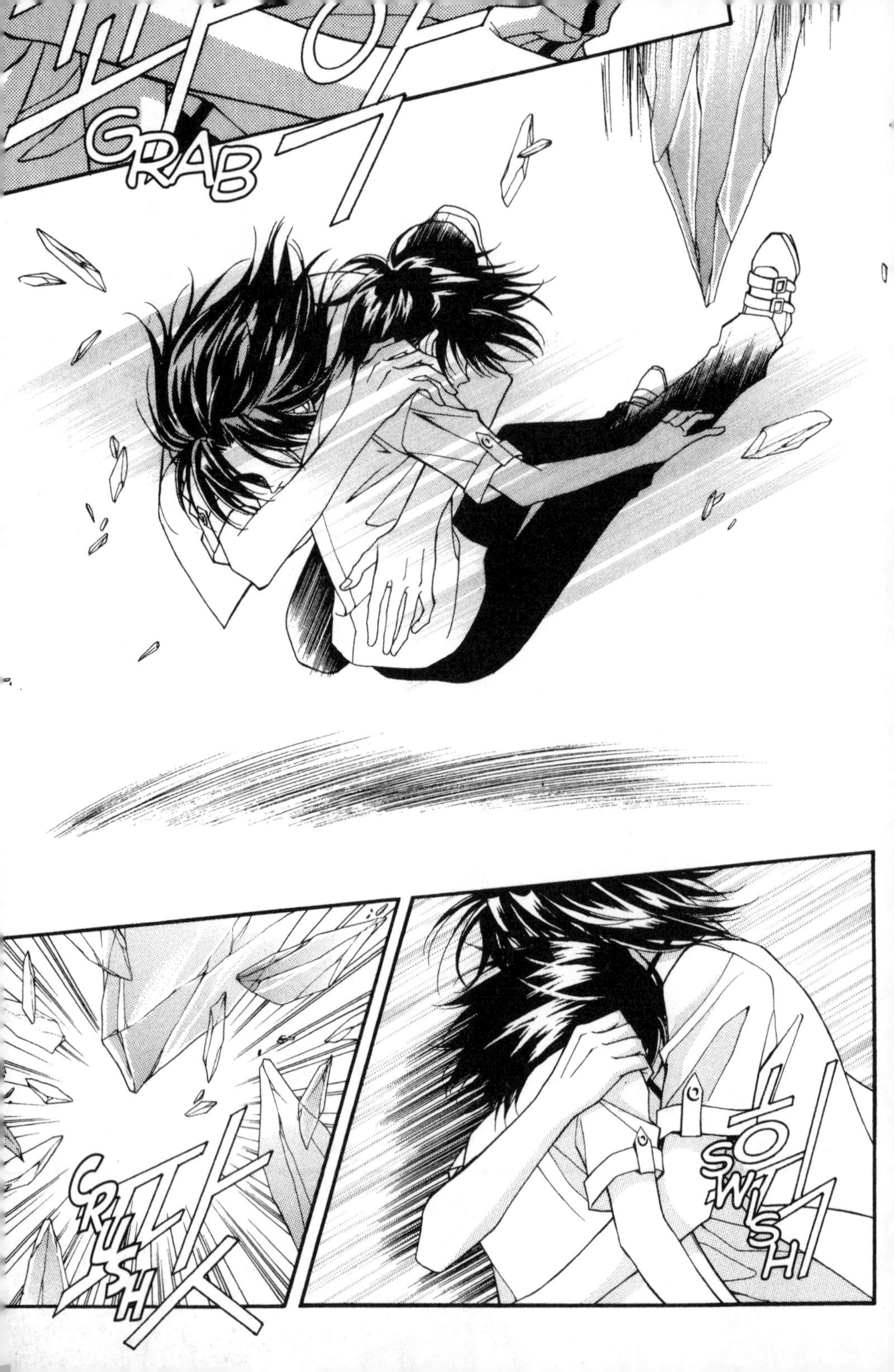
GRAB
CRUSH
SWISH

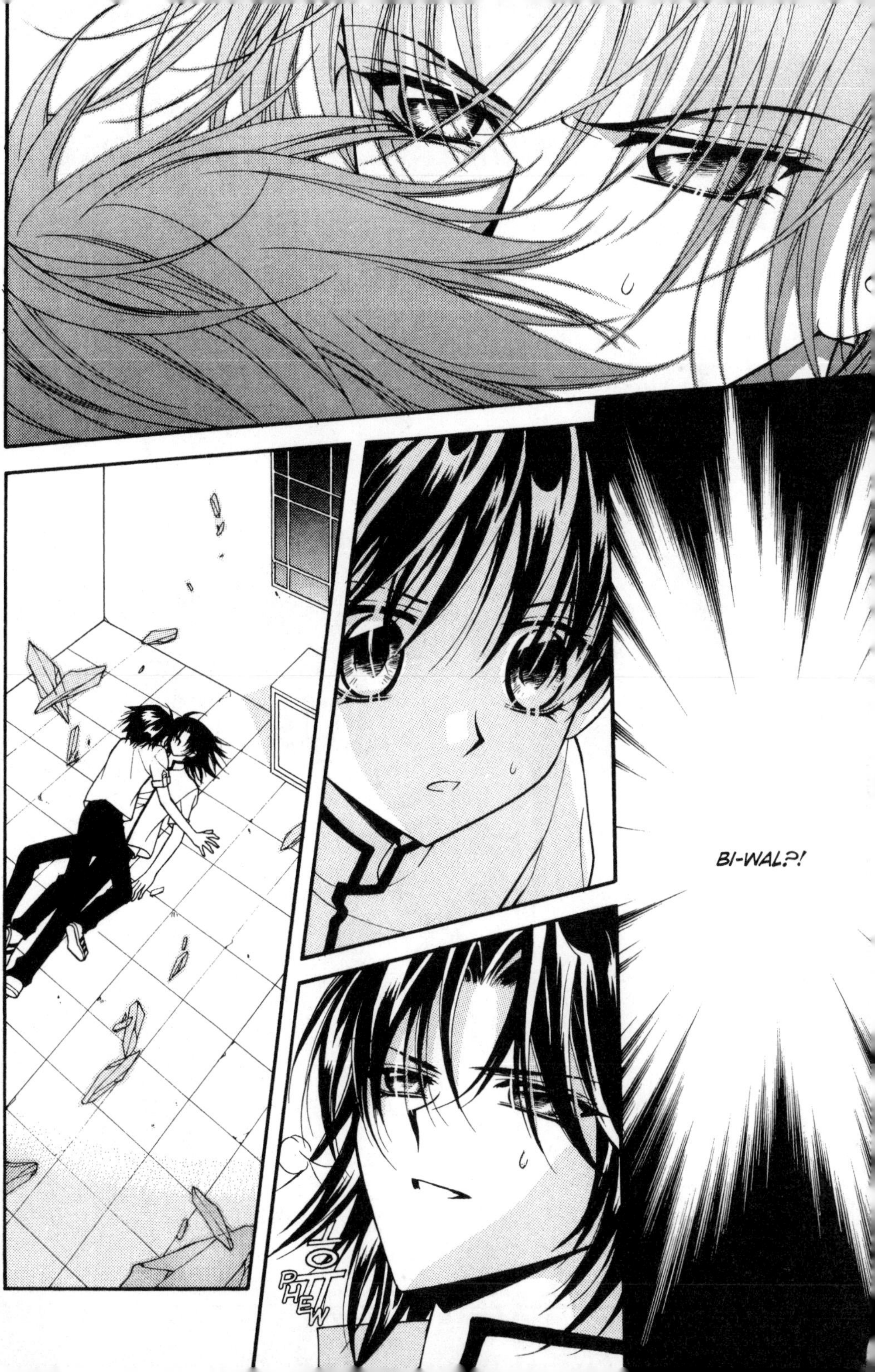
BI-WAL?!
PHEW

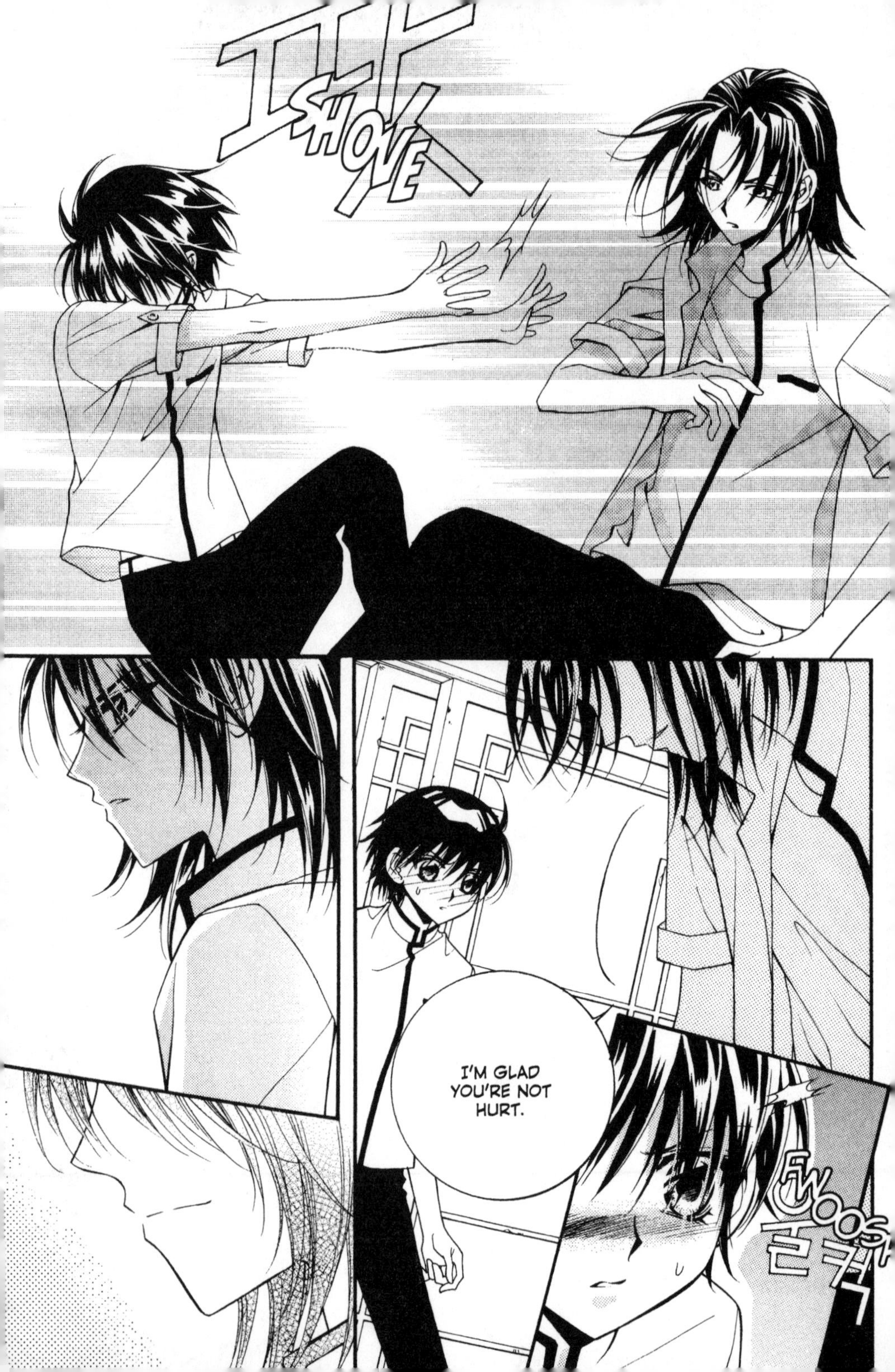
SHOVE
I'M GLAD YOU'RE NOT HURT.
FWOOSH

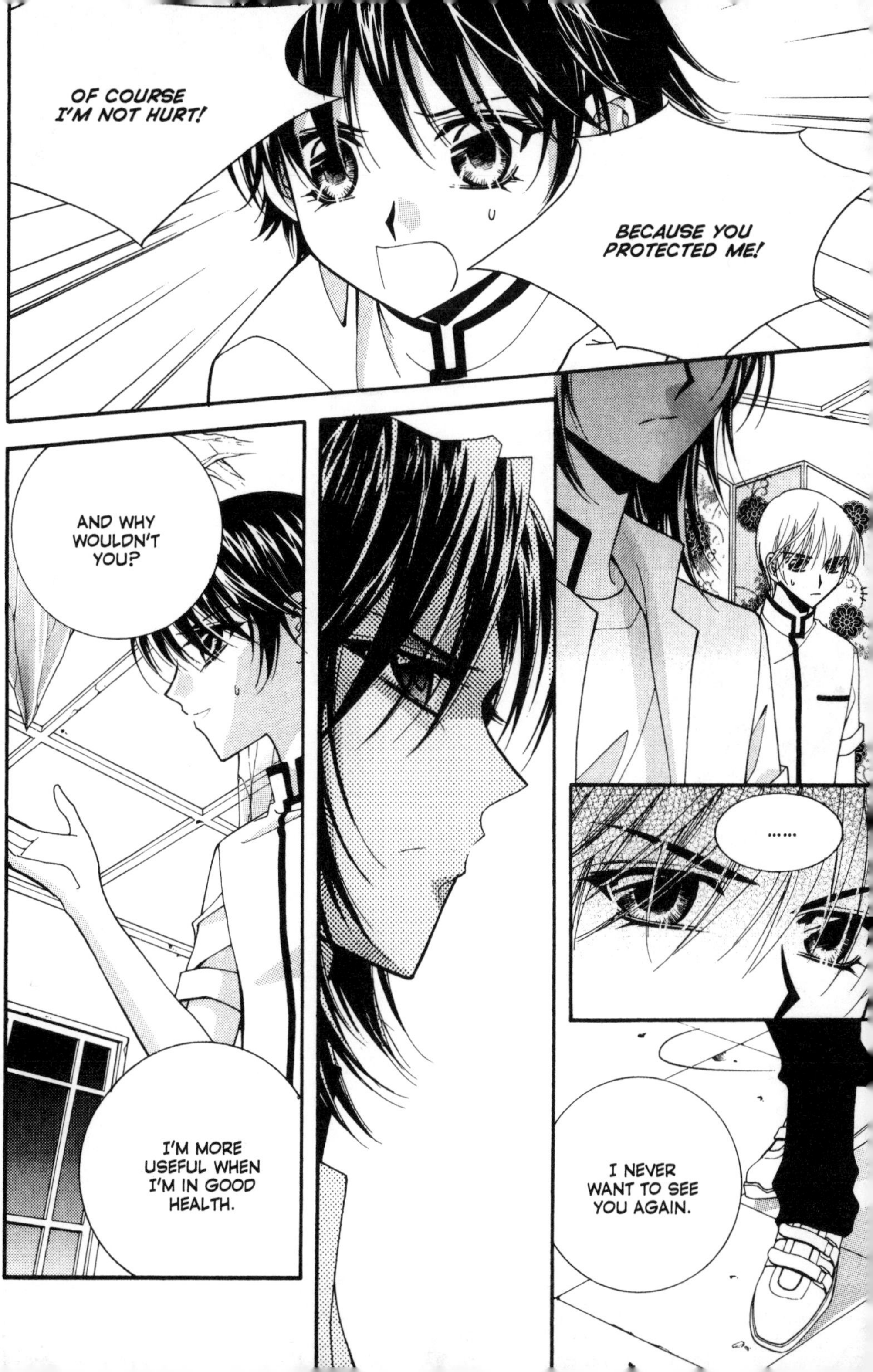
OF COURSE I'M NOT HURT!
BECAUSE YOU PROTECTED ME!
AND WHY WOULDN'T YOU?
I'M MORE USEFUL WHEN I'M IN GOOD HEALTH.
......
I NEVER WANT TO SEE YOU AGAIN.

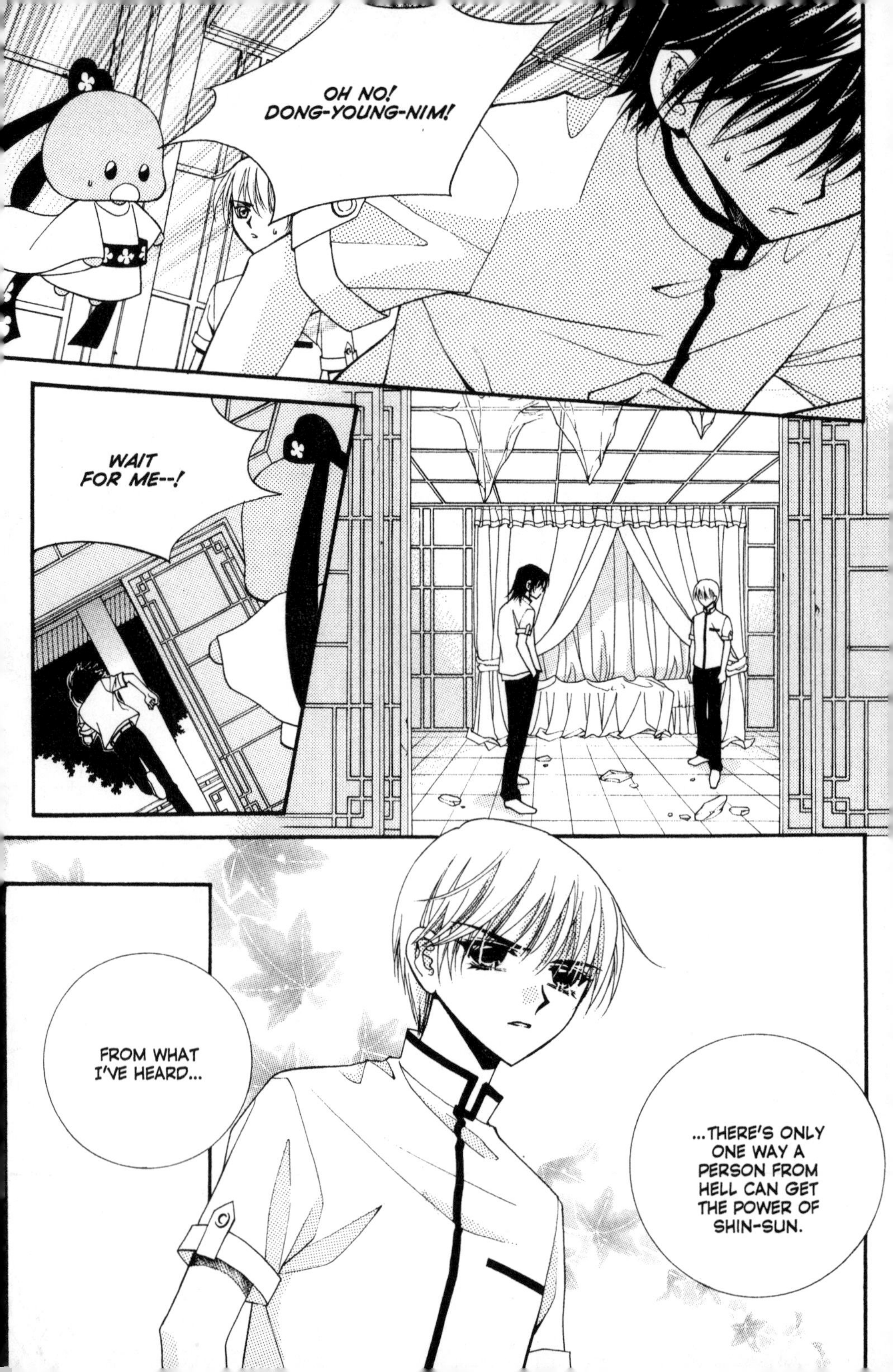
OH NO! DONG-YOUNG-NIM!
WAIT FOR ME--!
FROM WHAT I'VE HEARD...
...THERE'S ONLY ONE WAY A PERSON FROM HELL CAN GET THE POWER OF SHIN-SUN.

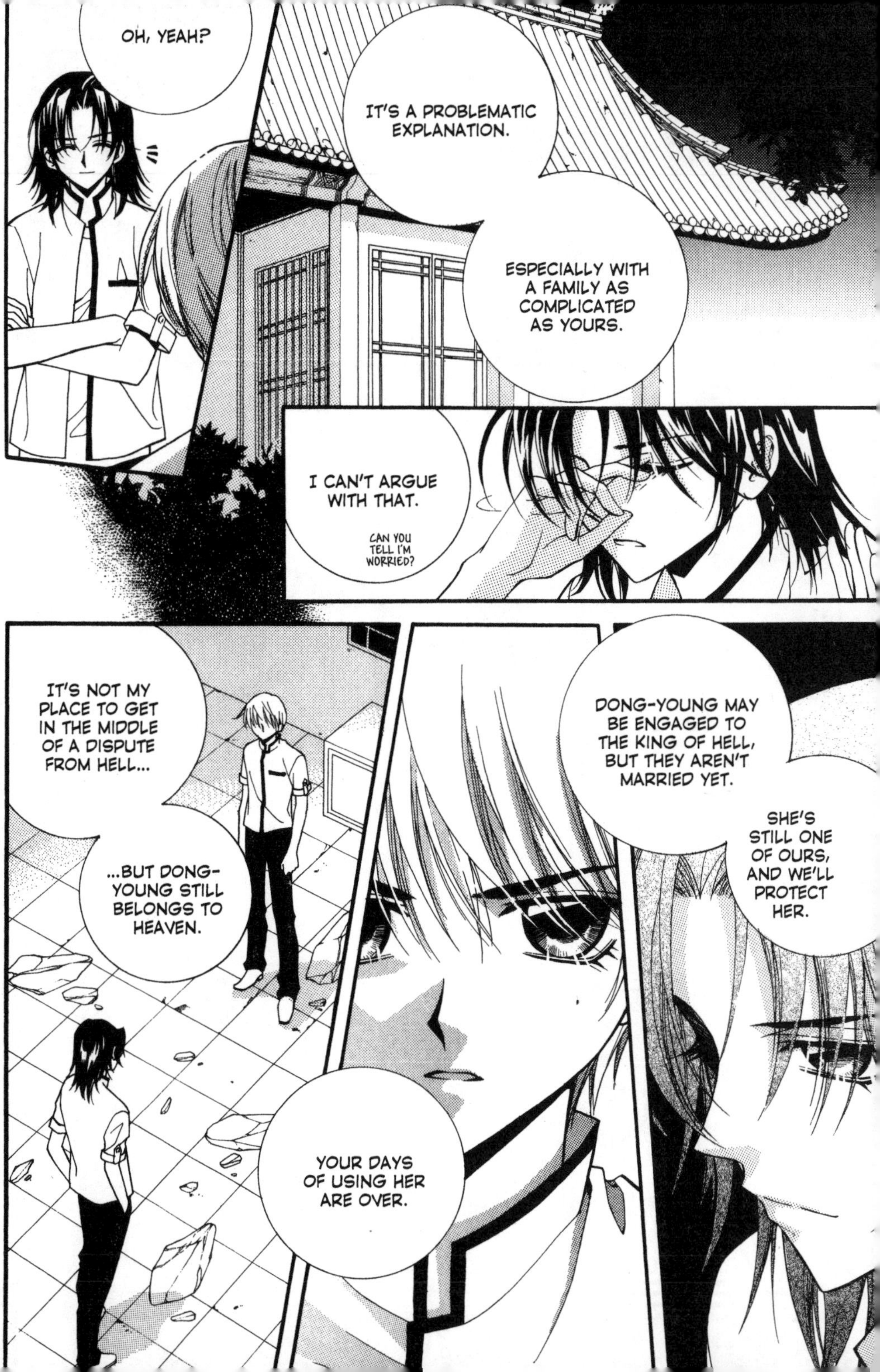
OH, YEAH?
IT'S A PROBLEMATIC EXPLANATION.
ESPECIALLY WITH A FAMILY AS COMPLICATED AS YOURS.
I CAN'T ARGUE WITH THAT.
CAN YOU TELL I'M WORRIED?
IT'S NOT MY PLACE TO GET IN THE MIDDLE OF A DISPUTE FROM HELL...
...BUT DONG-YOUNG STILL BELONGS TO HEAVEN.
DONG-YOUNG MAY BE ENGAGED TO THE KING OF HELL, BUT THEY AREN'T MARRIED YET.
SHE'S STILL ONE OF OURS, AND WE'LL PROTECT HER.
YOUR DAYS OF USING HER ARE OVER.

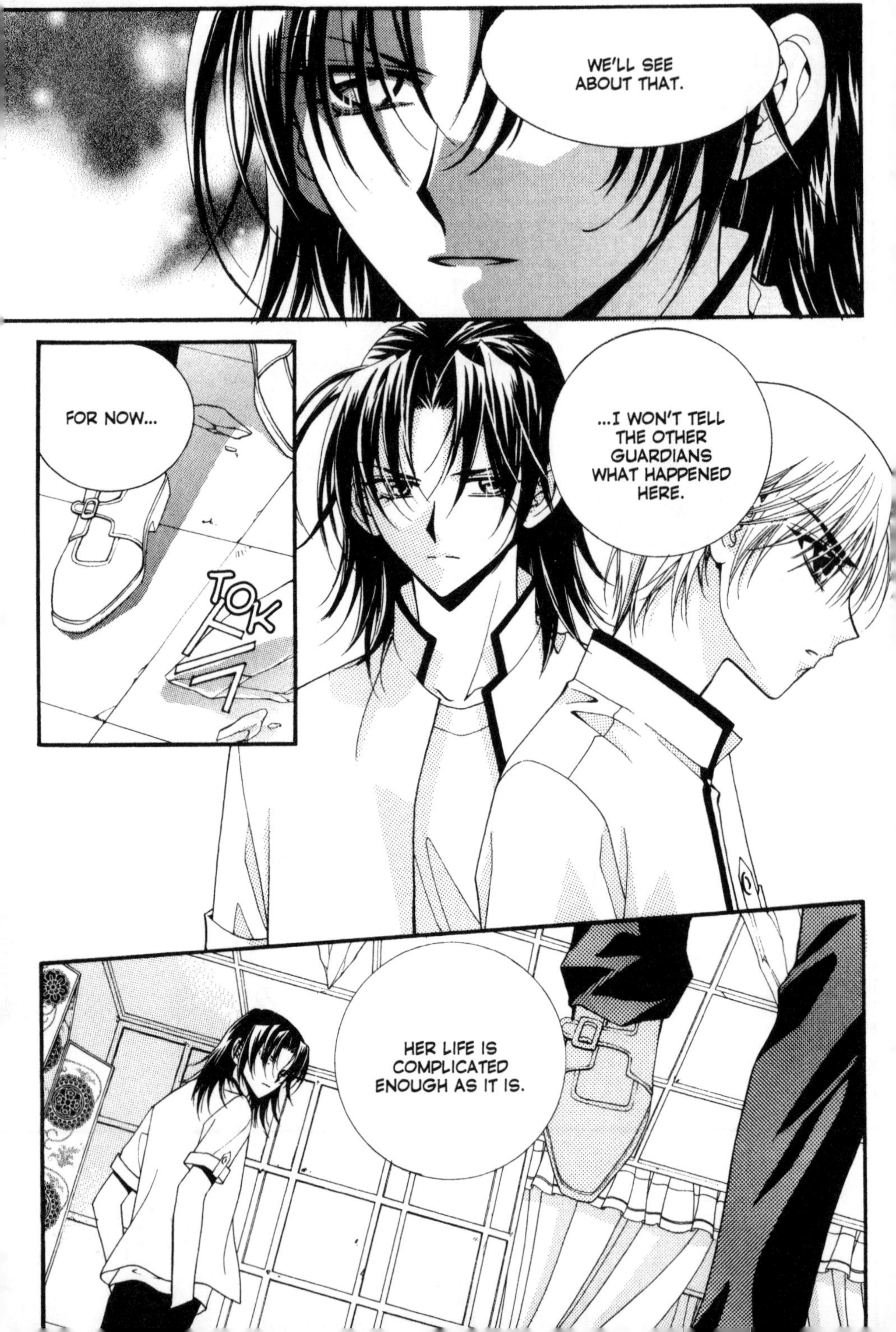
WE'LL SEE ABOUT THAT.
...I WON'T TELL THE OTHER GUARDIANS WHAT HAPPENED HERE.
FOR NOW...
TOK
HER LIFE IS COMPLICATED ENOUGH AS IT IS.

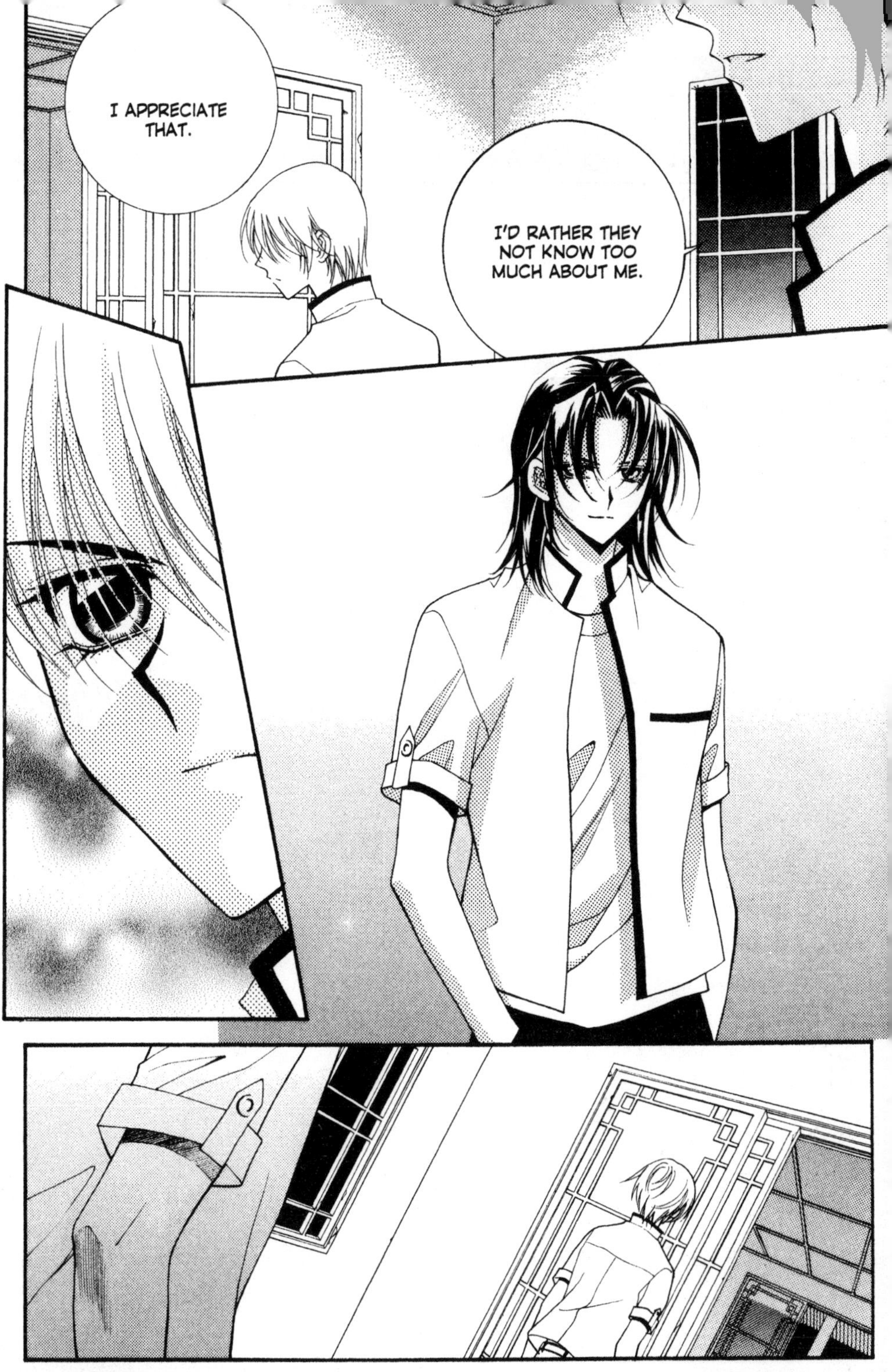
I'D RATHER THEY NOT KNOW TOO MUCH ABOUT ME.
I APPRECIATE THAT.

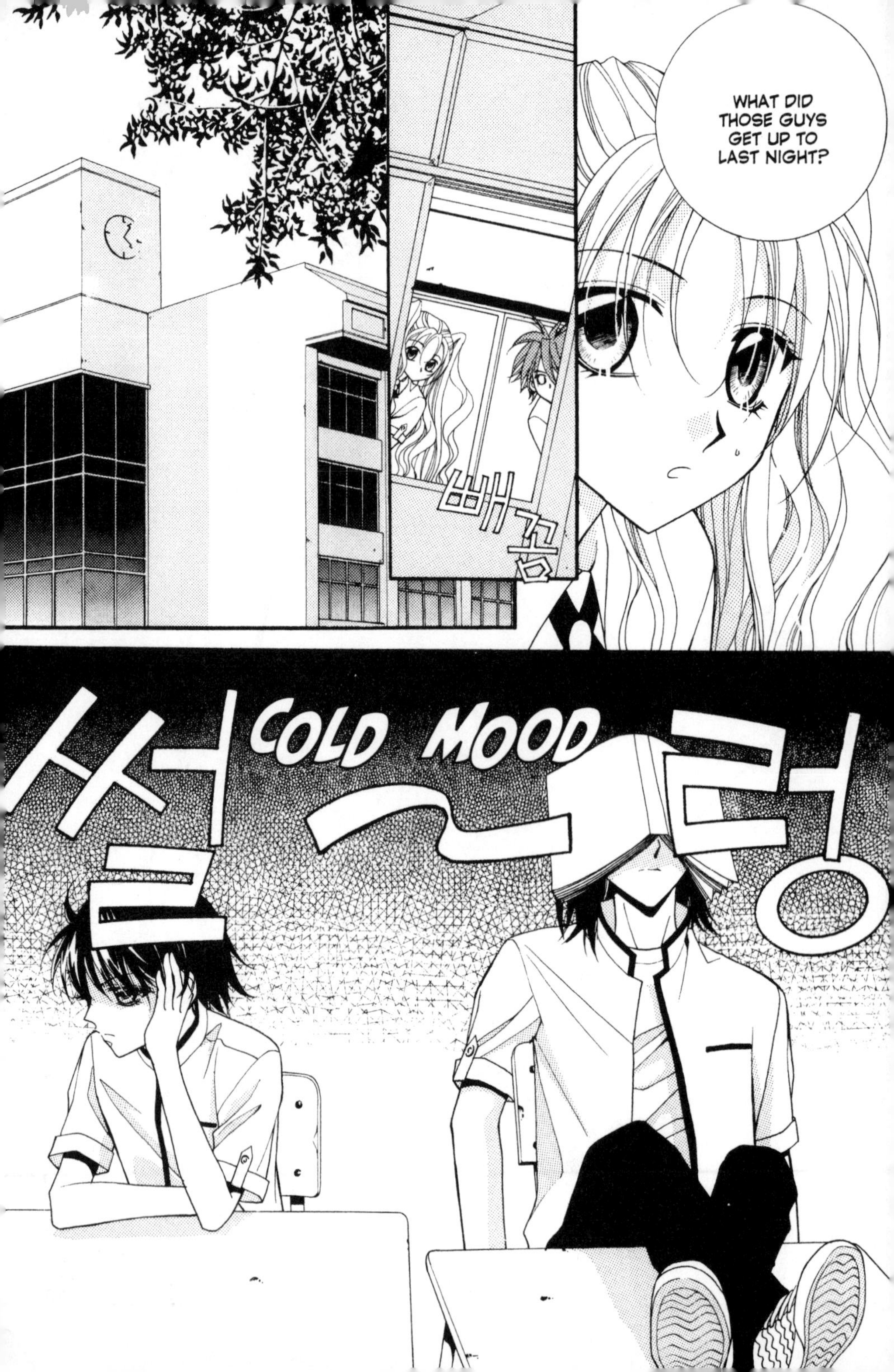
빼꼼
WHAT DID THOSE GUYS GET UP TO LAST NIGHT?
썰~렁
COLD MOOD

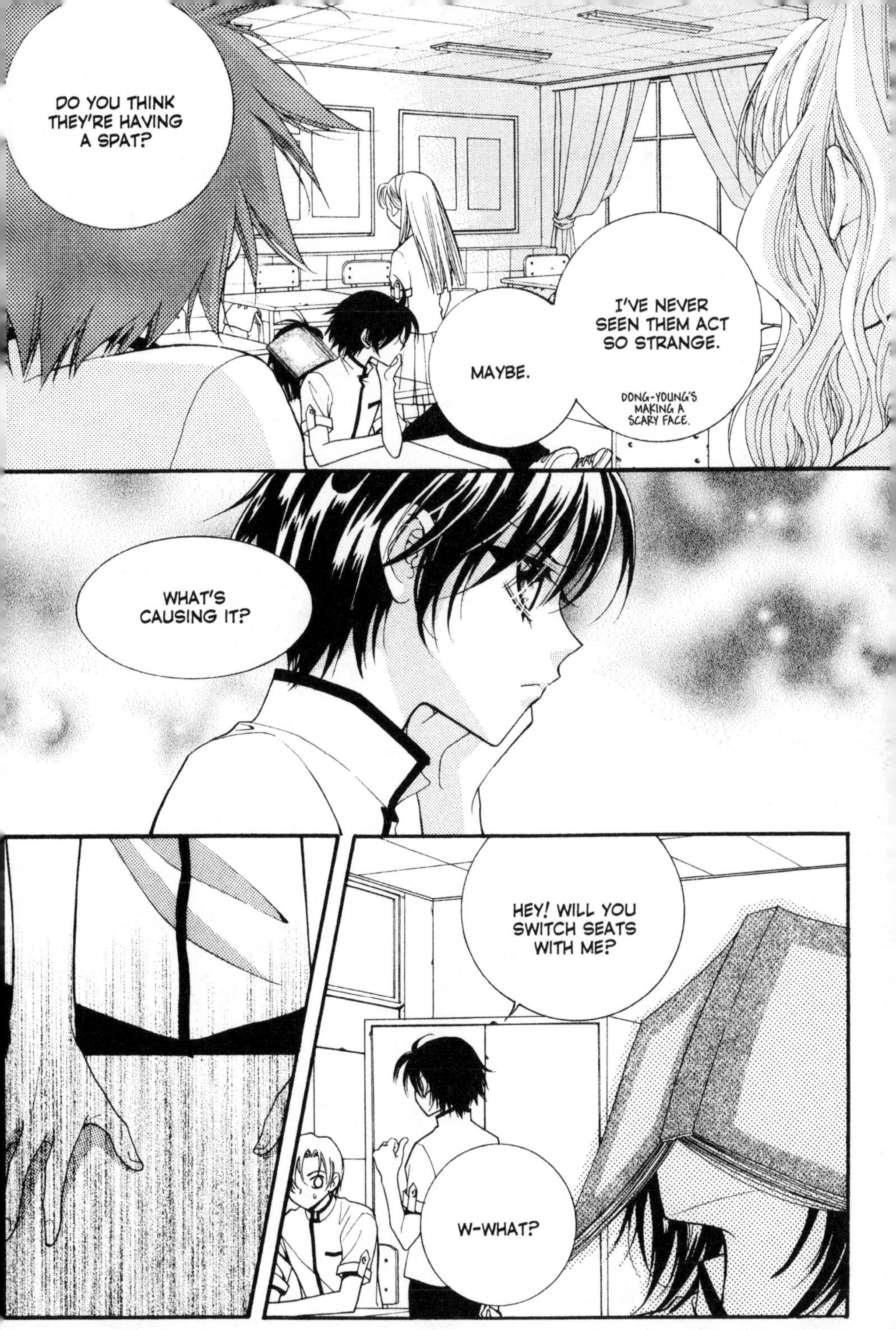
DO YOU THINK THEY'RE HAVING A SPAT?
I'VE NEVER SEEN THEM ACT SO STRANGE.
DONG-YOUNG'S MAKING A SCARY FACE.
MAYBE.
WHAT'S CAUSING IT?
HEY! WILL YOU SWITCH SEATS WITH ME?
W-WHAT?

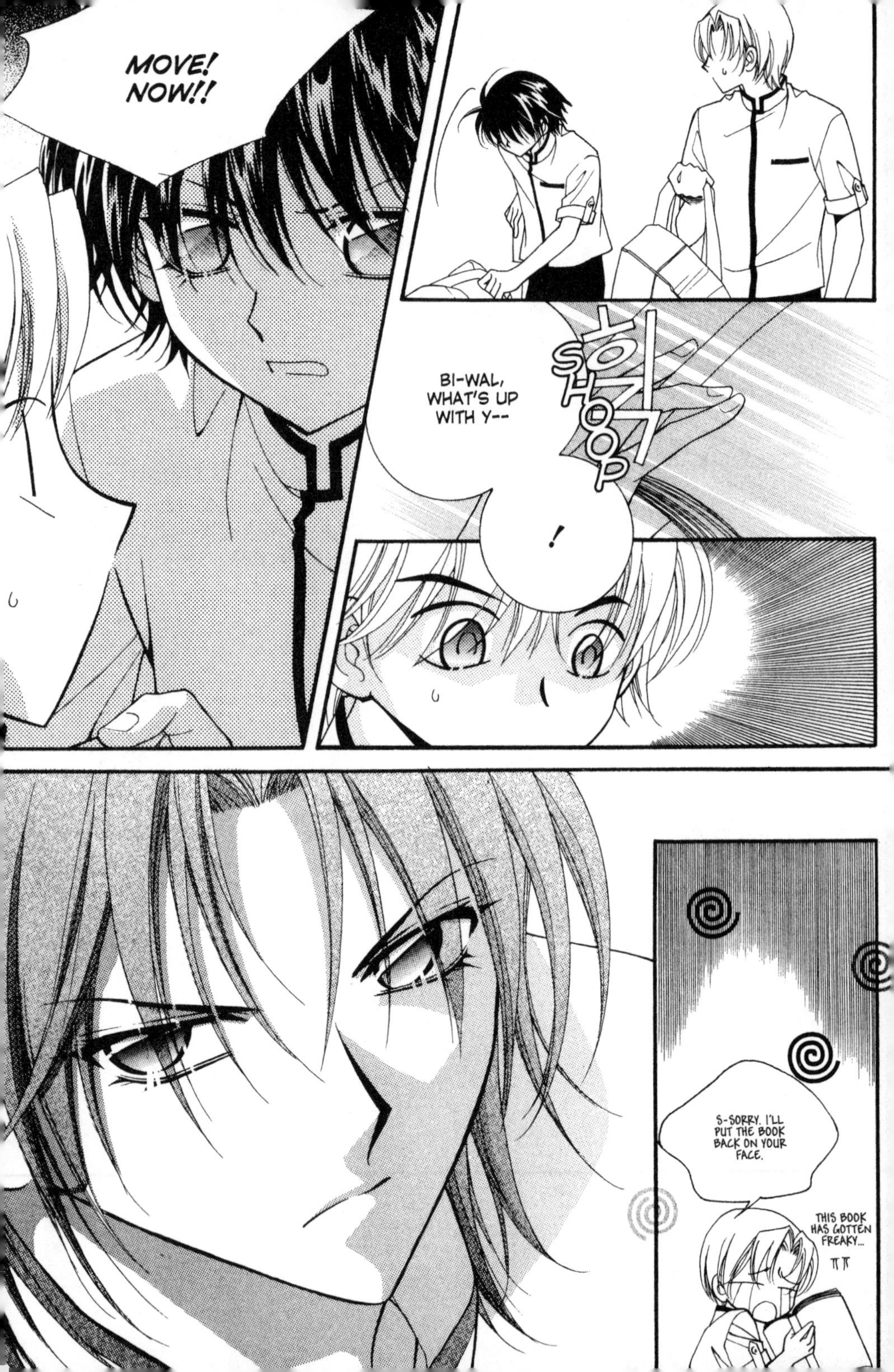
MOVE! NOW!!
BI-WAL, WHAT'S UP WITH Y--
SHOOP
!
S-SORRY. I'LL PUT THE BOOK BACK ON YOUR FACE.
THIS BOOK HAS GOTTEN FREAKY...

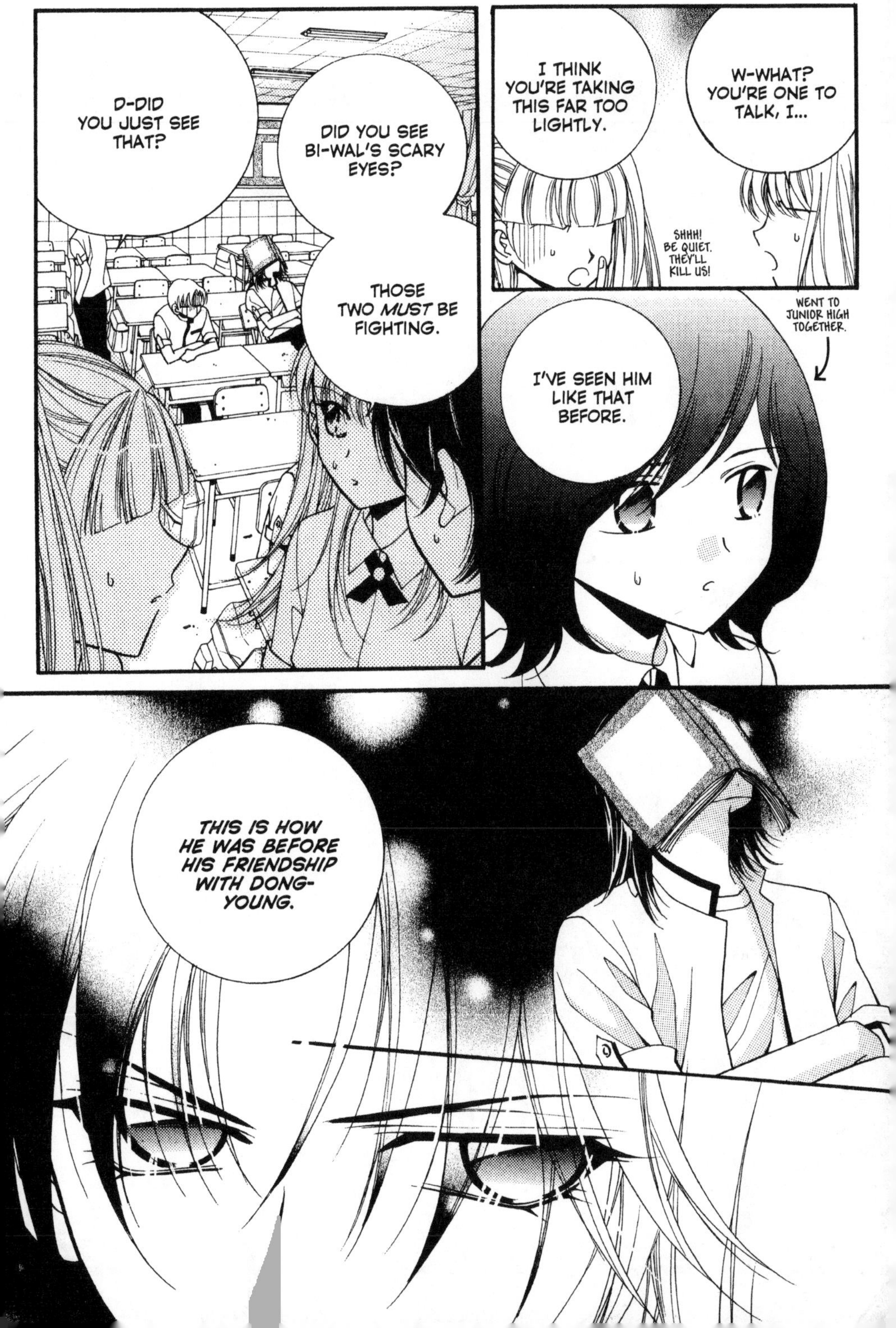
D-DID YOU JUST SEE THAT?
DID YOU SEE BI-WAL'S SCARY EYES?
THOSE TWO *MUST* BE FIGHTING.
I THINK YOU'RE TAKING THIS FAR TOO LIGHTLY.
W-WHAT? YOU'RE ONE TO TALK, I...
SHHH! BE QUIET. THEY'LL KILL US!
WENT TO JUNIOR HIGH TOGETHER.
I'VE SEEN HIM LIKE THAT BEFORE.
THIS IS HOW HE WAS BEFORE HIS FRIENDSHIP WITH DONG-YOUNG.

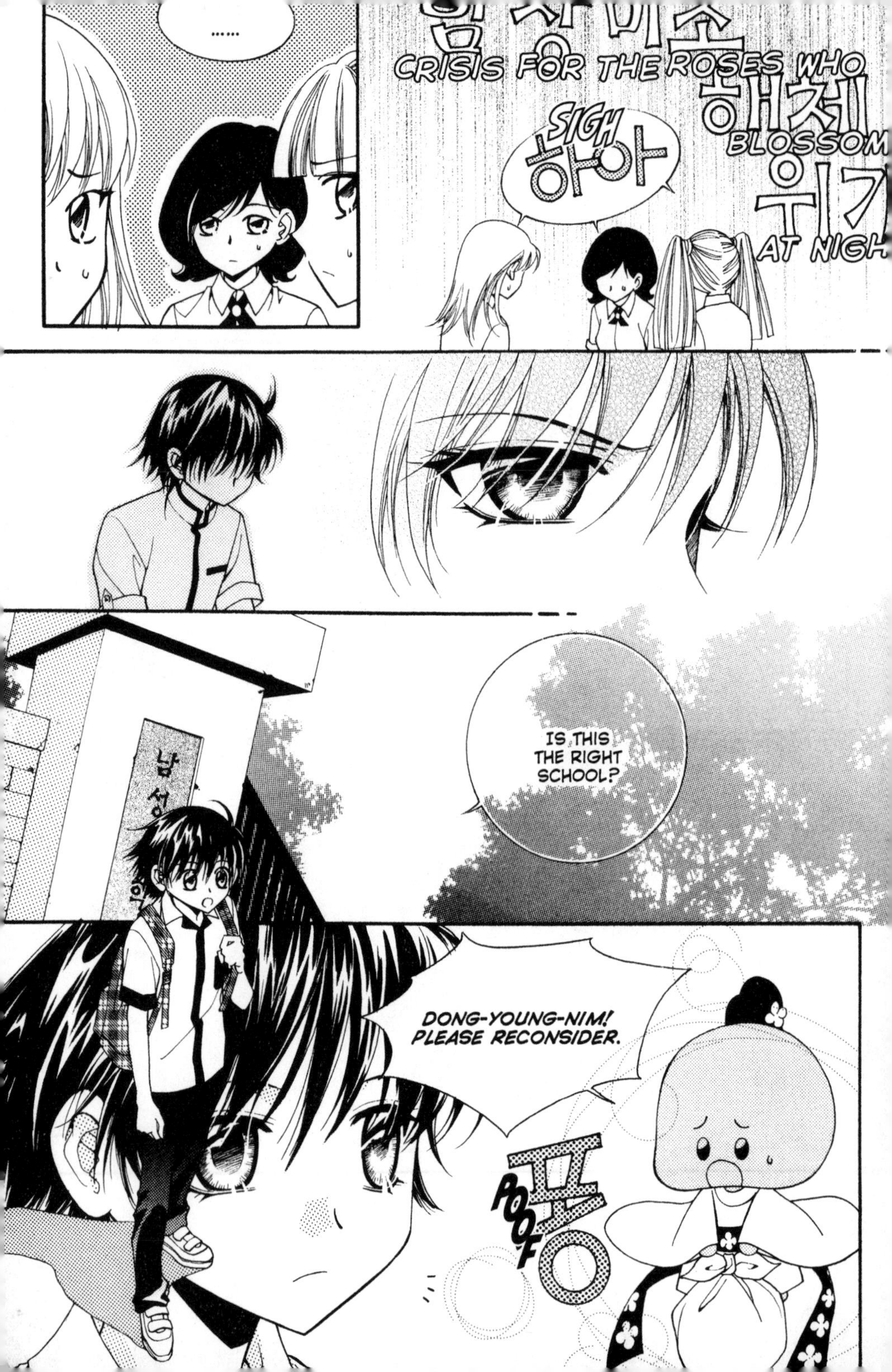
……
CRISIS FOR THE ROSES WHO
해체
BLOSSOM
위기
AT NIGH
SIGH
하아
IS THIS THE RIGHT SCHOOL?
DONG-YOUNG-NIM! PLEASE RECONSIDER.
POOF
퐁

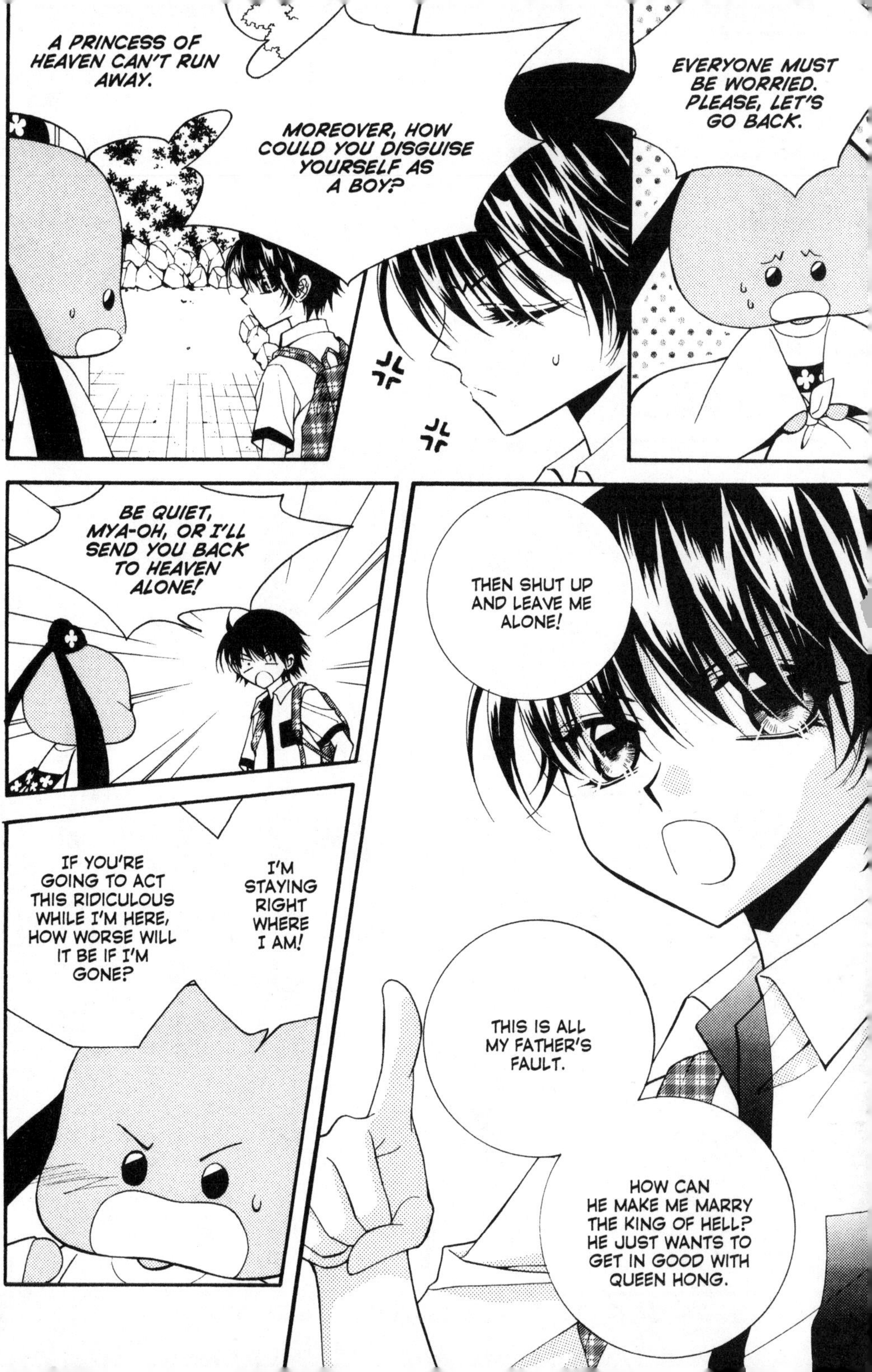
A PRINCESS OF HEAVEN CAN'T RUN AWAY.
MOREOVER, HOW COULD YOU DISGUISE YOURSELF AS A BOY?
EVERYONE MUST BE WORRIED. PLEASE, LET'S GO BACK.
BE QUIET, MYA-OH, OR I'LL SEND YOU BACK TO HEAVEN ALONE!
IF YOU'RE GOING TO ACT THIS RIDICULOUS WHILE I'M HERE, HOW WORSE WILL IT BE IF I'M GONE?
I'M STAYING RIGHT WHERE I AM!
THEN SHUT UP AND LEAVE ME ALONE!
THIS IS ALL MY FATHER'S FAULT.
HOW CAN HE MAKE ME MARRY THE KING OF HELL? HE JUST WANTS TO GET IN GOOD WITH QUEEN HONG.

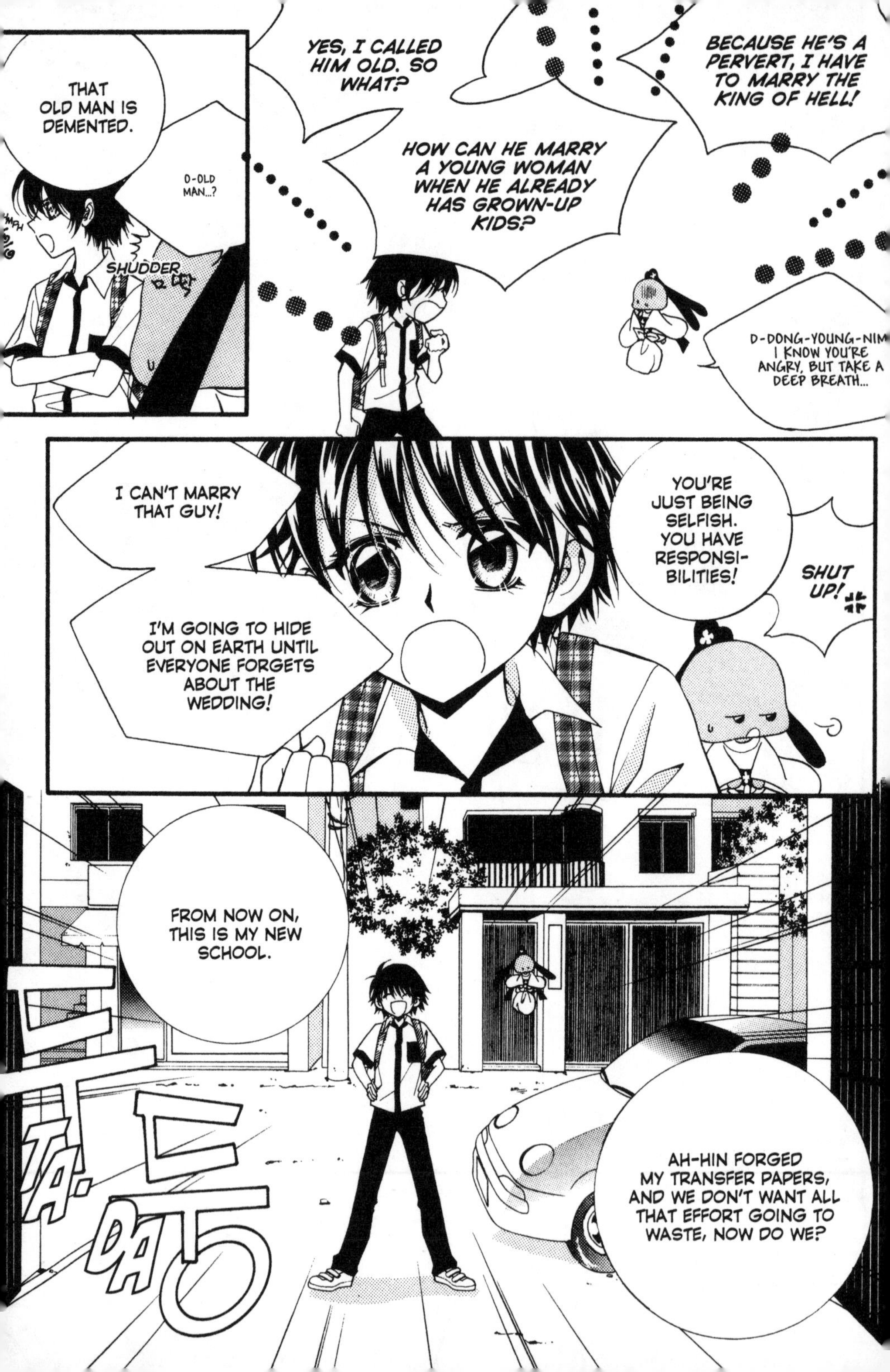

THAT OLD MAN IS DEMENTED.
D-OLD MAN...?
SHUDDER
YES, I CALLED HIM OLD. SO WHAT?
HOW CAN HE MARRY A YOUNG WOMAN WHEN HE ALREADY HAS GROWN-UP KIDS?
BECAUSE HE'S A PERVERT, I HAVE TO MARRY THE KING OF HELL!
D-DONG-YOUNG-NIM I KNOW YOU'RE ANGRY, BUT TAKE A DEEP BREATH...
I CAN'T MARRY THAT GUY!
I'M GOING TO HIDE OUT ON EARTH UNTIL EVERYONE FORGETS ABOUT THE WEDDING!
YOU'RE JUST BEING SELFISH. YOU HAVE RESPONSI-BILITIES!
SHUT UP!
FROM NOW ON, THIS IS MY NEW SCHOOL.
TA-DA
AH-HIN FORGED MY TRANSFER PAPERS, AND WE DON'T WANT ALL THAT EFFORT GOING TO WASTE, NOW DO WE?

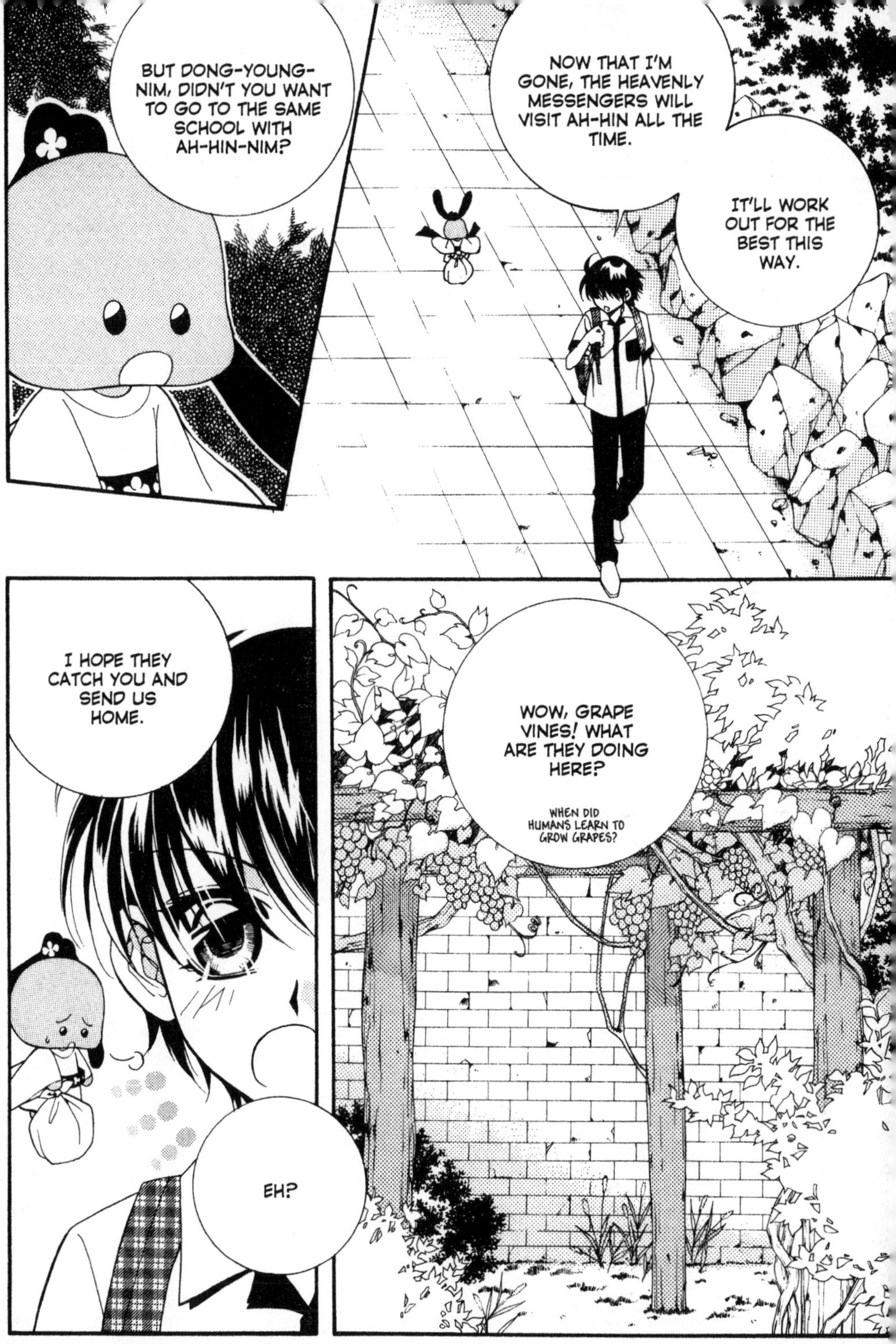
BUT DONG-YOUNG-NIM, DIDN'T YOU WANT TO GO TO THE SAME SCHOOL WITH AH-HIN-NIM?
NOW THAT I'M GONE, THE HEAVENLY MESSENGERS WILL VISIT AH-HIN ALL THE TIME.
IT'LL WORK OUT FOR THE BEST THIS WAY.
I HOPE THEY CATCH YOU AND SEND US HOME.
EH?
WOW, GRAPE VINES! WHAT ARE THEY DOING HERE?
WHEN DID HUMANS LEARN TO GROW GRAPES?

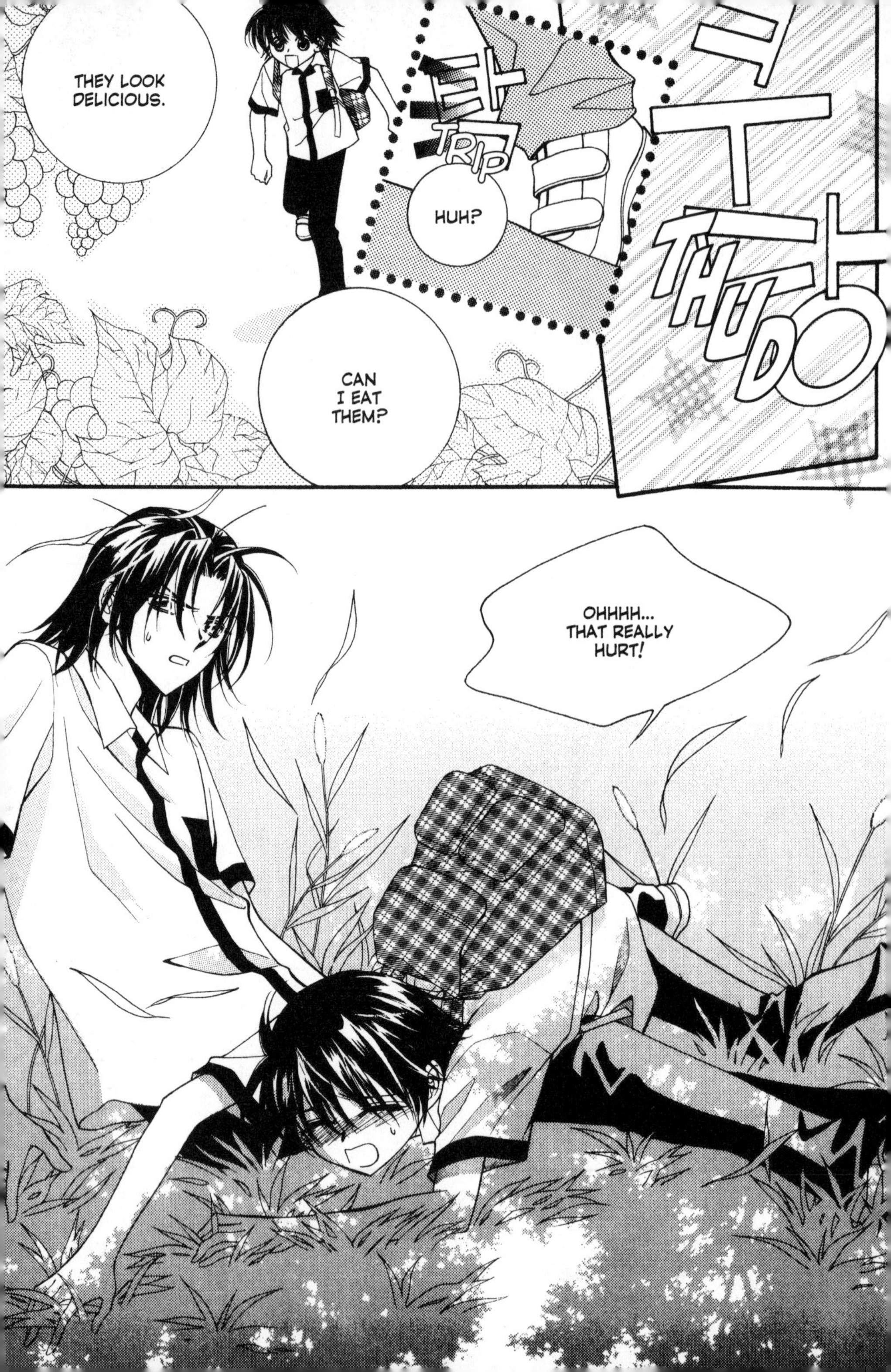

THEY LOOK DELICIOUS.
CAN I EAT THEM?
TRIP
HUH?
THUD
OHHHH... THAT REALLY HURT!

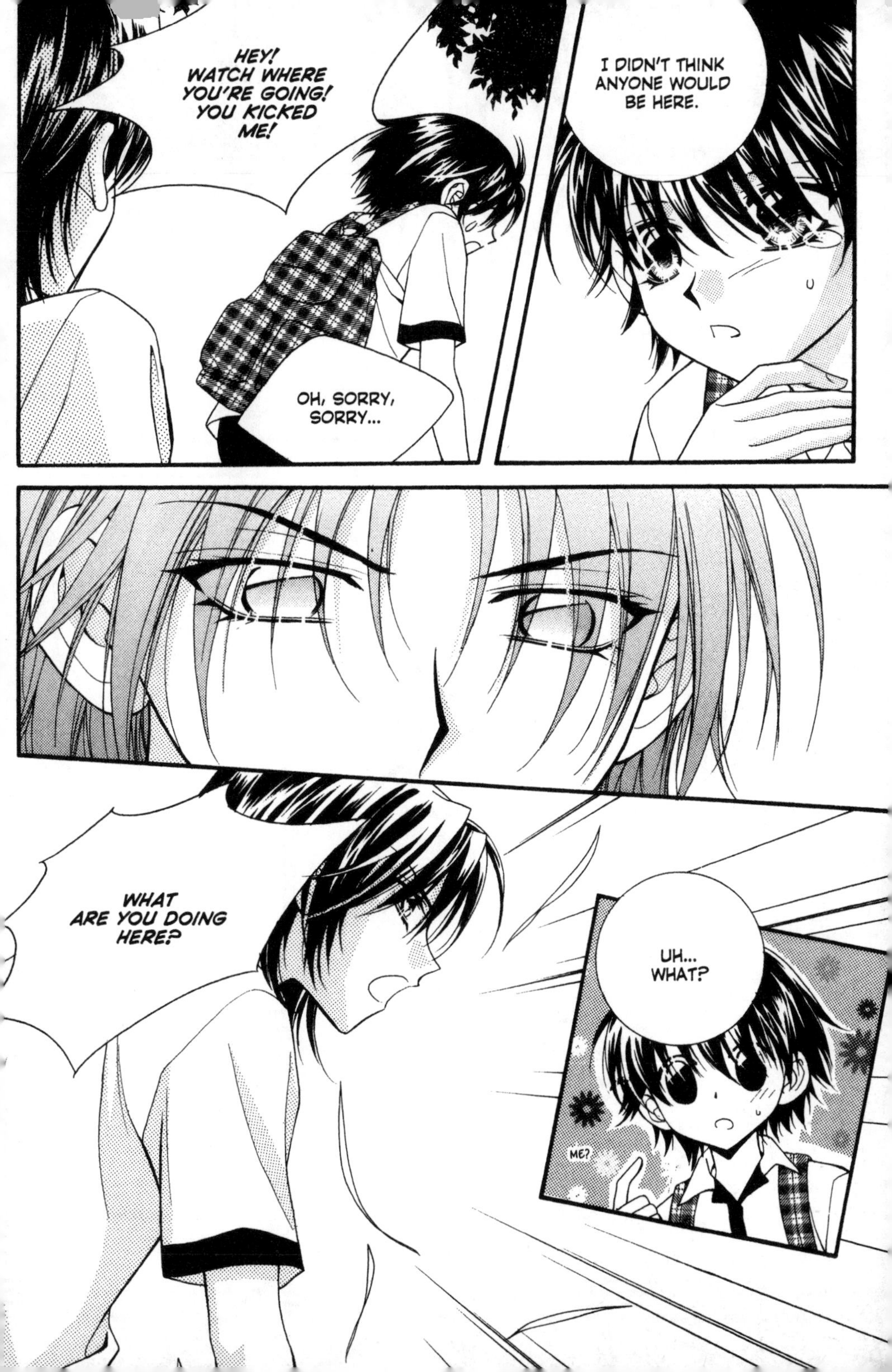
HEY! WATCH WHERE YOU'RE GOING! YOU KICKED ME!
OH, SORRY, SORRY...
I DIDN'T THINK ANYONE WOULD BE HERE.
WHAT ARE YOU DOING HERE?
UH... WHAT?
ME?

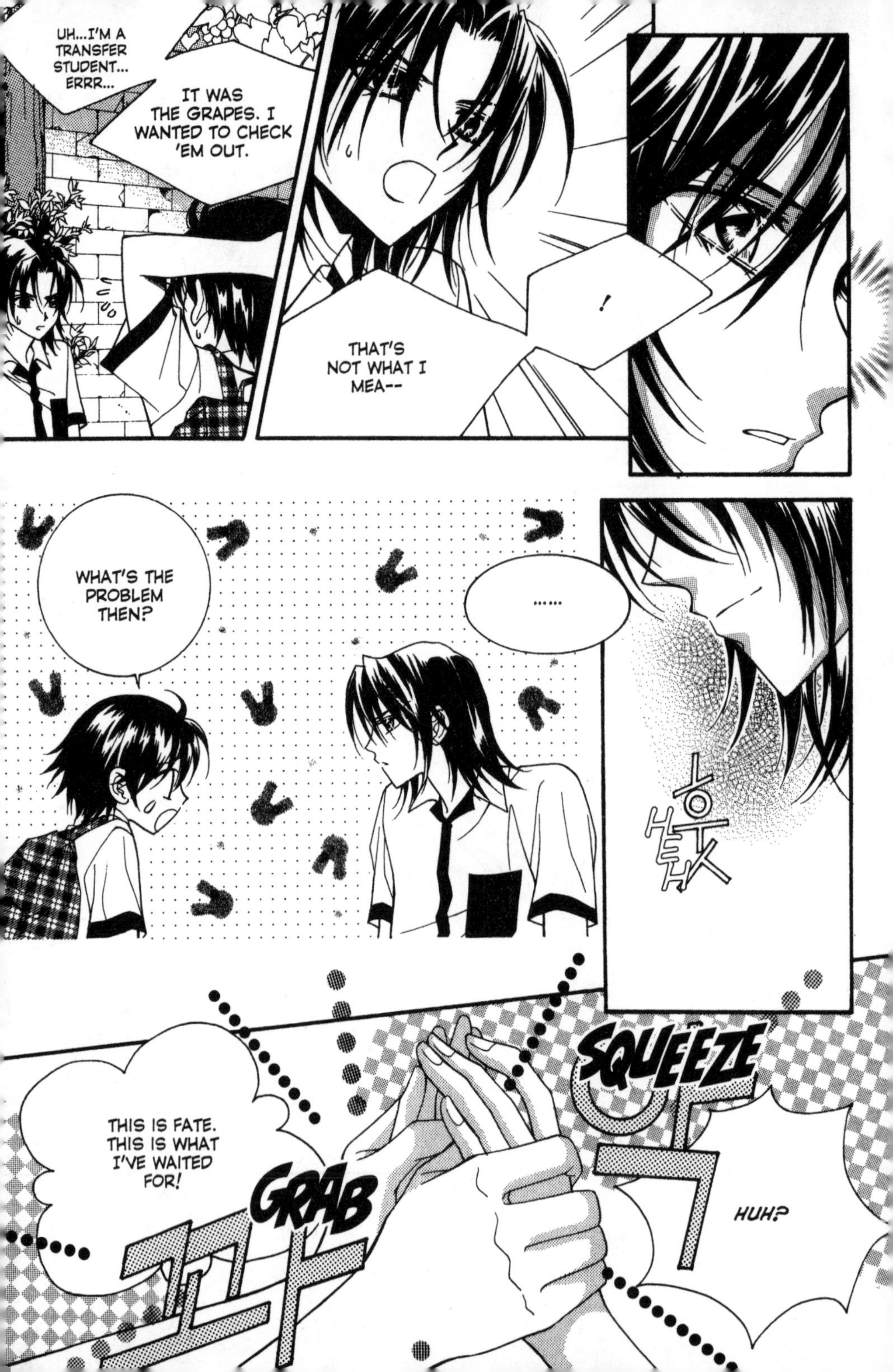
UH...I'M A TRANSFER STUDENT... ERRR...
IT WAS THE GRAPES. I WANTED TO CHECK 'EM OUT.
THAT'S NOT WHAT I MEA--
!
WHAT'S THE PROBLEM THEN?
......
THIS IS FATE. THIS IS WHAT I'VE WAITED FOR!
GRAB
SQUEEZE
HUH?

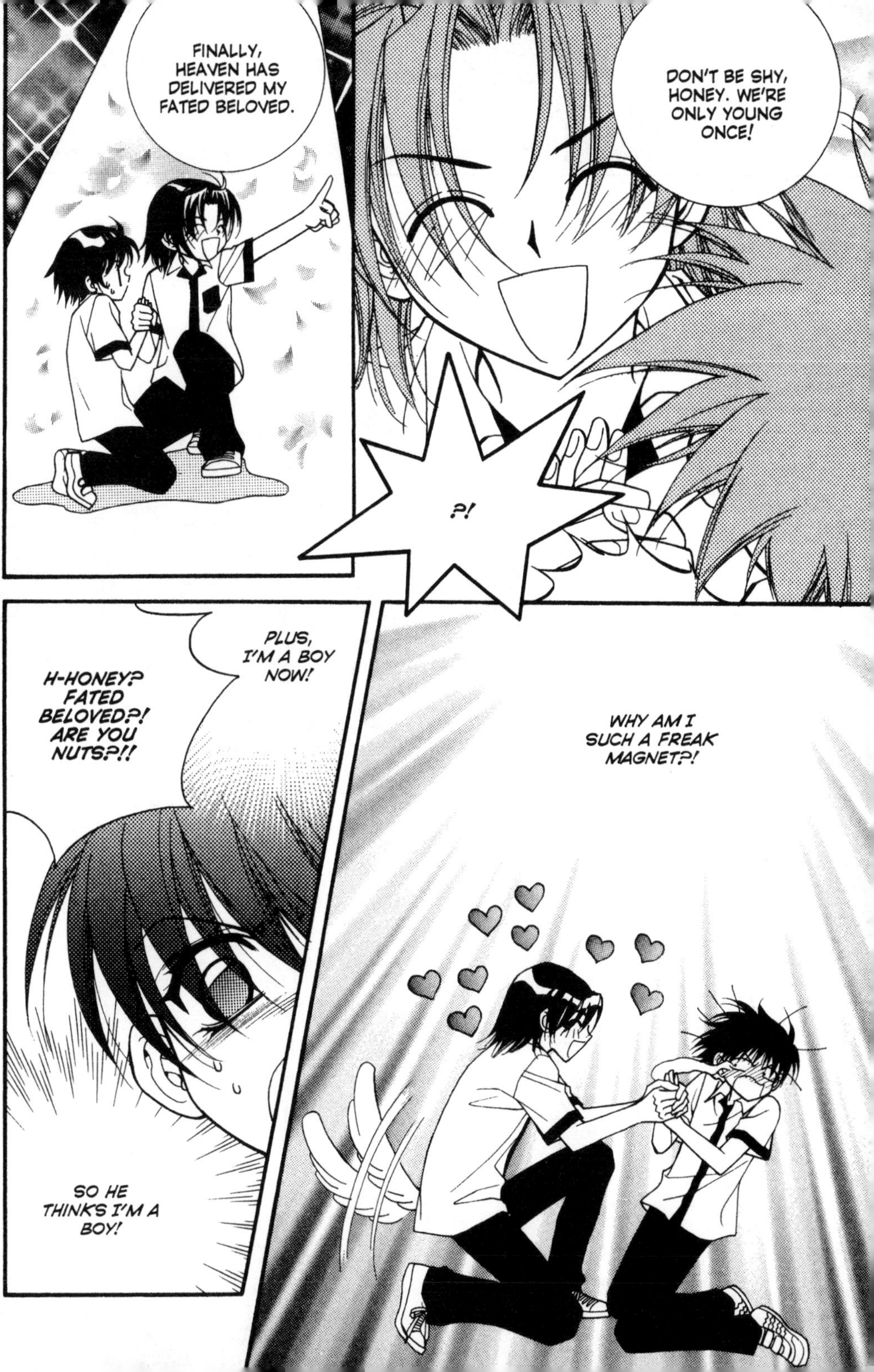
FINALLY, HEAVEN HAS DELIVERED MY FATED BELOVED.
DON'T BE SHY, HONEY. WE'RE ONLY YOUNG ONCE!
?!
H-HONEY? FATED BELOVED?! ARE YOU NUTS?!!
SO HE THINKS I'M A BOY!
PLUS, I'M A BOY NOW!
WHY AM I SUCH A FREAK MAGNET?!

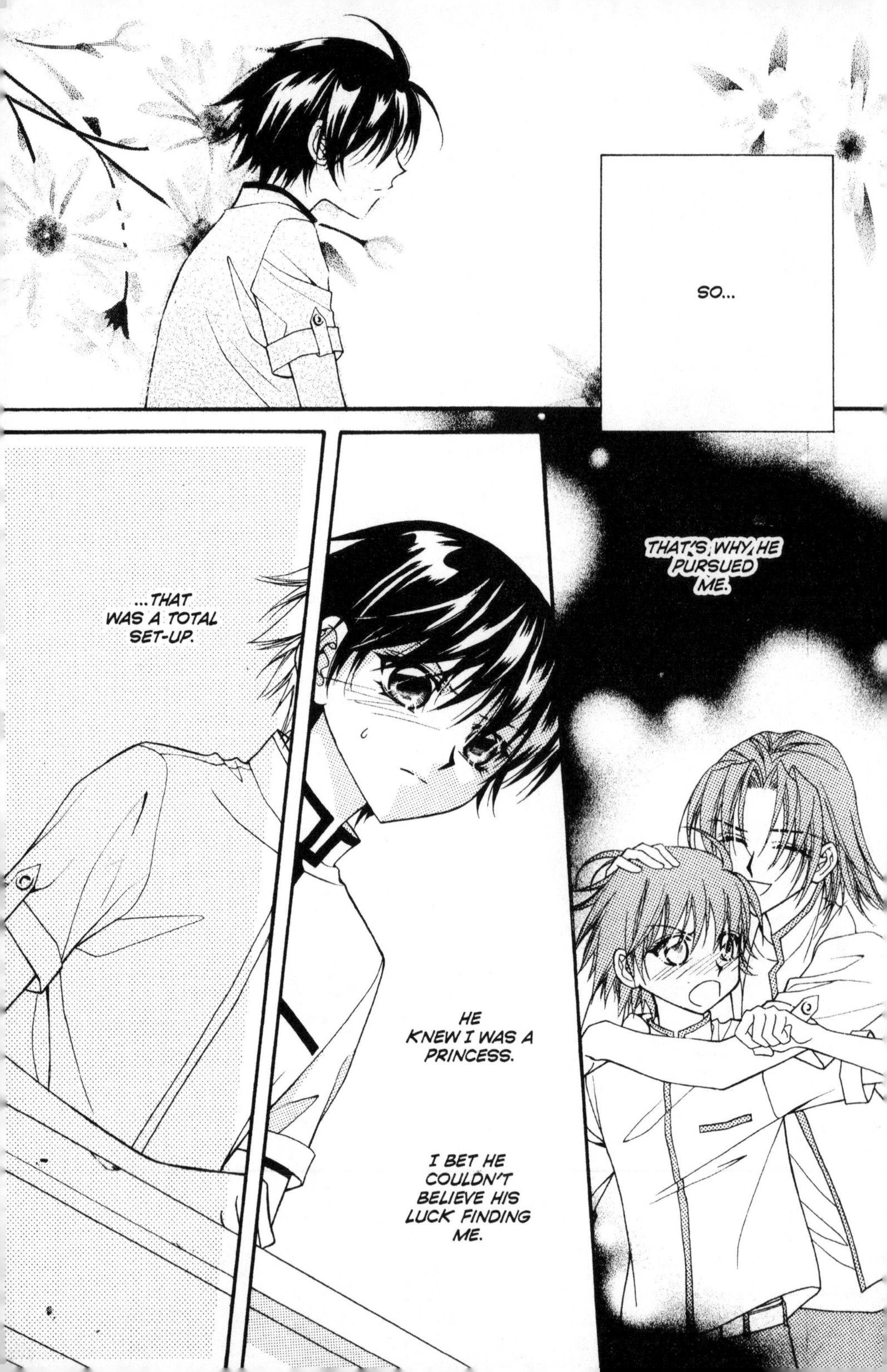
SO...
THAT'S WHY HE PURSUED ME.
HE KNEW I WAS A PRINCESS.
I BET HE COULDN'T BELIEVE HIS LUCK FINDING ME.
...THAT WAS A TOTAL SET-UP.

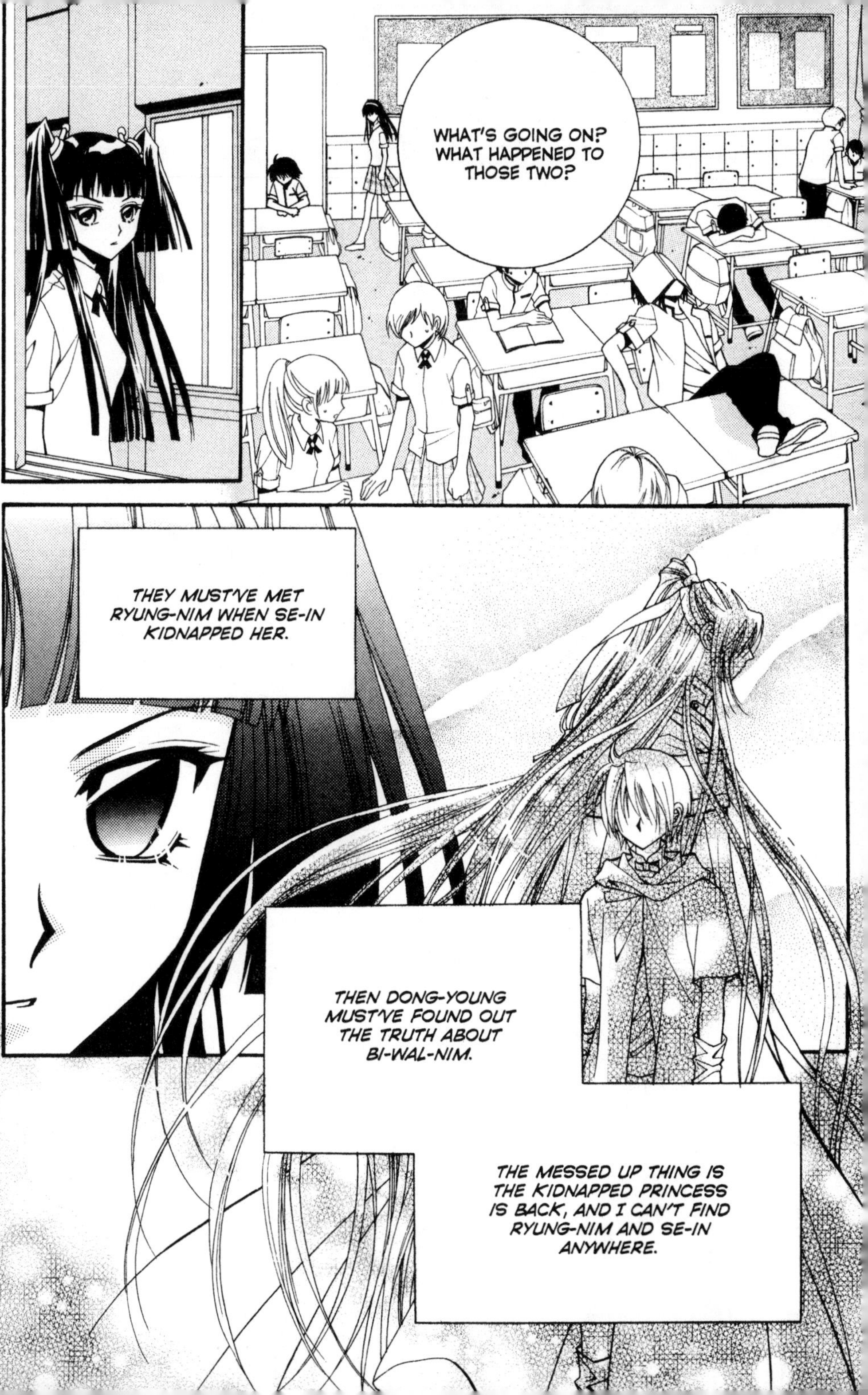
WHAT'S GOING ON? WHAT HAPPENED TO THOSE TWO?
THEY MUST'VE MET RYUNG-NIM WHEN SE-IN KIDNAPPED HER.
THEN DONG-YOUNG MUST'VE FOUND OUT THE TRUTH ABOUT BI-WAL-NIM.
THE MESSED UP THING IS THE KIDNAPPED PRINCESS IS BACK, AND I CAN'T FIND RYUNG-NIM AND SE-IN ANYWHERE.

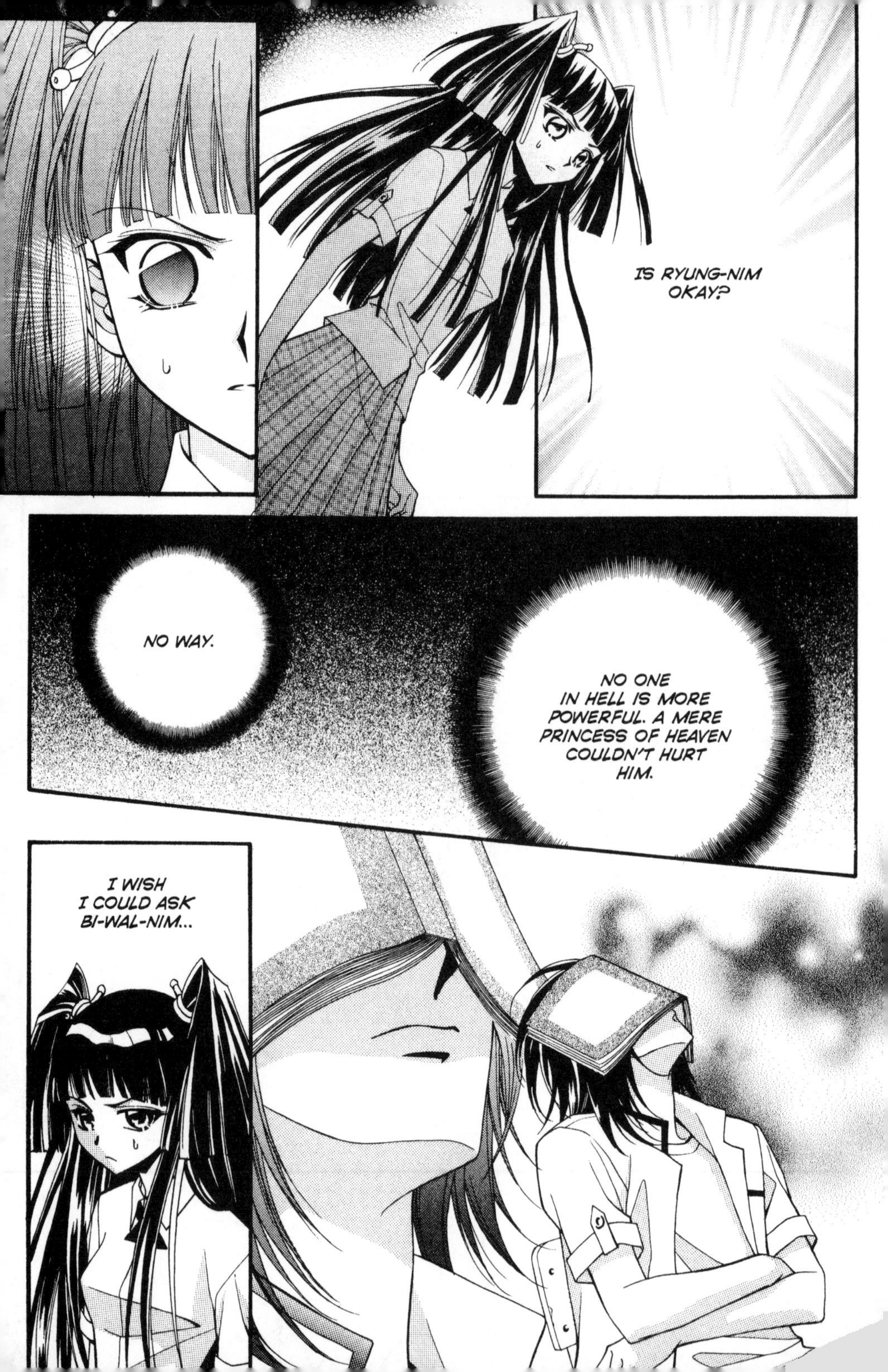
IS RYUNG-NIM OKAY?
NO WAY.
NO ONE IN HELL IS MORE POWERFUL. A MERE PRINCESS OF HEAVEN COULDN'T HURT HIM.
I WISH I COULD ASK BI-WAL-NIM...

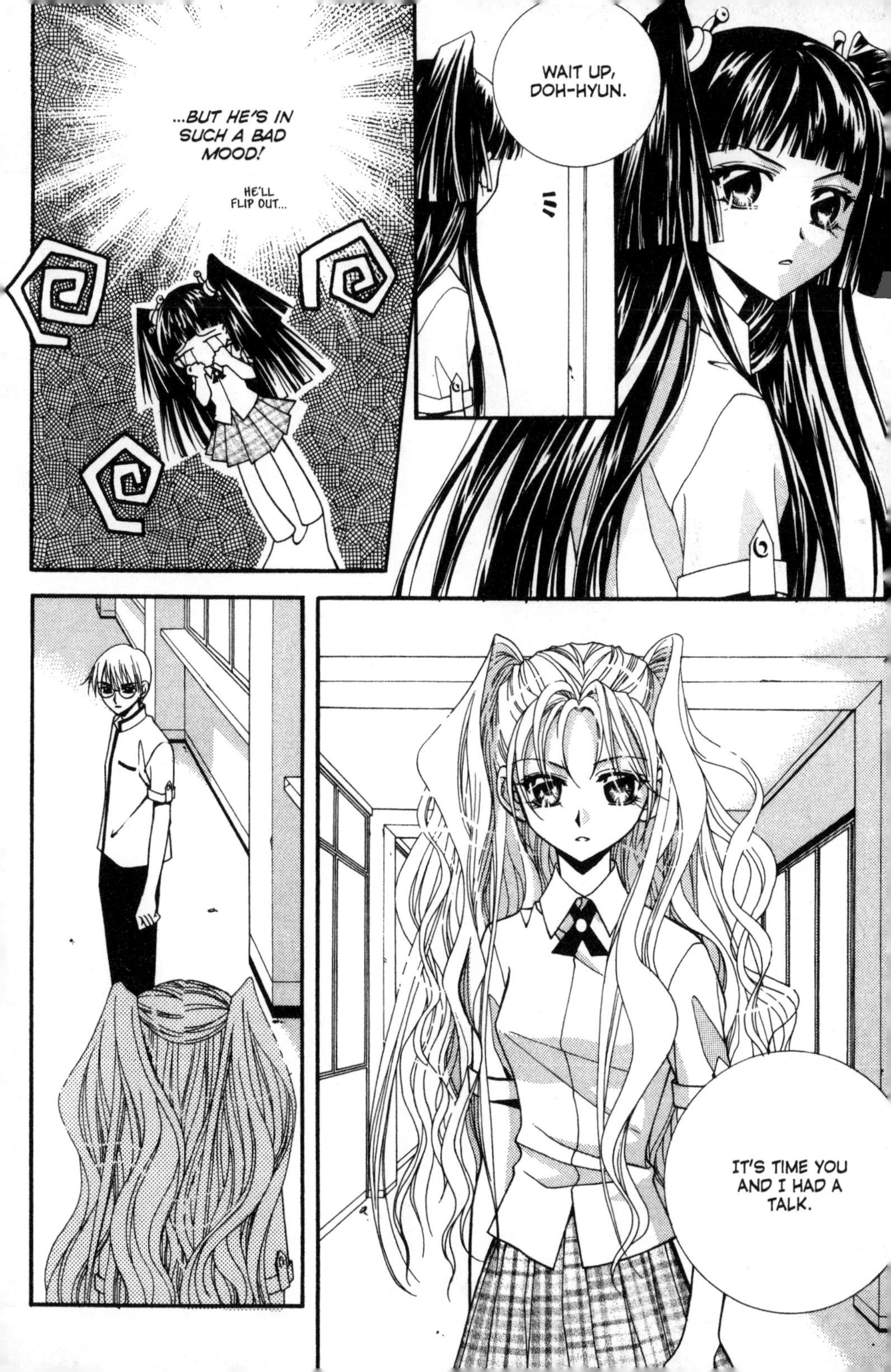
...BUT HE'S IN SUCH A BAD MOOD!
HE'LL FLIP OUT...
WAIT UP, DOH-HYUN.
IT'S TIME YOU AND I HAD A TALK.

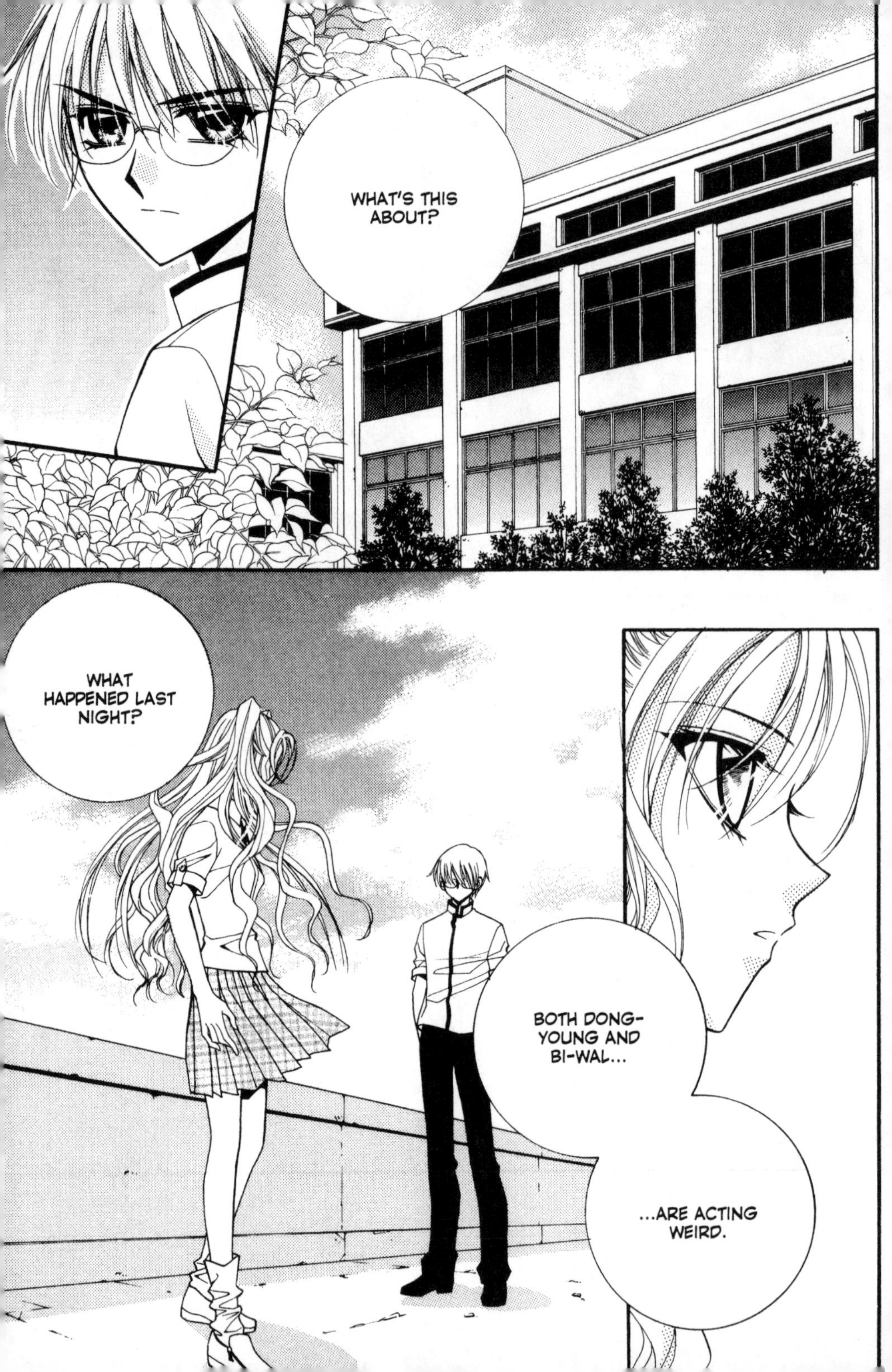
WHAT'S THIS ABOUT?
WHAT HAPPENED LAST NIGHT?
BOTH DONG-YOUNG AND BI-WAL...
...ARE ACTING WEIRD.

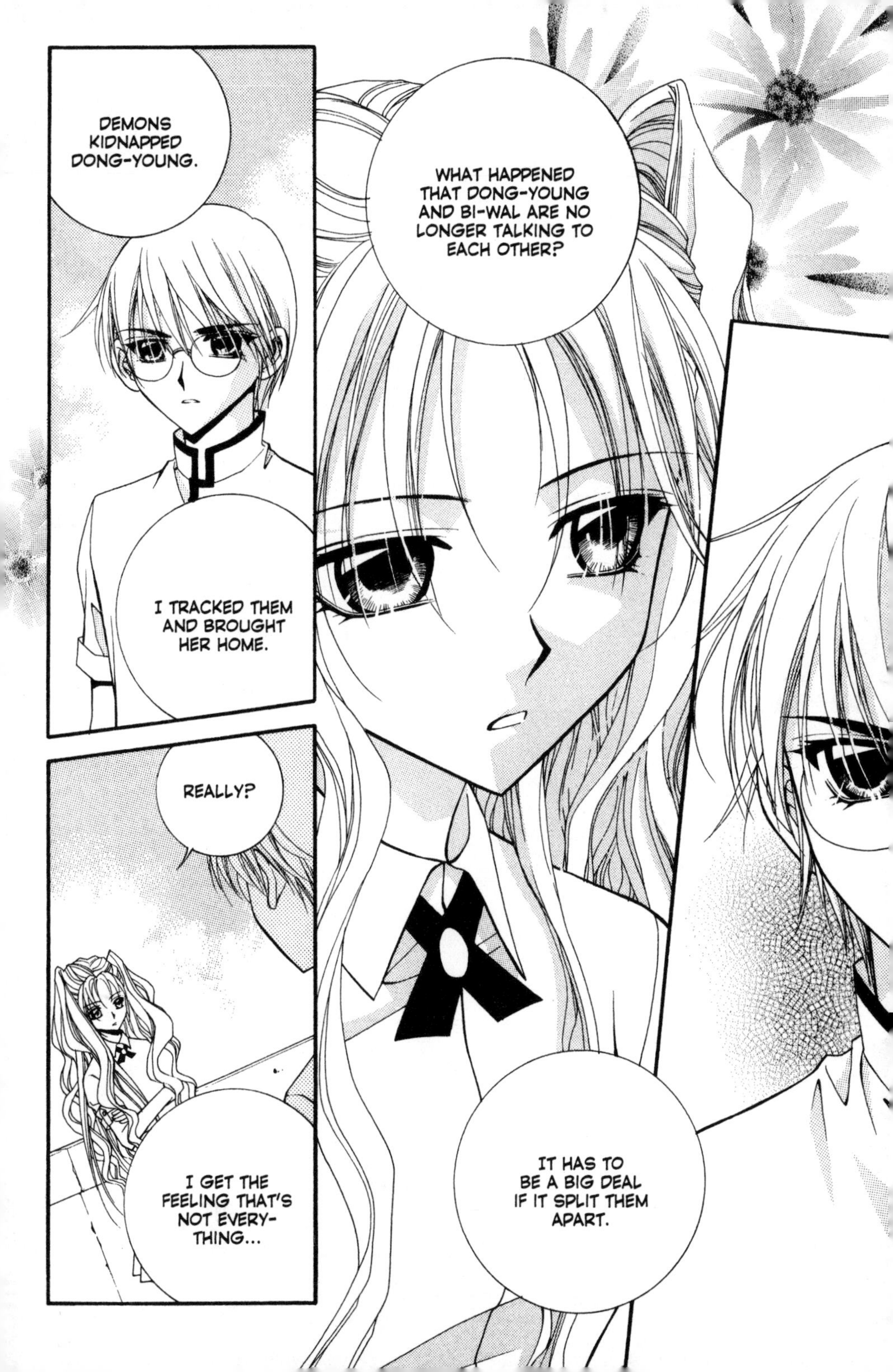
DEMONS KIDNAPPED DONG-YOUNG.
I TRACKED THEM AND BROUGHT HER HOME.
WHAT HAPPENED THAT DONG-YOUNG AND BI-WAL ARE NO LONGER TALKING TO EACH OTHER?
REALLY?
I GET THE FEELING THAT'S NOT EVERY-THING...
IT HAS TO BE A BIG DEAL IF IT SPLIT THEM APART.

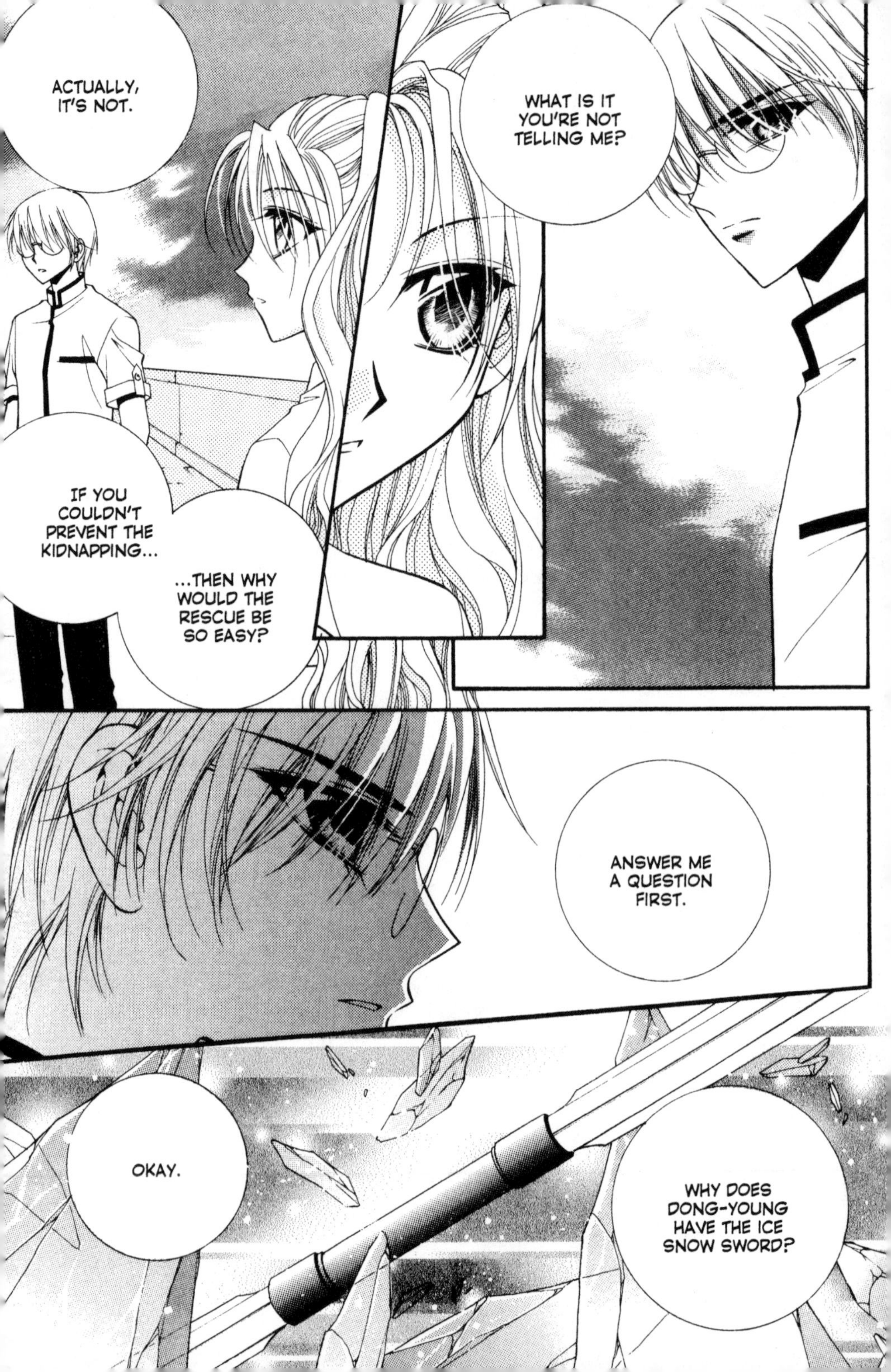
WHAT IS IT YOU'RE NOT TELLING ME?
ACTUALLY, IT'S NOT.
IF YOU COULDN'T PREVENT THE KIDNAPPING...
...THEN WHY WOULD THE RESCUE BE SO EASY?
ANSWER ME A QUESTION FIRST.
WHY DOES DONG-YOUNG HAVE THE ICE SNOW SWORD?
OKAY.

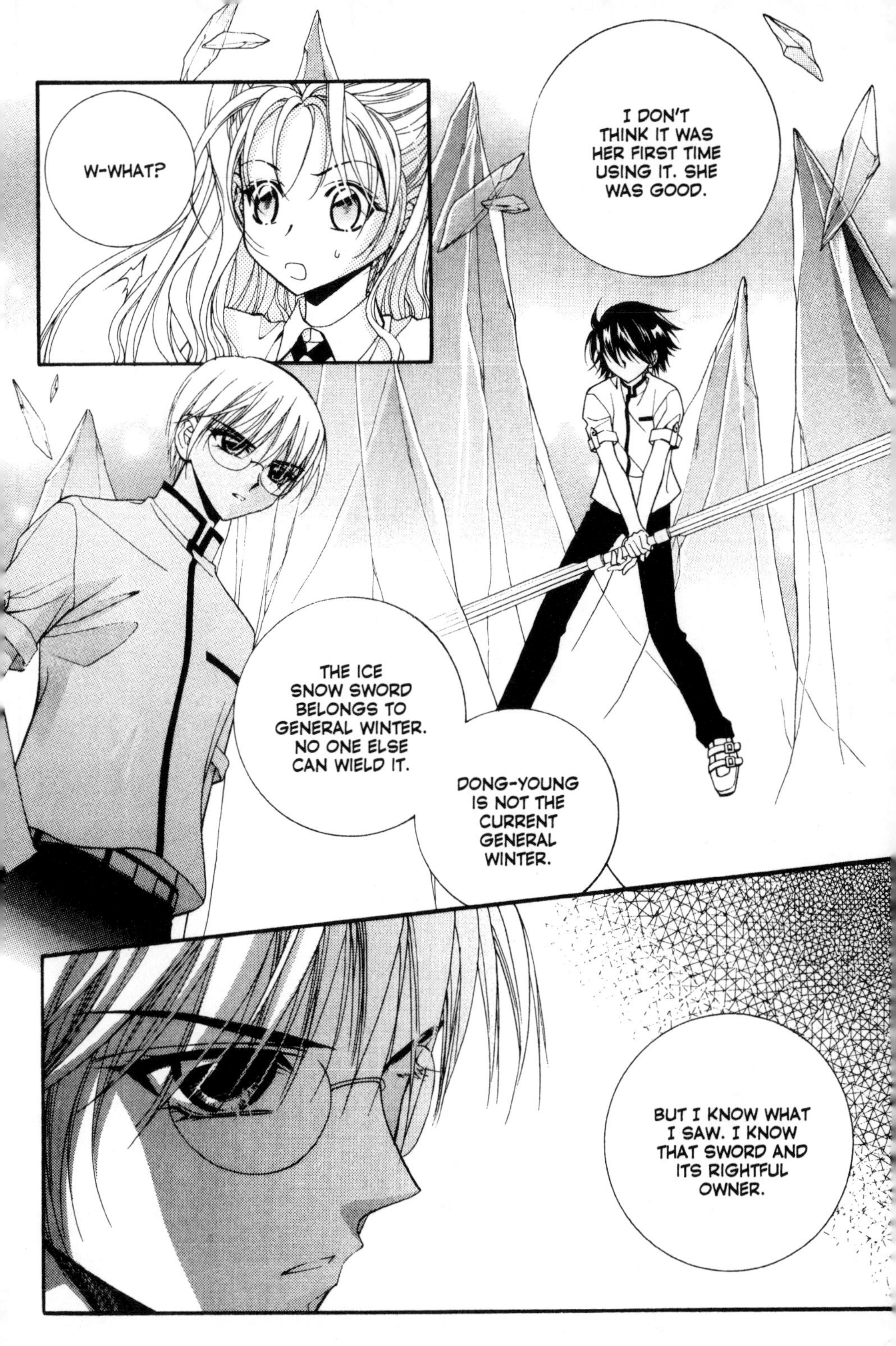
W-WHAT?
I DON'T THINK IT WAS HER FIRST TIME USING IT. SHE WAS GOOD.
THE ICE SNOW SWORD BELONGS TO GENERAL WINTER. NO ONE ELSE CAN WIELD IT.
DONG-YOUNG IS NOT THE CURRENT GENERAL WINTER.
BUT I KNOW WHAT I SAW. I KNOW THAT SWORD AND ITS RIGHTFUL OWNER.

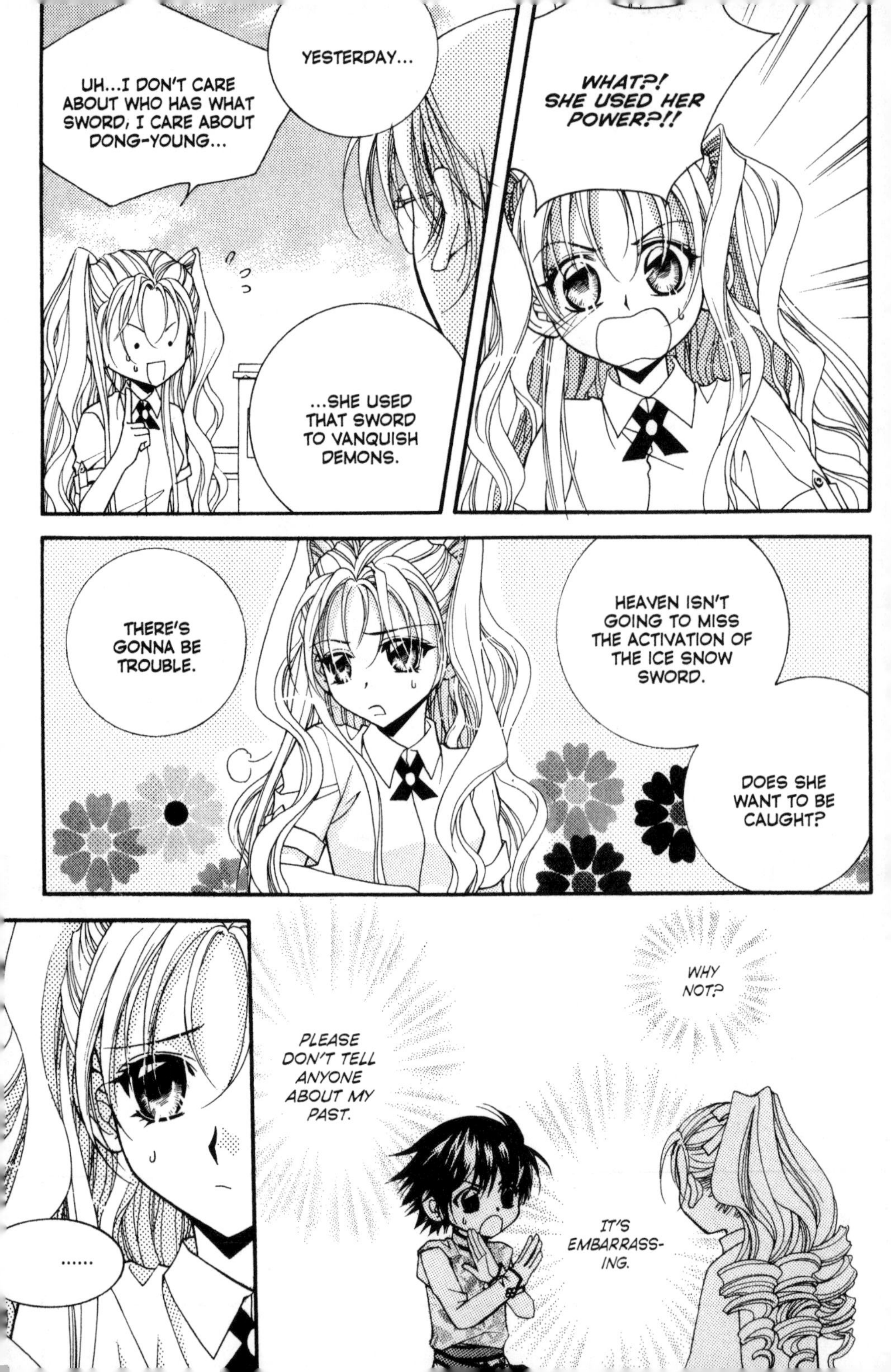
UH...I DON'T CARE ABOUT WHO HAS WHAT SWORD, I CARE ABOUT DONG-YOUNG...
YESTERDAY...
...SHE USED THAT SWORD TO VANQUISH DEMONS.
WHAT?! SHE USED HER POWER?!!
THERE'S GONNA BE TROUBLE.
HEAVEN ISN'T GOING TO MISS THE ACTIVATION OF THE ICE SNOW SWORD.
DOES SHE WANT TO BE CAUGHT?
......
PLEASE DON'T TELL ANYONE ABOUT MY PAST.
WHY NOT?
IT'S EMBARRASS-ING.

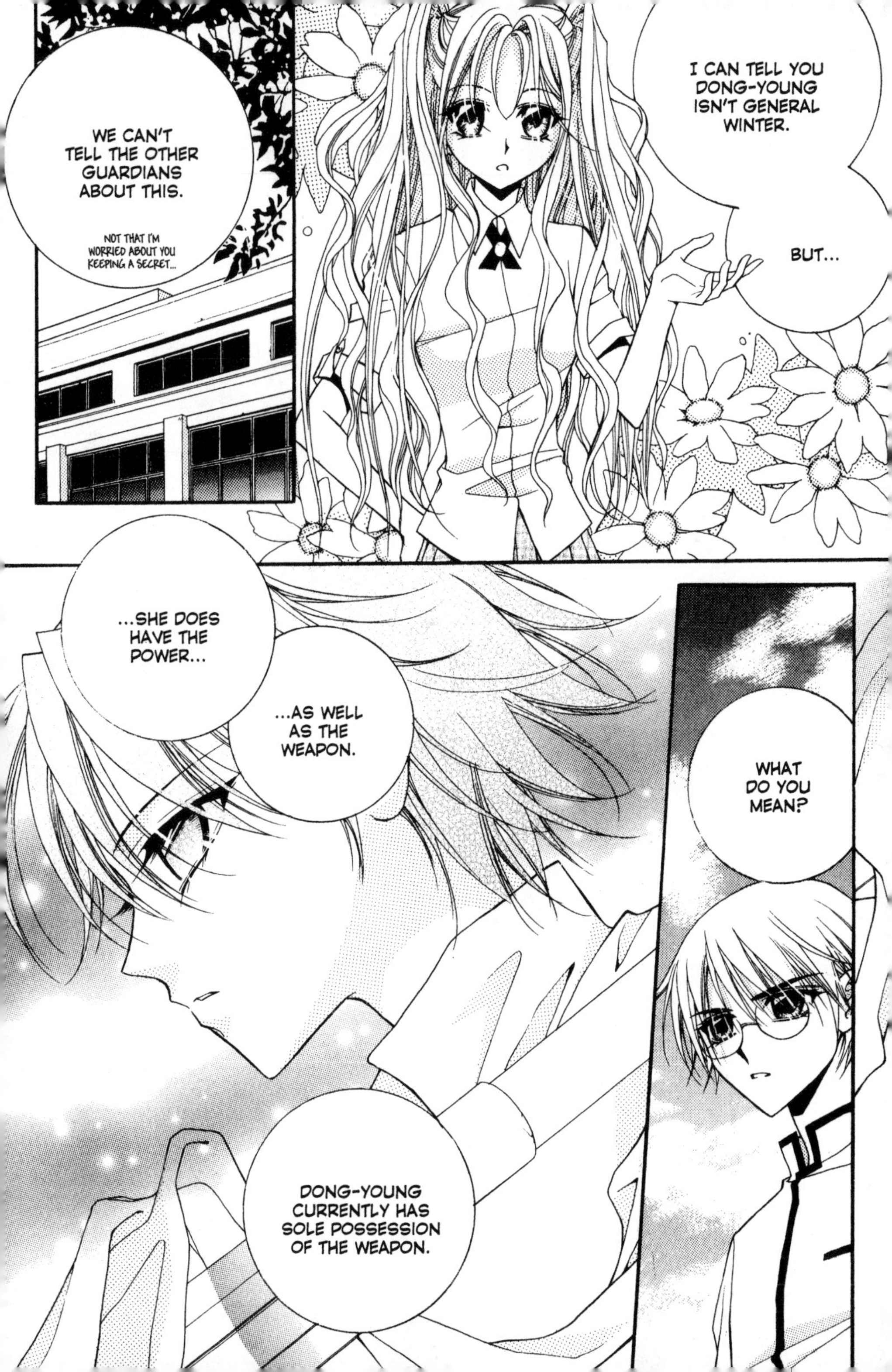
WE CAN'T TELL THE OTHER GUARDIANS ABOUT THIS.
NOT THAT I'M WORRIED ABOUT YOU KEEPING A SECRET...
I CAN TELL YOU DONG-YOUNG ISN'T GENERAL WINTER.
BUT...
...SHE DOES HAVE THE POWER...
...AS WELL AS THE WEAPON.
WHAT DO YOU MEAN?
DONG-YOUNG CURRENTLY HAS SOLE POSSESSION OF THE WEAPON.

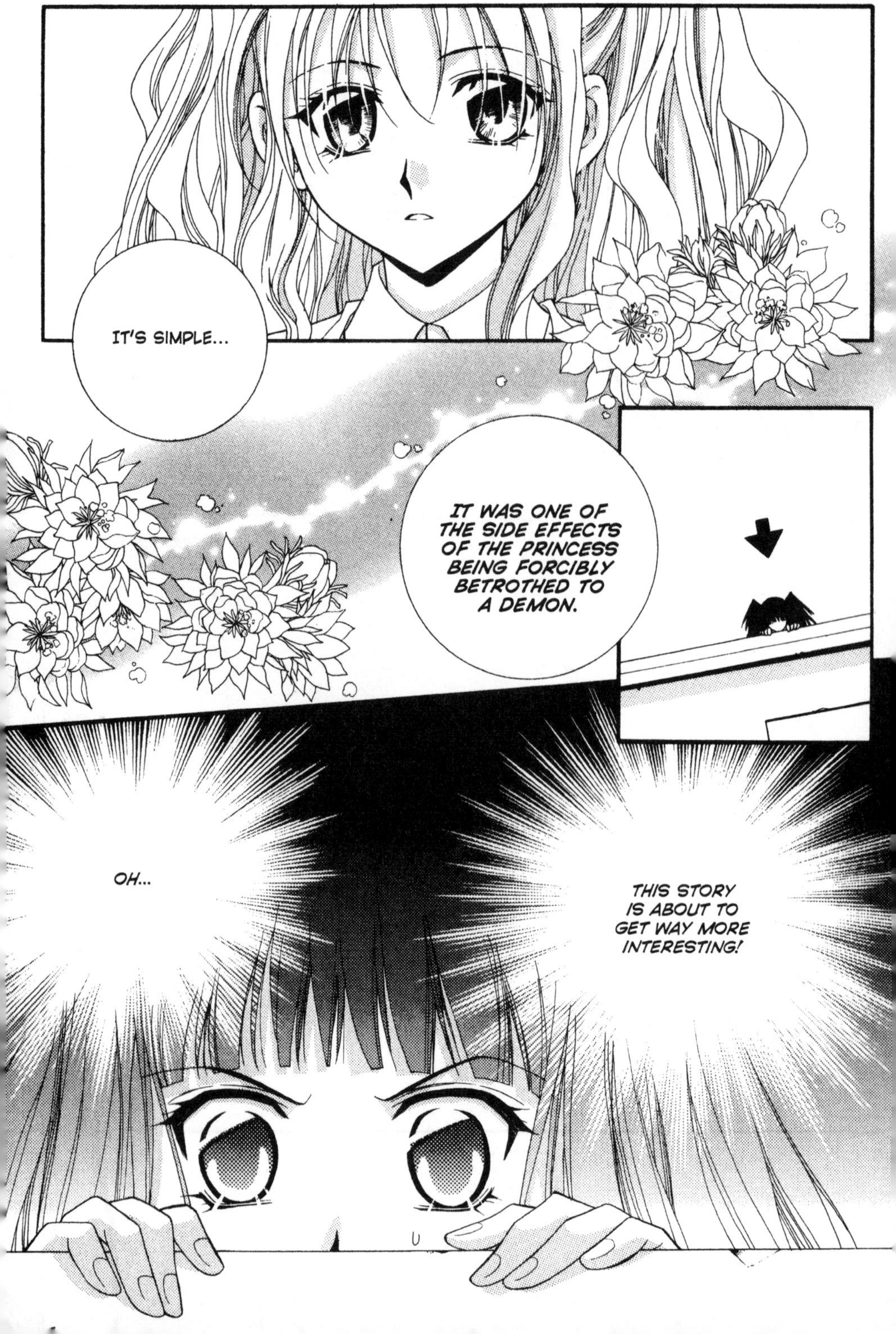
IT'S SIMPLE...
IT WAS ONE OF THE SIDE EFFECTS OF THE PRINCESS BEING FORCIBLY BETROTHED TO A DEMON.
OH...
THIS STORY IS ABOUT TO GET WAY MORE INTERESTING!

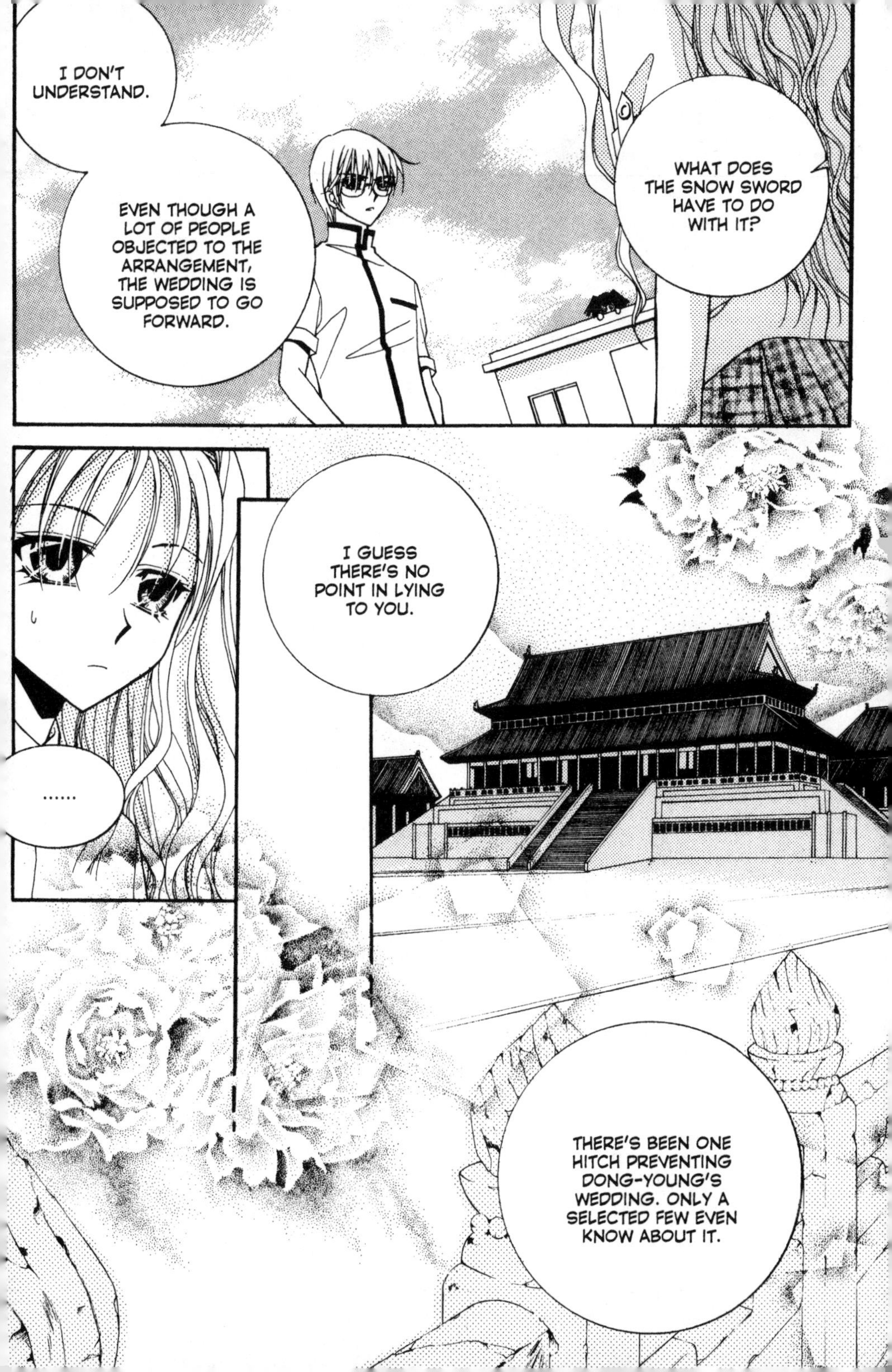
WHAT DOES THE SNOW SWORD HAVE TO DO WITH IT?
I DON'T UNDERSTAND.
EVEN THOUGH A LOT OF PEOPLE OBJECTED TO THE ARRANGEMENT, THE WEDDING IS SUPPOSED TO GO FORWARD.
I GUESS THERE'S NO POINT IN LYING TO YOU.
......
THERE'S BEEN ONE HITCH PREVENTING DONG-YOUNG'S WEDDING. ONLY A SELECTED FEW EVEN KNOW ABOUT IT.

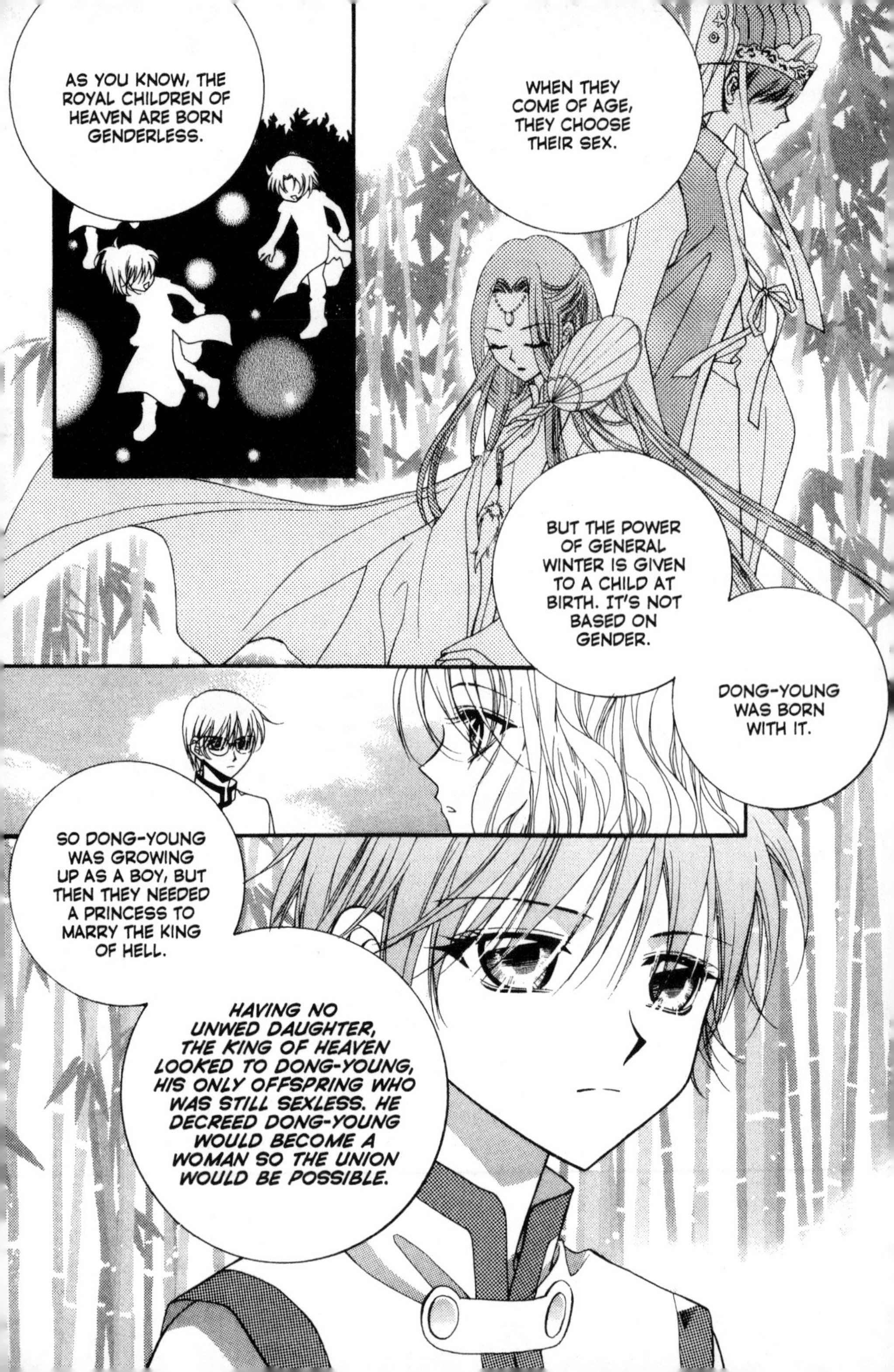

WHEN THEY COME OF AGE, THEY CHOOSE THEIR SEX.
AS YOU KNOW, THE ROYAL CHILDREN OF HEAVEN ARE BORN GENDERLESS.
BUT THE POWER OF GENERAL WINTER IS GIVEN TO A CHILD AT BIRTH. IT'S NOT BASED ON GENDER.
DONG-YOUNG WAS BORN WITH IT.
SO DONG-YOUNG WAS GROWING UP AS A BOY, BUT THEN THEY NEEDED A PRINCESS TO MARRY THE KING OF HELL.
HAVING NO UNWED DAUGHTER, THE KING OF HEAVEN LOOKED TO DONG-YOUNG, HIS ONLY OFFSPRING WHO WAS STILL SEXLESS. HE DECREED DONG-YOUNG WOULD BECOME A WOMAN SO THE UNION WOULD BE POSSIBLE.

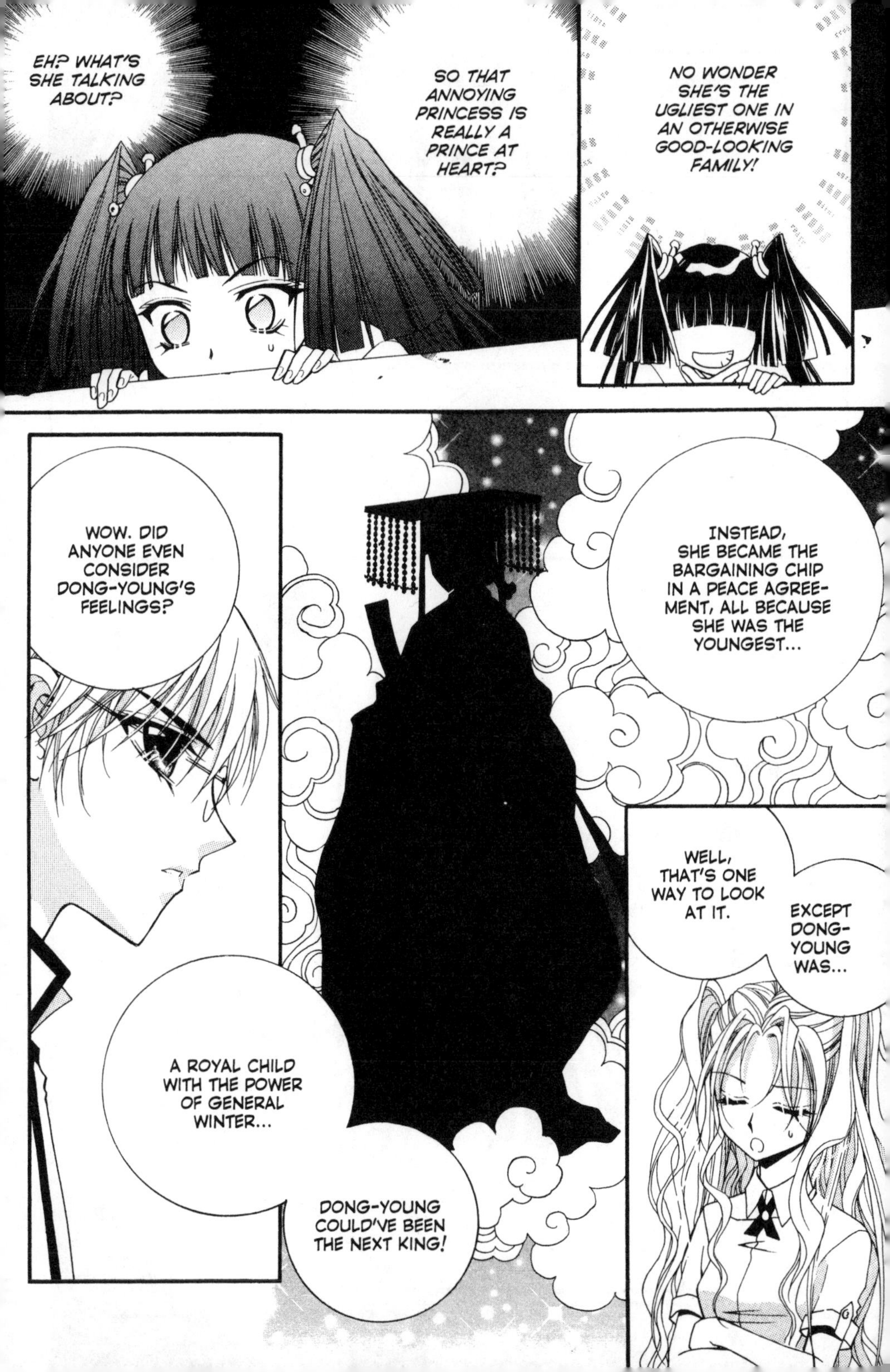
EH? WHAT'S SHE TALKING ABOUT?
SO THAT ANNOYING PRINCESS IS REALLY A PRINCE AT HEART?
NO WONDER SHE'S THE UGLIEST ONE IN AN OTHERWISE GOOD-LOOKING FAMILY!
WOW. DID ANYONE EVEN CONSIDER DONG-YOUNG'S FEELINGS?
INSTEAD, SHE BECAME THE BARGAINING CHIP IN A PEACE AGREE-MENT, ALL BECAUSE SHE WAS THE YOUNGEST...
WELL, THAT'S ONE WAY TO LOOK AT IT.
EXCEPT DONG-YOUNG WAS...
A ROYAL CHILD WITH THE POWER OF GENERAL WINTER...
DONG-YOUNG COULD'VE BEEN THE NEXT KING!

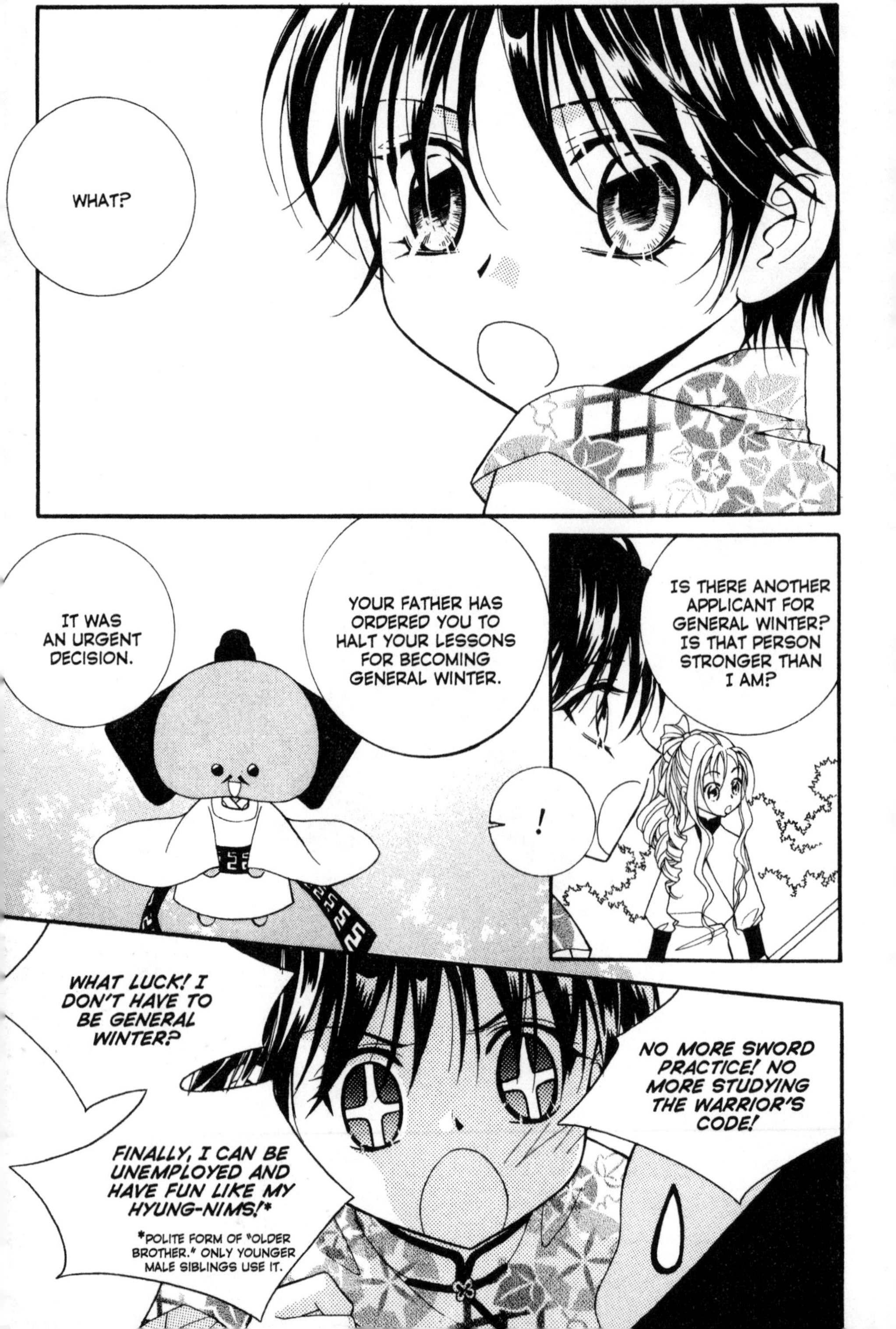
WHAT?
IT WAS AN URGENT DECISION.
YOUR FATHER HAS ORDERED YOU TO HALT YOUR LESSONS FOR BECOMING GENERAL WINTER.
IS THERE ANOTHER APPLICANT FOR GENERAL WINTER? IS THAT PERSON STRONGER THAN I AM?
!
WHAT LUCK! I DON'T HAVE TO BE GENERAL WINTER?
NO MORE SWORD PRACTICE! NO MORE STUDYING THE WARRIOR'S CODE!
FINALLY, I CAN BE UNEMPLOYED AND HAVE FUN LIKE MY HYUNG-NIMS!*
*POLITE FORM OF "OLDER BROTHER." ONLY YOUNGER MALE SIBLINGS USE IT.

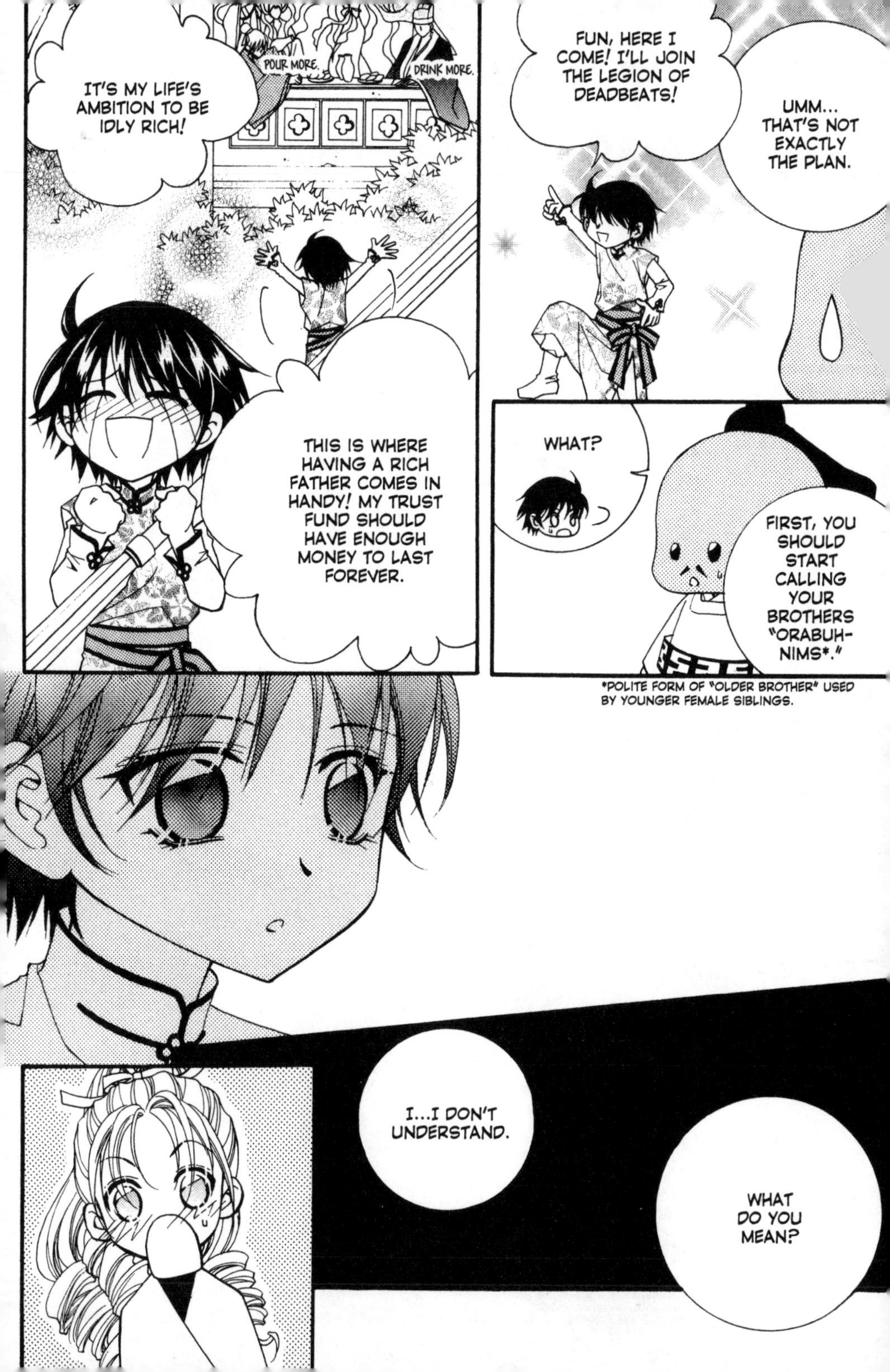
IT'S MY LIFE'S AMBITION TO BE IDLY RICH!
POUR MORE.
DRINK MORE.
THIS IS WHERE HAVING A RICH FATHER COMES IN HANDY! MY TRUST FUND SHOULD HAVE ENOUGH MONEY TO LAST FOREVER.
FUN, HERE I COME! I'LL JOIN THE LEGION OF DEADBEATS!
UMM... THAT'S NOT EXACTLY THE PLAN.
WHAT?
FIRST, YOU SHOULD START CALLING YOUR BROTHERS "ORABUH-NIMS*."
I...I DON'T UNDERSTAND.
WHAT DO YOU MEAN?

*POLITE FORM OF "OLDER BROTHER" USED BY YOUNGER FEMALE SIBLINGS.

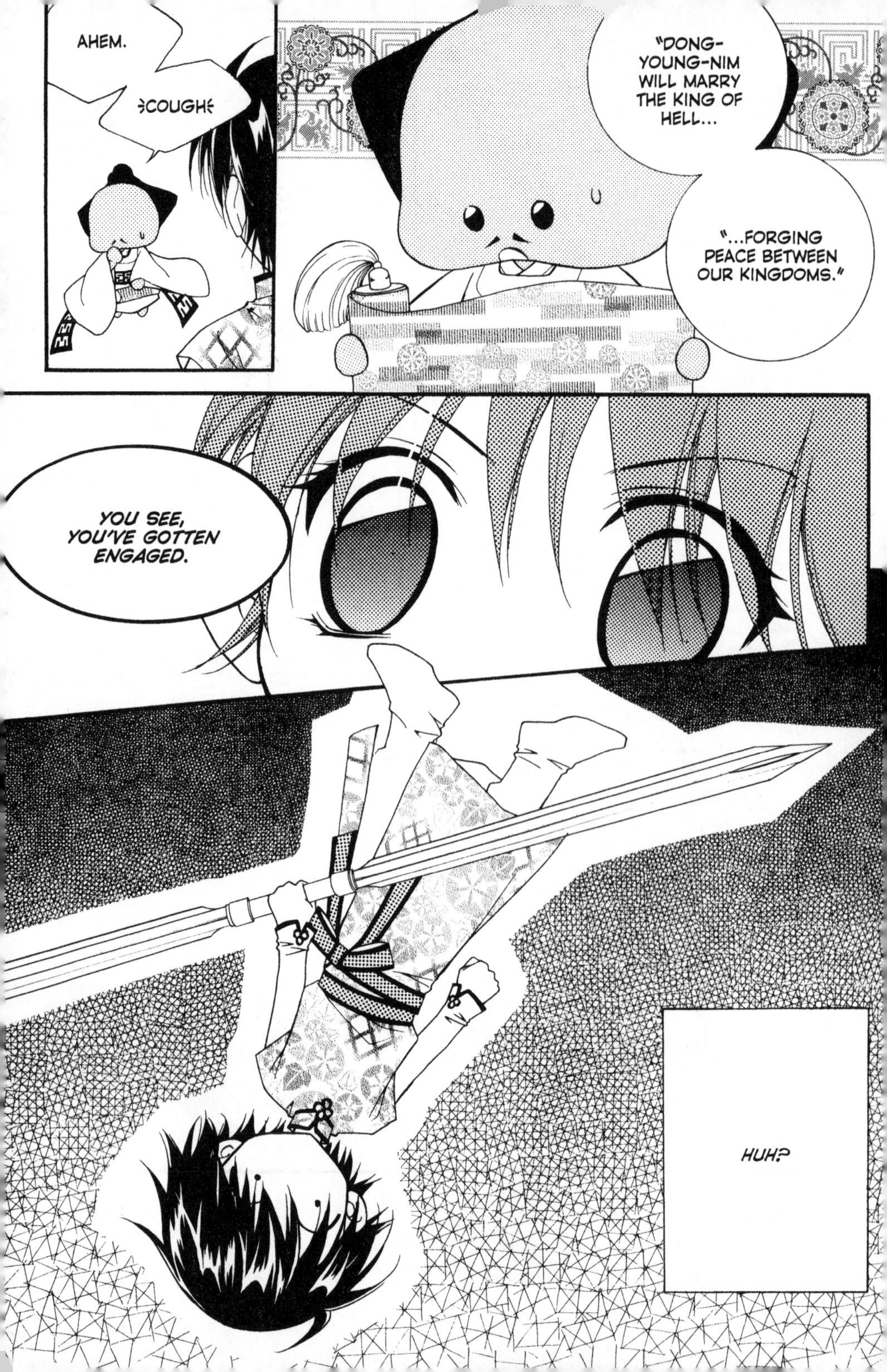
AHEM.
COUGH
"DONG-YOUNG-NIM WILL MARRY THE KING OF HELL...
"...FORGING PEACE BETWEEN OUR KINGDOMS."
YOU SEE, YOU'VE GOTTEN ENGAGED.
HUH?

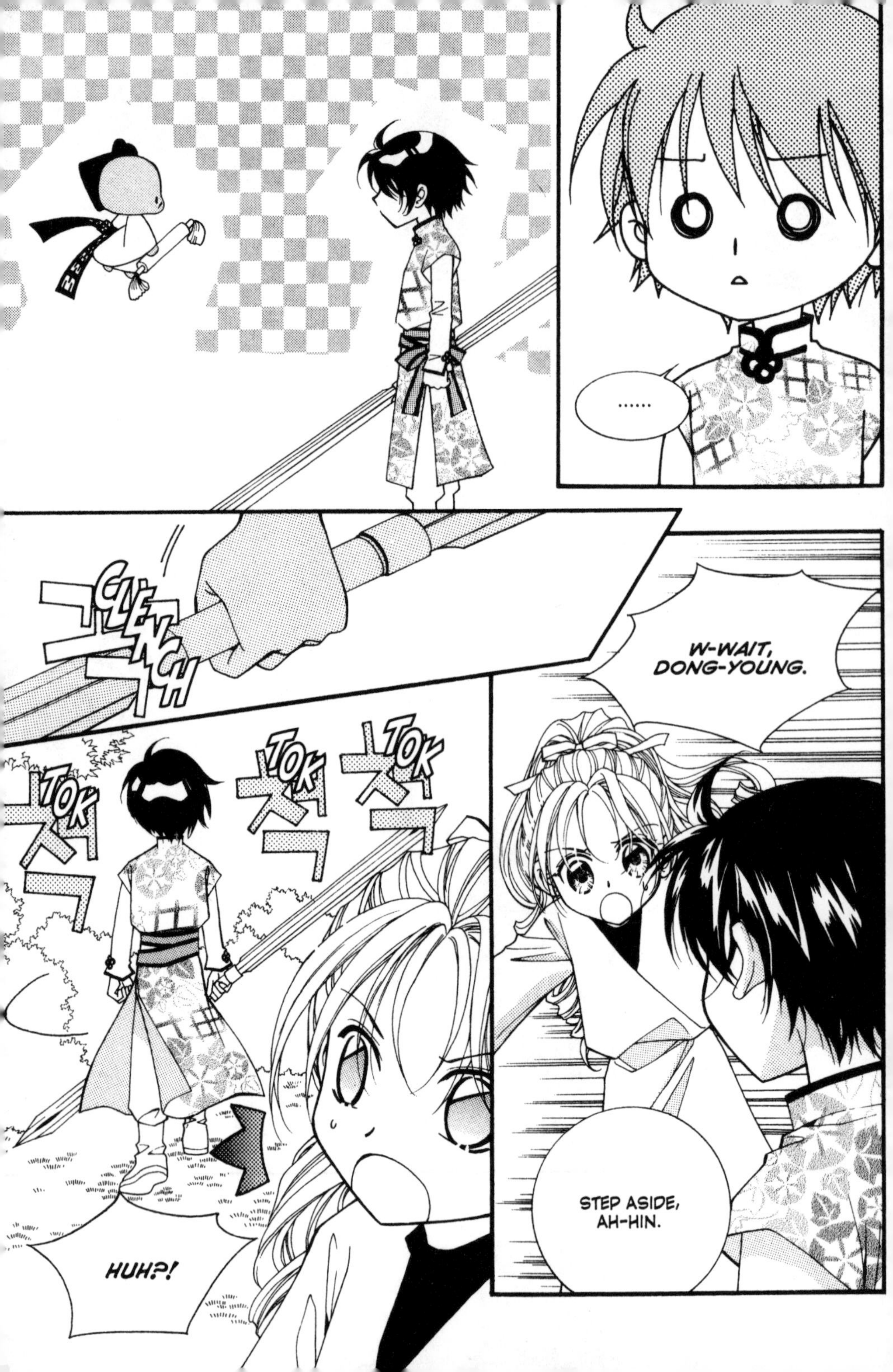
......
CLENCH
TOK
TOK
TOK
HUH?!
W-WAIT, DONG-YOUNG.
STEP ASIDE, AH-HIN.

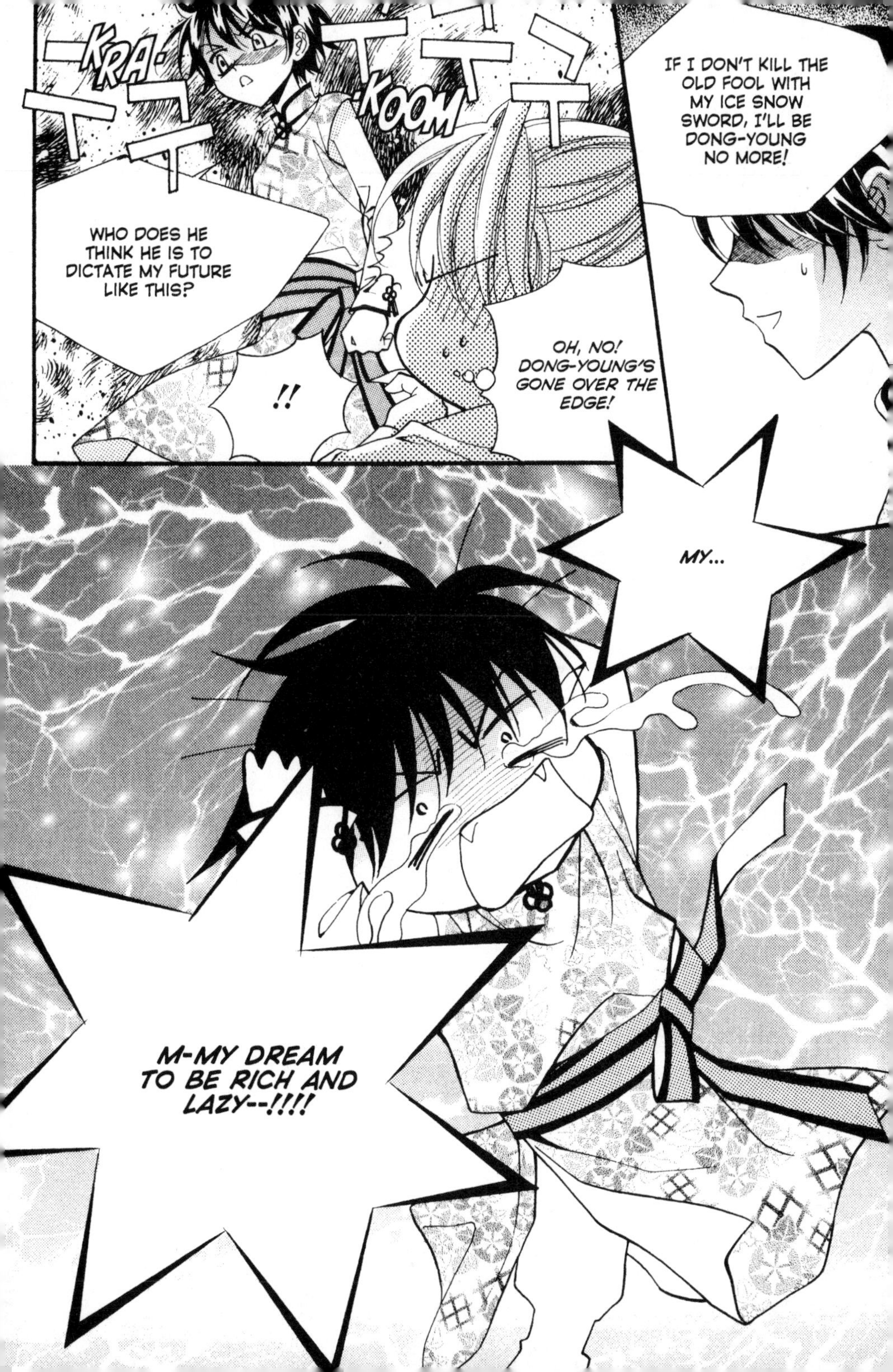
IF I DON'T KILL THE OLD FOOL WITH MY ICE SNOW SWORD, I'LL BE DONG-YOUNG NO MORE!
KRA-KOOM
WHO DOES HE THINK HE IS TO DICTATE MY FUTURE LIKE THIS?
OH, NO! DONG-YOUNG'S GONE OVER THE EDGE!
!!
MY...
M-MY DREAM TO BE RICH AND LAZY--!!!!

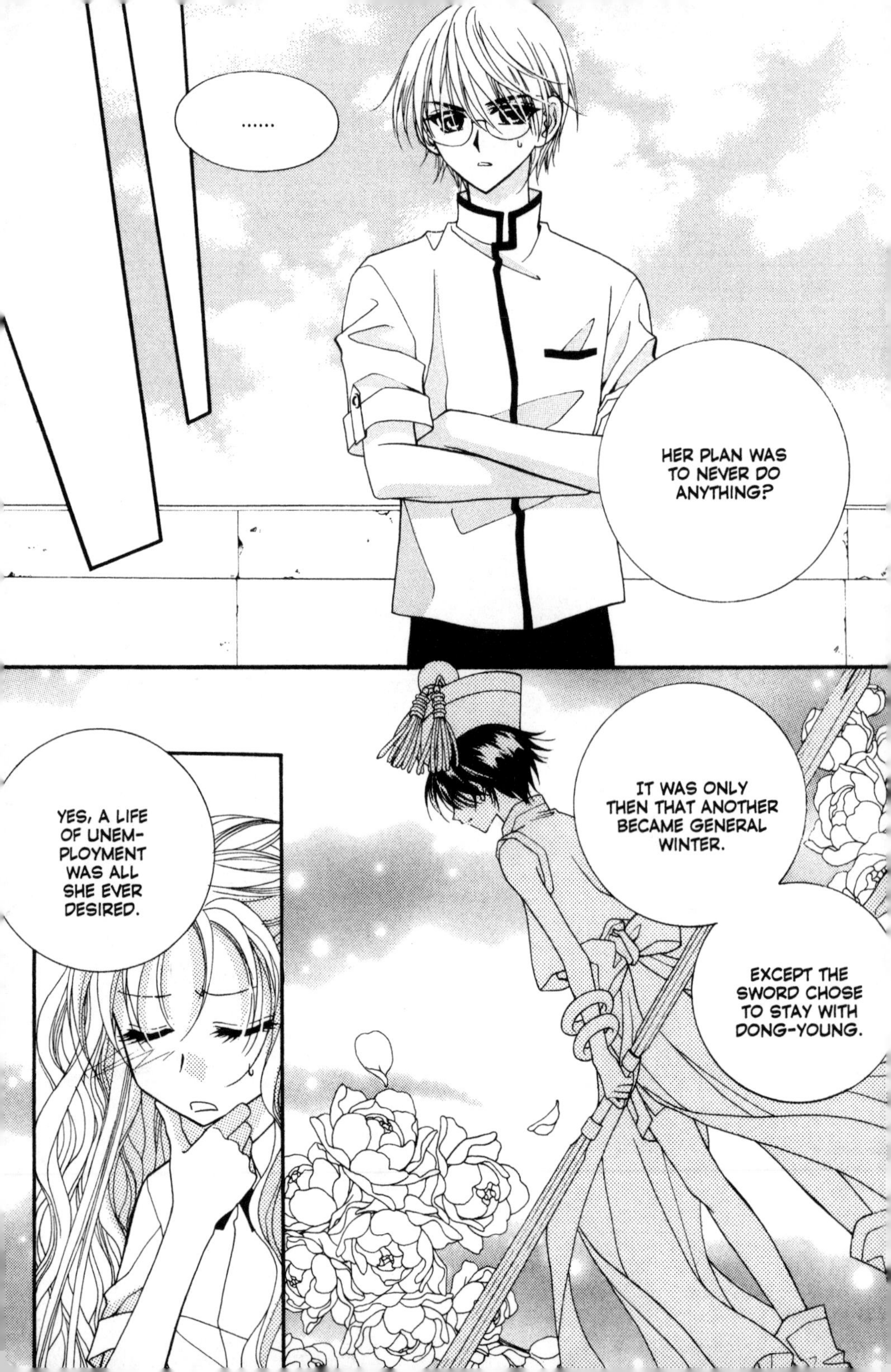
......
HER PLAN WAS TO NEVER DO ANYTHING?
IT WAS ONLY THEN THAT ANOTHER BECAME GENERAL WINTER.
EXCEPT THE SWORD CHOSE TO STAY WITH DONG-YOUNG.
YES, A LIFE OF UNEM-PLOYMENT WAS ALL SHE EVER DESIRED.

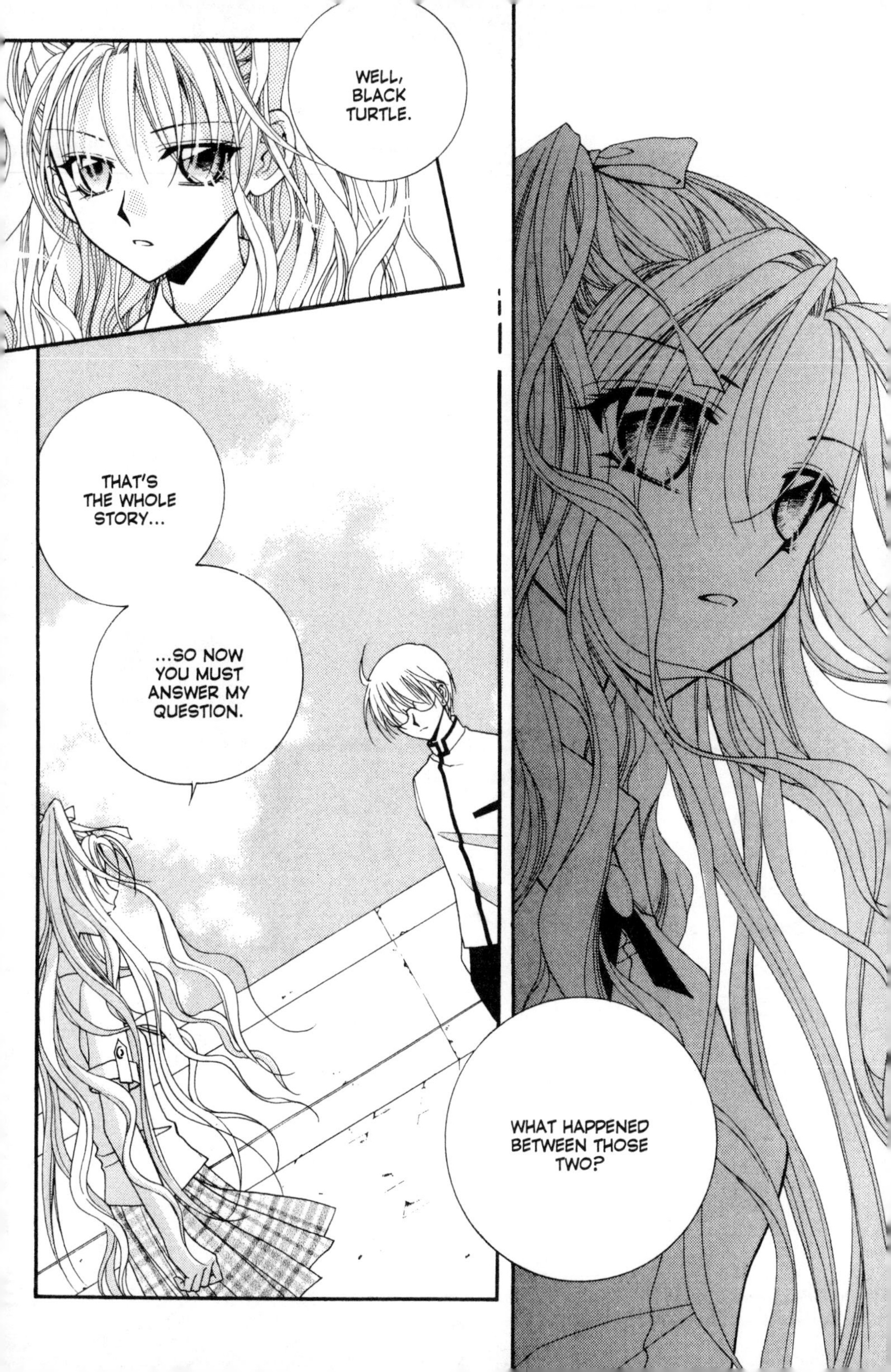
WELL, BLACK TURTLE.
THAT'S THE WHOLE STORY...
...SO NOW YOU MUST ANSWER MY QUESTION.
WHAT HAPPENED BETWEEN THOSE TWO?

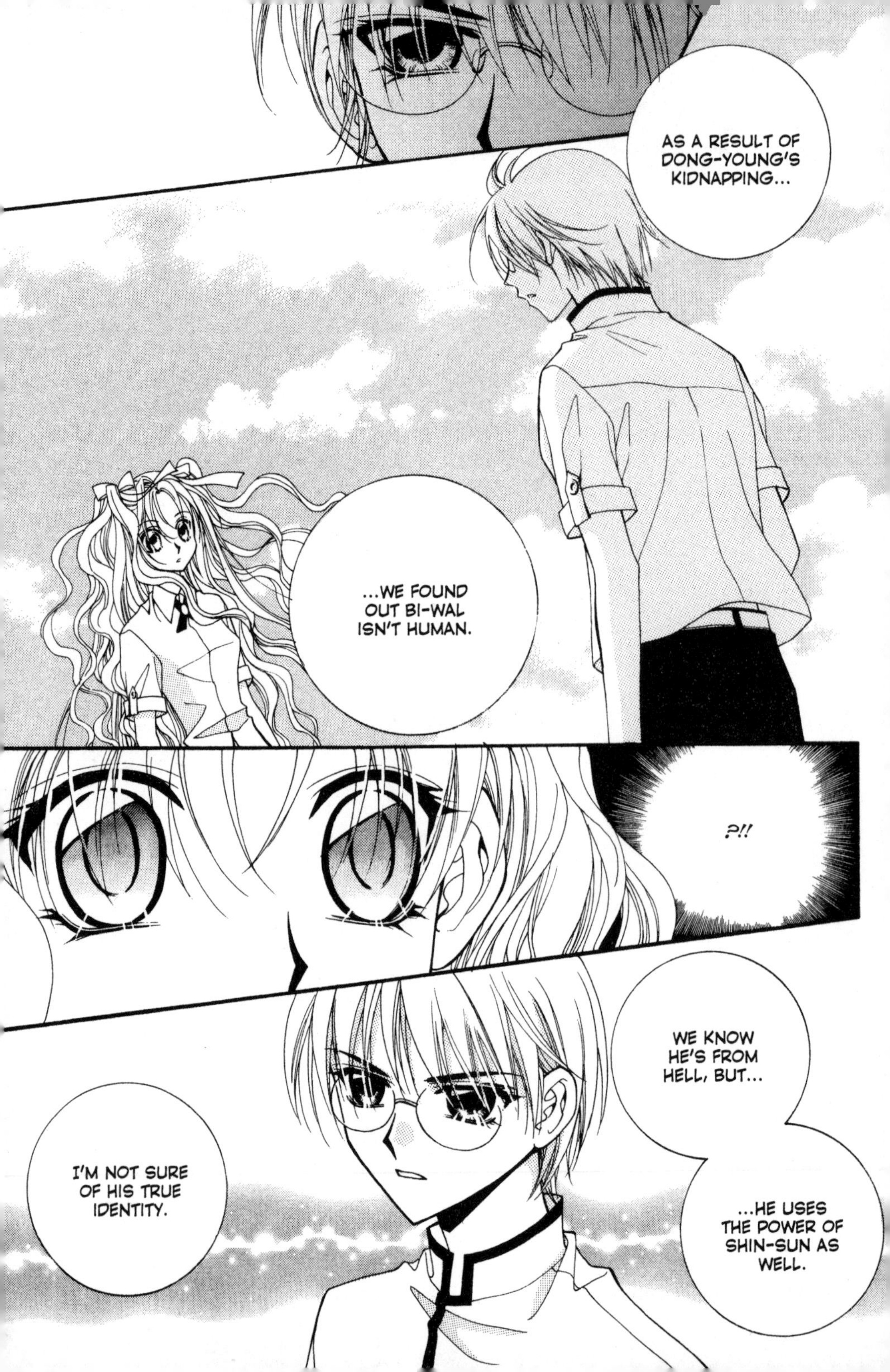
AS A RESULT OF DONG-YOUNG'S KIDNAPPING...
...WE FOUND OUT BI-WAL ISN'T HUMAN.
?!!
WE KNOW HE'S FROM HELL, BUT...
...HE USES THE POWER OF SHIN-SUN AS WELL.
I'M NOT SURE OF HIS TRUE IDENTITY.

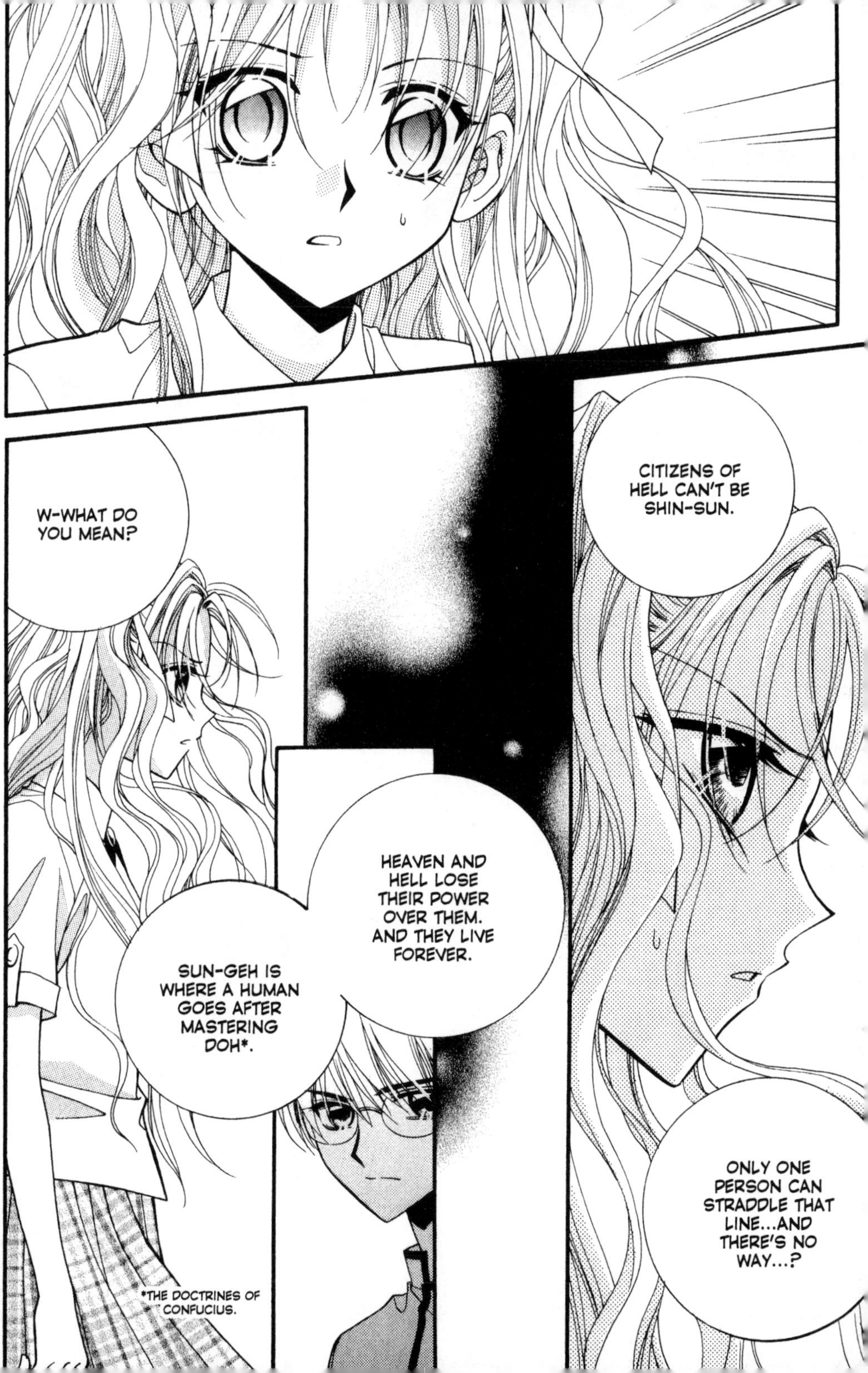
CITIZENS OF HELL CAN'T BE SHIN-SUN.
W-WHAT DO YOU MEAN?
SUN-GEH IS WHERE A HUMAN GOES AFTER MASTERING DOH*.
HEAVEN AND HELL LOSE THEIR POWER OVER THEM. AND THEY LIVE FOREVER.
ONLY ONE PERSON CAN STRADDLE THAT LINE...AND THERE'S NO WAY...?
*THE DOCTRINES OF CONFUCIUS.

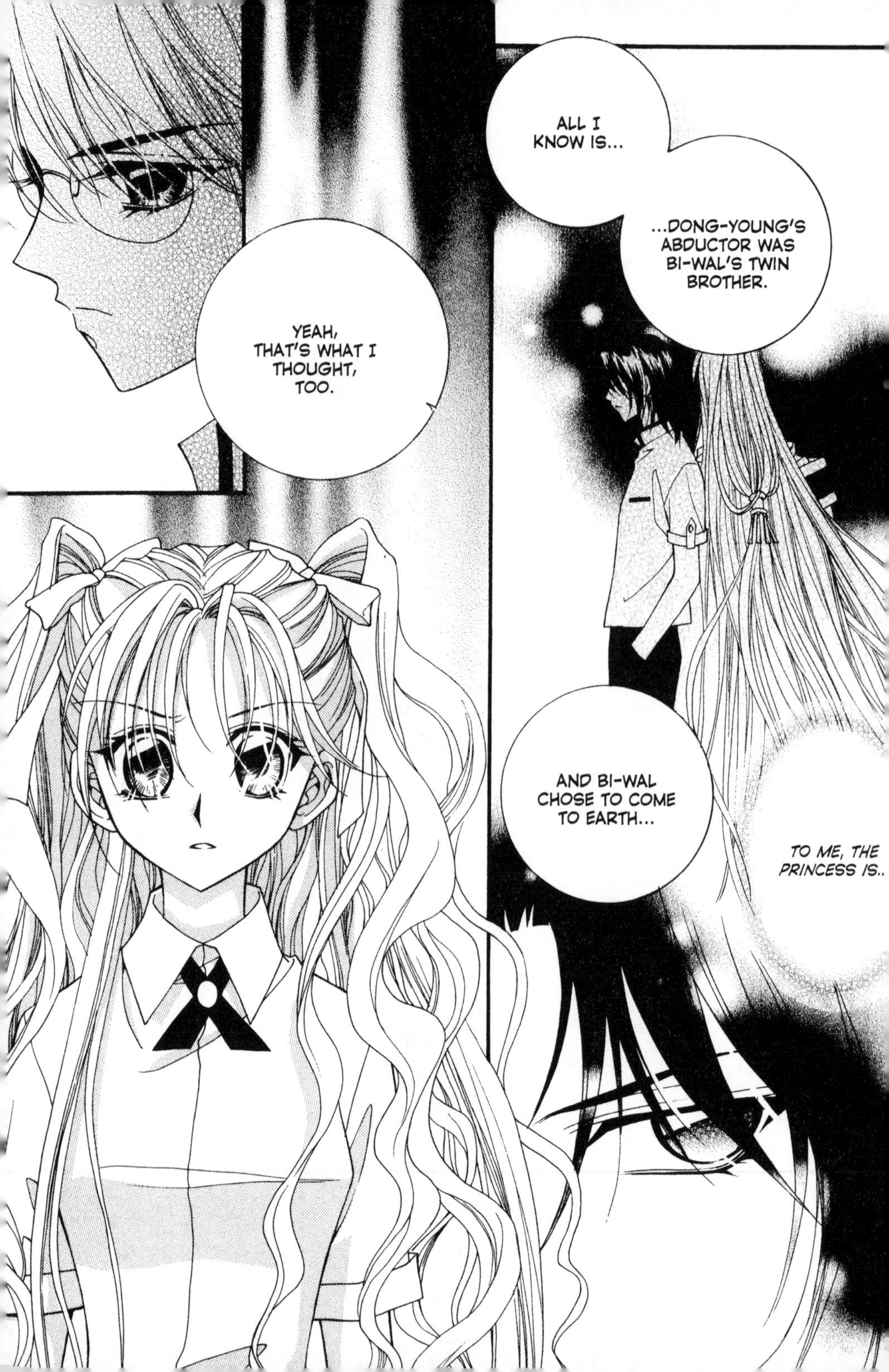
ALL I KNOW IS...
...DONG-YOUNG'S ABDUCTOR WAS BI-WAL'S TWIN BROTHER.
YEAH, THAT'S WHAT I THOUGHT, TOO.
AND BI-WAL CHOSE TO COME TO EARTH...
TO ME, THE PRINCESS IS..

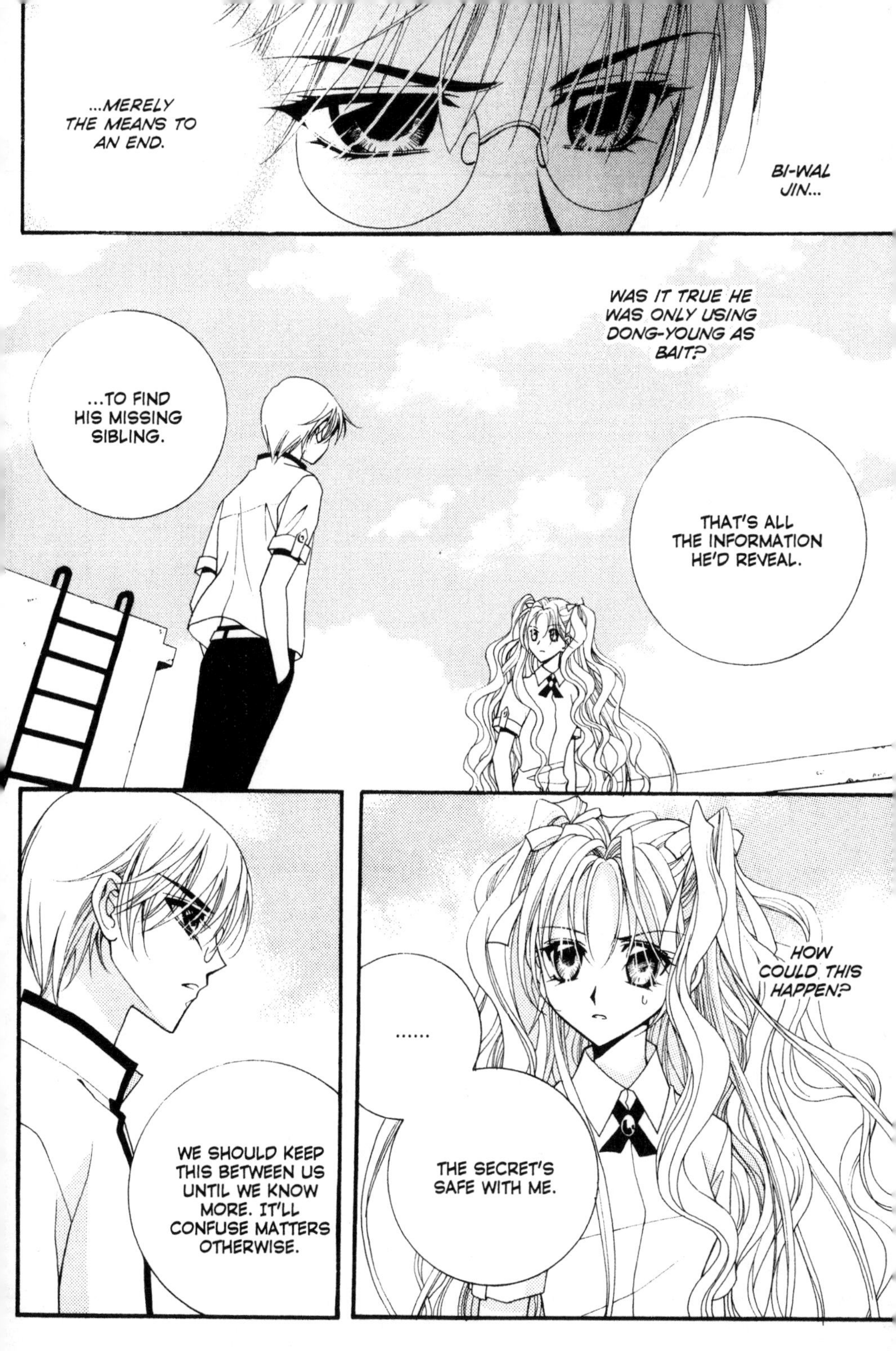
...MERELY THE MEANS TO AN END.
BI-WAL JIN...
WAS IT TRUE HE WAS ONLY USING DONG-YOUNG AS BAIT?
...TO FIND HIS MISSING SIBLING.
THAT'S ALL THE INFORMATION HE'D REVEAL.
HOW COULD THIS HAPPEN?
......
WE SHOULD KEEP THIS BETWEEN US UNTIL WE KNOW MORE. IT'LL CONFUSE MATTERS OTHERWISE.
THE SECRET'S SAFE WITH ME.

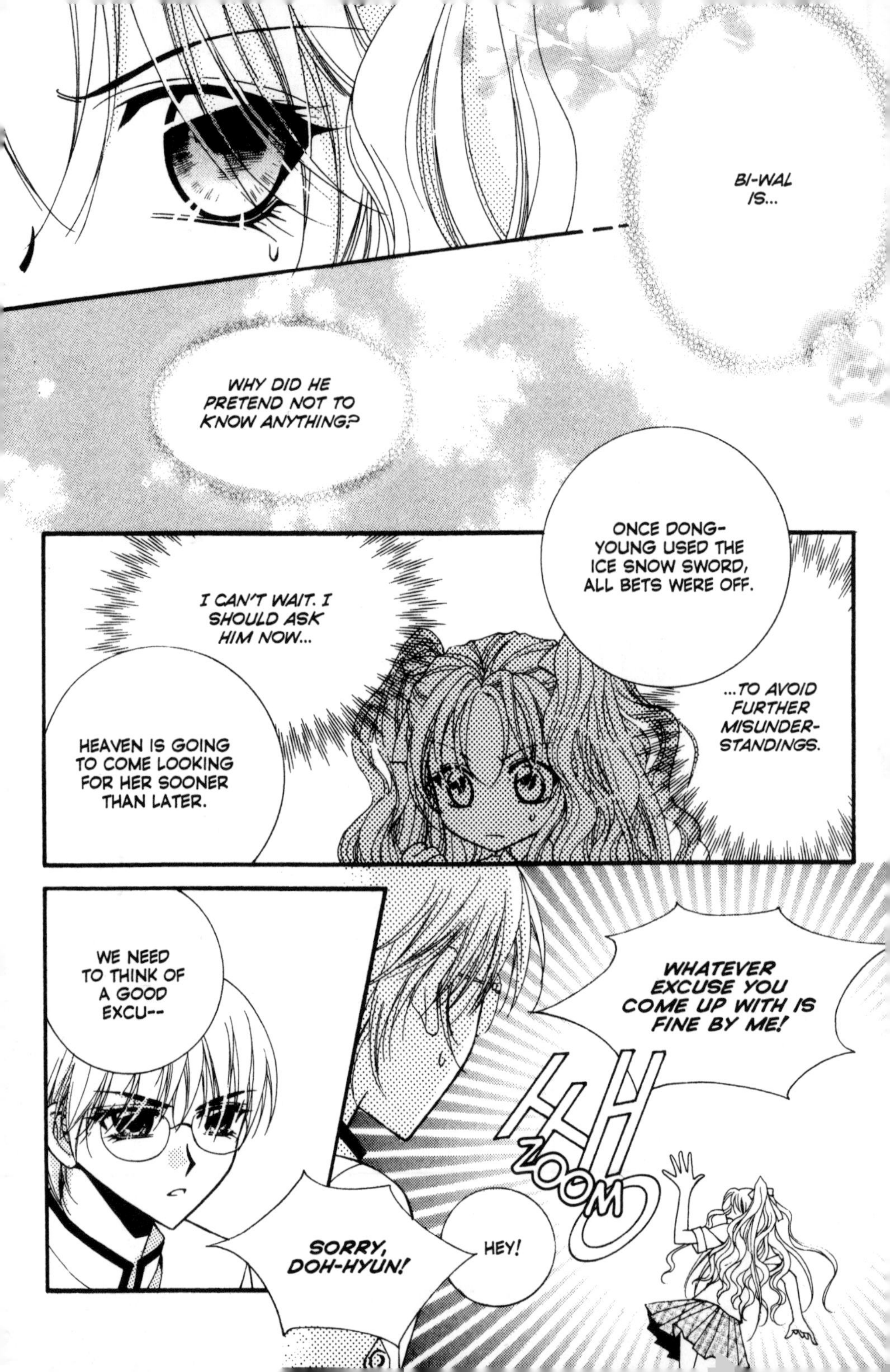

BI-WAL IS...
WHY DID HE PRETEND NOT TO KNOW ANYTHING?
ONCE DONG-YOUNG USED THE ICE SNOW SWORD, ALL BETS WERE OFF.
I CAN'T WAIT. I SHOULD ASK HIM NOW...
...TO AVOID FURTHER MISUNDER-STANDINGS.
HEAVEN IS GOING TO COME LOOKING FOR HER SOONER THAN LATER.
WE NEED TO THINK OF A GOOD EXCU--
WHATEVER EXCUSE YOU COME UP WITH IS FINE BY ME!
ZOOM
SORRY, DOH-HYUN!
HEY!

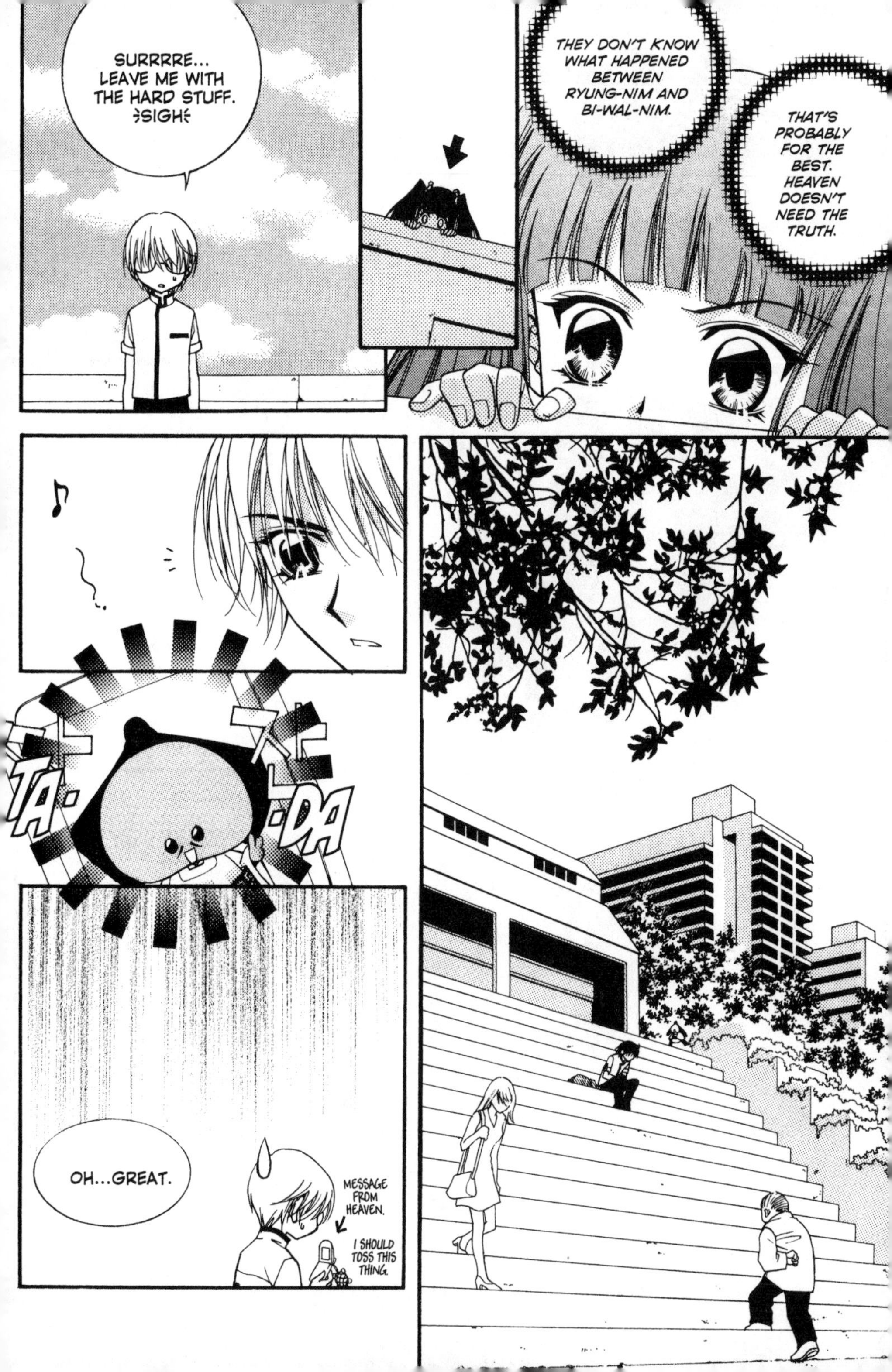
SURRRRE... LEAVE ME WITH THE HARD STUFF. SIGH
THEY DON'T KNOW WHAT HAPPENED BETWEEN RYUNG-NIM AND BI-WAL-NIM.
THAT'S PROBABLY FOR THE BEST. HEAVEN DOESN'T NEED THE TRUTH.
TA-DA
OH...GREAT.
MESSAGE FROM HEAVEN.
I SHOULD TOSS THIS THING.

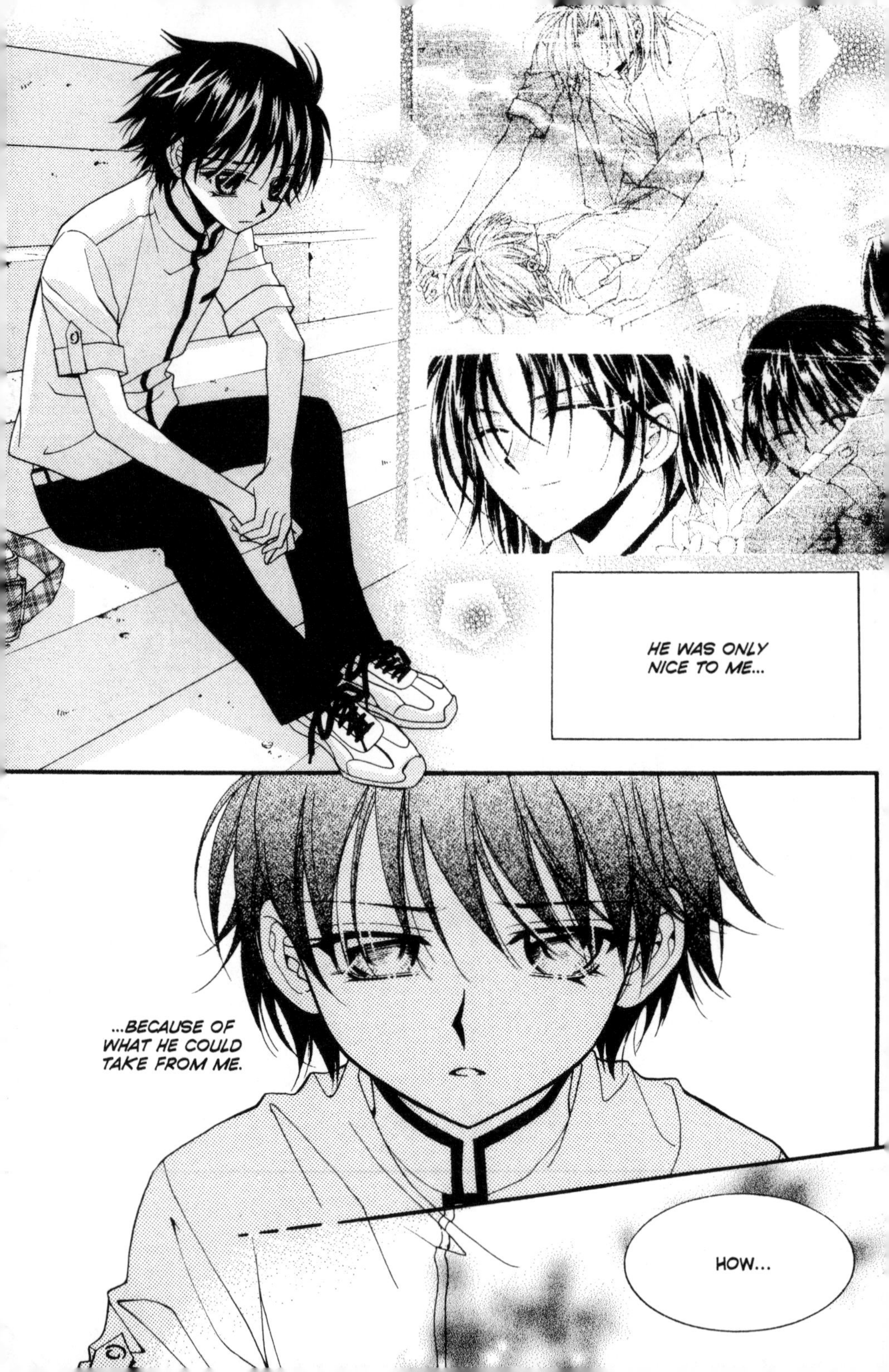
HE WAS ONLY NICE TO ME...
...BECAUSE OF WHAT HE COULD TAKE FROM ME.
HOW...

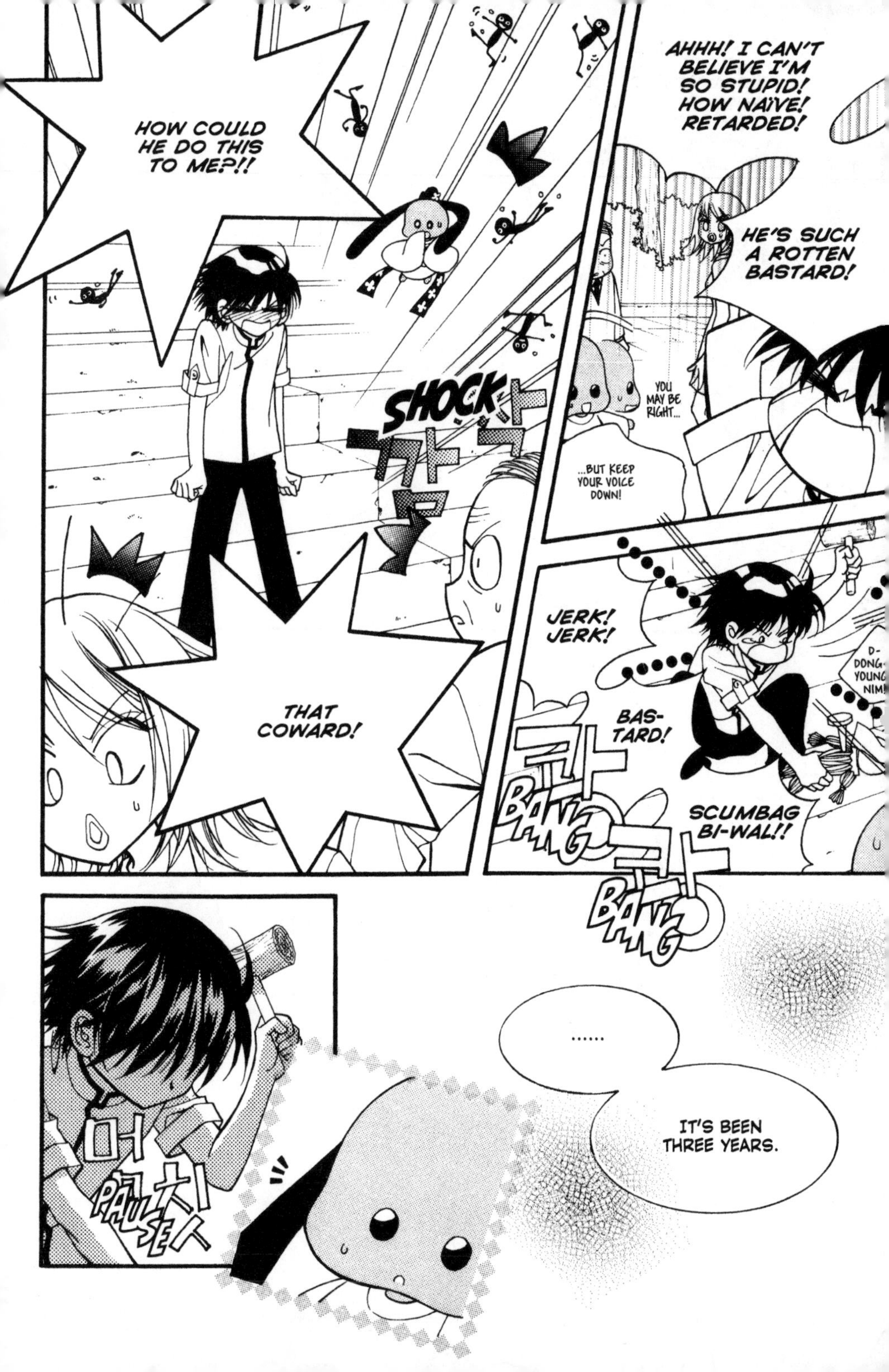
HOW COULD HE DO THIS TO ME?!!
SHOCK
THAT COWARD!
AHHH! I CAN'T BELIEVE I'M SO STUPID! HOW NAÏVE! RETARDED!
HE'S SUCH A ROTTEN BASTARD!
YOU MAY BE RIGHT...
...BUT KEEP YOUR VOICE DOWN!
JERK! JERK!
BAS-TARD!
SCUMBAG BI-WAL!!
D-DONG-YOUNG-NIM!
BANG
BANG
PAUSE
......
IT'S BEEN THREE YEARS.

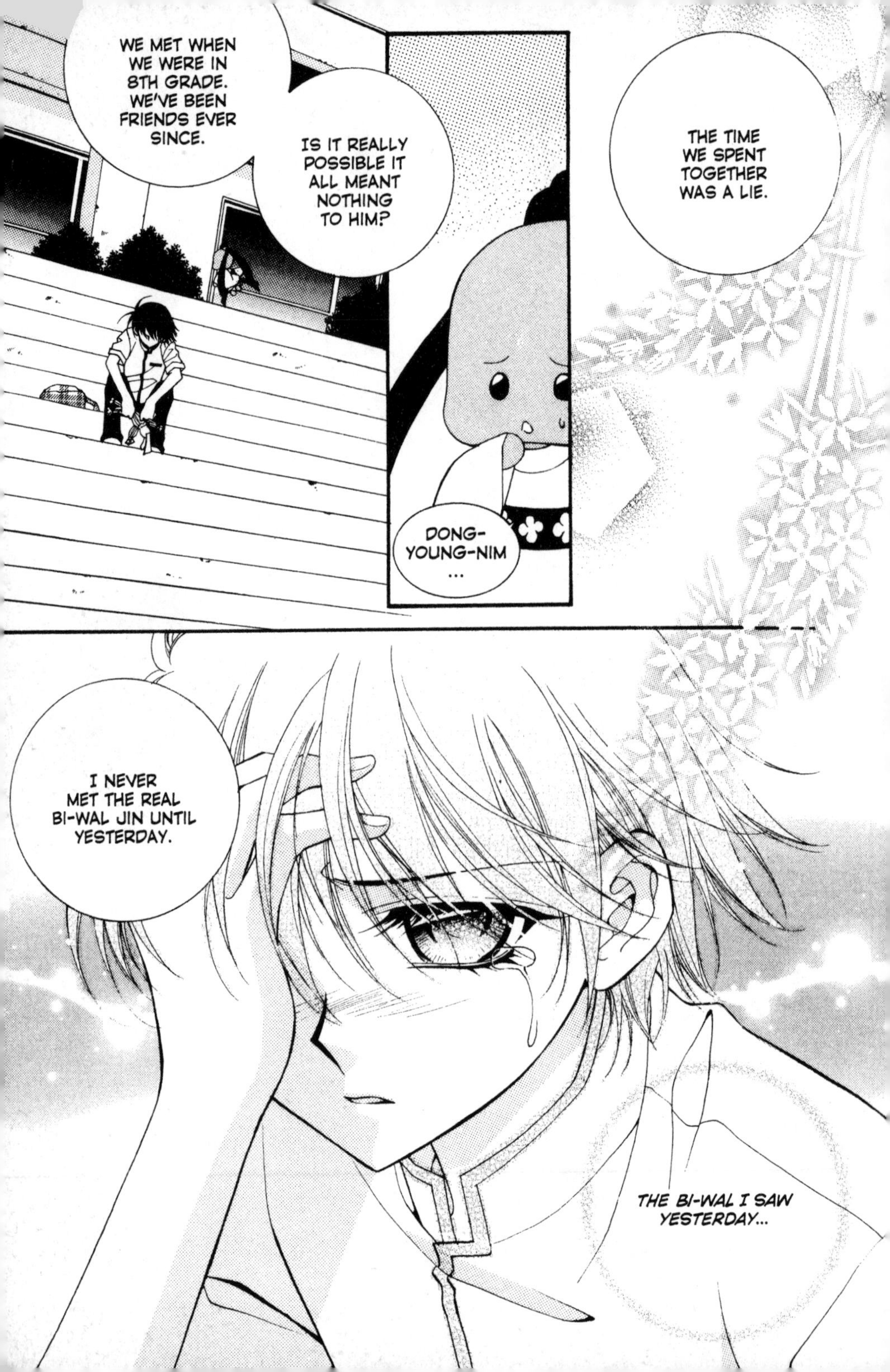
WE MET WHEN WE WERE IN 8TH GRADE. WE'VE BEEN FRIENDS EVER SINCE.
IS IT REALLY POSSIBLE IT ALL MEANT NOTHING TO HIM?
DONG-YOUNG-NIM ...
THE TIME WE SPENT TOGETHER WAS A LIE.
I NEVER MET THE REAL BI-WAL JIN UNTIL YESTERDAY.
THE BI-WAL I SAW YESTERDAY...

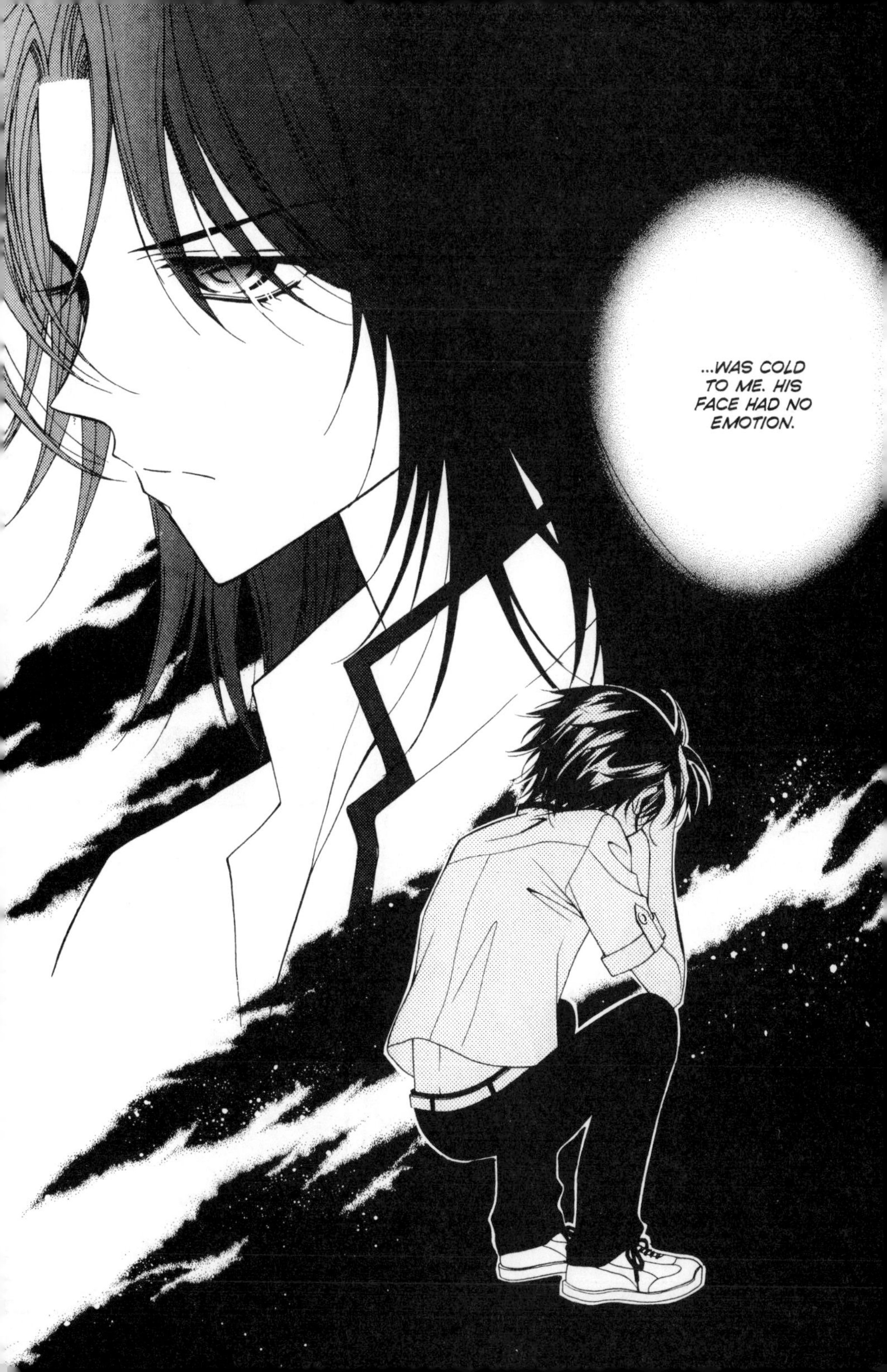
...WAS COLD TO ME. HIS FACE HAD NO EMOTION.

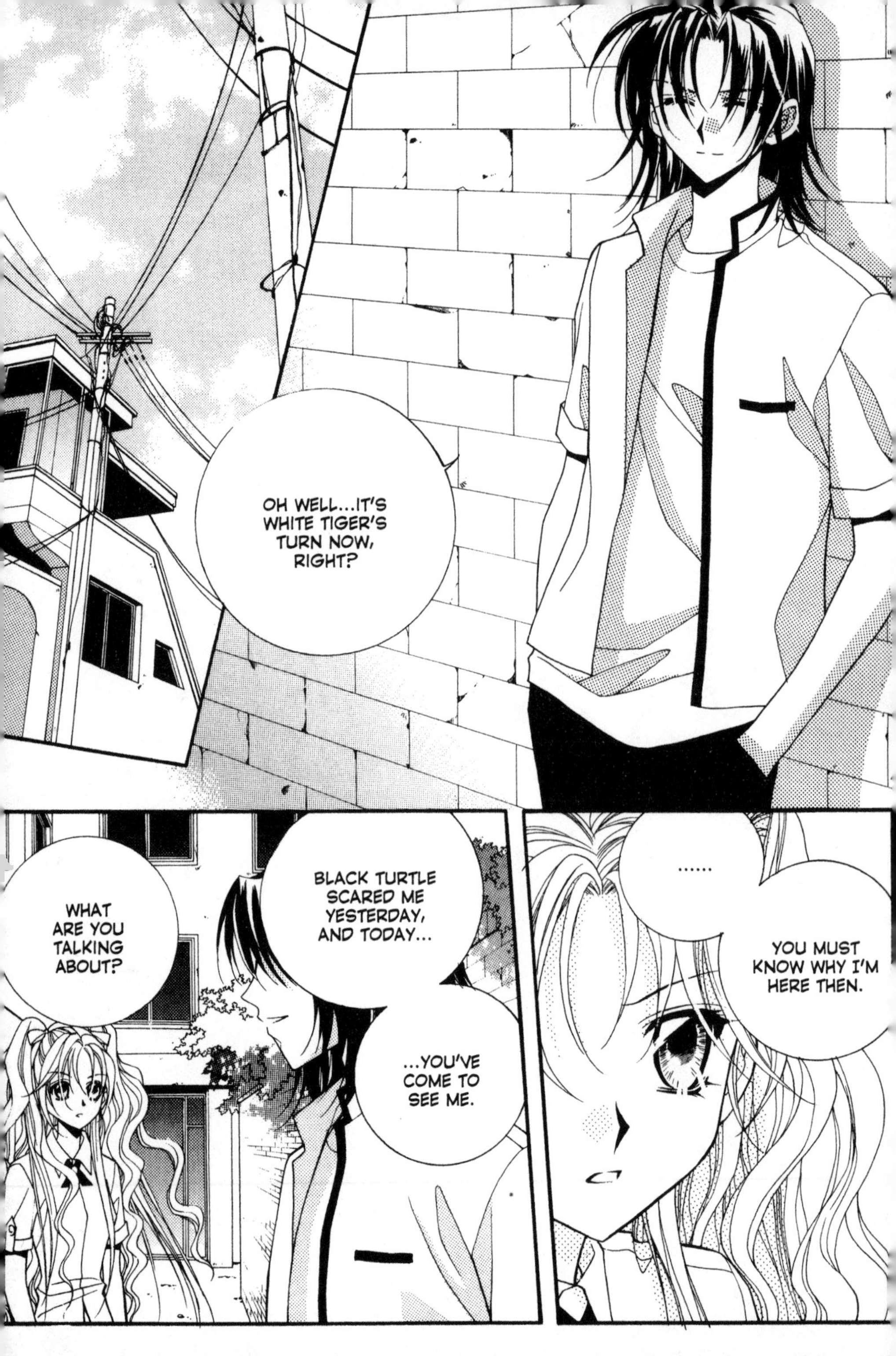
OH WELL...IT'S WHITE TIGER'S TURN NOW, RIGHT?
WHAT ARE YOU TALKING ABOUT?
BLACK TURTLE SCARED ME YESTERDAY, AND TODAY...
...YOU'VE COME TO SEE ME.
......
YOU MUST KNOW WHY I'M HERE THEN.

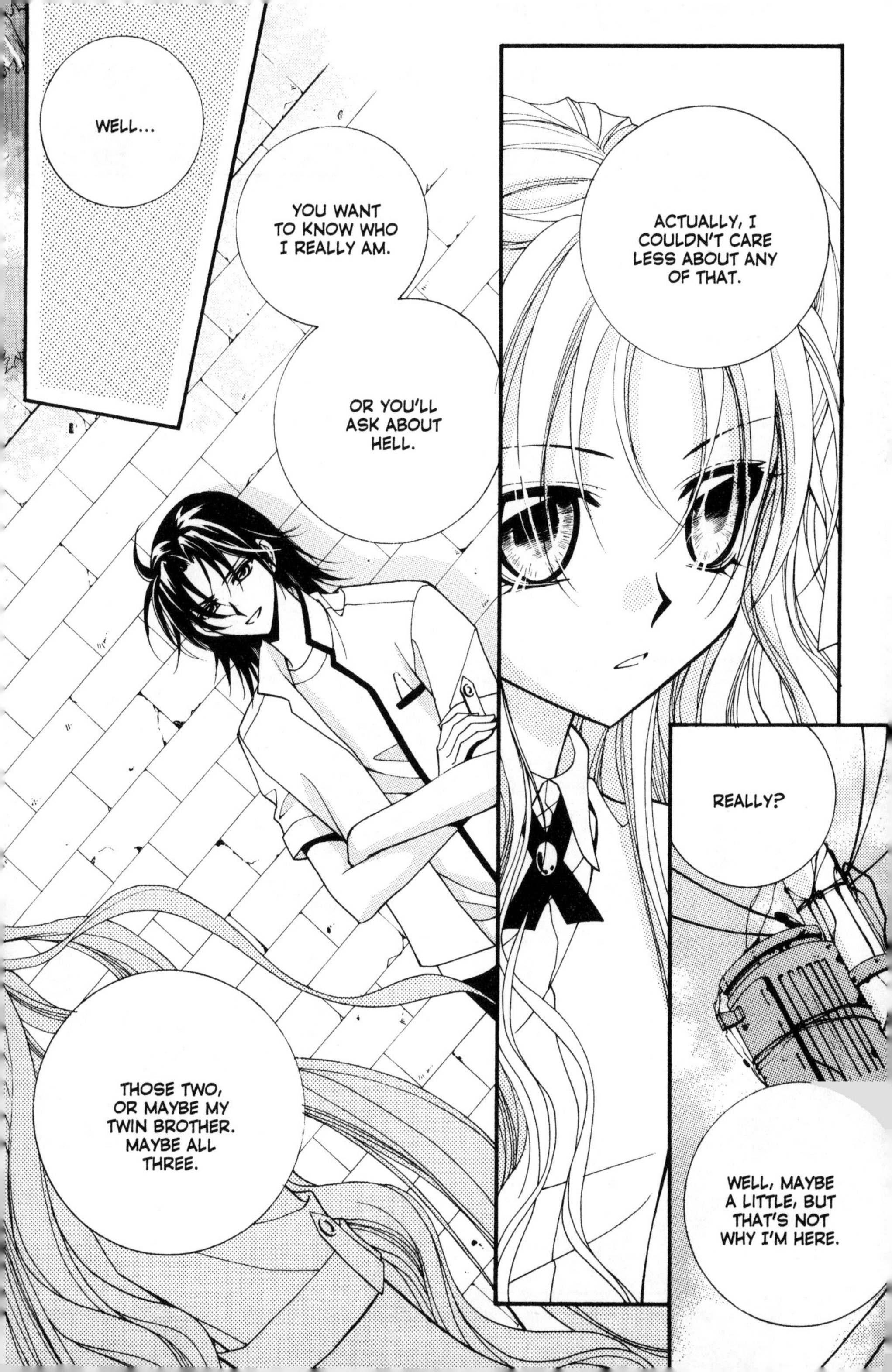
WELL...
YOU WANT TO KNOW WHO I REALLY AM.
OR YOU'LL ASK ABOUT HELL.
THOSE TWO, OR MAYBE MY TWIN BROTHER. MAYBE ALL THREE.
ACTUALLY, I COULDN'T CARE LESS ABOUT ANY OF THAT.
REALLY?
WELL, MAYBE A LITTLE, BUT THAT'S NOT WHY I'M HERE.

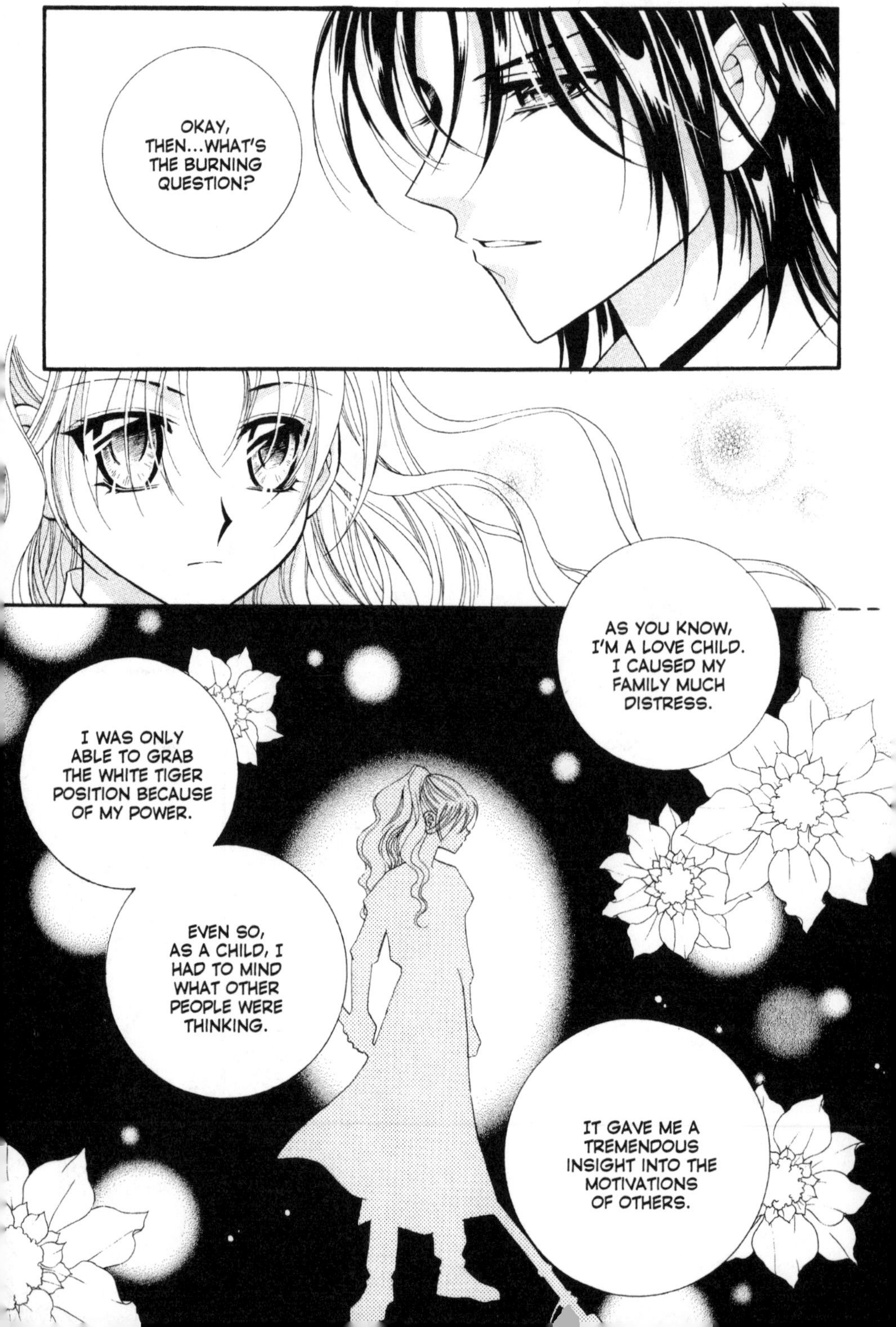
OKAY, THEN...WHAT'S THE BURNING QUESTION?
AS YOU KNOW, I'M A LOVE CHILD. I CAUSED MY FAMILY MUCH DISTRESS.
I WAS ONLY ABLE TO GRAB THE WHITE TIGER POSITION BECAUSE OF MY POWER.
EVEN SO, AS A CHILD, I HAD TO MIND WHAT OTHER PEOPLE WERE THINKING.
IT GAVE ME A TREMENDOUS INSIGHT INTO THE MOTIVATIONS OF OTHERS.

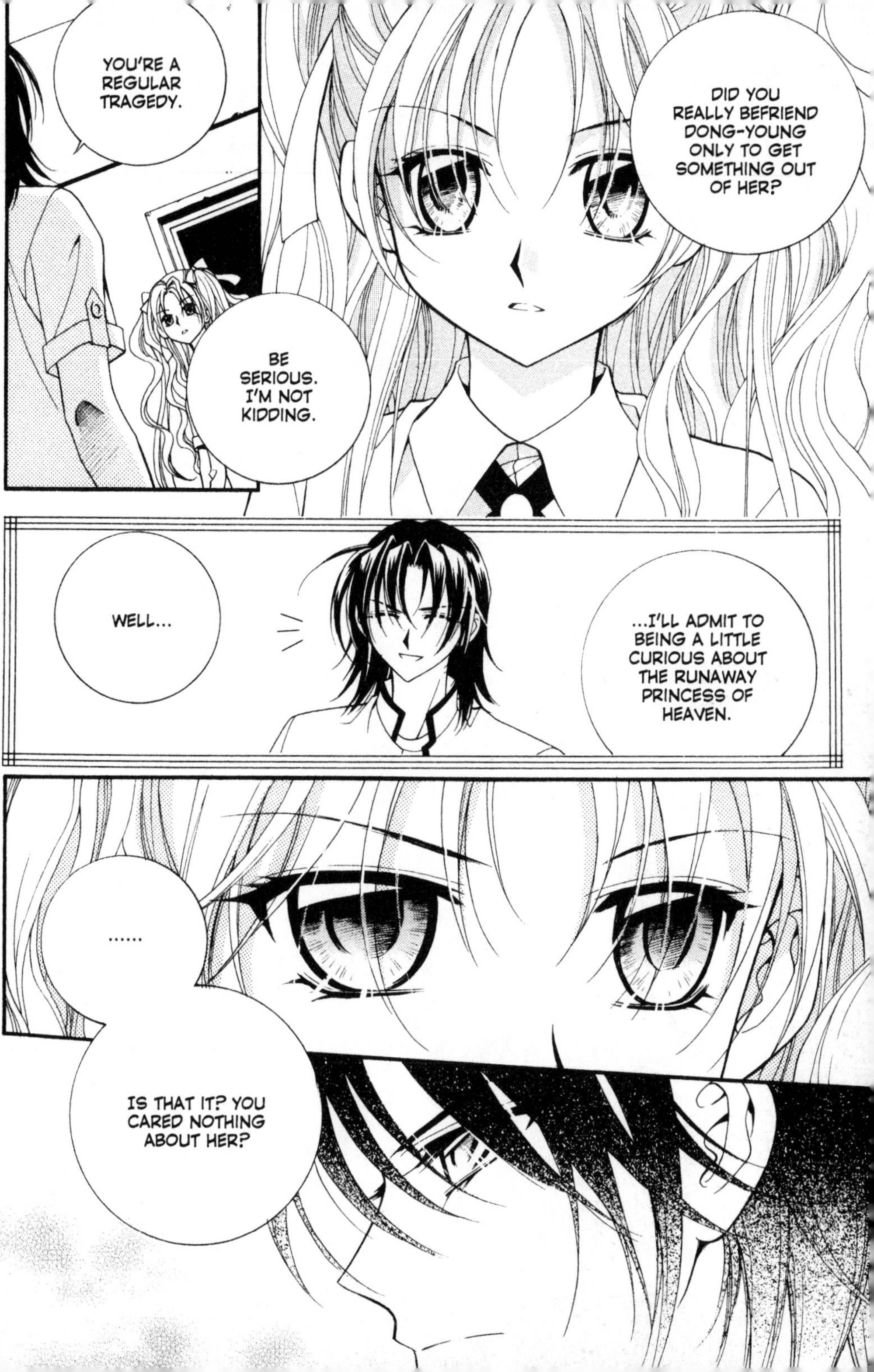
YOU'RE A REGULAR TRAGEDY.
BE SERIOUS. I'M NOT KIDDING.
DID YOU REALLY BEFRIEND DONG-YOUNG ONLY TO GET SOMETHING OUT OF HER?
WELL...
...I'LL ADMIT TO BEING A LITTLE CURIOUS ABOUT THE RUNAWAY PRINCESS OF HEAVEN.
......
IS THAT IT? YOU CARED NOTHING ABOUT HER?

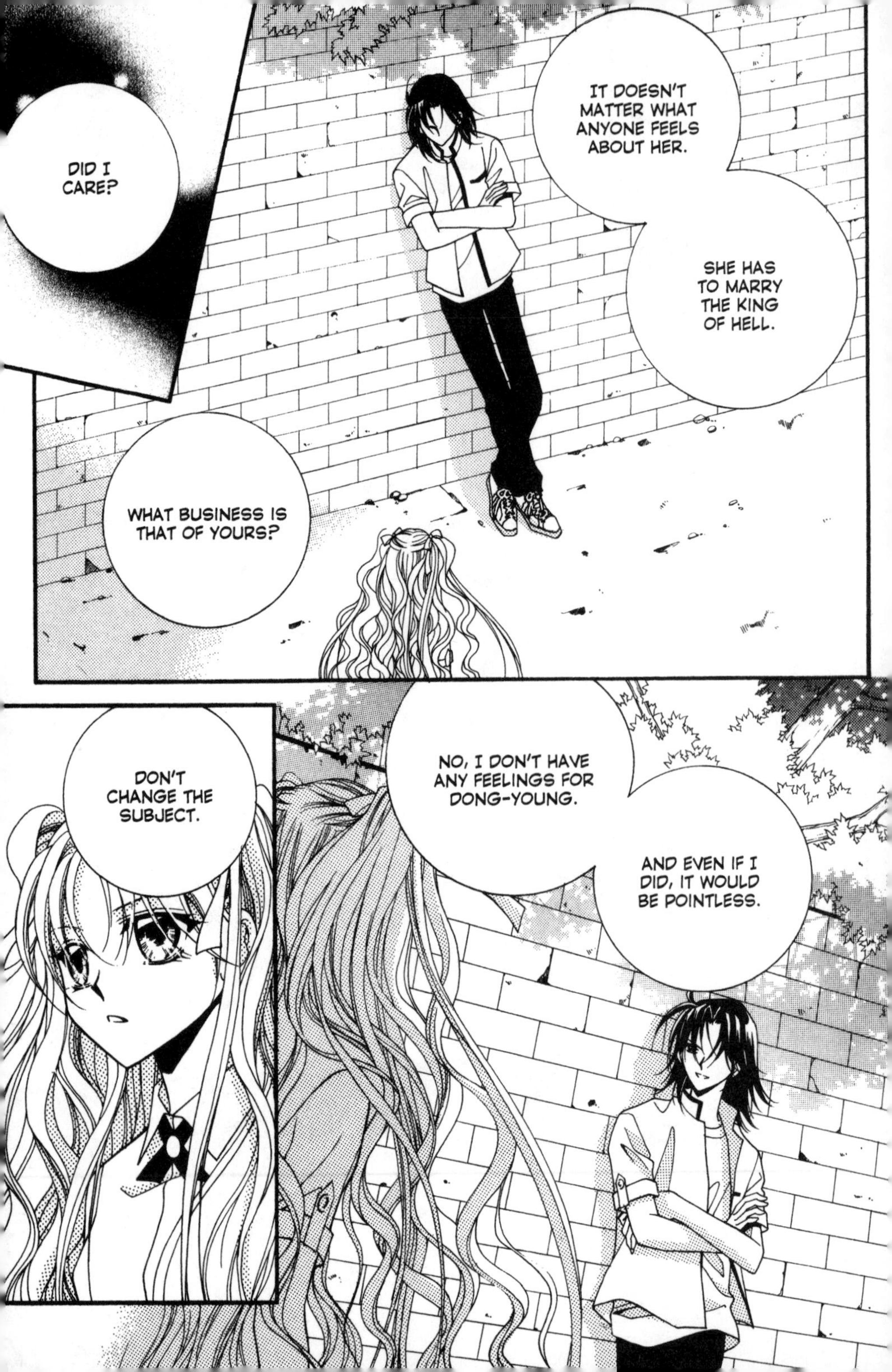
DID I CARE?
IT DOESN'T MATTER WHAT ANYONE FEELS ABOUT HER.
SHE HAS TO MARRY THE KING OF HELL.
WHAT BUSINESS IS THAT OF YOURS?
DON'T CHANGE THE SUBJECT.
NO, I DON'T HAVE ANY FEELINGS FOR DONG-YOUNG.
AND EVEN IF I DID, IT WOULD BE POINTLESS.

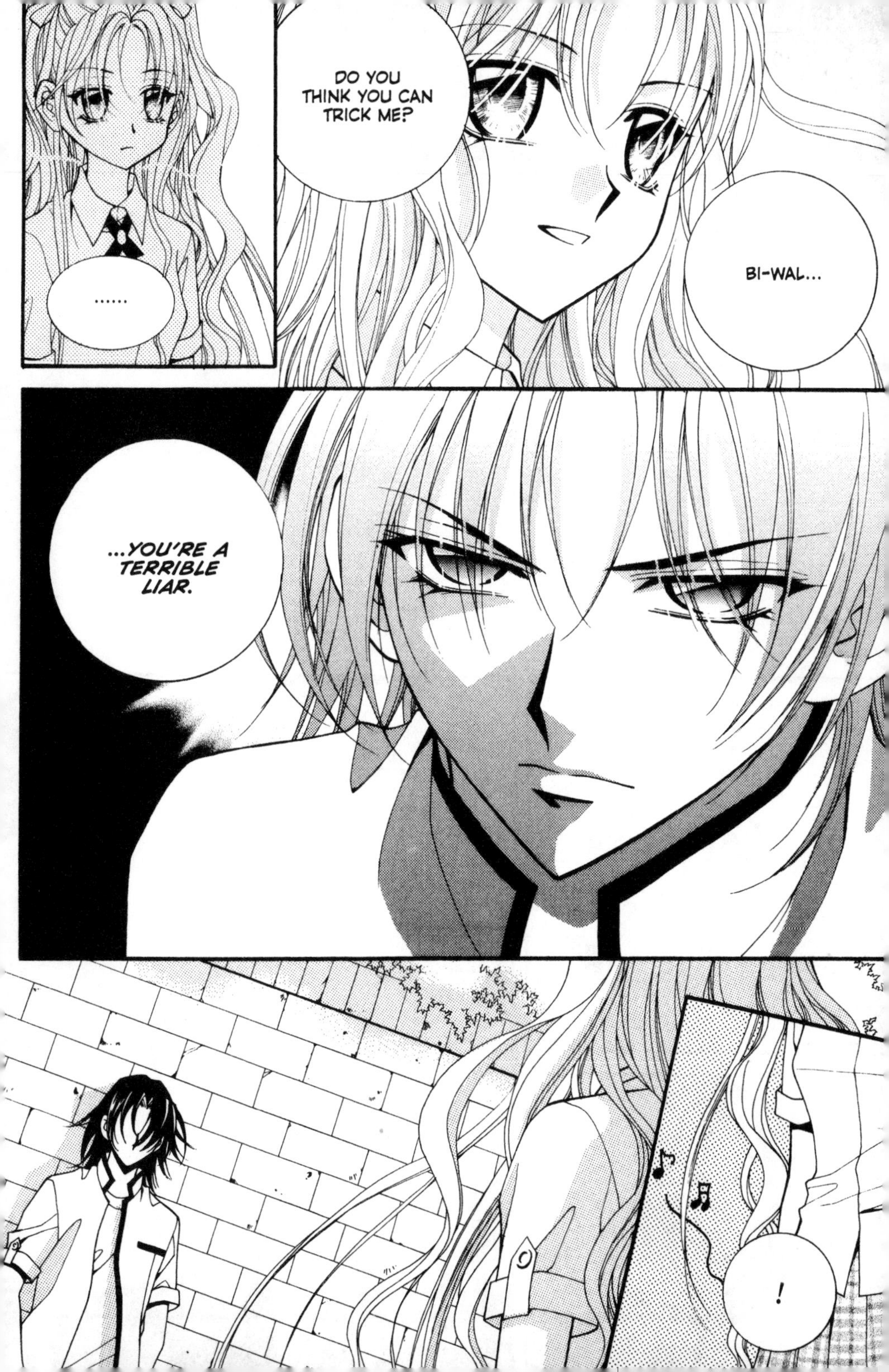
BI-WAL...
DO YOU THINK YOU CAN TRICK ME?
......
...YOU'RE A TERRIBLE LIAR.
!

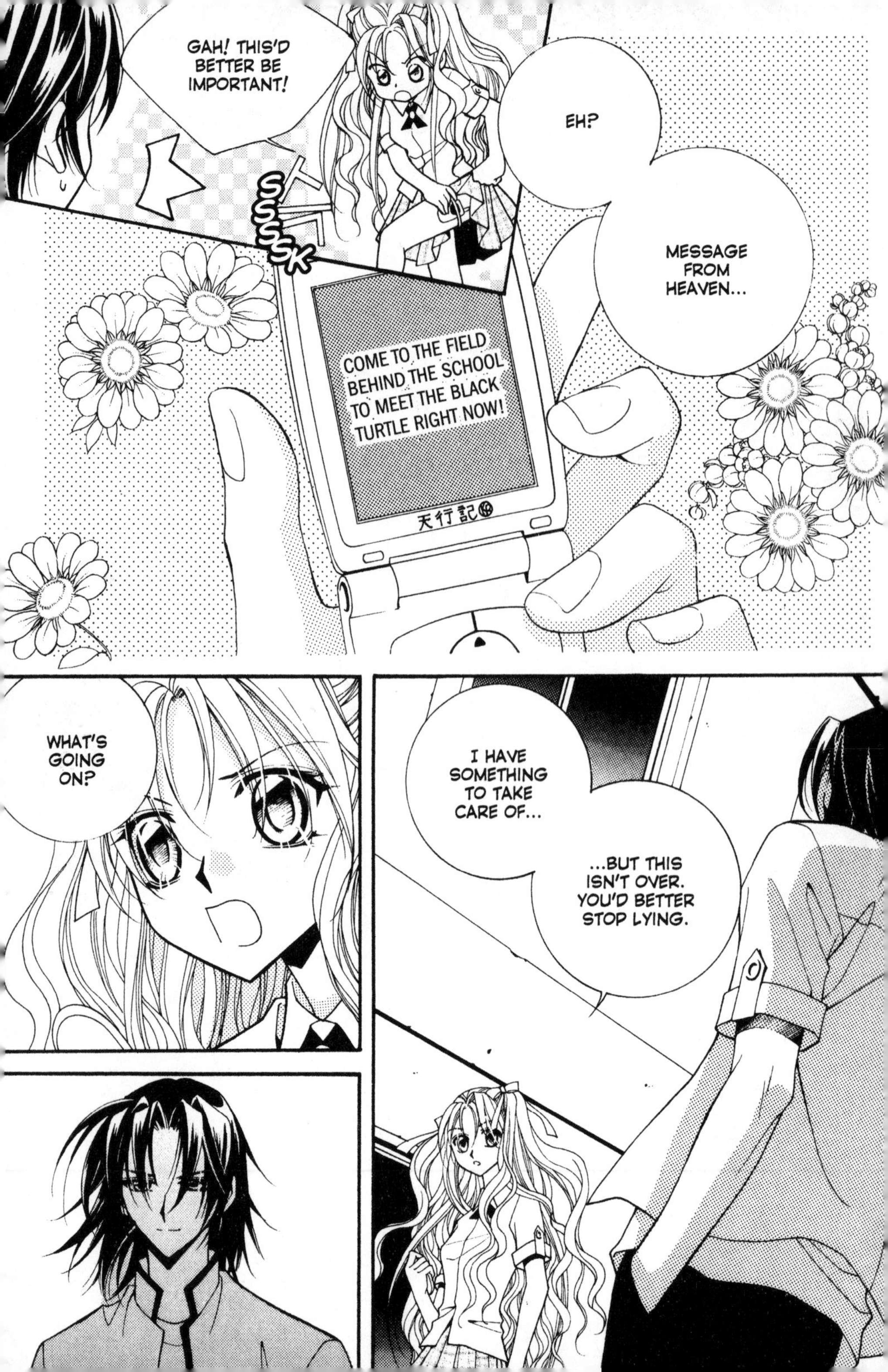
GAH! THIS'D BETTER BE IMPORTANT!
SSSSK
EH?
MESSAGE FROM HEAVEN...
COME TO THE FIELD BEHIND THE SCHOOL TO MEET THE BLACK TURTLE RIGHT NOW!
天行記
I HAVE SOMETHING TO TAKE CARE OF...
...BUT THIS ISN'T OVER. YOU'D BETTER STOP LYING.
WHAT'S GOING ON?

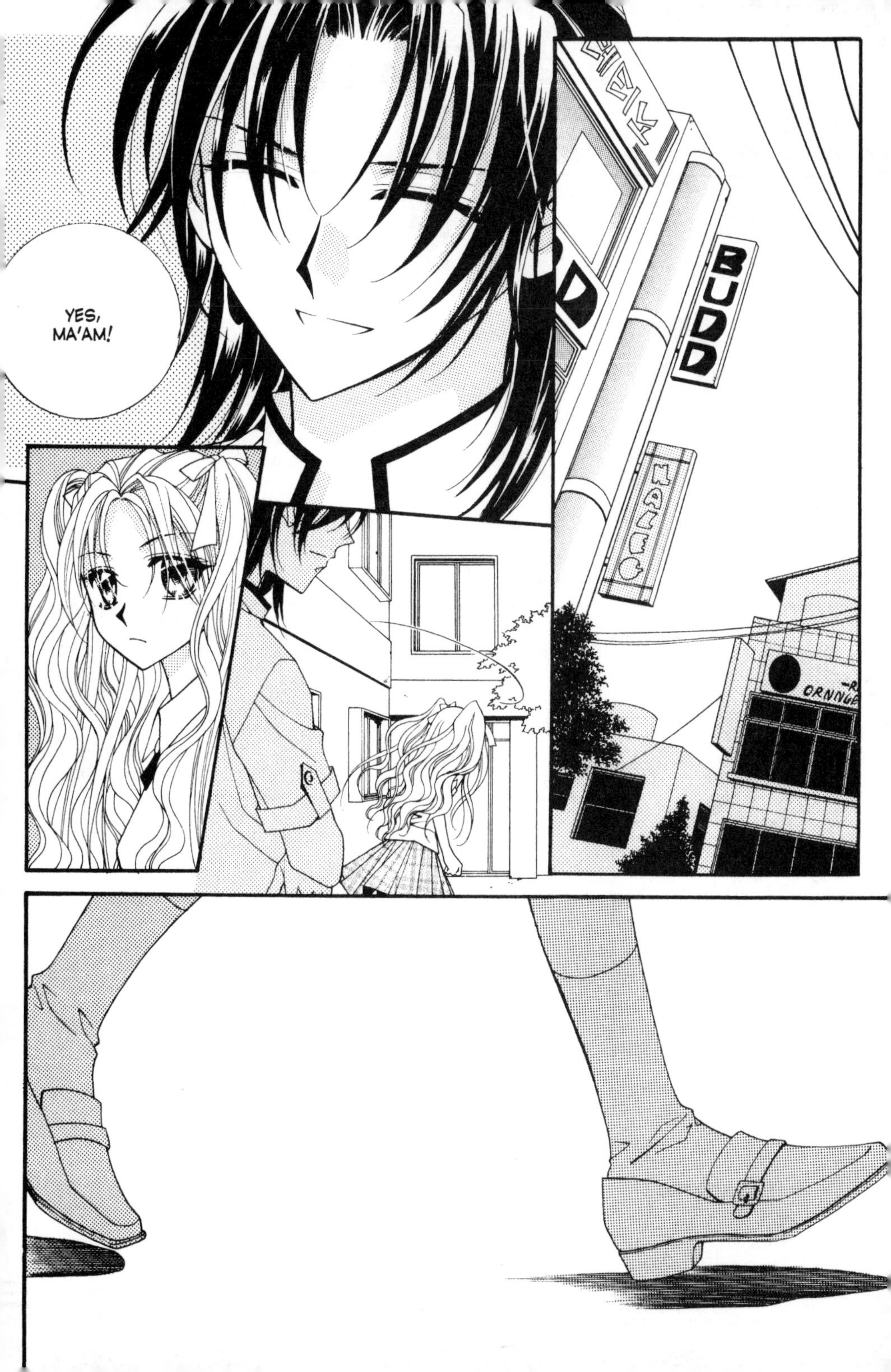
YES, MA'AM!
BUDD
ORNNGE

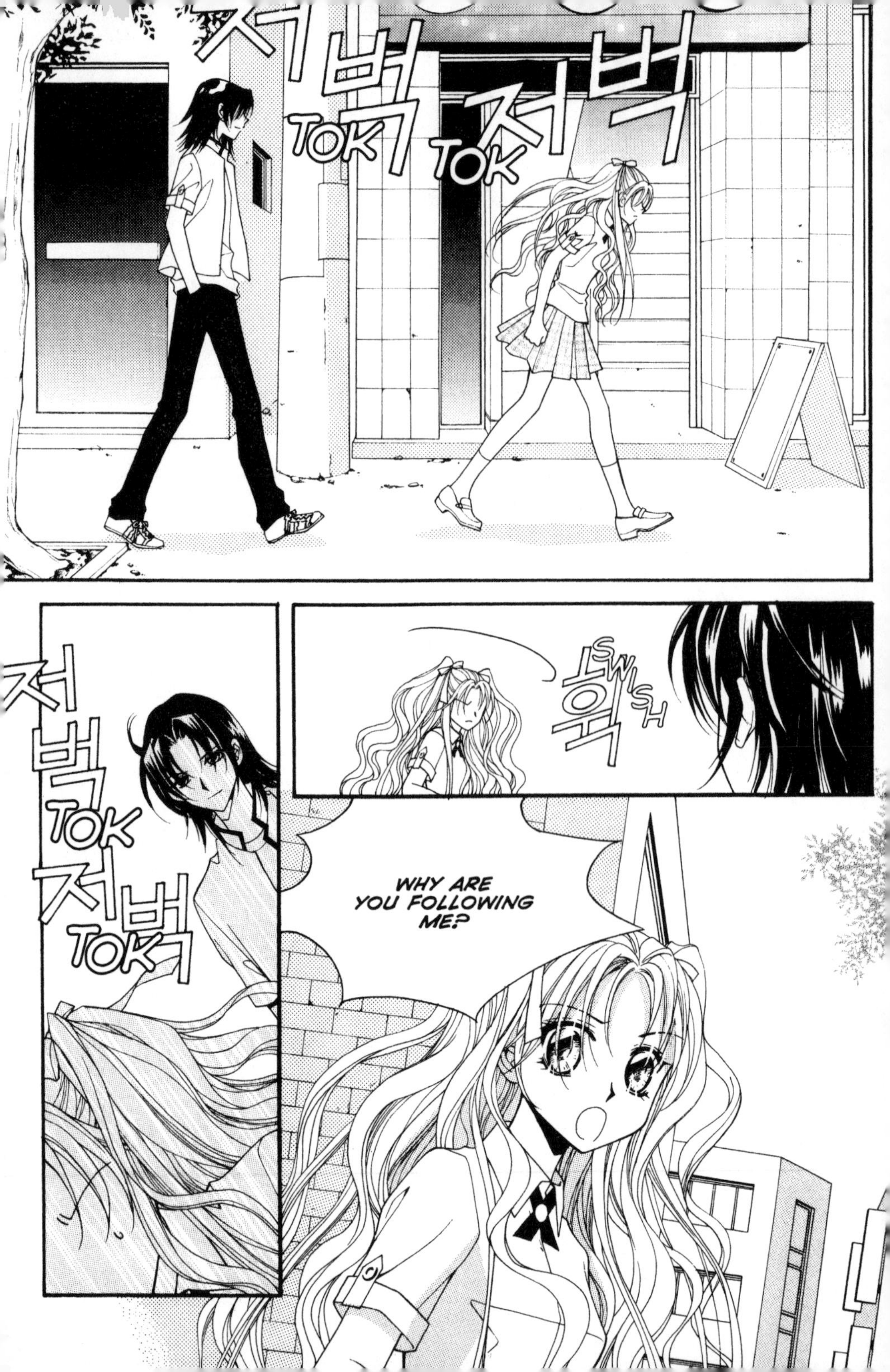
저벅
TOK
저벅
TOK
휘익
SWISH
저벅
TOK
저벅
TOK
WHY ARE YOU FOLLOWING ME?

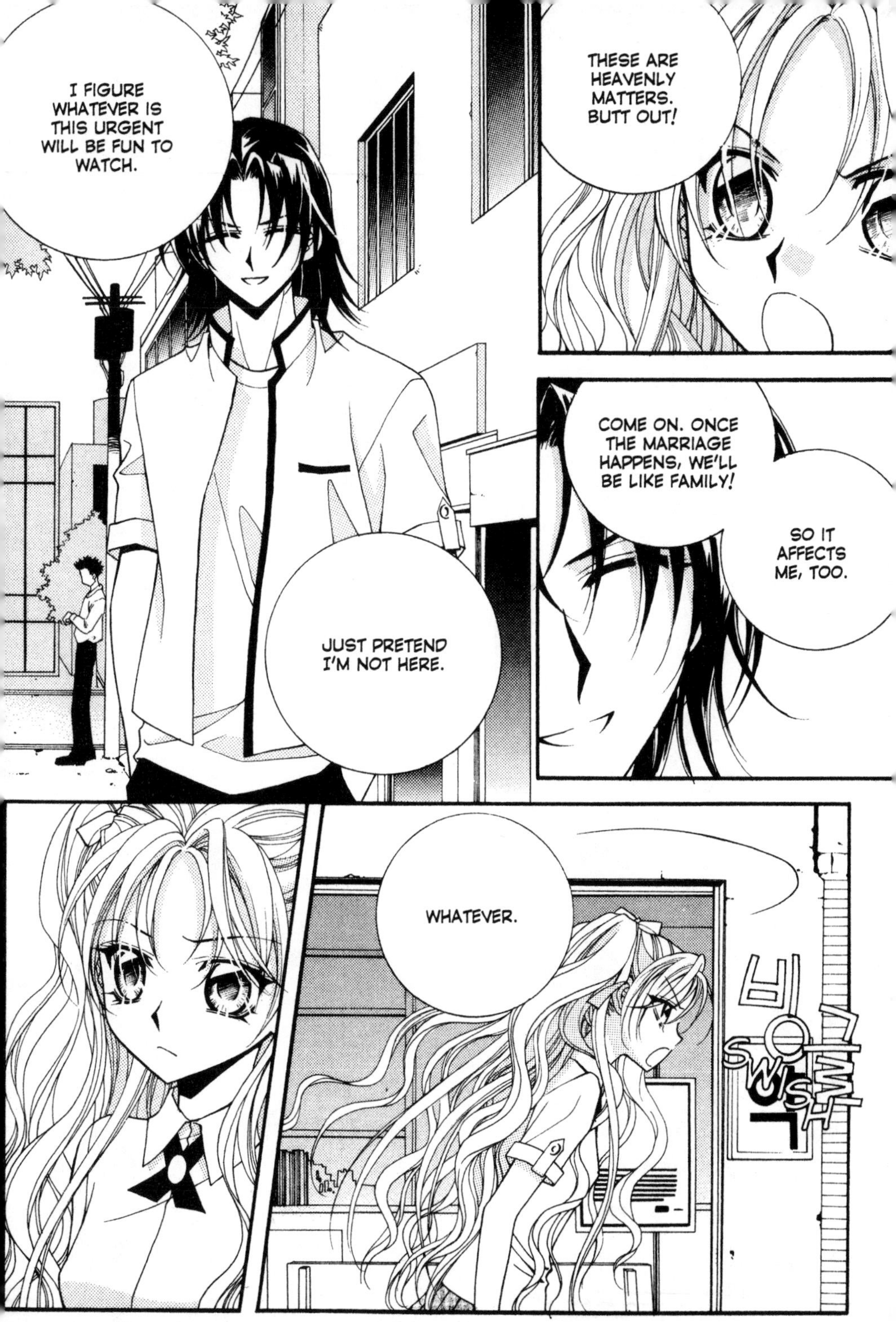
THESE ARE HEAVENLY MATTERS. BUTT OUT!
I FIGURE WHATEVER IS THIS URGENT WILL BE FUN TO WATCH.
JUST PRETEND I'M NOT HERE.
COME ON. ONCE THE MARRIAGE HAPPENS, WE'LL BE LIKE FAMILY!
SO IT AFFECTS ME, TOO.
WHATEVER.
SWISH

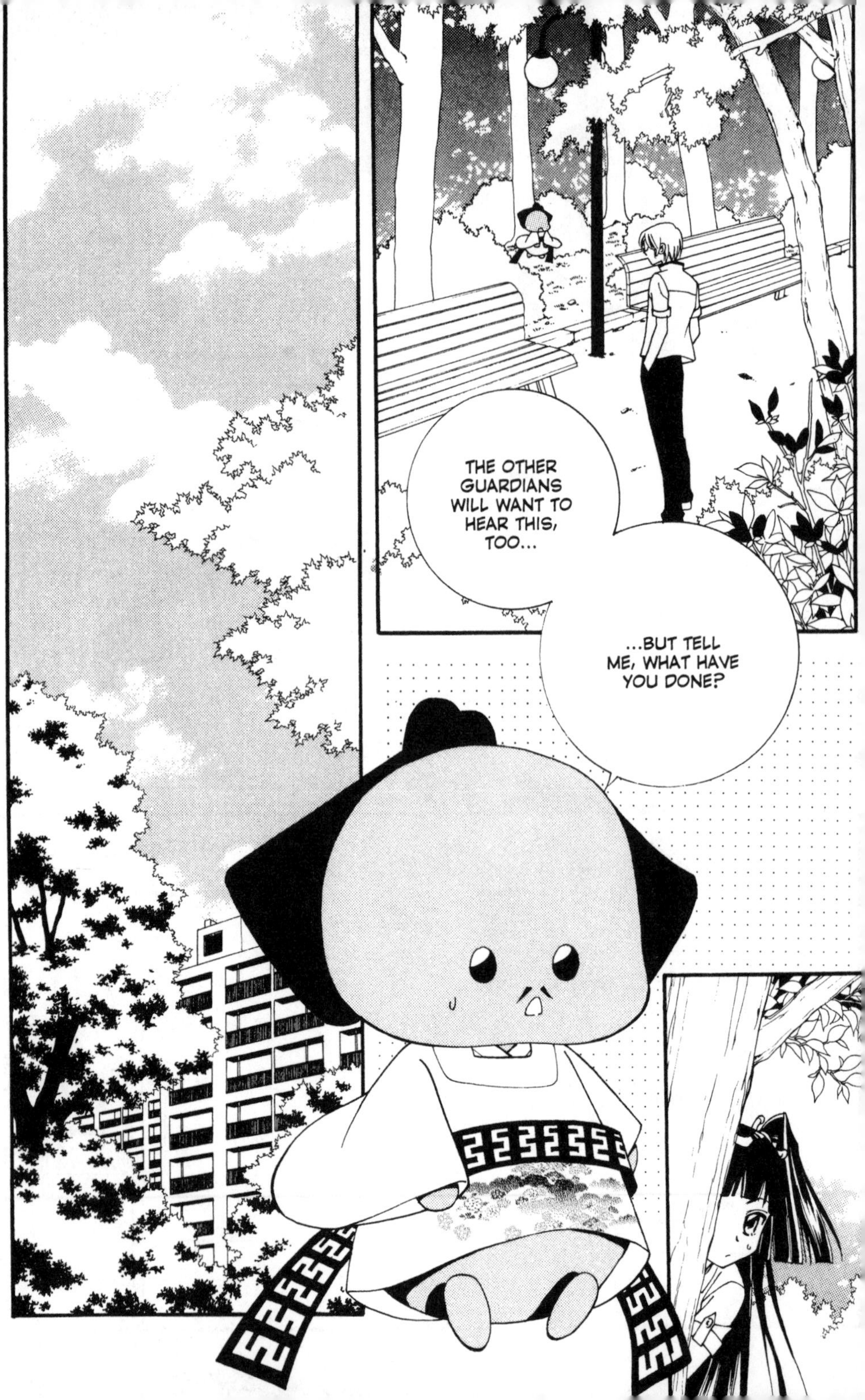
THE OTHER GUARDIANS WILL WANT TO HEAR THIS, TOO...
...BUT TELL ME, WHAT HAVE YOU DONE?

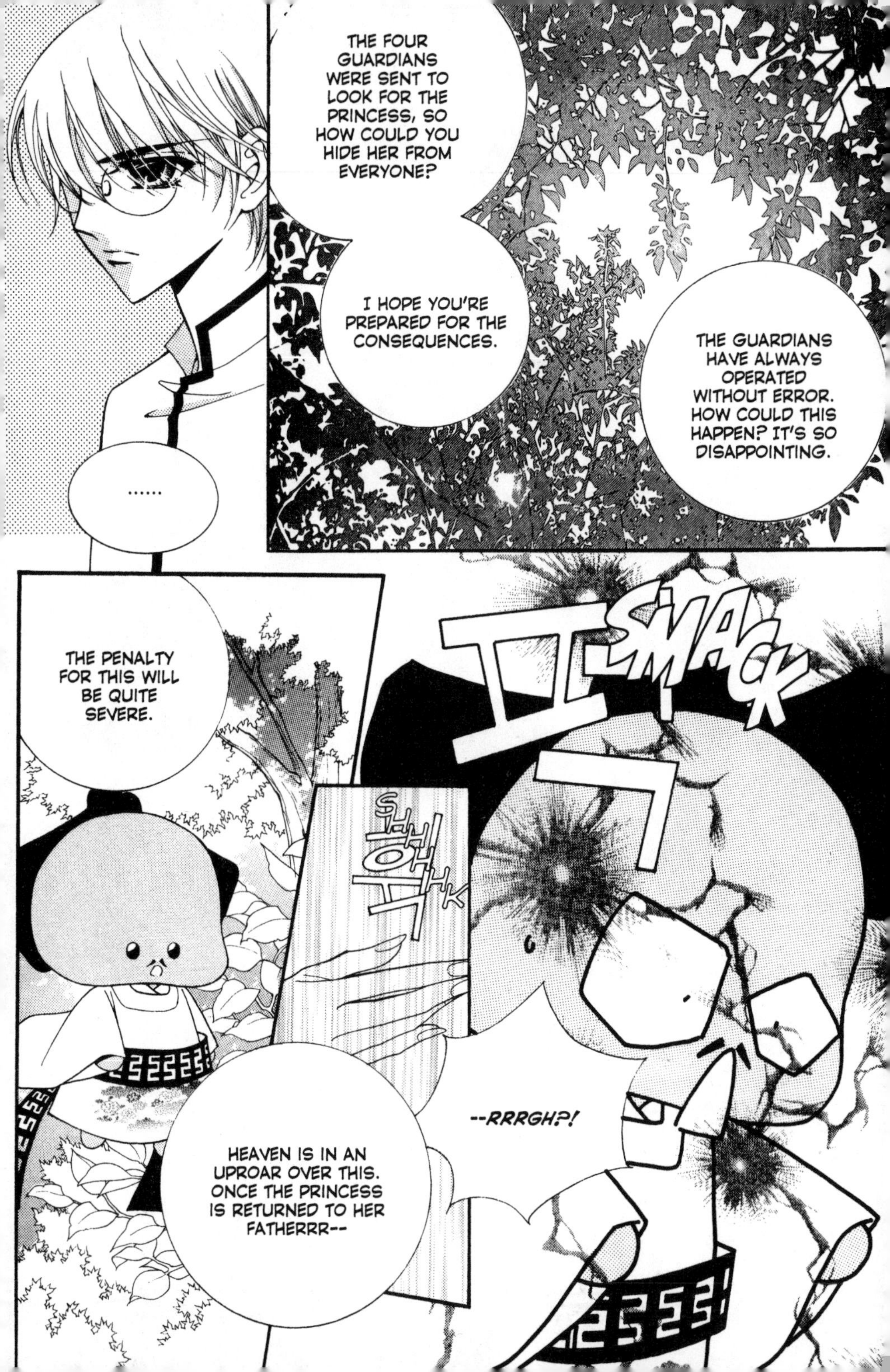
THE GUARDIANS HAVE ALWAYS OPERATED WITHOUT ERROR. HOW COULD THIS HAPPEN? IT'S SO DISAPPOINTING.
THE FOUR GUARDIANS WERE SENT TO LOOK FOR THE PRINCESS, SO HOW COULD YOU HIDE HER FROM EVERYONE?
I HOPE YOU'RE PREPARED FOR THE CONSEQUENCES.
......
THE PENALTY FOR THIS WILL BE QUITE SEVERE.
HEAVEN IS IN AN UPROAR OVER THIS. ONCE THE PRINCESS IS RETURNED TO HER FATHERRR--
SHHHOOHHHK
SMACK
--RRRGH?!

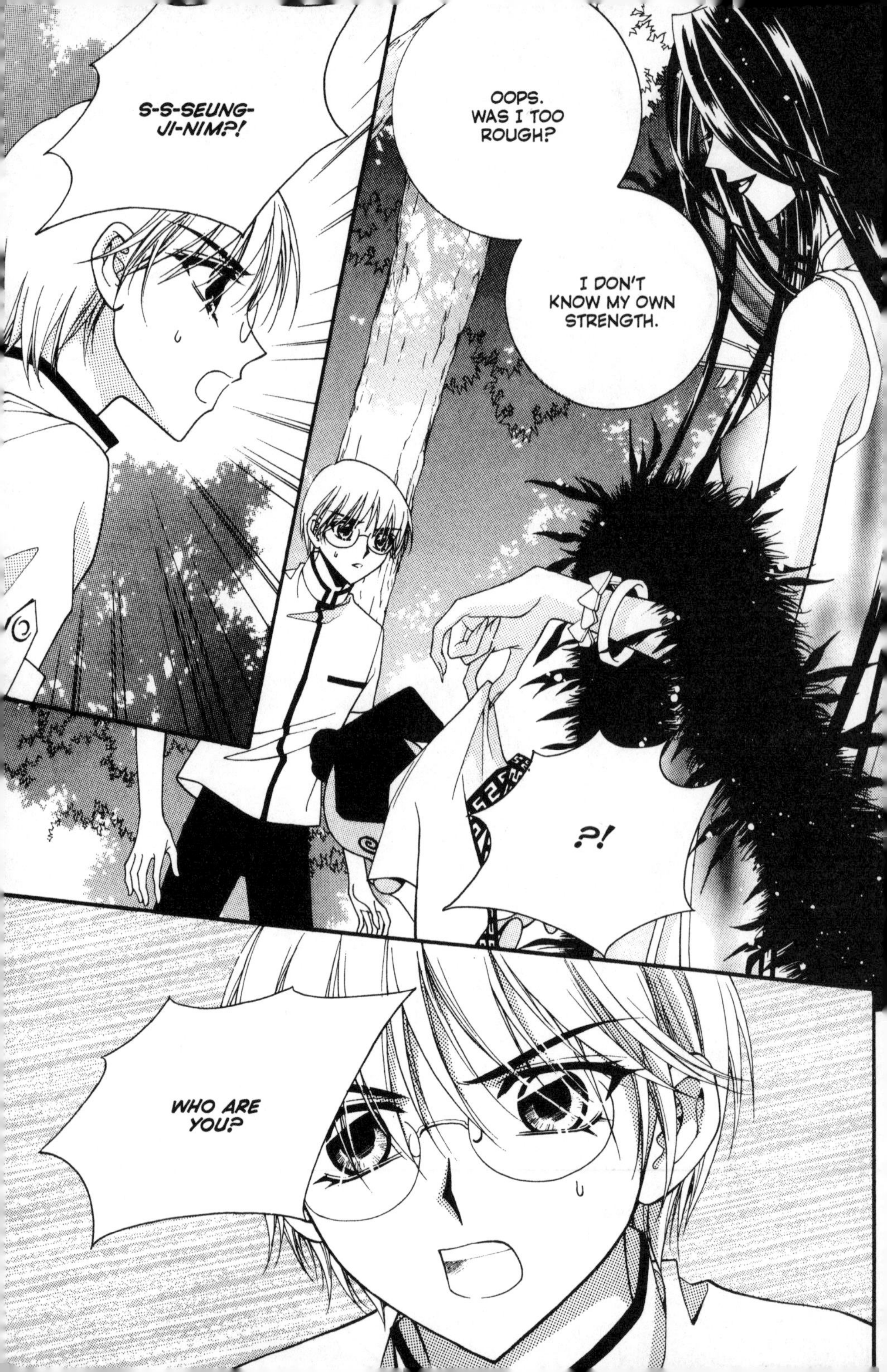
OOPS. WAS I TOO ROUGH?
I DON'T KNOW MY OWN STRENGTH.
S-S-SEUNG-JI-NIM?!
?!
WHO ARE YOU?

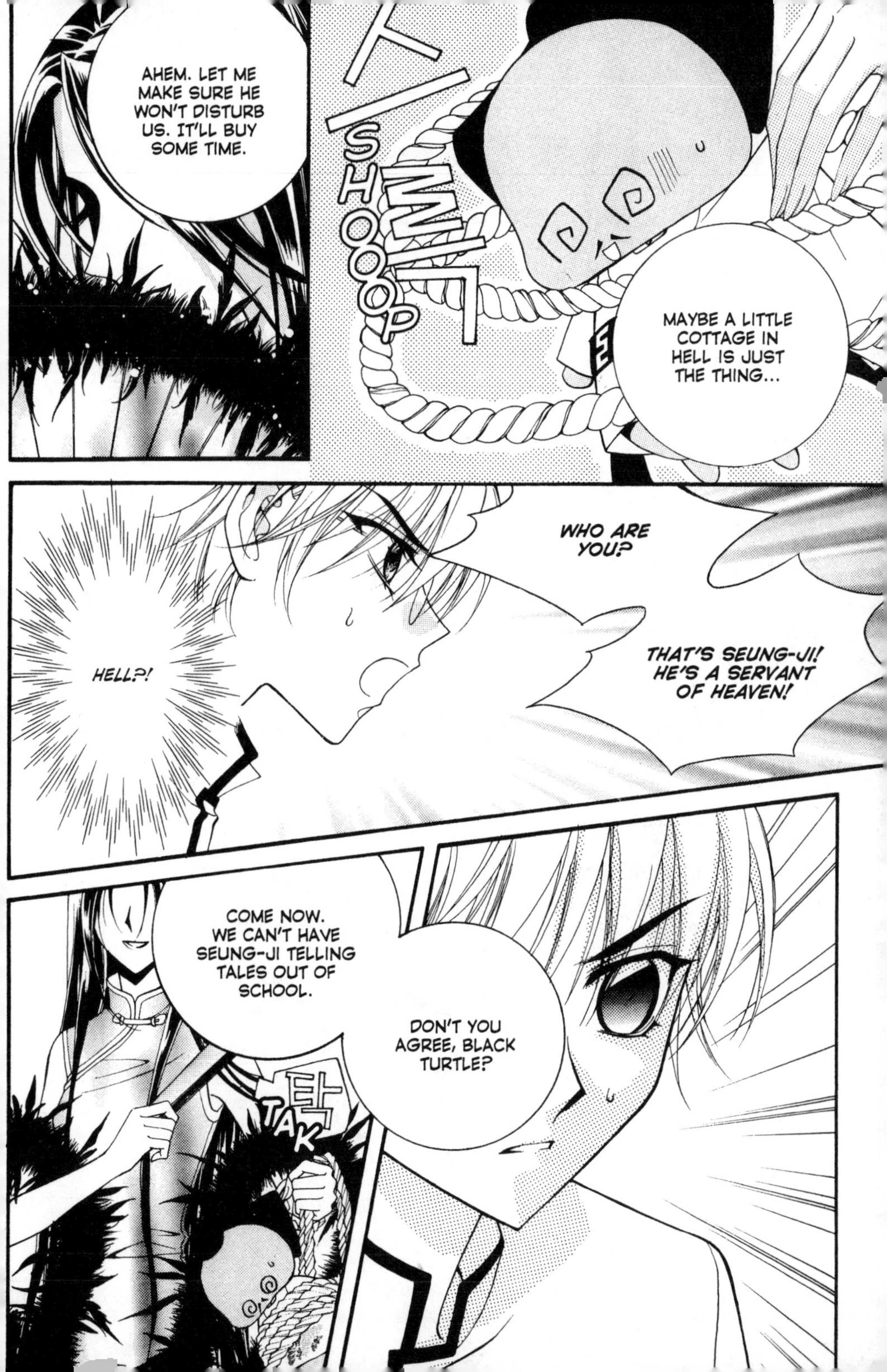

AHEM. LET ME MAKE SURE HE WON'T DISTURB US. IT'LL BUY SOME TIME.
SHOOOP
MAYBE A LITTLE COTTAGE IN HELL IS JUST THE THING...
HELL?!
WHO ARE YOU?
THAT'S SEUNG-JI! HE'S A SERVANT OF HEAVEN!
COME NOW. WE CAN'T HAVE SEUNG-JI TELLING TALES OUT OF SCHOOL.
DON'T YOU AGREE, BLACK TURTLE?
TAK

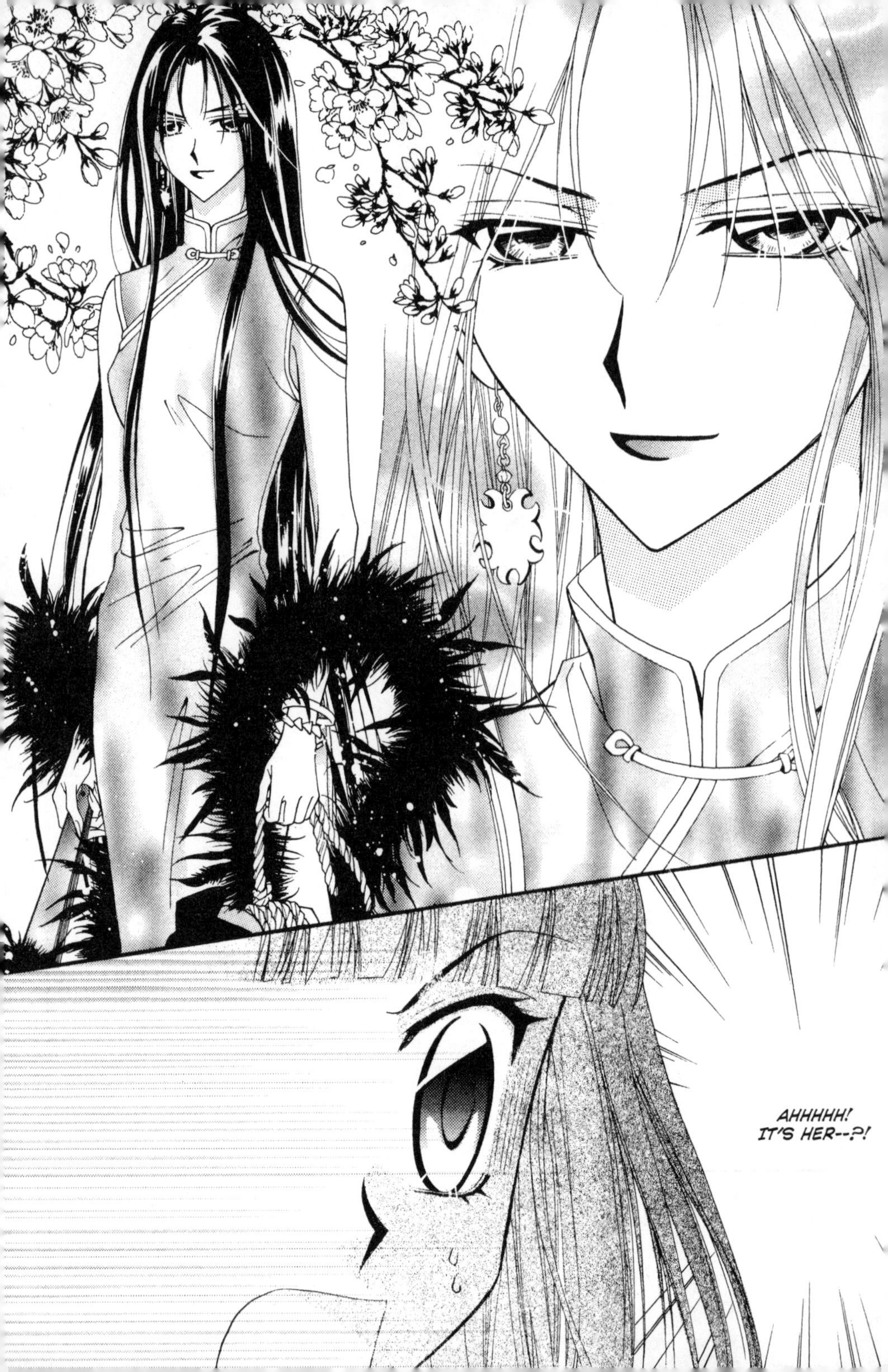
AHHHHH!
IT'S HER--?!

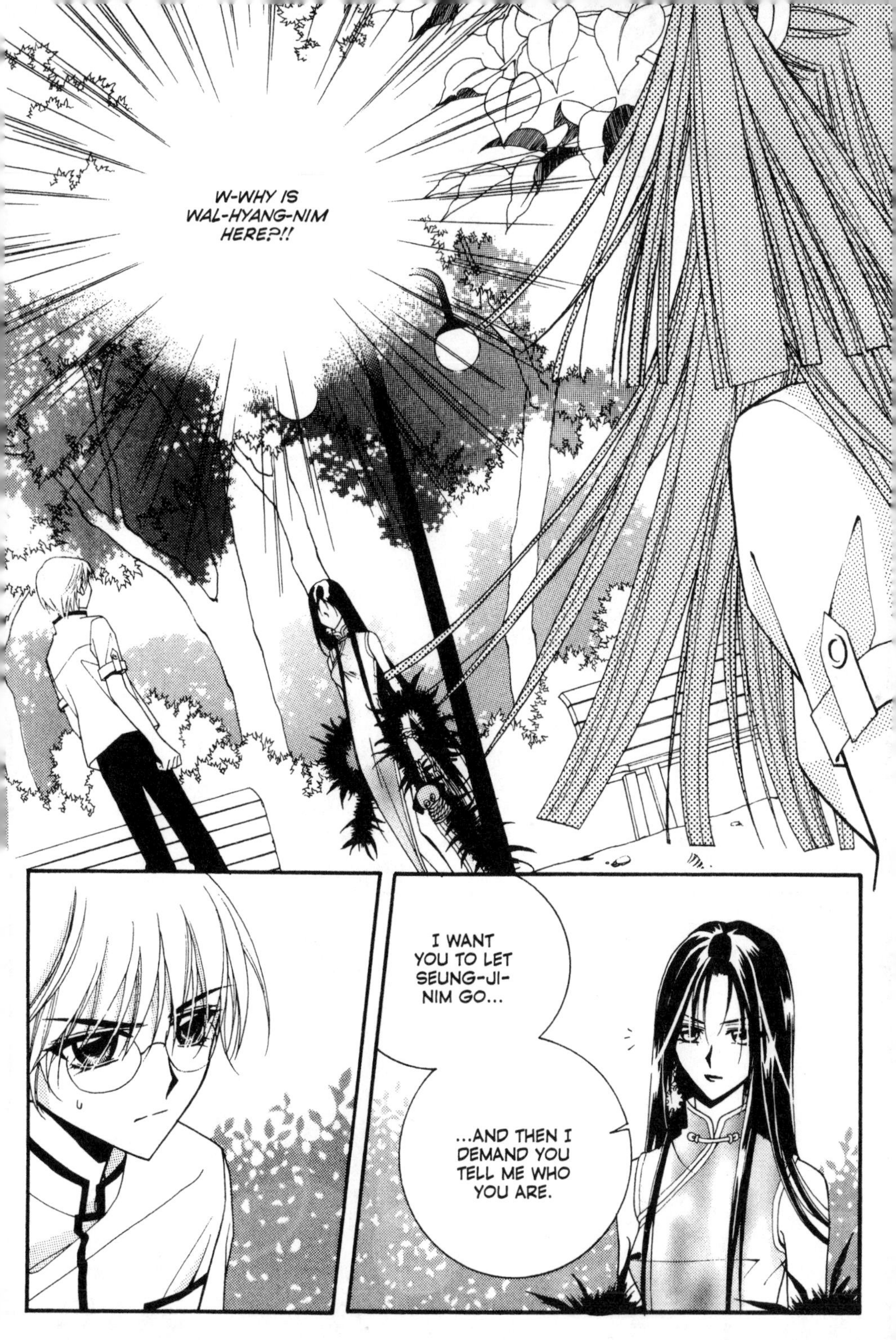
W-WHY IS WAL-HYANG-NIM HERE?!!
I WANT YOU TO LET SEUNG-JI-NIM GO...
...AND THEN I DEMAND YOU TELL ME WHO YOU ARE.

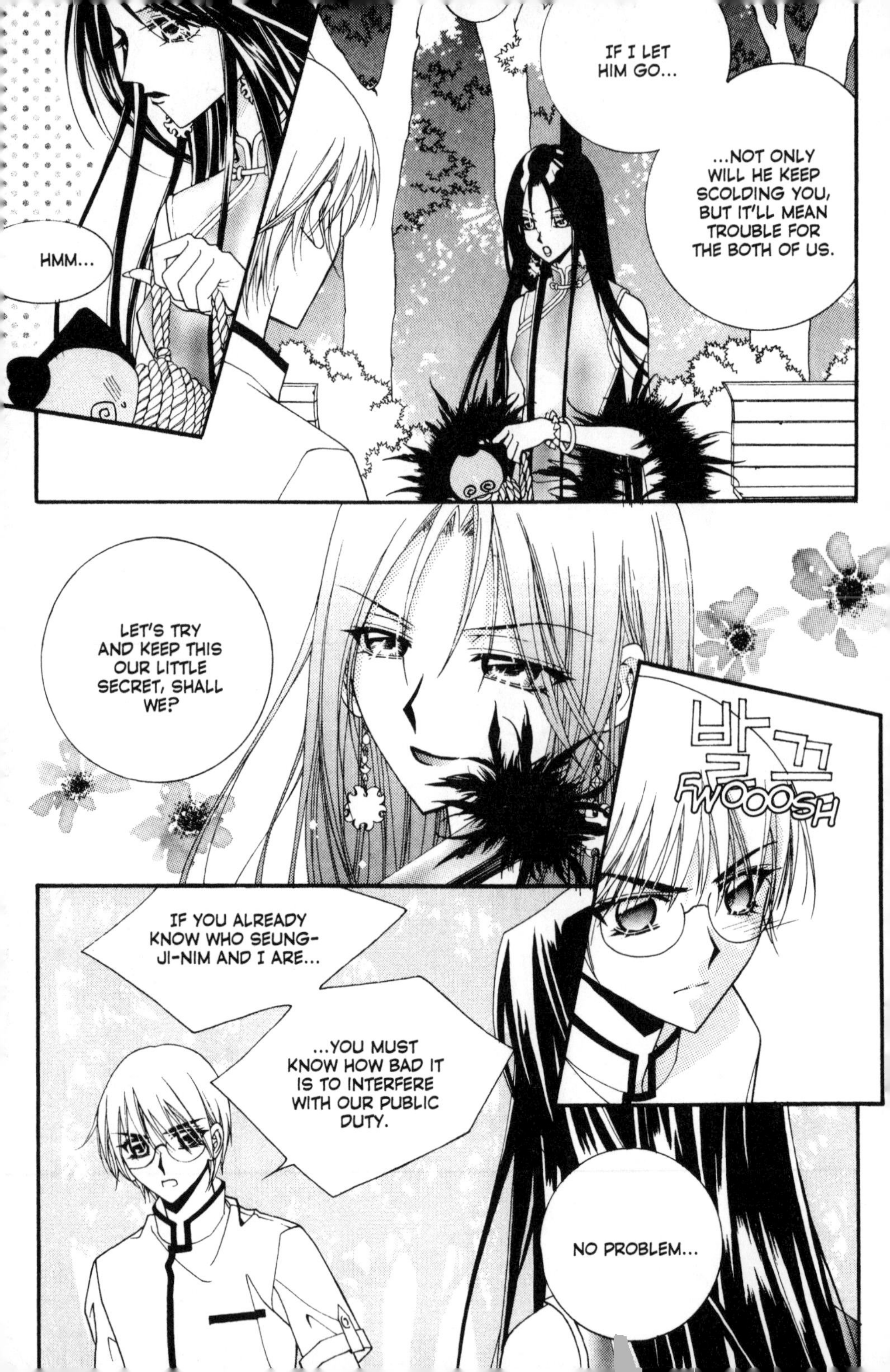
IF I LET HIM GO...
...NOT ONLY WILL HE KEEP SCOLDING YOU, BUT IT'LL MEAN TROUBLE FOR THE BOTH OF US.
HMM...
LET'S TRY AND KEEP THIS OUR LITTLE SECRET, SHALL WE?
발끈
FWOOOSH
IF YOU ALREADY KNOW WHO SEUNG-JI-NIM AND I ARE...
...YOU MUST KNOW HOW BAD IT IS TO INTERFERE WITH OUR PUBLIC DUTY.
NO PROBLEM...

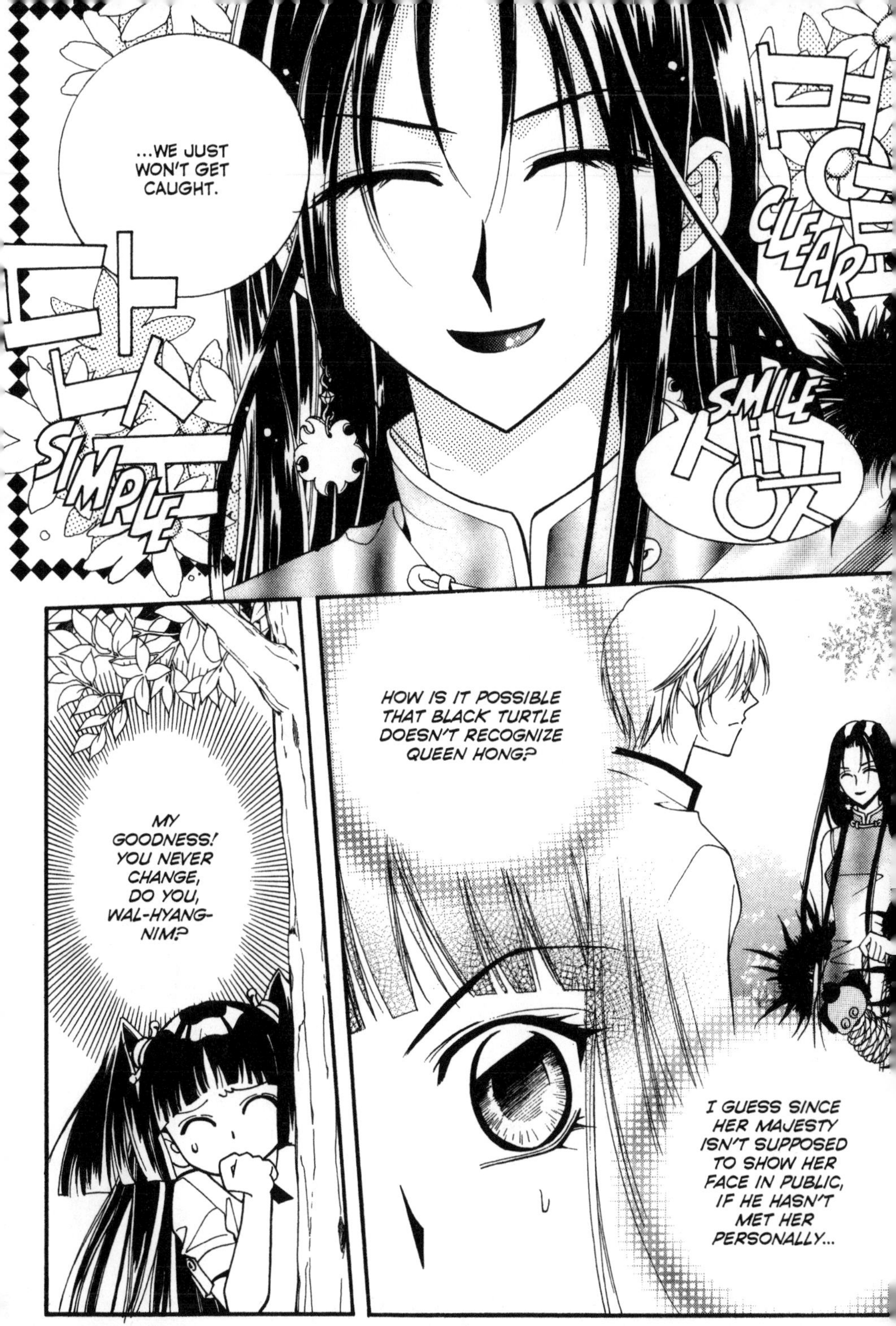
...WE JUST WON'T GET CAUGHT.
SIMPLE
CLEAR
SMILE
MY GOODNESS! YOU NEVER CHANGE, DO YOU, WAL-HYANG-NIM?
HOW IS IT POSSIBLE THAT BLACK TURTLE DOESN'T RECOGNIZE QUEEN HONG?
I GUESS SINCE HER MAJESTY ISN'T SUPPOSED TO SHOW HER FACE IN PUBLIC, IF HE HASN'T MET HER PERSONALLY...

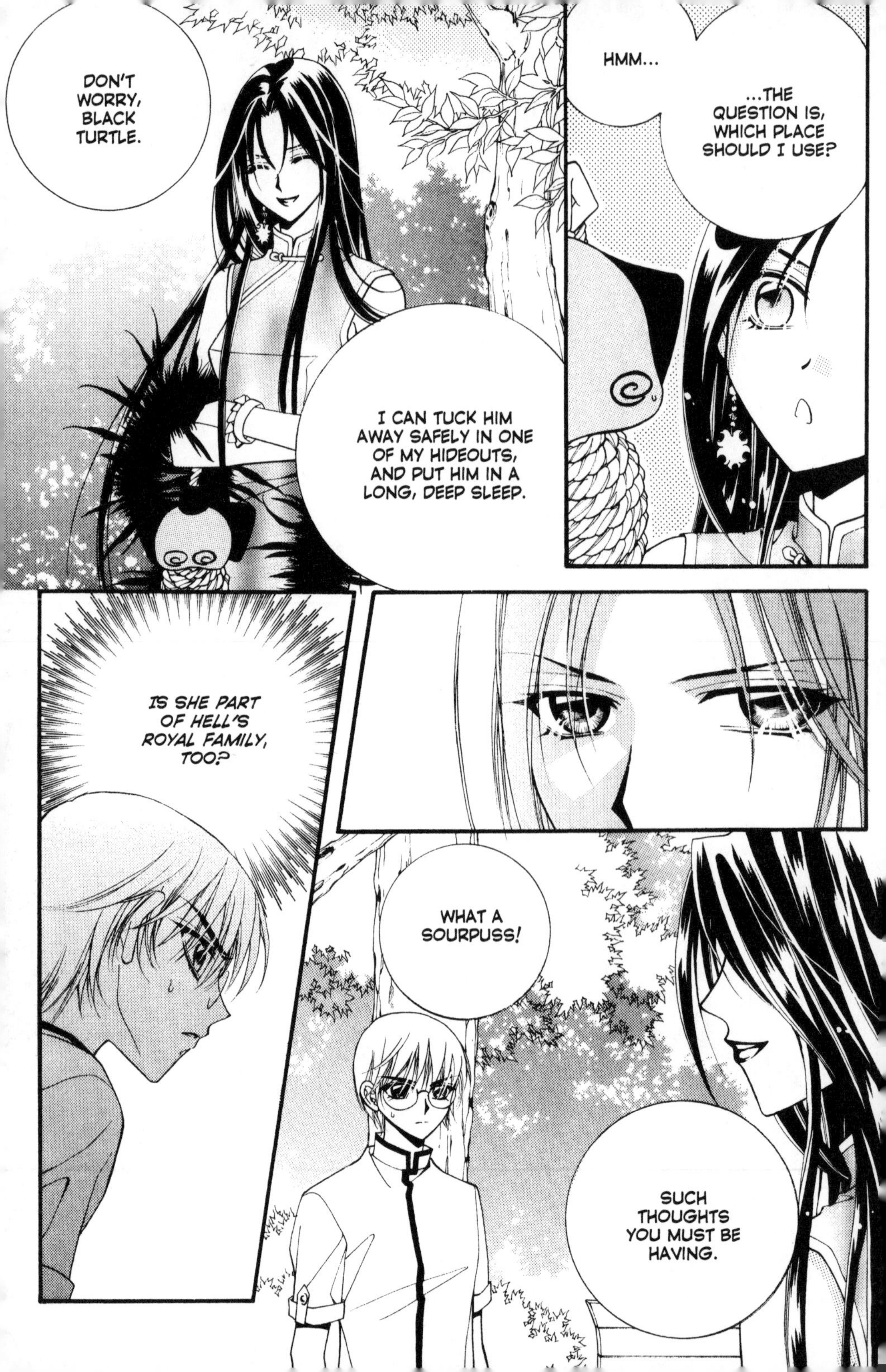
HMM...
...THE QUESTION IS, WHICH PLACE SHOULD I USE?
DON'T WORRY, BLACK TURTLE.
I CAN TUCK HIM AWAY SAFELY IN ONE OF MY HIDEOUTS, AND PUT HIM IN A LONG, DEEP SLEEP.
IS SHE PART OF HELL'S ROYAL FAMILY, TOO?
WHAT A SOURPUSS!
SUCH THOUGHTS YOU MUST BE HAVING.

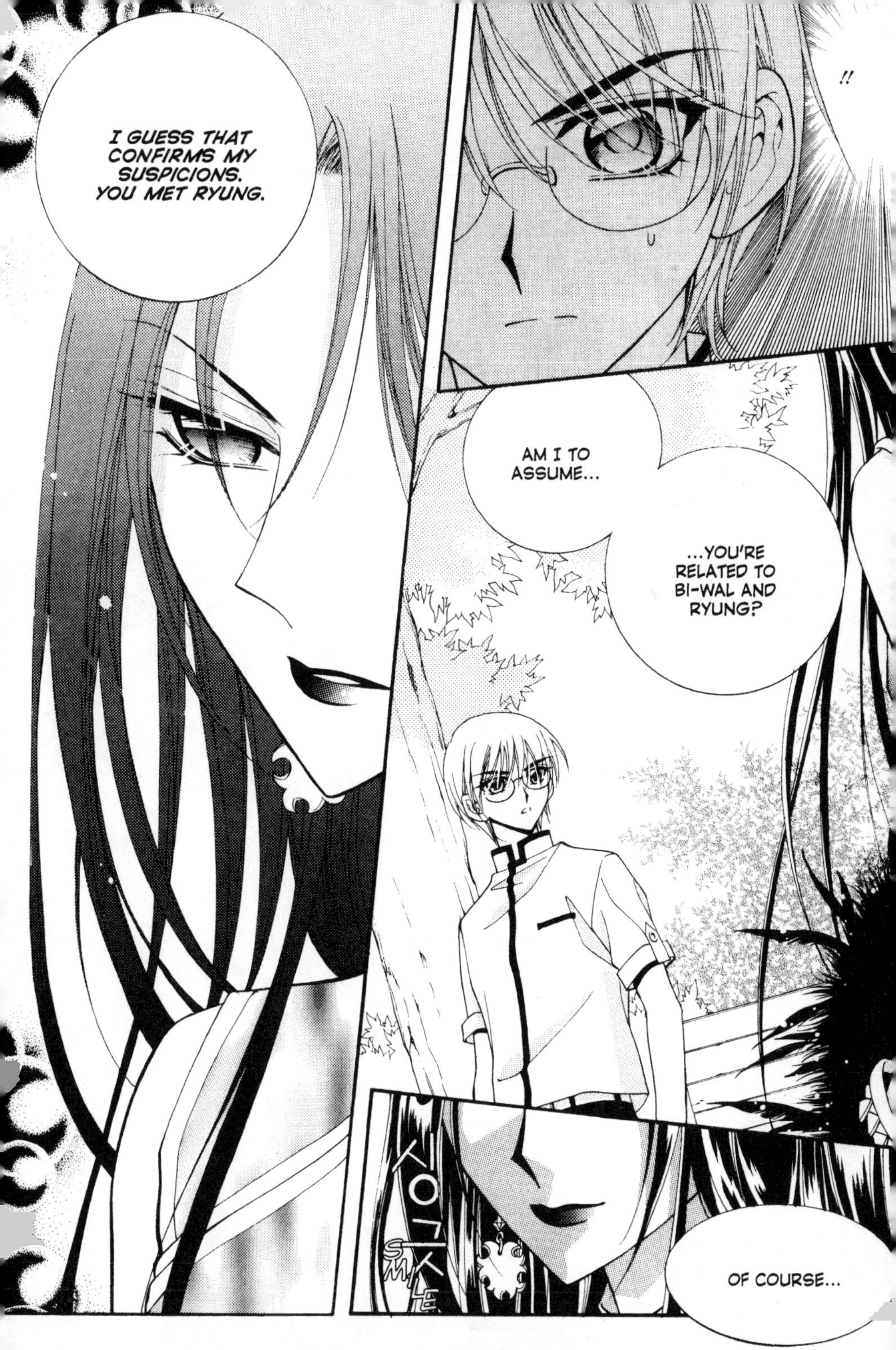

I GUESS THAT CONFIRMS MY SUSPICIONS. YOU MET RYUNG.
!!
AM I TO ASSUME...
...YOU'RE RELATED TO BI-WAL AND RYUNG?
SMILE
OF COURSE...

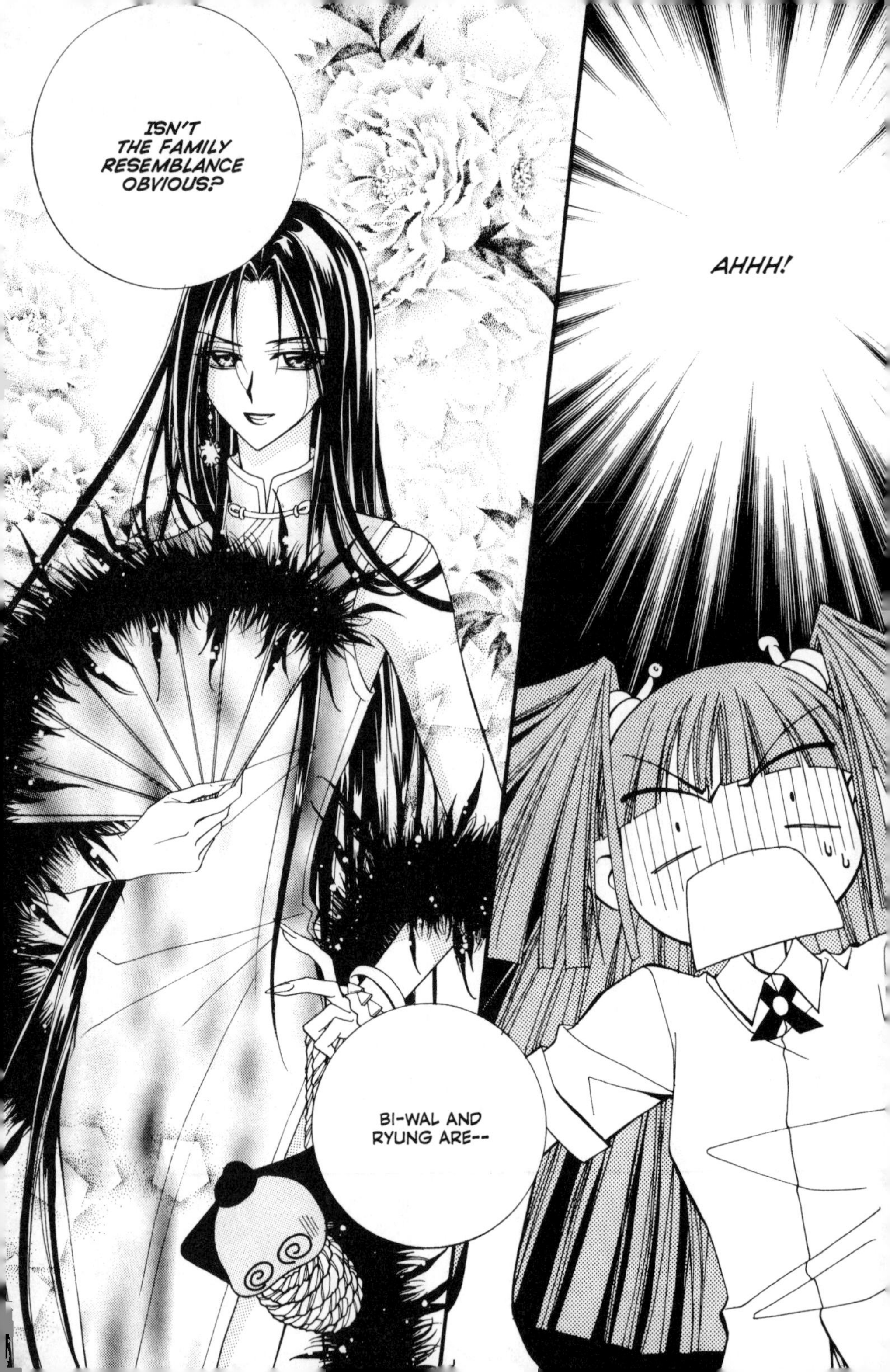
AHHH!
ISN'T THE FAMILY RESEMBLANCE OBVIOUS?
BI-WAL AND RYUNG ARE--

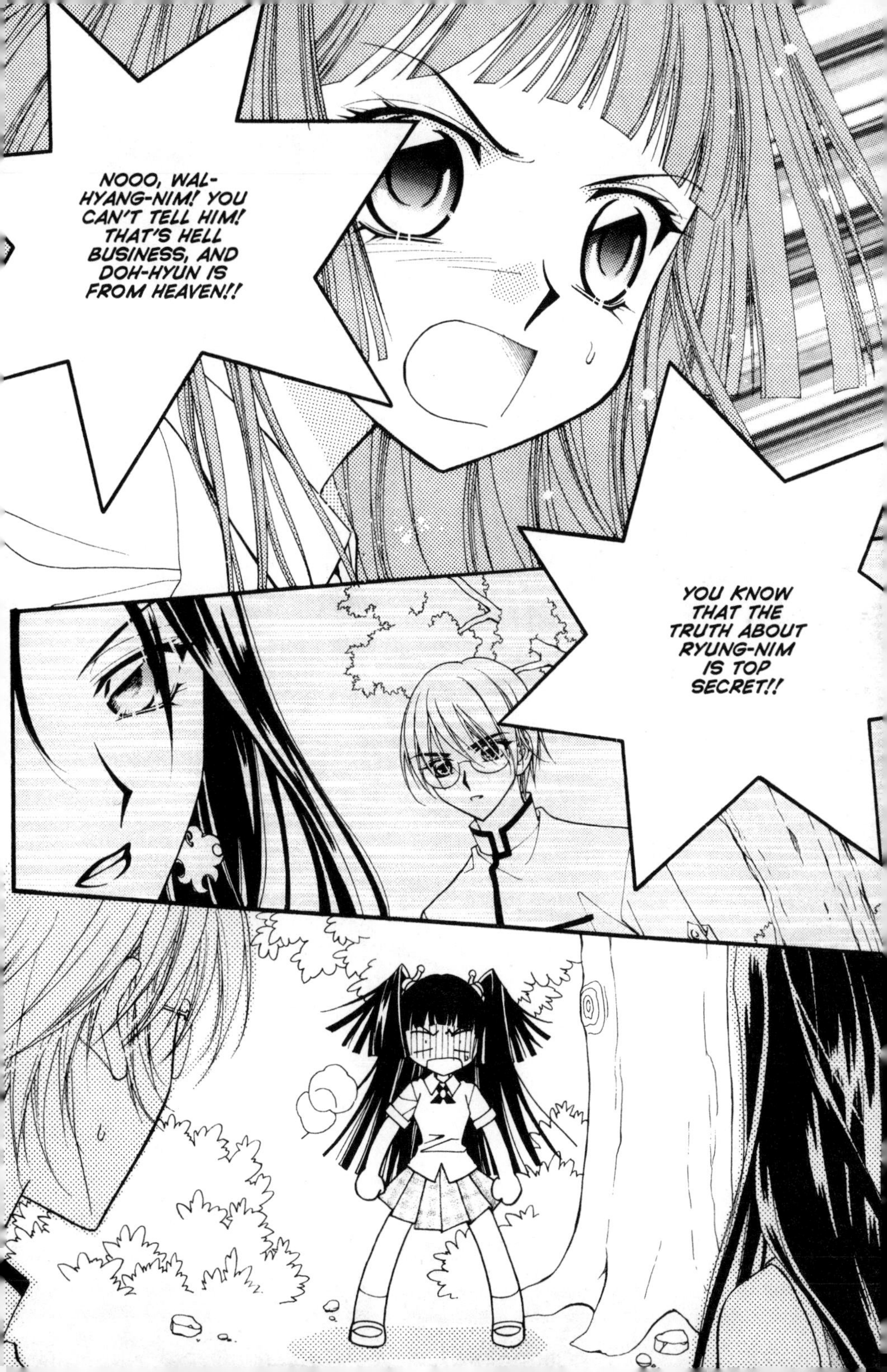
NOOO, WAL-HYANG-NIM! YOU CAN'T TELL HIM! THAT'S HELL BUSINESS, AND DOH-HYUN IS FROM HEAVEN!!
YOU KNOW THAT THE TRUTH ABOUT RYUNG-NIM IS TOP SECRET!!

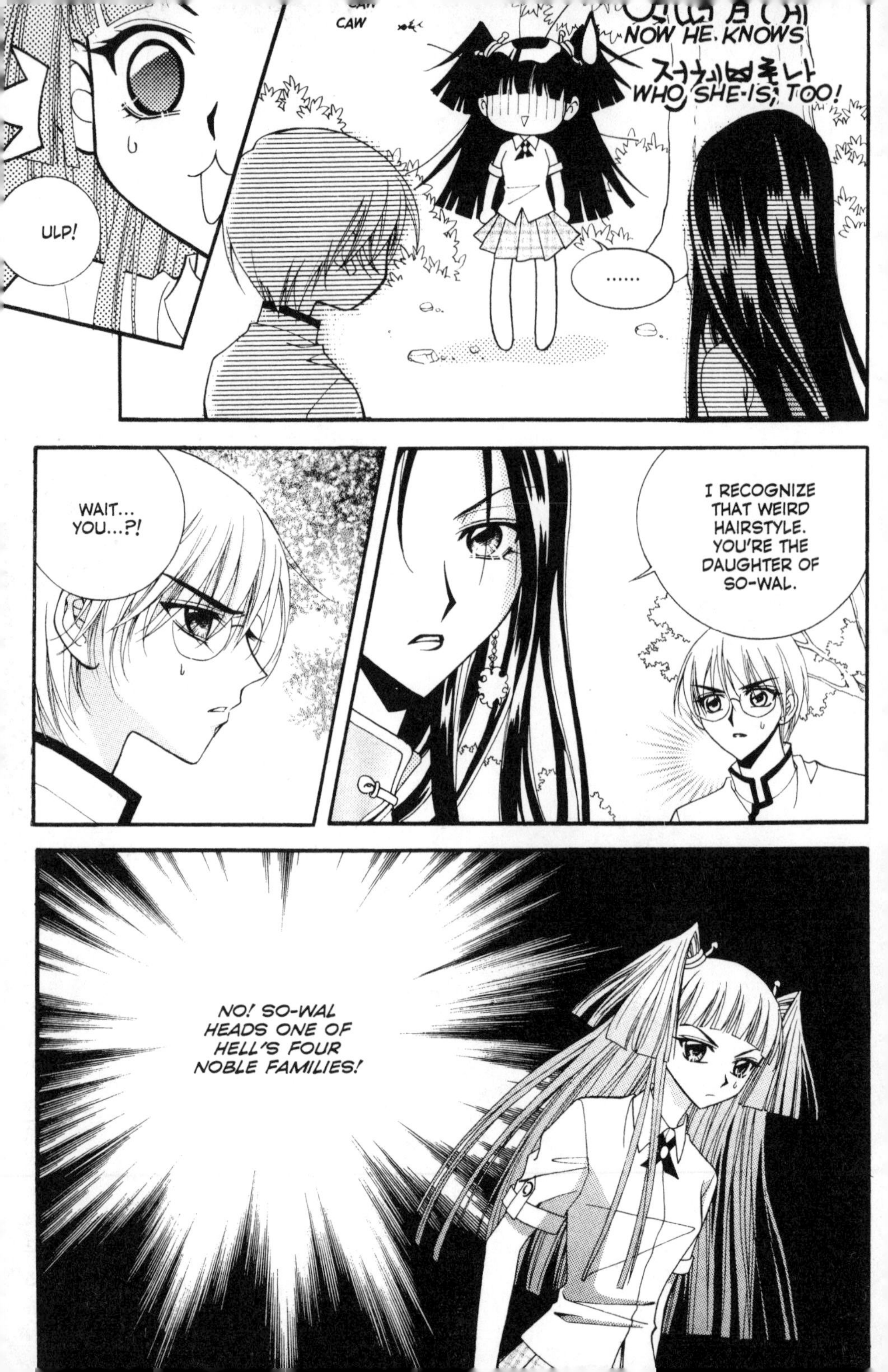

ULP!
CAW
NOW HE KNOWS
WHO SHE IS, TOO!
......
WAIT... YOU...?!
I RECOGNIZE THAT WEIRD HAIRSTYLE. YOU'RE THE DAUGHTER OF SO-WAL.
NO! SO-WAL HEADS ONE OF HELL'S FOUR NOBLE FAMILIES!

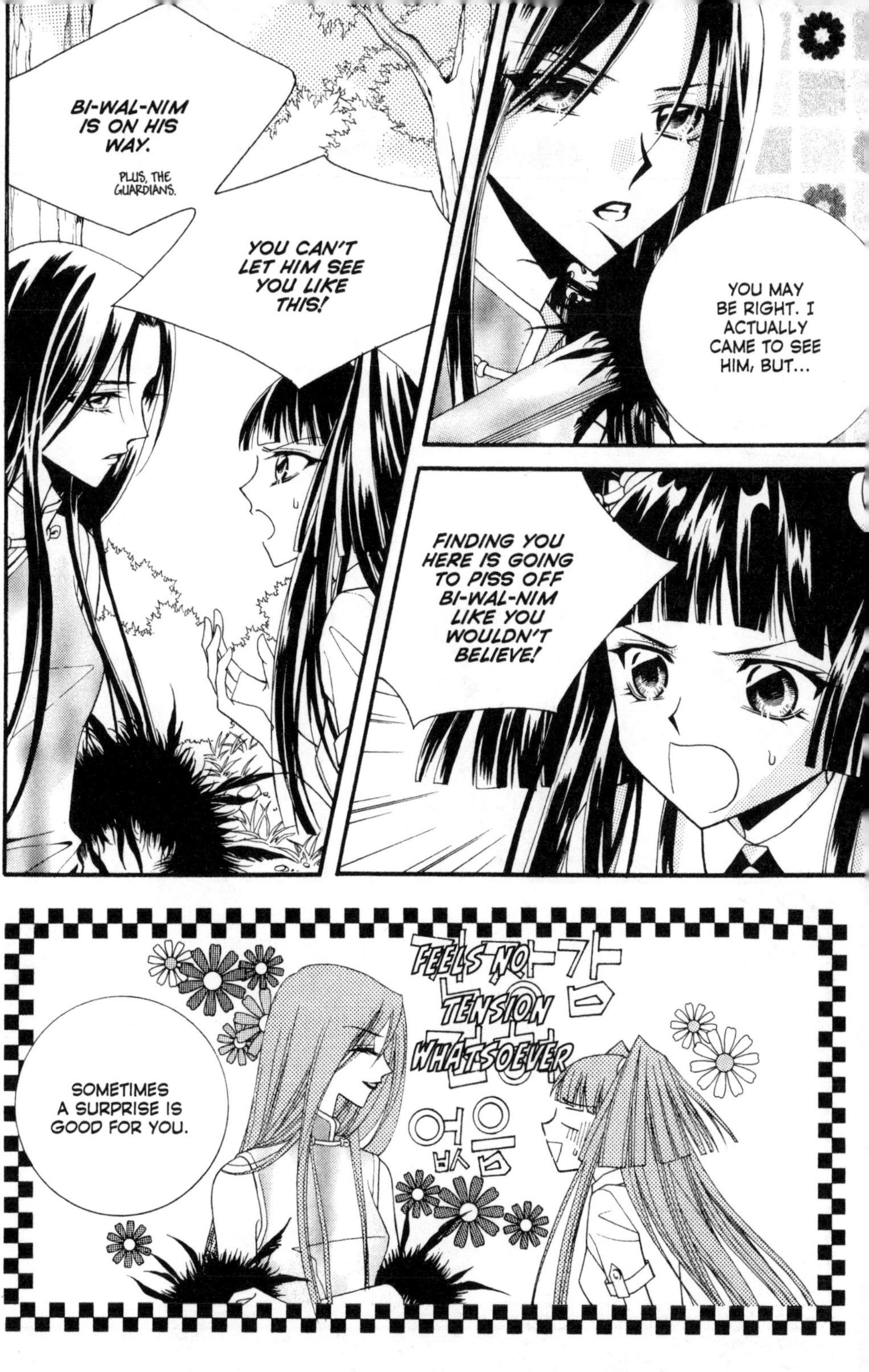
BI-WAL-NIM IS ON HIS WAY.
PLUS, THE GUARDIANS.
YOU CAN'T LET HIM SEE YOU LIKE THIS!
YOU MAY BE RIGHT. I ACTUALLY CAME TO SEE HIM, BUT...
FINDING YOU HERE IS GOING TO PISS OFF BI-WAL-NIM LIKE YOU WOULDN'T BELIEVE!
SOMETIMES A SURPRISE IS GOOD FOR YOU.
FEELS NO TENSION WHATSOEVER

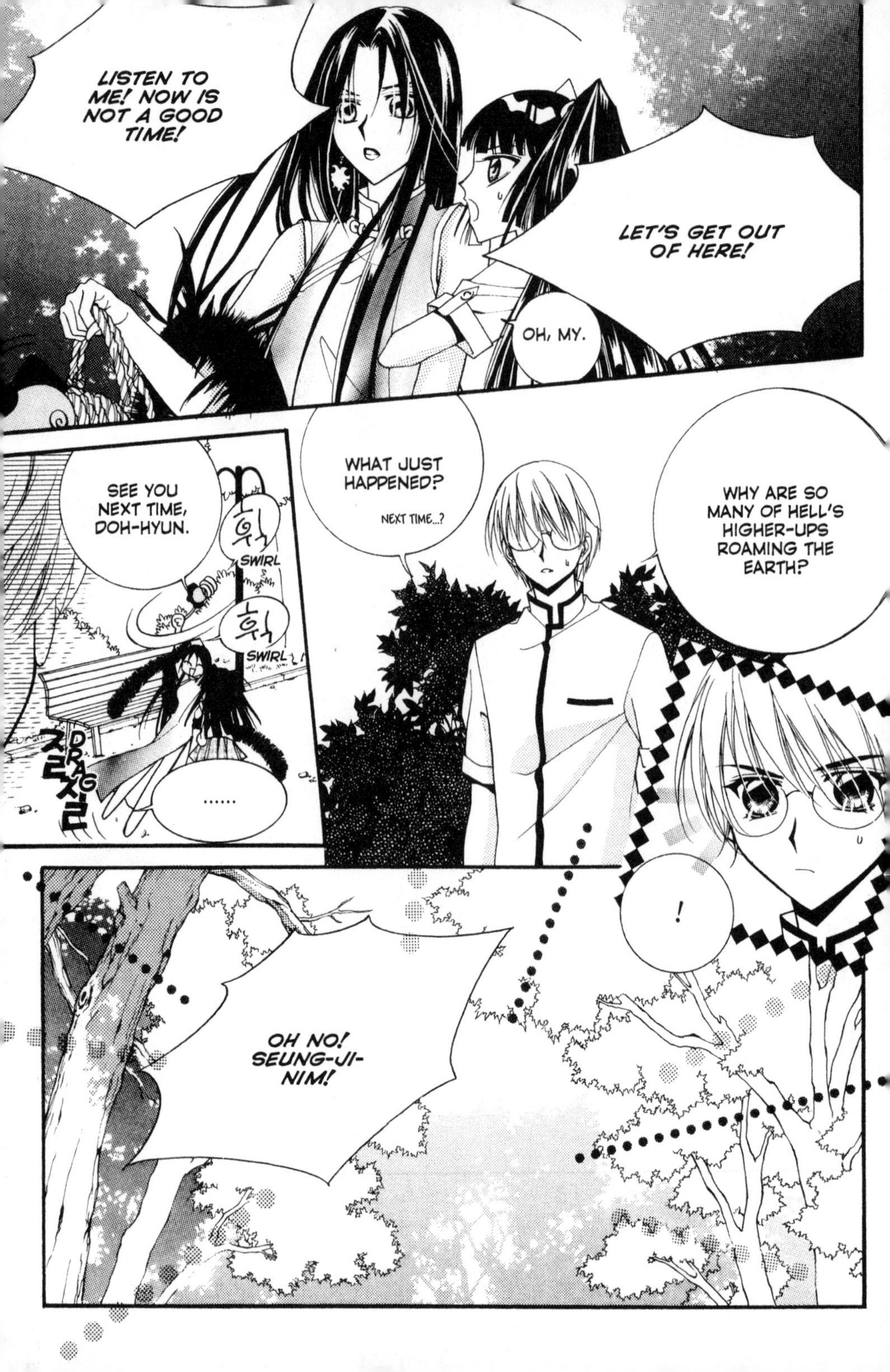
LISTEN TO ME! NOW IS NOT A GOOD TIME!
LET'S GET OUT OF HERE!
OH, MY.
SEE YOU NEXT TIME, DOH-HYUN.
SWIRL
SWIRL
DRAG
......
WHAT JUST HAPPENED?
NEXT TIME...?
WHY ARE SO MANY OF HELL'S HIGHER-UPS ROAMING THE EARTH?
!
OH NO! SEUNG-JI-NIM!

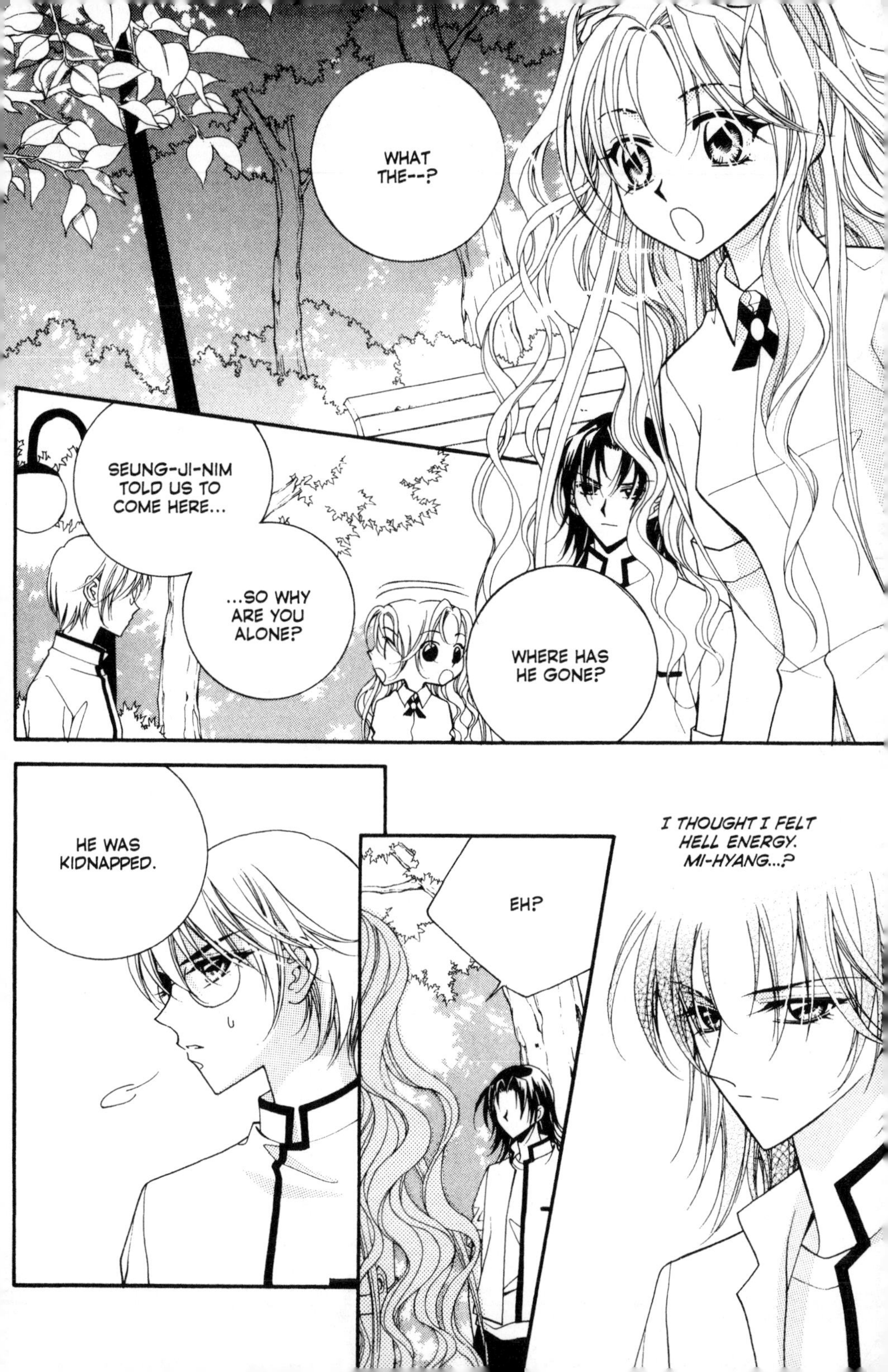
WHAT THE--?
SEUNG-JI-NIM TOLD US TO COME HERE...
...SO WHY ARE YOU ALONE?
WHERE HAS HE GONE?
HE WAS KIDNAPPED.
EH?
I THOUGHT I FELT HELL ENERGY. MI-HYANG...?

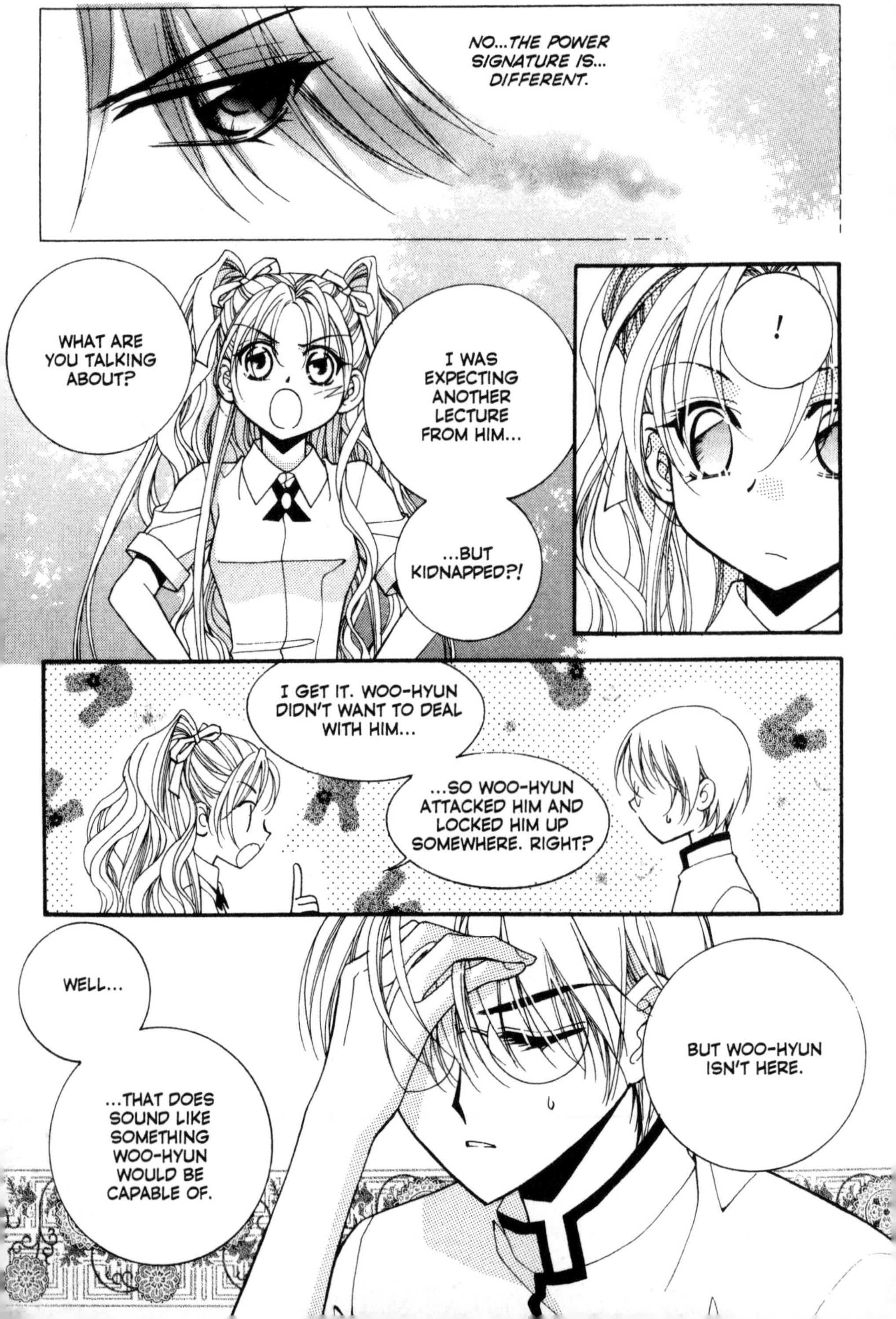
NO...THE POWER SIGNATURE IS... DIFFERENT.
!
I WAS EXPECTING ANOTHER LECTURE FROM HIM...
...BUT KIDNAPPED?!
WHAT ARE YOU TALKING ABOUT?
I GET IT. WOO-HYUN DIDN'T WANT TO DEAL WITH HIM...
...SO WOO-HYUN ATTACKED HIM AND LOCKED HIM UP SOMEWHERE. RIGHT?
BUT WOO-HYUN ISN'T HERE.
WELL...
...THAT DOES SOUND LIKE SOMETHING WOO-HYUN WOULD BE CAPABLE OF.

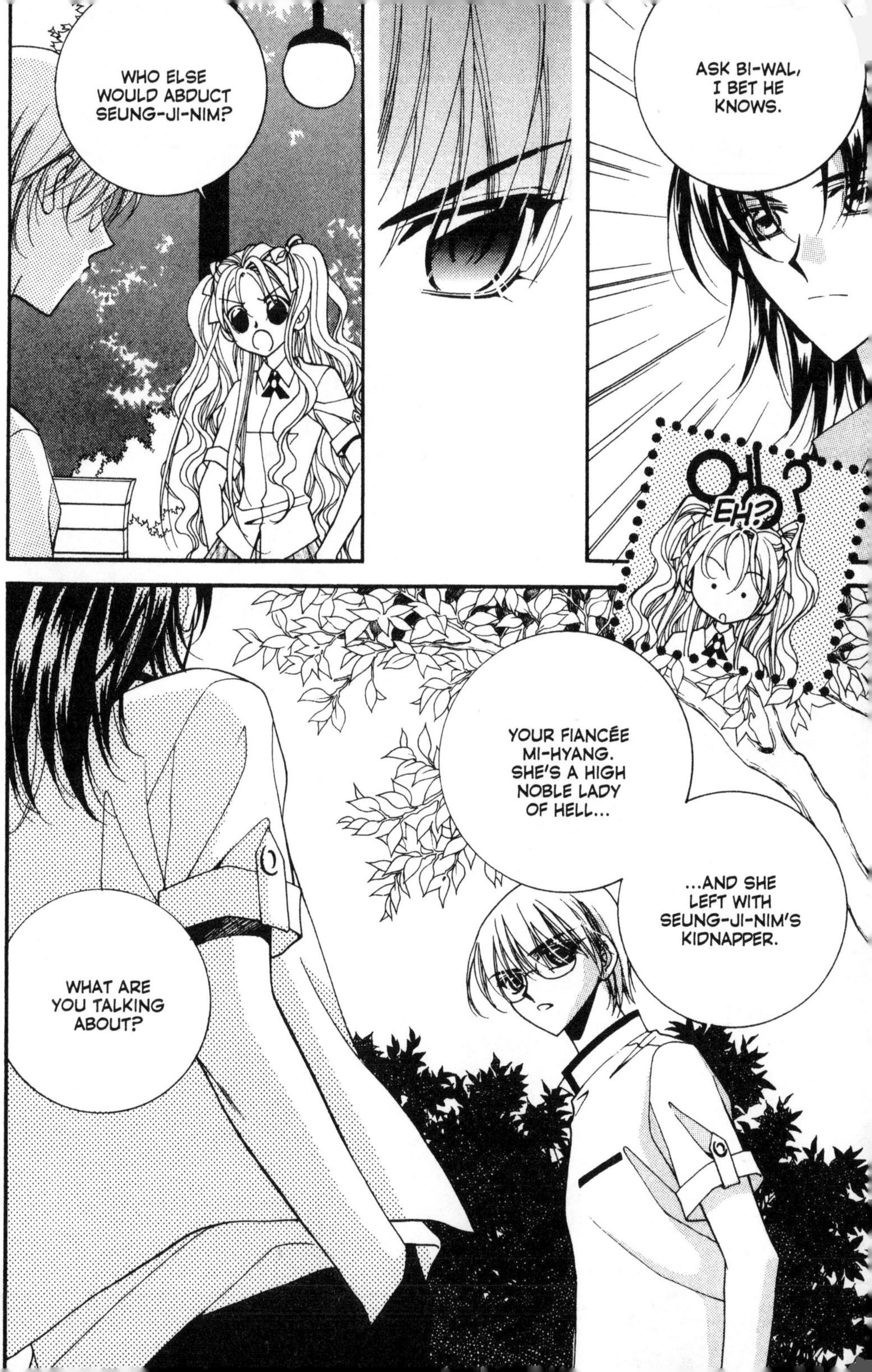
WHO ELSE WOULD ABDUCT SEUNG-JI-NIM?
ASK BI-WAL, I BET HE KNOWS.
EH?
YOUR FIANCÉE MI-HYANG. SHE'S A HIGH NOBLE LADY OF HELL...
...AND SHE LEFT WITH SEUNG-JI-NIM'S KIDNAPPER.
WHAT ARE YOU TALKING ABOUT?

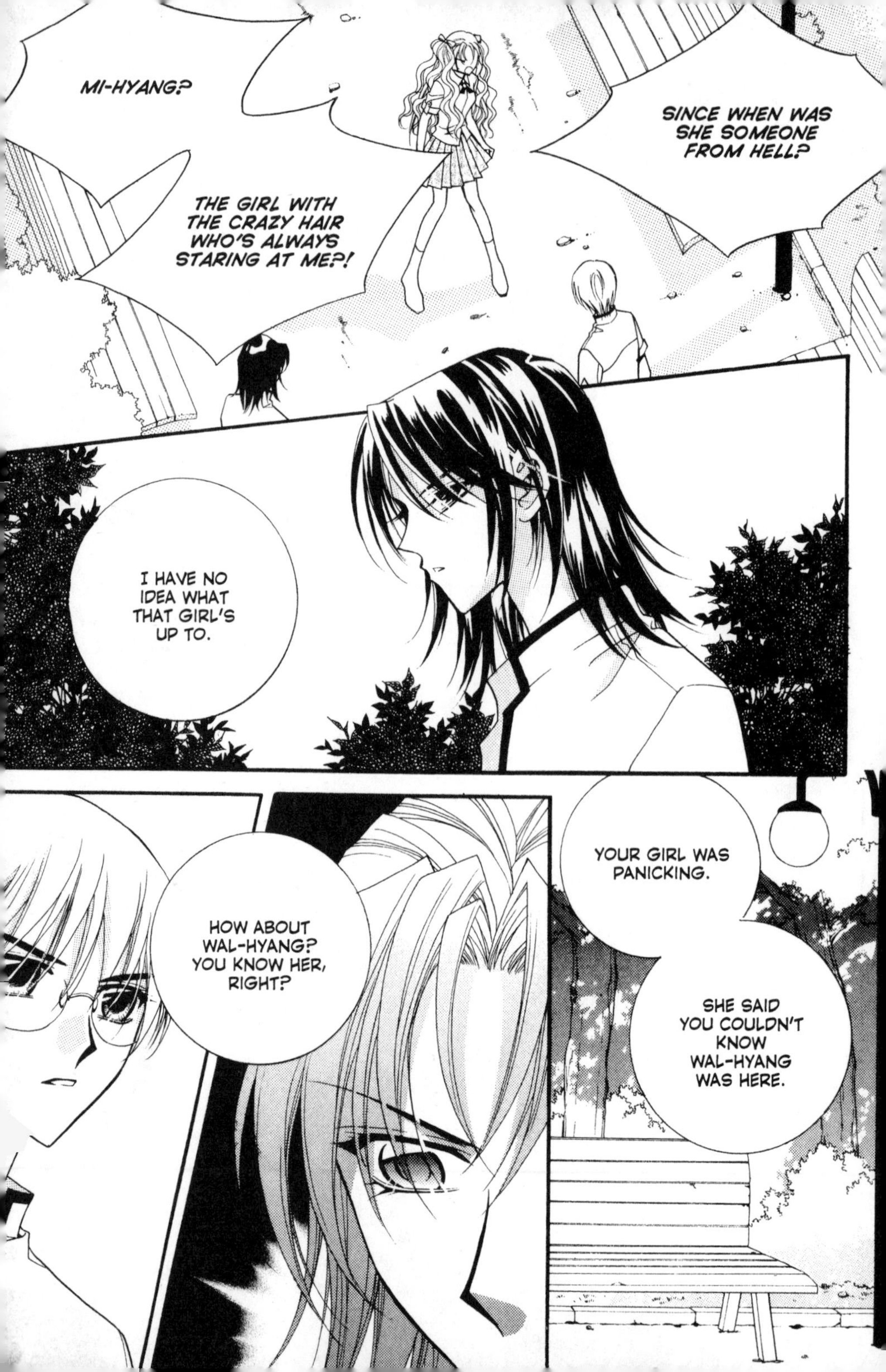
SINCE WHEN WAS SHE SOMEONE FROM HELL?
MI-HYANG?
THE GIRL WITH THE CRAZY HAIR WHO'S ALWAYS STARING AT ME?!
I HAVE NO IDEA WHAT THAT GIRL'S UP TO.
YOUR GIRL WAS PANICKING.
SHE SAID YOU COULDN'T KNOW WAL-HYANG WAS HERE.
HOW ABOUT WAL-HYANG? YOU KNOW HER, RIGHT?

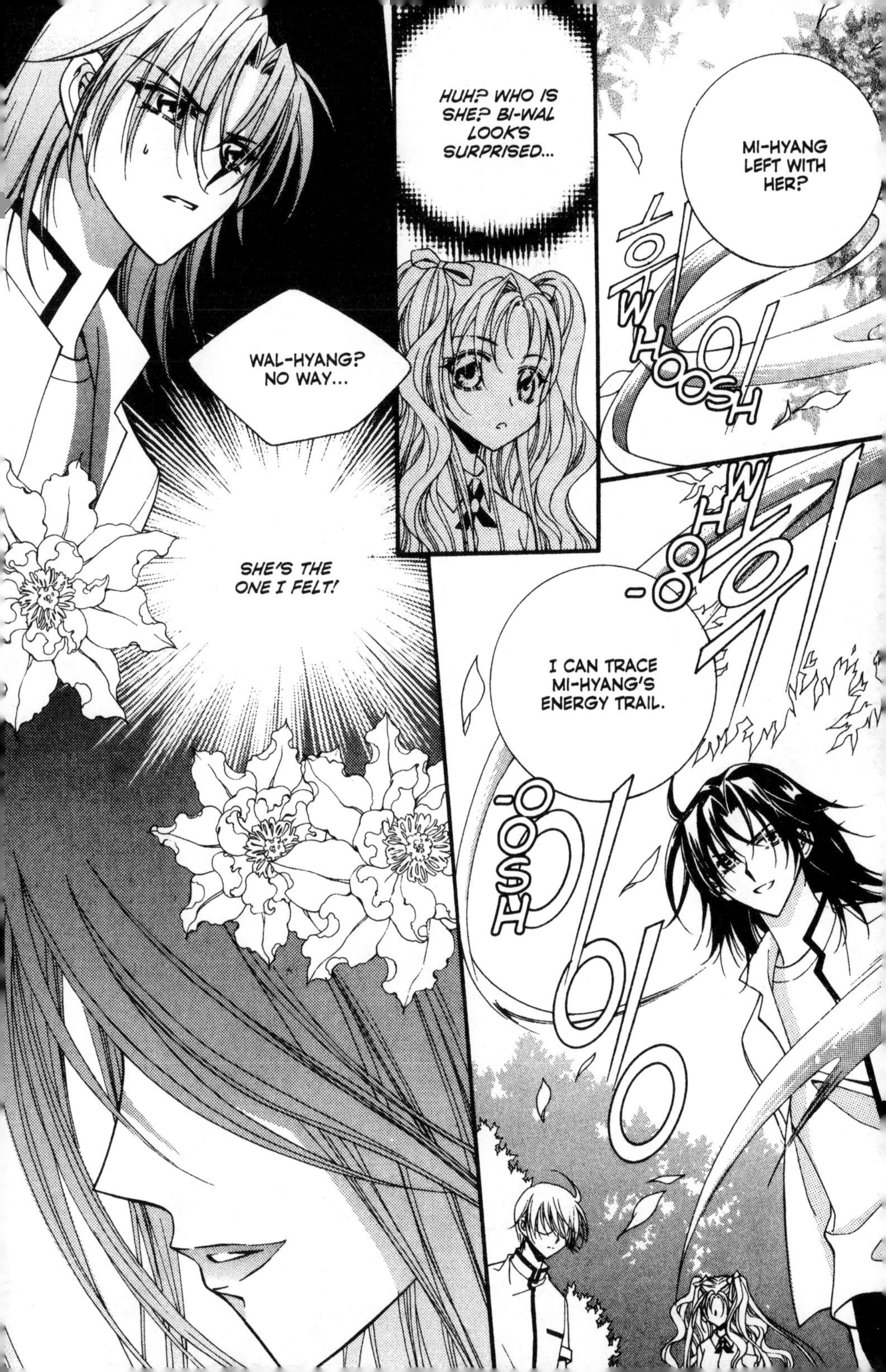
MI-HYANG LEFT WITH HER?
WHOOSH
HUH? WHO IS SHE? BI-WAL LOOKS SURPRISED...
WAL-HYANG? NO WAY...
SHE'S THE ONE I FELT!
WHOO-
I CAN TRACE MI-HYANG'S ENERGY TRAIL.
-OOSH

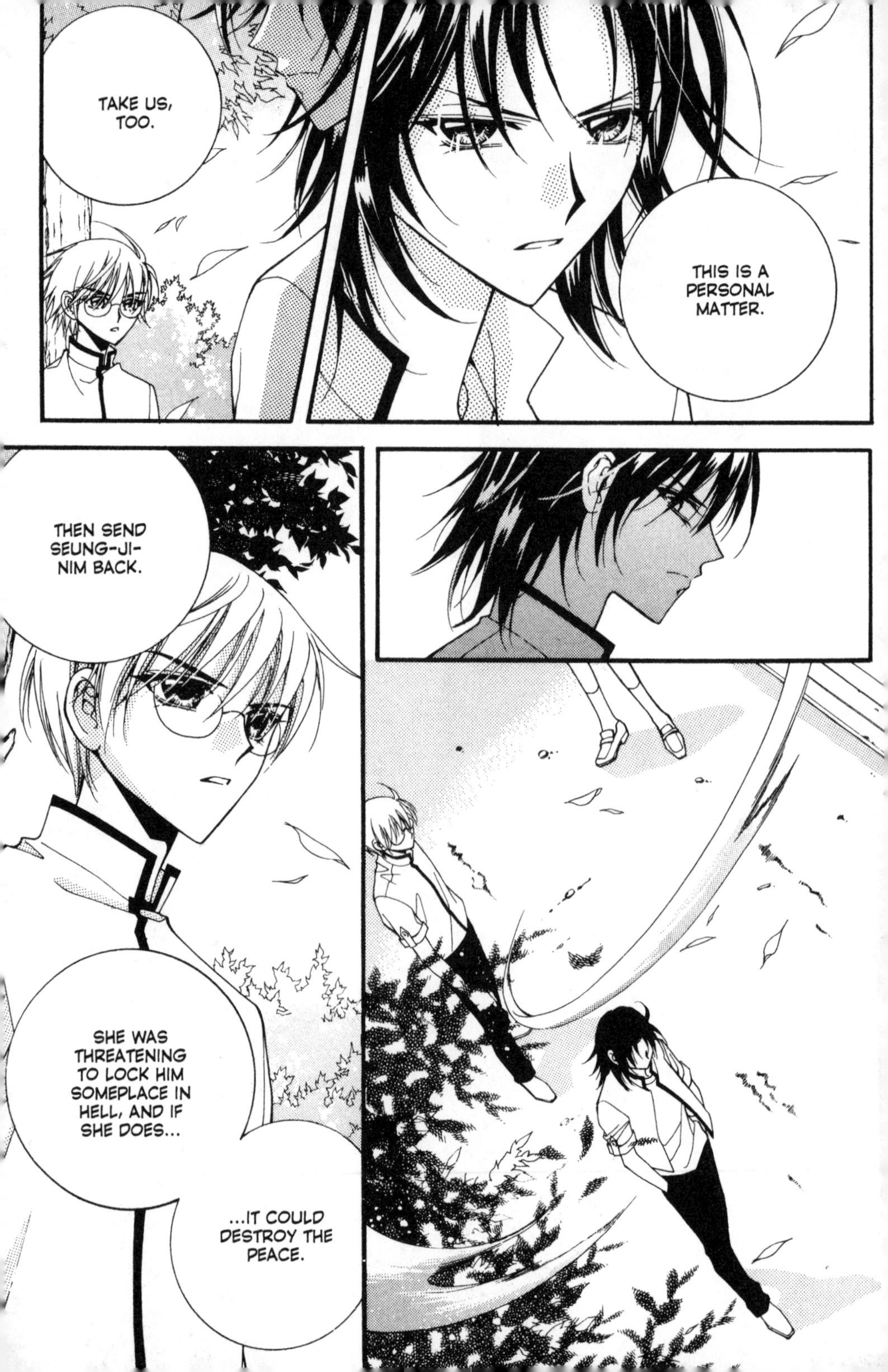
TAKE US, TOO.
THIS IS A PERSONAL MATTER.
THEN SEND SEUNG-JI-NIM BACK.
SHE WAS THREATENING TO LOCK HIM SOMEPLACE IN HELL, AND IF SHE DOES...
...IT COULD DESTROY THE PEACE.

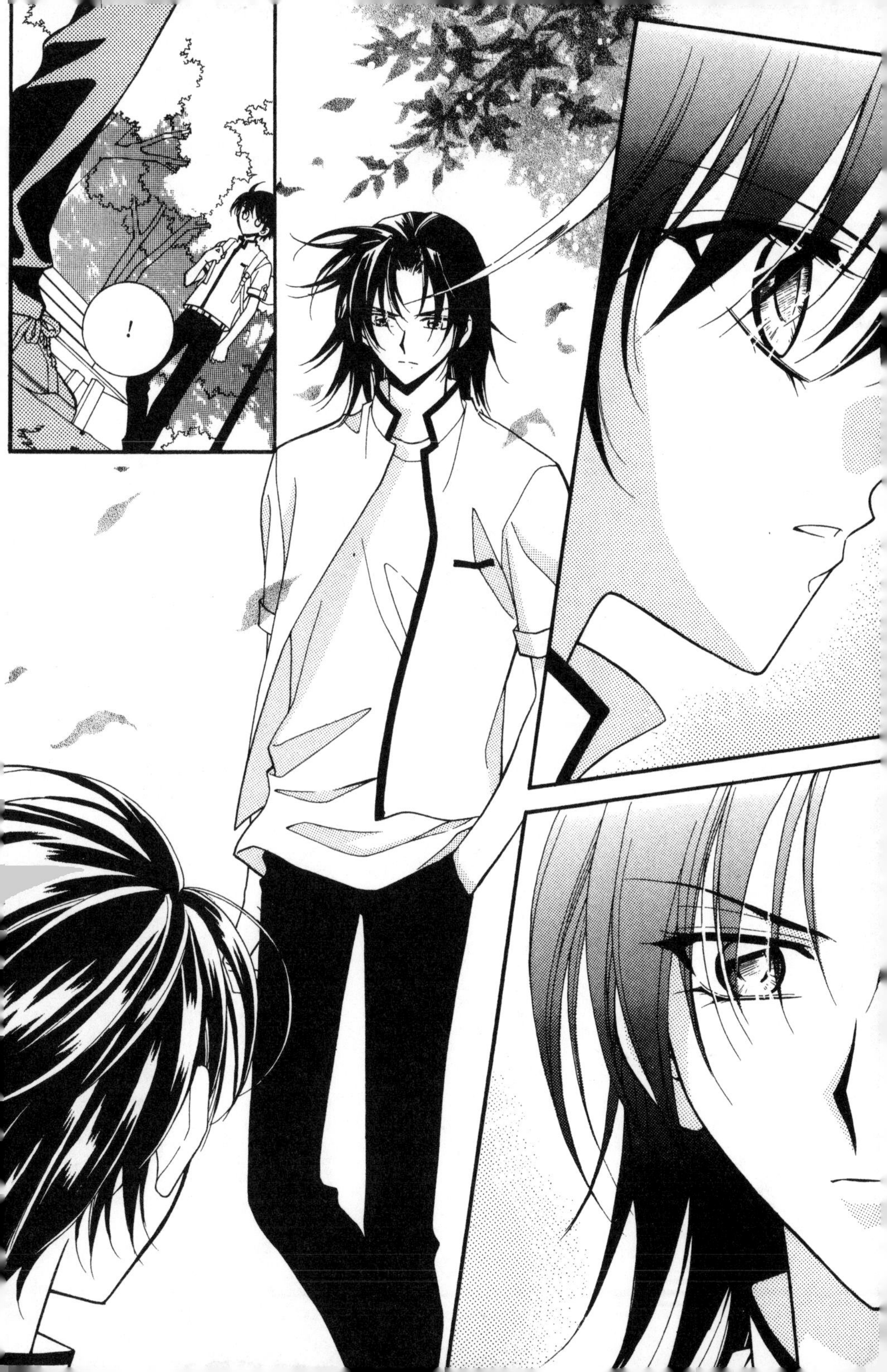
!

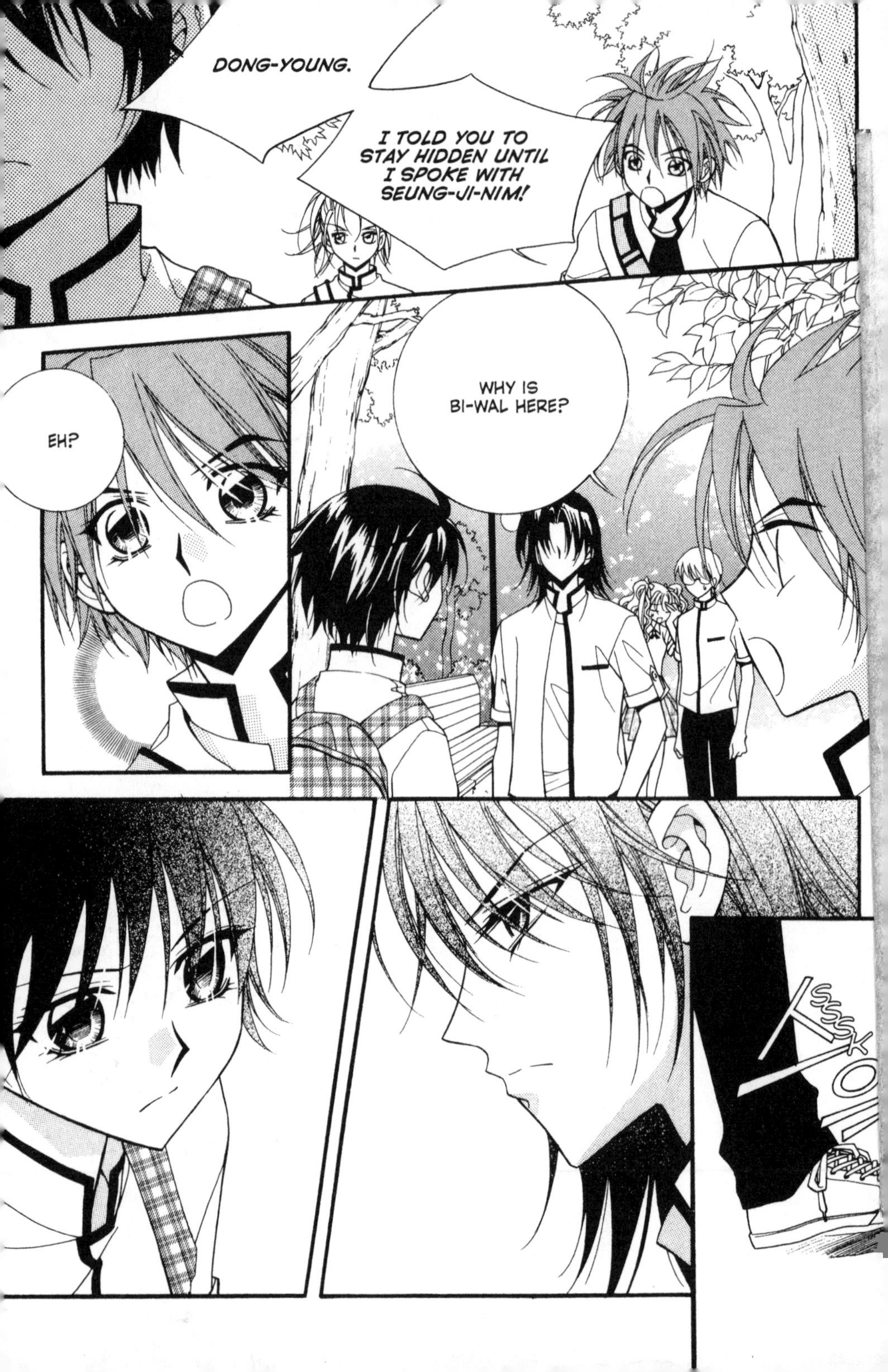
DONG-YOUNG.
I TOLD YOU TO STAY HIDDEN UNTIL I SPOKE WITH SEUNG-JI-NIM!
WHY IS BI-WAL HERE?
EH?
KSSSK

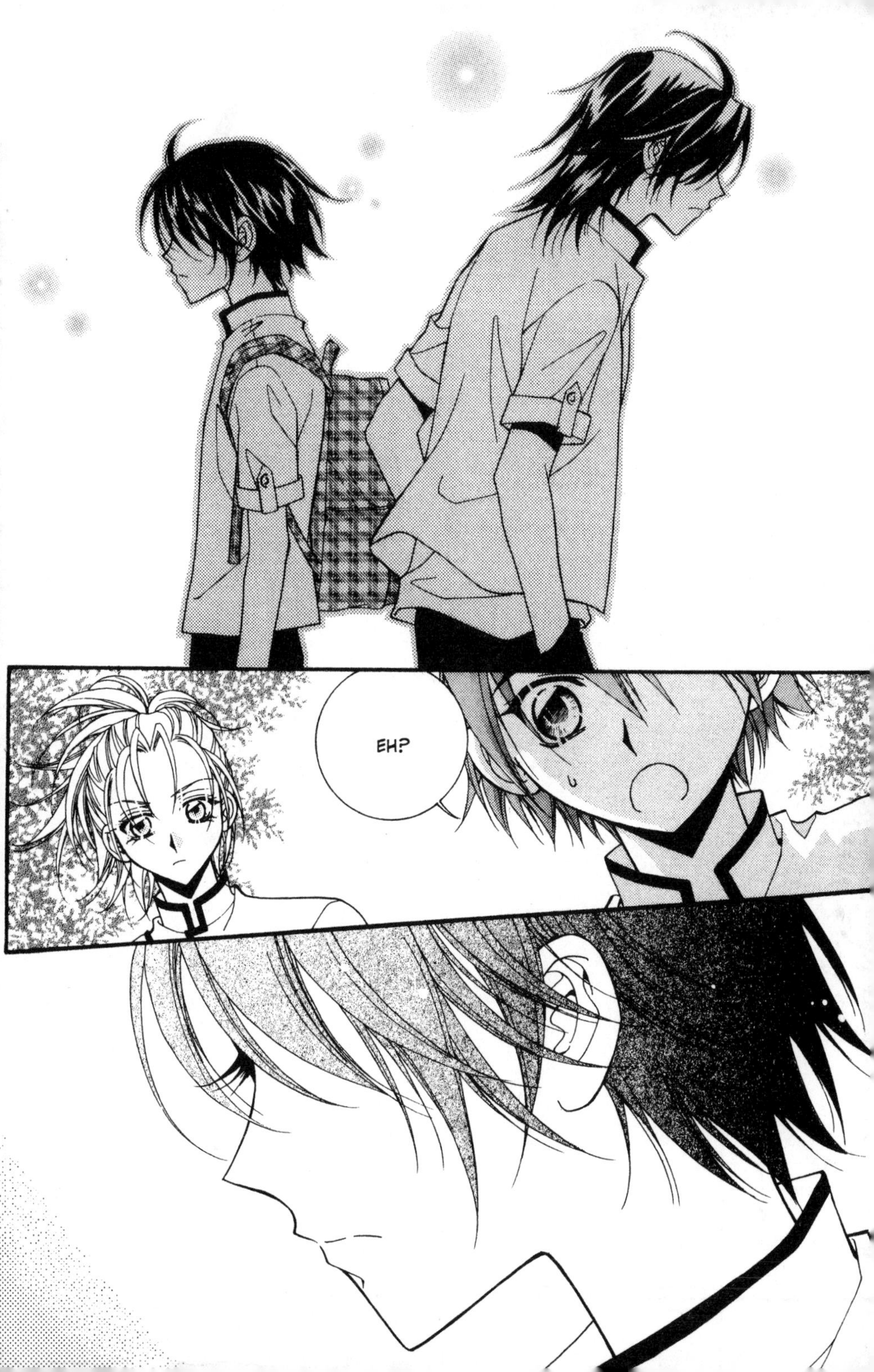
EH?

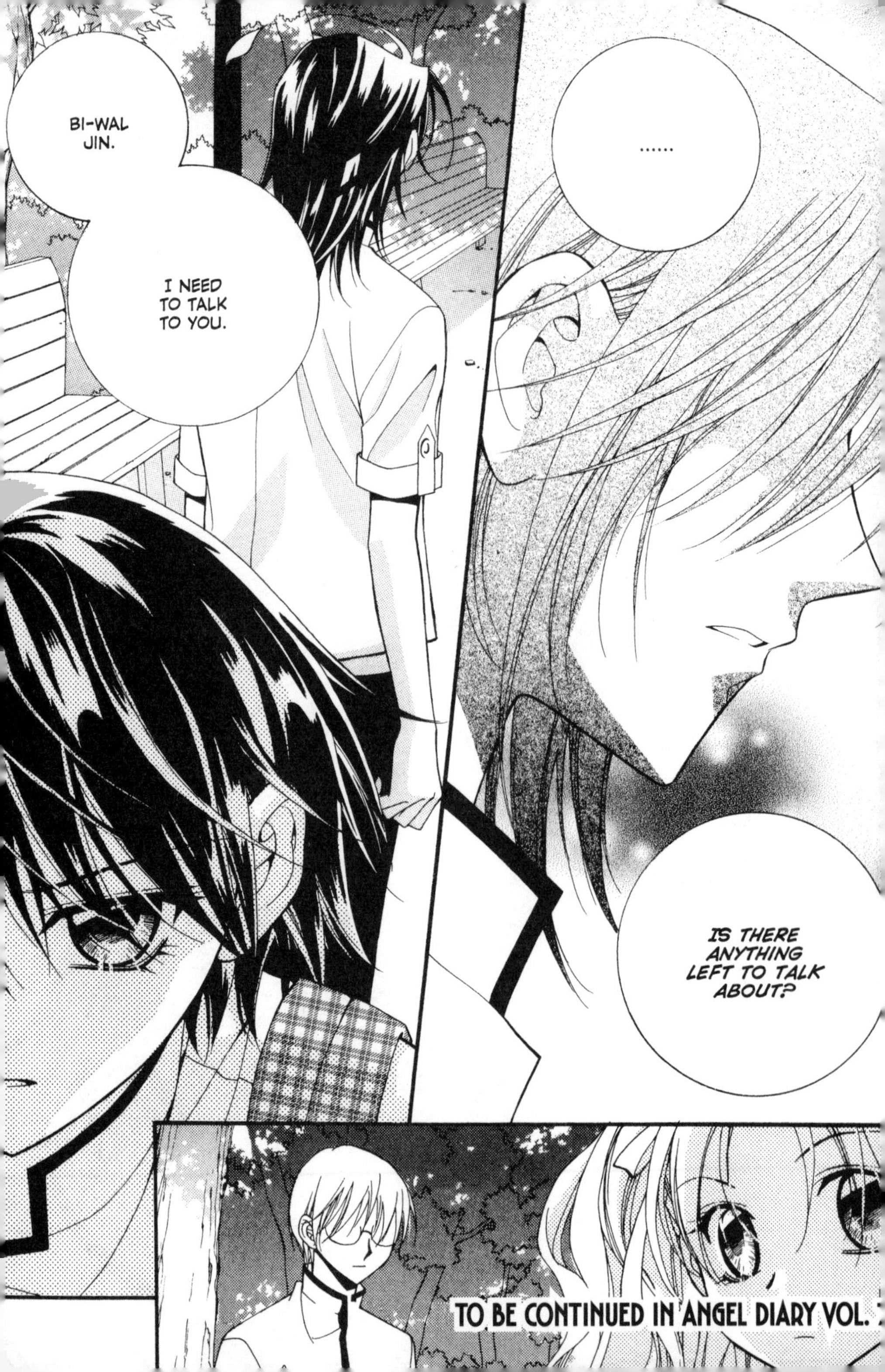
......
BI-WAL JIN.
I NEED TO TALK TO YOU.
IS THERE ANYTHING LEFT TO TALK ABOUT?
TO BE CONTINUED IN ANGEL DIARY VOL.

HAPPY NEW YEAR! ~♥

Yen Press
www.yenpress.com

The newest title from the creators of <Demon Diary> and <Angel Diary>!

Once upon a time, a selfish king summoned the monstrous Bulkirin into the real world. The monster killed half of all human beings, leaving the rest helpless as to what to do. That is, until one day when a hero appeared and defeated the Bulkirin with the legendary "Seven Blade Sword." But···what does all this have to do with 8th grader Eun-Gyo Sung?! First, she gets suspended from school for fighting. Then, she runs away from home. The last thing she needed was to be kidnapped—and whisked into the past by a mysterious stranger named No-Ah!

Available at bookstores near you!

Legend 2

K a r a · W o o S o o J u n g

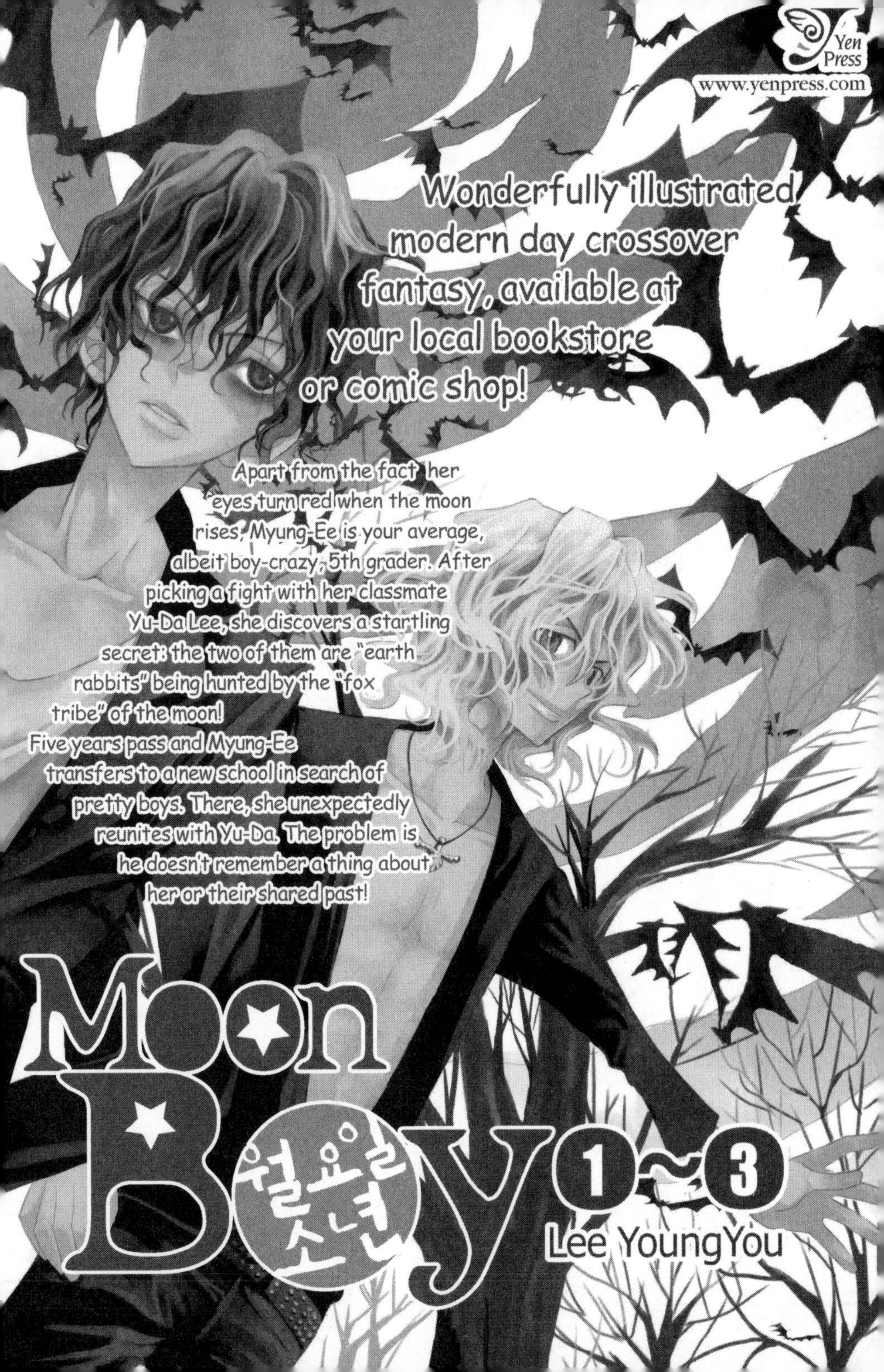
Yen Press
www.yenpress.com
Wonderfully illustrated modern day crossover fantasy, available at your local bookstore or comic shop!
Apart from the fact her eyes turn red when the moon rises, Myung-Ee is your average, albeit boy-crazy, 5th grader. After picking a fight with her classmate Yu-Da Lee, she discovers a startling secret: the two of them are "earth rabbits" being hunted by the "fox tribe" of the moon!
Five years pass and Myung-Ee transfers to a new school in search of pretty boys. There, she unexpectedly reunites with Yu-Da. The problem is he doesn't remember a thing about her or their shared past!
Moon Boy 1~3
월요일 소년
Lee YoungYou

What will happen when a tomboy meets a bishonen?

Tomboy Mi-ha is an extremely active and competitive girl who hates to lose. She's such a tomboy that boys fear her—exactly the way her evil brother wanted and trained her to be. It took him six long years to transform her into this pseudo-military style girl in order to protect her from anyone else.

Bishonen Seung-suh is a new transfer student who's got the looks, the charm, and the desire to sweep her off her feet. Will this male beauty be able to tame the beast? Will the evil brother of the beast let them be together and live happily ever after? Bring it on!

Available at bookstores near you!

Bring it on! 1~5
FINAL

Baek HyeKyung

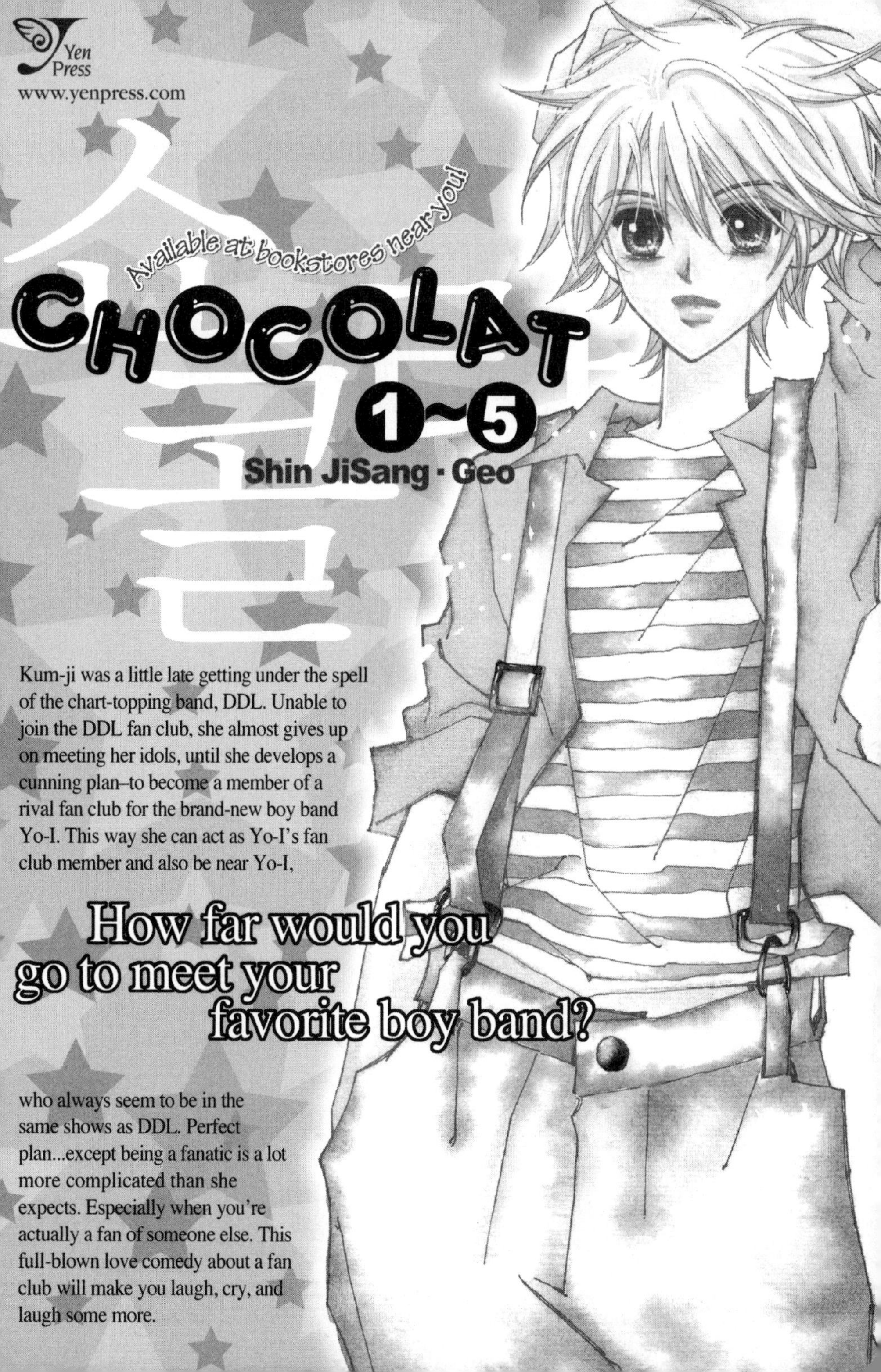
Yen Press
www.yenpress.com
Available at bookstores near you!
CHOCOLAT
1~5
Shin JiSang · Geo
Kum-ji was a little late getting under the spell of the chart-topping band, DDL. Unable to join the DDL fan club, she almost gives up on meeting her idols, until she develops a cunning plan–to become a member of a rival fan club for the brand-new boy band Yo-I. This way she can act as Yo-I's fan club member and also be near Yo-I,
How far would you go to meet your favorite boy band?
who always seem to be in the same shows as DDL. Perfect plan...except being a fanatic is a lot more complicated than she expects. Especially when you're actually a fan of someone else. This full-blown love comedy about a fan club will make you laugh, cry, and laugh some more.

Totally new Arabian nights, where Shahrazad is a guy!

Everyone knows the story of Shahrazad and her wonderful tales from the Arabian Nights. For one thousand and one nights, the stories that she created entertained the mad Sultan and eventually saved her life. In this version, Shahrazad is a guy who wanted to save his sister from the mad Sultan by disguising himself as a woman. When he puts his life on the line, what kind of strange and unique stories would he tell? This new twist on one of the greatest classical tales might just keep you awake for another ONE THOUSAND AND ONE NIGHTS.

Available at bookstores near you!

One thousand and one nights 1~4

Han SeungHee · Jeon JinSeok

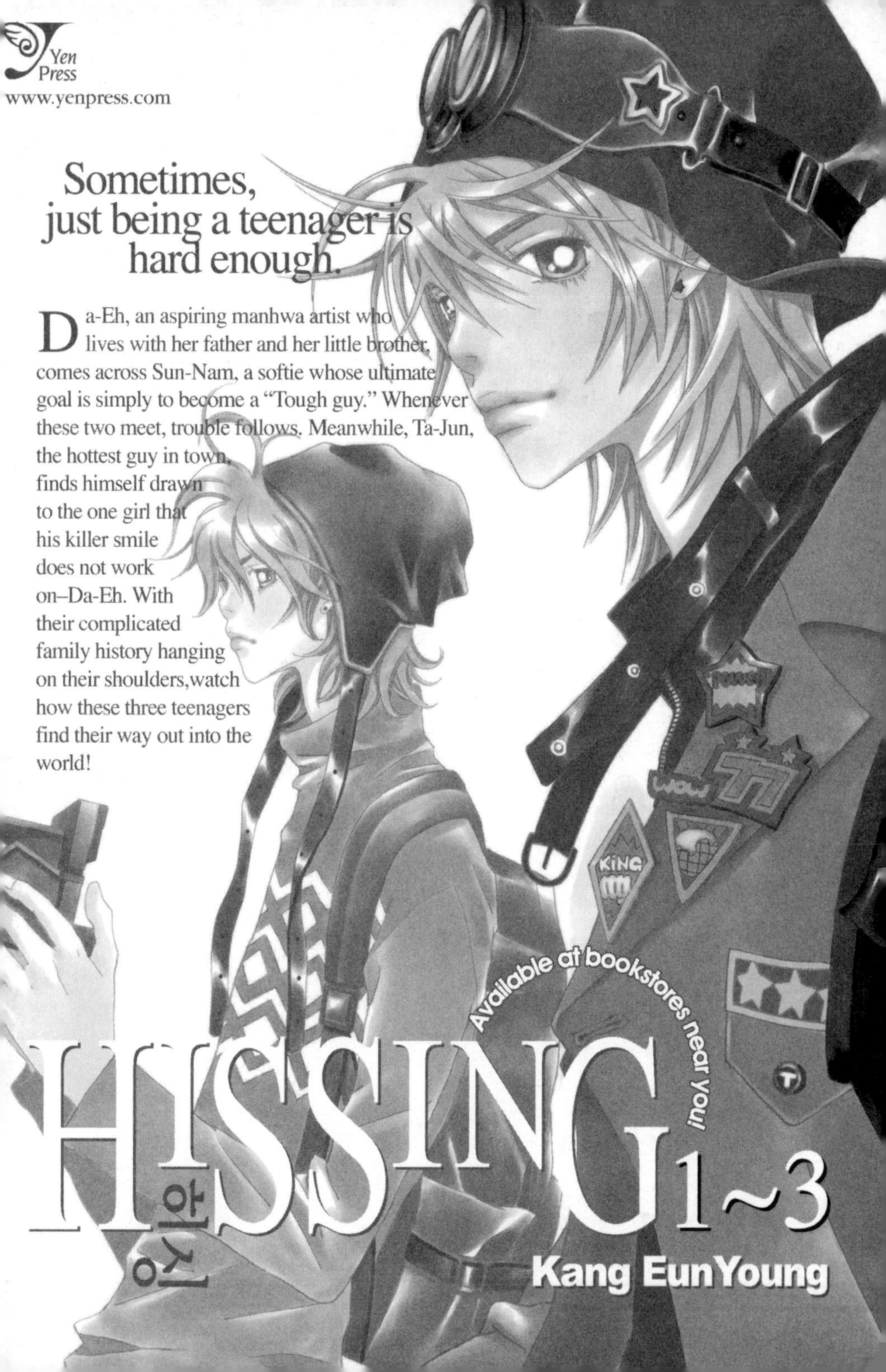
Yen Press
www.yenpress.com
Sometimes, just being a teenager is hard enough.
Da-Eh, an aspiring manhwa artist who lives with her father and her little brother, comes across Sun-Nam, a softie whose ultimate goal is simply to become a "Tough guy." Whenever these two meet, trouble follows. Meanwhile, Ta-Jun, the hottest guy in town, finds himself drawn to the one girl that his killer smile does not work on–Da-Eh. With their complicated family history hanging on their shoulders,watch how these three teenagers find their way out into the world!
Available at bookstores near you!
HISSING 1~3
하이싱
Kang EunYoung

Angel Diary vol. 6

Story by YunHee Lee
Art by Kara

Translation: HyeYoung Im
English Adaptation: Jamie S. Rich
Lettering: Marshall Dillon, Terri Delgado

Yen Press
Hachette Book Group USA
237 Park Avenue, New York, NY 10017

Visit our Web sites at www.HachetteBookGroupUSA.com and www.YenPress.com.

Yen Press is an imprint of Hachette Book Group USA, Inc. The Yen Press name and logo are trademarks of Hachette Book Group USA, Inc.

First Yen Press Edition: July 2008

ISBN-10: 0-7595-2904-3
ISBN-13: 978-0-7595-2904-5

10 9 8 7 6 5 4 3 2 1

BVG

Printed in the United States of America